LENIN (Samizdat) 150

2nd edition, revised and expanded

Hjalmar Jorge Joffre-Eichhorn (editor)

Patrick Anderson (language editor)

Johann Salazar (photography)

Daraja Press

Published by
Daraja Press
https://darajapress.com

Lenin150 (Samizdat)
2nd Edition, revised and expanded
ISBN 978-1988832-87-6

© 2021 Hjalmar Jorge Joffre-Eichhorn & Patrick Anderson
All rights reserved

Photographs © Johann Peter Salazar
Unless otherwise indicated

Copyright of all texts, translations and images
are retained by the respective authors

Lenin150 (Samizdat) was first published in 2020
By KickAss Books
ISBN 978-3000662-12-6

Library and Archives Canada Cataloguing in Publication

Title: Lenin 150 (Samizdat) / Hjalmar Jorge Joffre-Eichhorn (ed.) ; Patrick Anderson (language ed.) ; Johann Salazar (photo.).
Other titles: Lenin150 | Lenin one hundred and fifty
Names: Joffre-Eichhorn, Hjalmar Jorge, 1977- editor. | Anderson, Patrick, 1970- editor. | Salazar, Johann, 1987- editor.
Description: Second, expanded edition. | Includes bibliographical references and index. | Some chapters translated into English from various languages.
Identifiers: Canadiana (print) 20200376578 | Canadiana (ebook) 20200376675 | ISBN 9781988832876 (softcover) | ISBN 9781988832883 (ebook)
Subjects: LCSH: Lenin, Vladimir Il'ich, 1870-1924. | LCSH: Lenin, Vladimir Il'ich, 1870-1924—Influence. | LCSH: Lenin, Vladimir Il'ich, 1870-1924—Anniversaries, etc. | LCSH: Communism.
Classification: LCC DK254.L447 L46 2020 | DDC 947.084/1092—dc23

"A fascinating and surprisingly uplifting intellectual endeavour – analytically sharp yet wide-ranging. This collection of essays and images invites readers to reflect, from a multitude of perspectives and approaches, on one of history's central revolutionaries. More importantly, it encourages us to reflect on our own time in revolutionary ways. Its academic readership should also be inspired by its samizdat creation – there are ways to engage in intellectual conversations outside of the mainstream publication business."
– **Rebecca Selberg**, Lund University

"Wide-ranging, topical and sometimes provoking interpretations of Lenin reflecting different political standpoints."
– **David Lane**, Emeritus Fellow, Emmanuel College, Cambridge University.

"This wonderfully designed book provides an original and insightful contribution to academic discussions on Lenin, one that does justice to his legacy."
– **Joe Pateman**, University of Nottingham, UK

"A compelling volume for revolutionary-minded activists who are part of the radical ferment animating waves of dissent and protest sweeping the world – but also of genuine interest to anyone seeking information and ideas about one of the great political figures of the twentieth century."
– **Paul LeBlanc**, Professor of History, La Roche University, Author of *Lenin and the Revolutionary Party and October Song: Bolshevik Triumph, Communist Tragedy, 1917-1924*

"What an exciting culmination of the recent Lenin editorial revival! This explosive mix between images of Soviet relics and thoughtful insights about Leninism brilliantly dusts off the legacy of the October Revolution leader…"
– **Adrien Minard**, Independent Researcher

"'Consciousness not only reflects the objective world, but creates it,' Lenin wrote before the revolution. In analogy we might say, like Patti Smith once did: 'We created it, let's take it over!' This book is a tribute to revolutionary thought on the one hand and pure rock 'n' roll on the other!"
– **Ronald Matthijssen**, Lifetime communist voter and actor, social justice advocate and writer in the making

"I am not an admirer of Lenin. However, as a historian I believe that it is impossible to understand the contemporary world without a renewed effort to understand the emergence of the Soviet Union and its global legacy, including in the formation of "Western" Europe. This book pleasantly brings us memorial landscapes from Kyrgyzstan, both built and lyrical, originally articulating the latter with a diversity of scholarly and activist perspectives on the figure of Lenin. It is an important step towards a postcolonial debate on the history of the Soviet Union."
– **Tiago Castela**, University of Coimbra

"…an inspiring book, which gives a thought-provoking, prismatic picture of Lenin, both as a historic figure and an actual theoretician of change and revolution…"
– **Vesa Oittinen**, University of Helsinki

"I acquired this very unusual samizdat (self-published) 150th birthday present for Lenin as soon as I heard of it, and enthusiastically endorse its second edition. Not least because it is the product of one of my favourite countries, Kyrgyzstan, with many colour photos of Stalinist representations of Lenin (and Marx) taken in 2019 in the "Switzerland of Central Asia"; 22 chapters by authors from 15 countries, 4 from the USA, but also from the global South and 3 from Kyrgyzstan; poetry from a Kyrgyz revolutionary poet; and ending with a new translation of Bertolt Brecht's thrilling 'To Those Born After (An die Nachgeborenen).' Vladimir Ilich would have been delighted."
– **Bill Bowring**, Birkbeck College, University of London

"A great source of inspiration for those suffering from the corona dictatorships. Governments trying to freeze societies in their tracks will find revolution is around the corner."
– **Kees van der Pijl**, Prof of International Relations (retired), latest book, *Flight MH17, Ukraine and the New Cold War. Prism of Disaster*

"[The editors have] found exactly the right tone and the right team to bring Lenin into 21st century discussions. It is self-ironic, humorous, unpretentious, serious, wide-ranging, and well designed. As intended, the authors, of usually short pieces, come 'from all continents, from people of colour, different sexual orientations and gender identities.' Here we are almost as far away from the doxa of "Marxism-Leninism" as possible."
– **Göran Therborn**, Professor Emeritus of Sociology, Cambridge University

"I will return and I will be millions."
Tupac Katari

Contents

Hjalmar Jorge Joffre-Eichhorn, *Preface to the 2nd Edition* xi

The Politburo, *About This Book* xvii

Patrick Anderson, *In Search of Meaning –
A Note from the Translator* xxiii

Hjalmar Jorge Joffre-Eichhorn, *Introduction:
The Kyrgyz Lenin – From Spectre to Attractor (and Back)* 1

1. Leon Trotsky, *V.I. Lenin – On His Fiftieth Birthday* 11
2. Alain Badiou, *Lenin, Founder of the Modern Meaning
   of the Word 'Politics'* 15
3. Elvira Concheiro Bórquez, *Lenin Does Not Mean Leninism* 23
4. Michael Brie, *Learning from Lenin – and Doing It Differently* 31
5. Mauricio Sandoval Cordero, *Lenin from Latin America – Towards a
   Reactivation of the Marxism of Political Organisation and Strategy* 39
6. Vashna Jagarnath, *Peace! Land! Bread! – We are not going to die of
   Coronavirus, we are going to die of hunger!* 51
7. Atilio A. Boron, *Notes on "Left-Wing" Communism:
   An Infantile Disorder* 61
8. Owen Hatherley, *Dead Russians on the Wall* 79
9. Marcos Del Roio, *Engels and Lenin in Latin America:
   Yesterday and Today* 87
10. Kevin B. Anderson, *A Note on Lenin and the Dialectic* 97
11. Roland Boer, *Lenin and Non-Antagonistic Contradictions* 103
12. Georgy Mamedov, *How Is Internationalism to Be Understood?
    A Leninist Perspective on Identity Politics* 111
13. Jodi Dean, *Lenin's Desire: Reminiscences of Lenin
    and the Desire of the Comrade* 125

Poetic Interlude – Joomart Bokonbaev
Three Communist Poems 134

14. Ursina Lardi, *Playing Lenin –
    A Conversation about Lenin and Theatre* 143
15. Oxana Timofeeva, *What Lenin Teaches Us About Witchcraft* 149
16. Tora Lane, *Lenin, the Revolution, and the Uncertainties
    of Communism in the Work of Platonov* 163
17. Thomas Rudhof-Seibert,
    Eleven Theses on Lenin in the Corona Era 171
18. Matthieu Renault,
    On Revolutionary Prudence, or the Wisdom of Lenin 191
19. Michael Neocosmos, *Lenin's 'Turn to the Masses' (1921-1923)* 203
20. Molaodi Wa Sekake, *Lenin: A Man of Action
    and a Defender of the Integrity of Revolutionary Thought* 213
21. Matthew T. Huber, *Electric Communism:
    The Continued Importance of Energy to Revolution* 225
22. Mohira Suyarkulova,
    City of Lenin and the Social(ist) Life of a River 238
23. Ronald Grigor Suny, *A Whole River of Blood: Lenin and Stalin* 255
24. Wang Hui, *The Revolutionary Personality and The Philosophy
    of Victory – Commemorating the 150th Anniversary
    of Lenin's Birth* 261
25. Darko Suvin, *In the Shadows of Never-Ending Warfare:
    On the Use-Value of Lenin today* 279
26. Slavoj Žižek, *Lenin? – Which Lenin?* 291
27. Vijay Prashad,
    For Comrade Lenin on His 150th Birth Anniversary 295

Johann Salazar, *I Believe in Yesterday – A Photographer's Note
on Remembering an Alternative Future* 303

Bertolt Brecht, *To Those Born After* 313

The Central Committee 319
The Politburo 327
Index 329

List of Images

x	Photograph of 1969 Soviet postcard (Artist: Nikolai Zhukov)
xvi	Central Lenin monument in Bishkek, close to National History Museum
xxii	Lenin street somewhere between Tokmok and Bishkek, one of many in Kyrgyzstan
xxiv	Postcard of the Lenin monument, now replaced by the monument of the Kyrgyz National Hero Manas, in front of the National History Museum, Bishkek
9	Monument of the Kyrgyz National Hero Manas in front of the National History Museum, Bishkek
10	Lenin bust at a local bookshop opposite the Manas monument
14	Monument to the soldiers who lost their lives in WWII bearing the face of Lenin, Bishkek
21	Lenin statue in Luxemburg, Chuy Oblast
22	A split image of the Lenin statue in Luxemburg, Chuy Oblast
30	Lenin statue hidden from sight in the backyard of the Sport Palace Kozhomkul, Bishkek
31	Lenin statue hidden from sight in the backyard of the Sport Palace Kozhomkul, Bishkek
38	Lenin in Cholpon-Ata, Issyk-Kul Oblast (Photographer: Ulan Ashimov)
50	Lenin monument outside a former conference centre on the outskirts of Bishkek (Photographer: Dastan Kozhomuratov)
60	Internationalist mural on Soviet-era residential building in Bishkek
78	A monument with the face of Lenin in Bishkek
86	Marx and Engels monument in Bishkek juxtaposed with the Lenin monument in Osh
95	Marx and Engels monument in Bishkek
96	Close-up of Marx, Marx and Engels monument in Bishkek
102	Soviet era bus stop with a mosaic of the Kyrgyz horse on the road to Kant, Chuy Oblast
110	Distorted image of Lenin statue in thrift shop, Bishkek
124	Lenin statue in a factory compound in Kant, Chuy Oblast
134	Poetic Interlude: Panorama of the Ala-Too Mountains outside Bishkek
142	Image of Ursina Lardi as Lenin (Photographer: Thomas Aurin)
144	Image of Ursina Lardi as Lenin (Photographer: Thomas Aurin)
148	Lenin on repeat
162	Soviet monument in Bishkek

170	Lenin statue in Soviet sanatorium in a village outside Bishkek
188	"Lenin is with us" mosaic in Bishkek (Artist: Lidia Il'ina)
189	"Lenin is with us" mosaic in Bishkek (Artist: Lidia Il'ina)
202	Lenin monument in Osh, Osh Oblast (Photographer: Askat Ismailov)
212	One-hand Lenin statue in Kant, Chuy Oblast
224	Photograph of 1973 Soviet postcard (Artist: Boris Parmeev)
238	Ca. 1975 staged image by TASS photographer Simchenko
242	Lithograph by V. Pilpeniuk
244	Monument to Lenin on the right bank of Syr Darya in Leninabad, Soviet Tajikistan
245	Women picking pomegranates in Soviet Tajikistan
254	Lenin and Stalin artefacts in Bishkek thrift shop
260	Lenin monument in the Intergelpo neighbourhood of Bishkek
278	Lenin inside Bishkek train station (Photographer: Dastan Kozhomuratov)
281	The Light Bulb Of Ilyich 1 (Lampochka Ilicha; Source: http://vm.sovrhistory.ru)
281	The Light Bulb Of Ilyich 2 (Lampochka Ilicha; Photographer: Arkady Shaikhet)
290	Statue of Lenin in front of school in Luxemburg, Chuy Oblast
294	Lenin statue in Tokmok, Chuy Oblast
302	A FED 5 camera, made in the USSR
312	Small Lenin bust on sale at Orto-Say flea market in Bishkek
317	Back to the front: Lenin relocated to the back of National History Museum in Bishkek

All photographs by Johann Salazar unless otherwise mentioned

Preface to the 2nd Edition
Breathing for the Revolution – Toward an Oxygenic Communism

> *Lenin walks around the world.*
> *The sun sets like a scar.*
> *Between the darkness and the dawn*
> *There rises a red star.*[1]
> Langston Hughes[2]

> *I can't breathe.*
> Eric Garner, George Floyd and too many others

> *[I]n Russia if a person is allowed to breathe it is called freedom!*
> V.I. Lenin[3]

For all the official historiographic efforts at forging a mythologised image of Vladimir Ilyich Ulyanov as the austere, no-nonsense, professional revolutionary, the really existing flesh and blood Lenin understood and appreciated that the most materialist action an individual must carry out without fault to metabolise the struggle for communism is to breathe. Not just biologically respire but consciously breathe. Breathe for oneself and breathe for and with others.

On a personal level, this translated into Ilyich "forcing his lungs into a more active condition"[4] by "walking around the world" and especially walking and hiking in forests, steppes and mountains, "often [...] over 20 kilometres a day"[5] while singing "with courage, comrades, we go on marching,"[6] from the Swiss Alps and the Volski Forest to the Siberian Sayan. Lenin was fond of fresh and clean air, where "breathing is so easy,"[7] and naturally he had no qualms about pestering and advising relatives and comrades to follow his lead and do some relaxigorating walking and

---
1 Hughes in Rampersad and Roessel 1995: 318.
2 Intriguingly, during his only trip to the USSR Hughes deliberately visited Soviet Central Asia, "a coloured land moving into orbits hitherto reserved for whites," (Hughes 2003: 135) for a total of five months between September 1932 and January 1933. During his stay, apart from marvelling at a variety of large-scale modernisation projects and witnessing an embryonic version of the 1936-38 Moscow Trials, he met "with a broad range of poets, writers, musicians, artists and other cultural figures, who received him with enthusiasm." (Chioni Moore 2002: 1125) Some of his impressions were later published in *A Negro Looks at Soviet Central Asia* (1934) and *I wonder as I wander* (1956). Although existing research suggests otherwise, it is extremely tempting to imagine a face-to-face meeting – a veritable poetry slam, "rhym[ing] the Five-Year-Plan" (Hughes 2003: 137) and/or bringing to life a Central Asian "Leninist Blues" (Flatley 2020: 314) – between Hughes and the lyrical protagonist of this book, Kyrgyz revolutionary poet Joomart Bokonbaev, who composed many of his verses in the same 1930s. Other important Afro-American writers to visit the region in later years were W.E.B. DuBois and Audre Lorde, attending the 1958 and 1976 African-Asian Writers' Conference in Tashkent (Uzbek SSR), respectively. For a critically entertaining and at times deeply poignant account of the latter's impressions, see Lorde 2007.
3 Lenin 1972: 428.
4 Lepeshinskaya in Deutscher 1976: 52.
5 Elwood 2011: 144.
6 Lepeshinsky in Deutscher 1976: 54.
7 Lenin 1975: 92.

breathing of their own, as a number of his private letters reveal.[8]

On a politico-philosophical level, a variety of literal as well as metaphoric references to the act of breathing were perhaps surprisingly common in his everyday incendiary parlance, from the need for or lack of a tactical "breathing space" for political action among his own ranks to the sarcastic slandering of his political enemies as bearers of the "breath of death"[9] and "breath[ing] the odour of the dead."[10] And while the legacy of his 1909 *Materialism and Empiro-criticism* is at best contested, the superficially not overly breath-taking "before we perceive, we breathe; we cannot exist without air, food and drink"[11] may just deserve to be appreciated in all its radical simplicity, especially when thought-felt together with Lenin's linking the act of breathing to freedom and the absence thereof to suffocation and/or strangulation. In other words, the struggle for socialism was at one of its cores informed by a will to, at long last, "breathe freely" as opposed to continue "being strangled in the embrace of the imperialist bourgeoisie"[12] in a "Russia [that] is suffocating under the yoke of oppression and tyranny."[13]

Now, clearly even those of us inclined to (grudgingly? zealously? finally?) defend certain aspects of the 70+ year legacy of the USSR and other Communist experiments would hesitate to describe the overall atmosphere in Soviet society as one of persistent comfortable breathing for all its citizens, whether in political or environmental terms. On the contrary, the fact that the Soviet Union was decidedly not oxygenic enough surely contributed decisively to its demise. Then again, if there was ever a time colonised by a general sentiment of "physical and psychological breathlessness,"[14] an epoch "when breathing together grew dangerous, everybody was obliged to breathe alone and the rhythm of individual respiration was obliged to follow the pace of economic competition,"[15] it is today's era dominated by an ultra-totalitarian onto-civilisational model of production that feeds on sucking the lifeblood out of all of us – human and non-human – every fucking second of our lives. So yes, we cannot breathe, and thanks to the last words of our slain brother-comrades Eric Garner, George Floyd and way too many others, we now have a new rallying cry for letting our barbarian masters know that we will no longer allow that our lives be trumped by the same old, forever toxic logic of profit over people, white over non-white and heterosexual man over everyone else.

---

8 See, for example, Lenin's letters to his sister Maria Ilyinichna: "You ought to force yourself to take a walk for about two hours every day. It is not worthwhile poring over your lessons so industriously – you will ruin your health," (Ibid: 68) and to his mother Maria Alexandrovna: "It is a good thing that you have found an apartment near the Zemstvo offices. But is the air breathable in such places? Isn't it too dusty and stuffy?" (Ibid: 456)
9 Lenin 1977a: 448.
10 Lenin 1977b: 431.
11 Lenin 1977c: 142.
12 Lenin 1974: 338.
13 Lenin 1978: 421.
14 Berardi 2018: 15.
15 Ibid: 74.

Therefore, if it is indeed our desire to breathe new life into the long choking red star, a new oxygenic Communist politics of walking and breathing is what we must aspire to, inspire, respire and encourage, the latter in the sense of the Spanish verb "alentar," to give breath to someone. A "walking with the comrades"[16] nourished by an "asthmatic solidarity,"[17] "open to all the breaths of the world"[18] and striving towards the liberation of our individual and collective breathing apparatuses as the most fundamental means of production, which must at all times be totally unfettered. There can be no compromise on this. No breathing, no revolution. As simple as that. Tovarish Lenin knew this a century ago. Let's strap him on our backs and go on marching.

Hjalm(ar) Jorge Joffre-Eichhorn
Liepaja, Former Latvian CCP, 28 November 2020
(Engels is dead, long live Engels!)

References

Berardi, Franco "Bifo" (2018), *Breathing. Chaos. Poetry*. South Pasadena: Semiotext(e).
Chioni Moore, David (2002), "Colored Dispatches from the Uzbek Border, Langston Hughes' Relevance, 1933-2002," Callaloo, 25.4, 1115-1135.
Deutscher, Tamara (ed.) (1976), *Not By Politics Alone – The Other Lenin*. Westport: Lawrence Hill and Company.
Elwood, Carter (2011), *The Non-Geometric Lenin: Essays on the Development of the Bolshevik Party 1910-1914*. New York: Anthem Press.
Fanon, Frantz (2008), *Black Skin, White Mask*. London: Pluto Press.
Flatley, Jonathan (2020), "'Beaten, but Unbeatable:' On Langston Hughes's Black Leninism," *in* Amelia Glaser and Steven S. Lee (eds.), *Comintern Aesthetics*. Toronto: University of Toronto Press, 313-351.
Hughes, Langston (1934), *A Negro Looks at Soviet Central Asia*. Moscow: Co-Operative Publishing Society of Foreign Workers in the USSR.
Hughes, Langston (2003), *I wonder as I wander*. Columbia: University of Missouri Press.
Lenin, V.I. (1972), *Collected Works Vol. 11*. Moscow: Progress Publishers.
Lenin, V.I. (1974), *Collected Works Vol. 21*. Moscow: Progress Publishers.
Lenin, V.I. (1975), *Collected Works Vol. 37*. Moscow: Progress Publishers.
Lenin, V.I. (1977a), *Collected Works Vol. 17*. Moscow: Progress Publishers.
Lenin, V.I. (1977b), *Collected Works Vol. 26*. Moscow: Progress Publishers.
Lenin, V.I. (1977c), *Collected Works Vol. 14*. Moscow: Progress Publishers.
Lenin, V.I. (1978), *Collected Works Vol. 18*. Moscow: Progress Publishers.

---

16 See Roy 2014.
17 Berardi 2018: 15.
18 Césaire in Fanon 2008: 94.

Lepeshinskaya, Olga (1976), "The Siberian Deportee II," *in* Tamara Deutscher (ed.), *Not By Politics Alone – The Other Lenin*. Westport: Lawrence Hill and Company, 52-53.

Lepeshinsky, P.N. (1976), "A kind of Baritone," *in* Tamara Deutscher (ed.), *Not By Politics Alone – The Other Lenin*. Westport: Lawrence Hill and Company, 54-55.

Lorde, Audre (2007), *Sister Outsider*. New York: Random House.

Rampersad, Arnold, and David Roessel (1995), *The Collected Poems of Langston Hughes*. New York: Vintage Classics.

Roy, Arundhati (2011), *Walking with the Comrades*. New Delhi: Penguin Books India.

About This Book

Lenin150 (Samizdat) is the product of a rather leisurely executed 9-year plan. The original idea was conceived in 2011 as a result of a visit to the former Soviet republic of Kyrgyzstan, one of the few places in the world where almost every major town still hosts a monument to the great *vozhd* (leader) of the world proletariat. Subsequent visits cemented the desire to do 'something' about the generous existence of Lenin in the Kyrgyz public space and the format soon became clear. Given Ilyich's own obsession with the written word, 'it' had to become a book, though in this case his visual omnipresence in the erstwhile Kirghiz SSR needed to be taken into account, and hence an illustrated volume quickly emerged as the most reasonable and in fact exciting solution. What was missing was a suitable occasion – a communist horizon so to speak – for publication. Fortunately, 2017 was around the corner. 100 years of the October Revolution. Perfect.

To cut a long story short: it did not work out. Too many events and books were already in the process of being organised and most of the people we contacted to contribute texts were either too busy or had (temporarily) exhausted their Leninist repertoire in previously published volumes such as *Lenin Rediscovered, Lenin Reloaded: Toward a Politics of Truth, The Dilemmas of Lenin* and *Lenin 2017: Remembering, Repeating, and Working Through*. Too bad, we thought, but no reason to throw the idea into the dustbin of history just yet – new opportunities would undoubtedly arise very soon. In the meantime, in the spirit of Marx, Bensaïd, and Lacan, the stubborn old mole burrowed on, not giving up on its desire. What was needed now was a concrete analysis of the concrete situation.

Sure enough, additional special occasions were soon identified, starting with the 250th anniversary of *Das Kapital* (2017), followed by the bicentenary of Marx (2018) and yes, the 150th anniversary in 2020 of the birth of Vladimir Ilyich Ulyanov on April 22, 1870. 150 years of Lenin. Hell yeah. Seek and ye shall find. The former V. Ilyin, alias Lenin, was right: "Old Truths [That] Are Ever New".[1] It was now or never, but we had to move quickly. No "One step forward, two steps back"[2] allowed. In October 2019, a Politburo of three was quickly convened though the division of labour/separation of powers was done in rather bourgeois fashion. Paraphrasing the old Ilyich, we had to create the book, not with abstract human material, or with human material specially prepared by us, but with the human material bequeathed to us by capitalism, that is, Us. Oh dear. Что делать? What to do? The answer was ultimately straightforward: "From each according to his ability, to each according to his needs," i.e. one of us would look after the written content, the second would take care of the visual elements and the third member of the group had full control of all language-related aspects

1 Lenin 1977a: 211.
2 Lenin 1977b: 472.

of the book. The need part, on the other hand, was taken care of by a mysterious fourth member – let's call him the invisible hand or, more politically correct, a contemporary Engels – who agreed to support us financially via the contribution of travel-related expenses for our return trip to Kyrgyzstan in late 2019 plus the purchase of multiple Soviet cameras and film. Other than that, there was no money in *Lenin150 (Samizdat)*. With the exception of a few custodians of Lenin paraphernalia in Kyrgyzstan and the wonderful translator of the verses of Kyrgyz Communist poet Joomart Bokonbaev (1910-1944), nobody was paid. The motto was "all you need is love" and at least some of us surely did feel something akin to a strong comradely affection to the old, non-white man.

There were now two main tasks cut out for us: i) Lenin-hunting in Kyrgyzstan; and ii) the (s)election of the Central Committee of our (birthday) party. To start with the bad news, the former was severely cut short by the advent of the Coronavirus and the at least temporary impossibility of our return to Kyrgyzstan in early 2020 to further document Lenin in his natural habitat. The latter, on the other hand, was hampered by the recent going-out-of-fashion of forced labour, i.e. the sad truth that we could do very little about the fact that many potential candidates had once again to decline due to other revolutionary commitments. Another complication entailed from our desire to adopt a decolonised and depatriarchalised internationalist approach to the composition of the book: in other words, we aimed to include contributions from all continents, from people of colour, different sexual orientations and gender identities and of course, we were determined to have a strong presence of female voices. Now that the book is done and looking at the table of contents, the final result is slightly sobering, as clearly there is a certain Eurocentric and male bias to the authors. Nevertheless, we are damn proud of each person who did eventually show up at the birthday blast, including a distinguished guest from a previous anniversary occasion, and we can only say спасибо (in Russian) or рахмат (in Kyrgyz), i.e. an old-fashioned thank you, to everyone who put in the effort to write a text at extremely short notice and – in most cases – specifically for the occasion.

Speaking of the texts, the themes of the contributions were neither subject to principles of democratic centralism nor was there an overarching party line to follow. Instead, the invitation to write was based on two straightforward requests: one, critical solidarity with Lenin, and two, writing with joy. The former request had to do with the fact that we did not want to add to the canon of "balanced" accounts of Lenin's life and work, i.e. 'Lenin, the Antichrist' books. Given the dire state of 21st century capitalism even before the Corona crisis, it is understandable that liberal and conservative "paper tigers" would want to divert attention from the ever so "civilised

About This Book

barbarism"³ caused by their multiple systems of oppression via the conjuring of the bloody spectre of communism and its helmsmen. To invite some of these "liquidators" to the party, however, would have violated all current social and ideological distancing rules. In short: "Let them gloat, let them perform their clownish antics,"⁴ but not in our book. The latter request, on the other hand, was not an absurd attempt at undermining Lenin's much-cited anguished love for Beethoven's *Appassionata* by asking the authors to compose their texts while listening to the same prodigy's *Ode to Joy* aka the Anthem of (Capitalist) Europe. No, the invitation was simply – even if only for a brief moment – to refuse to obey the incessant neoliberal colonisation and depletion of our time and energy resources, with the attendant pressure of always having to function and perform, and just enjoy chillin' with Lenin. Consequently, we encouraged the authors to write in whatever style came most naturally to them, whether academic, journalistic, polemical or even lyrical. While most members of the CC ultimately ended up writing in a more traditional academic format, we hope that the creation process itself was nonetheless joyful, and we invite the reader to adopt a reading style that – without relinquishing our Leninist capacity for critical thinking – is inspired by a similar spirit of chilled solidarity. Vladimir Ilyich himself was, after all, quite given to the odd moment of joy and relaxation, such as the occasional nerve-soothing walk in the forest or in the mountains, preferably in the company of his beloved Krupskaya.

Mountains and Nadezhda Konstantinovna, that brings us back to the beautiful country of Kyrgyzstan, the site of our anniversary festivities. Since the idea for the book was born here, we wanted to make sure that the country and people would be 'shown' not only through the potentially colonising gaze of a bunch of foreigners, and so we were intent on inviting as many Kyrgyz friends as possible to co-host the party. Once again, we may not have been entirely successful, but we are grateful to our Kyrgyzstan-based comrades Georgy Mamedov, Mokhira Suyarkulova, Darika Amanbaeva, Dastanbek Kozhomuratov, Tynchtykbek Bakytov, Elnura Isabaeva, Valentina, Alexander, Nurkan, Rahat, Yulia, Nika, Noorila, Askat Ismailov, Ulan Ashimov, Aisuluu Kokoyeva and Charles Buxton for their invaluable contributions and support, material and immaterial, and to all those Kyrgyz citizens who pointed us in the direction – or not – of Lenin monuments and relics in and around Bishkek and Chuy *oblast*, some of which are illustrated in this book. большое спасибо / Чоң рахмат.

Finally, and to conclude this overture, every birthday deserves a toast. Ours will be spoken by a special guest, expressing himself in English for the first time, the aforementioned Kyrgyz revolutionary poet Joomart Bokonbaev. Three of his poems have been included in *Lenin150 (Samizdat)*; it is with a stanza from his 1939 work "To N.K. Krupskaya," in which the author

---
3 Lenin 1977c: 388.
4 Lenin 1973: 211.

honours both Nadezhda and Volodya for their tireless revolutionary efforts, that our journey into past and future shall begin…

"But those who struggled for the good of people
Will never die, they will burn like candles."

С днем рождения, Ильич !
Happy Birthday, Ilyich!

The Politburo

Postscriptum: It turns out that publishing an openly partisan, not exclusively academic book about Lenin in 2020 is no easy feat. Frankly, some of the experiences we made with the publishing winter palaces of our time were rather demoralising, but clearly this is not the space to wash our dirty lenin in public. On the contrary, we were always very explicit with our comrade-authors that samizdat (Russian for 'self-publishing') was a concrete option since for us the entire initiative, right from its inception, was above all about investing in Lenin in the year of his 150th anniversary. *Samizdat* = investing in Lenin: intellectually, emotionally, psychologically, physically and yes, if needed, financially. The returns will depend on all of us daring to "dream dangerously."[5]

References

Ali, Tariq (2017), *The Dilemmas of Lenin: Terrorism, War, Empire, Love, Revolution*. London: Verso.
Budgen, Sebastian, Kouvelakis, Stathis, and Slavoj Žižek (eds.) (2007), *Lenin Reloaded: Toward a Politics of Truth*. Durham: Duke University Press.
Lenin, V.I. (1973), *Collected Works Vol. 33*. Moscow: Progress Publishers.
Lenin, V.I. (1977a), *Collected Works Vol. 17*. Moscow: Progress Publishers.
Lenin, V.I. (1977b), *Collected Works Vol. 7*. Moscow: Progress Publishers.
Lenin, V.I. (1977c), *Collected Works Vol. 19*. Moscow: Progress Publishers.
Lih, Lars T. (2008), *Lenin Rediscovered: What Is To Be Done?* Chicago: Haymarket Books.
Žižek, Slavoj (2012), *The Year of Dreaming Dangerously*. London: Verso.
Žižek, Slavoj (2017), *Lenin 2017: Remembering, Repeating, and Working Through*. London: Verso.

---

5 See Žižek 2012.

Ленин
көчөсү

In Search of Meaning – A Note from the Translator

Patrick Anderson

The translator's task, always and of necessity, exists in the realm between rigid authenticity and whimsical adaptation. It is like crossing a river on a narrow plank with a weighty sack in each hand: in one, faithfulness to the original work, written in the language, that is to say the verbal expression of the history and culture, of the author; in the other, the idioms and inherent beauty of the target language, without which the translation becomes at best stilted, at worst devoid of real meaning.

The rendering of the text thus requires a constant balancing act between these two demands, whose ultimate goal is not perfection – an impossibility in the circumstances – but rather a kind of earnest devotion to reproduce the content and spirit of the author's creation in a manner accessible to those with a different language, history and culture.

This is by no means an easy endeavour, but a rewarding one, at times even exhilarating. There is a sense of adventure in plumbing the depths of another writer's thought and style, entering the often foreign world of the subject matter, facing the occasional demon in the form of a truly untranslatable word or concept and, above all, resisting the hubristic temptation to make the translation so elegant as to betray the original yet continuing to strive for the most accurate and compelling possible rendition.

In all of this, I am oddly reminded of Lenin himself, as he is revealed in the essays in this book: balancing the demands of adherence and adaptability; confronting crises that called for urgent yet thoughtful innovation; succumbing at times to condescension, a belief in exclusive access to truth, albeit with the noblest of intentions. Perhaps, in his way, Lenin too was a translator of sorts – of ideology into praxis, of imagined possibility into material action. While his successes and failures continue to be the subject of debate, there is no doubting his devotion.

I am grateful to Hjalmar for inviting me to join this project, which gave me the opportunity to enhance my patchy knowledge of the period, an unprecedented and remarkable chapter in human history. To the authors whose work I translated, I hope you will find some satisfaction in my imperfect rendition of your words, and pleasure in the knowledge that others who do not share your language can now share in your passion, conviction and erudition.

Zurich, April 2020

Introduction: The Kyrgyz Lenin – From Spectre to Attractor (and Back)

Hjalmar Jorge Joffre-Eichhorn

> *Strike me dead, the track has vanished,*
> *Well, what now? We've lost the way,*
> *Demons have bewitched our horses,*
> *Led us in the wilds astray.*
> A. Pushkin

> *Oh we,*
> *Who wished to lay the ground for kindness*
> *Could not ourselves be kind.*
> *But you, when the time comes at last*
> *That wo/man is helper to wo/man*
> *Think of us*
> *With forbearance.*
> B. Brecht

Kyrgyzstan, May 2011. Lenin everywhere. What a trip, or rather treat, or probably both. In any case, I was flabbergasted and at the same time strangely happy. It felt really good to keep running into him wherever we went. Not the real Lenin of course, but the statues, relics and images of him in central squares, on buildings and paintings. Clearly, the flesh-and-blood Vladimir Ilyich would have sternly disapproved of such cultish veneration, but truth be told, after having had to endure for years the incessant hubristic chatter about "the end of history" and the well-deserved triumph of so-called freedom and democracy, i.e. unfettered capitalist barbarism, it was just so nice to see him sticking around long after the demise of his very own offspring, the ever so Evil Empire aka the Union of Soviet Socialist Republics or *CCCP*.

Later on in that first visit, I was told by my Kyrgyz friends that basically every main town in the former Kirghiz SSR still hosts a monument to *tovarish* Ulyanov,[1] and over the years as I returned to the country time and again, I was privileged to confirm first-hand the ubiquity of the former н. Ленин in the cities and countryside, in some people's hearts and other people's minds, and certainly on people's tongues, at least if you asked them directly about what Lenin meant for them both historically and in today's times. Needless to say, there was a wide range of, generally quite passionately embodied, views about him, from total reverence to equally outright rejection, from a desperate holding on to the dream of a resurrection of the USSR – times have not been easy for many citizens since independence – to a just as fierce clinging to

---
[1] For the story of one particular Lenin monument in Kyrgyzstan, see Cummings 2013.

the yet unfulfilled promises of the brave new world of liberal democracy and globalised capitalism. As was to be expected, by and large the former views were expressed by those who had experienced the beauties and pains of actually existing socialism, while the advocates of the latter were generally people whose lives had unfolded in post-Soviet times, marked by multiple political revolutions, mass-scale economic migration to Russia, ethnic strife, the highly ambivalent benefits of simultaneously hosting both US and Russian military bases but also new forms of grassroots resistance, especially from women's rights and queer activists, to name just a few "trivial" details of quotidian 21st century Kyrgyz life.

So far, so unsurprising. Both the adulation and demonisation of Lenin belong to the "usual suspects" category of remembering him, in Kyrgyzstan and beyond, although there is undoubtedly something quite mysterious and mind-blowing about the visceral intensity with which praise and slurs continue to be bestowed on VIU a staggering 150 years after his birth in unsuspecting Simbirsk. In fact, even people's frequently voiced indifference towards him was expressed in rather engaged – or was it resigned? – terms. How to (ir)rationally explain this never-ending hysteria? A strange case of Leninitis? False Consciousness? Post-Traumatic Socialist Disorder? Cold War Syndrome? Left-Wing Melancholia?[2] The spectre of communism? How about self-fulfilling prophecy? Enter the scene: the anguished bard of Communism, Vladimir Vladimirovich Mayakovsky and his four-poem Lenin cycle immortalised by a single line:

"Ленин жил, Ленин жив, Ленин будет жить."
"Lenin lived, Lenin lives, Lenin will live."

If you ask me, I like this reasoning the most, at least when thinking about Lenin from a Left perspective. I admit that it is neither particularly scientific nor particularly materialist and, really, not particularly dialectical either. On the contrary, it is rather plain and kitschy, and hence one might be tempted to call it idealist or utopian, replete with opioid undertones. No doubt, if it had not been published posthumously, Lenin himself would have showered unceasing abuse on Mayakovsky and then spent the next few days and nights writing *Materialism and Empirio-Criticism 2.0* to refute his own immortality once and for all. But at the risk of myself becoming the subject of people's ridicule and even wrath – people with more intellectual and Communist prowess than me – I do believe that there is value in Mayakovsky's deification of Lenin, especially if taken together with another lowbrow historic utterance that united writer, Plutarch, and General Secretary, Julius Caesar: "*Veni, Vidi, Vici.*" "I came, I saw, I won."

Because that is really what Lenin did and what makes him live forever,

---

2 See Traverso 2016 for an important recent engagement with left-wing melancholy.

Introduction

isn't it? He came, he saw, he won. Not just him, of course. Lenin's name has always stood for the expression of a collective project, and as such his quest for the realisation of the Marxian Kingdom of Freedom was and continues to be conducted, loved and vilified, in different personal pronouns and linguistic expressions: from the slandering "They are Leninists" to the self-ennobling "We are all Lenin," or to put it in contemporary terms – #blamelenin, #beleninbehappy. In fact, at least in the English language, we might want to consider making the distinction between lenin with a small "l," referring to the ultimately ordinary man living a quite extraordinary life, "a life that speaks for itself,"[3] and Lenin with a capital "L," standing in as a Left-wing floating signifier for everything that was, is and will always be good about (Communists like) us. You know, our capacity to think, feel, dream, analyse, state the truth, prepare, organise, imagine, strategise, create, intervene, struggle, be in solidarity with each other, fuck up, persevere, and yes, we must not forget, win.

The man lenin was a winner. He had, as the Germans say, the *Sieger-Gen*, the innate capacity and will to win. And while all this might sound terribly deterministic and mechanical – sorry, Vladimir Ilyich – what I am getting at here is simply the fact that "Lenin lived, Lenin lives, Lenin will live" has not only a propagandistic and (vaguely) lyrical but also an ontological dimension that I believe should not be reduced to the eternal paying homage to lenin the actually existing revolutionary, though we may do that too, but rather to make his *Sieger-Gen* the psycho-material foundation of our own individual and collective DNA, our fighting spirit so to speak. In other words, we need to claim and make genetically ours precisely this Leninist drive to engage the dialectic of victory, i.e. to "accelerate the vicissitude of the times," to take, when needed, "One Step Forward, Two Steps Back," to understand that sometimes the rule must be "Better fewer, but better," to disregard the "malicious joy" of our "true friends" whenever we fail, to learn not to "give way to despondency" on our treacherous way to the summit, and finally, to dare to declare victory, put down our flag, raise our fists, throw back a few shots of vodka or cognac, sing and dance to "The Internationale" and get back to work.

Speaking of the latter, and at the risk of turning into a Leninist Killjoy,[4] we must return to the streets of Kyrgyzstan once more. This time anno 2015. Because admittedly my initial excitement about the surreal presence of Lenin everywhere was soon complemented, replaced even, by a deep sense of defeat and loss. While at first seeing his statues in places like Osh, Bishkek or Batken had an incredibly invigorating and mobilising effect on me – sparks were flying and I was ready to "Leap, Leap, Leap" – on closer inspection, as I noticed their general state of advanced decay – a missing hand, a broken nose, a barely legible plaque – his monuments began to

---

3 Loginov 2019: 7.
4 With regard to Sara Ahmed and her notion of the Feminist Killjoy.

have exactly the opposite effect: they weighed on me, evoking an eerie sense of disillusionment and political paralysis. In short, I was no longer at ease. Instead of Mayakovsky's exalting hymns, suddenly the sobering laments and warnings of comrades like Andrey Platonov, Victor Serge,[5] Walter Benjamin, Stuart Hall, Daniel Bensaïd, Pepetela,[6] Bifo Berardi and Mark Fisher – yes, all of them male, I wonder why – came hammering into my head, epitomised by Hall's "History is not waiting in the wings to catch up your mistakes into another inevitable success. You lose because you lose because you lose." Mind you, it was not the premonitory nature of Hall's sentence that caused me the greatest despair – speaking with Fisher I am "senselessly hopeful" that we will get another shot at "failing again and failing better" soon enough – but rather the encroaching realisation that the recent decades of revolutionary setbacks and defeats, symbolised by the bruised and battered Kyrgyz Lenin statues lingering on in "a place stained by time,"[7] not only failed to bring about the much anticipated withering away of all kinds of practices of oppression but instead resulted – for many of us – in the increasing mutilation of our once so beautiful (left-) wings. #leninistired.

As all of us who struggle for a better world are viscerally aware, such feelings of despair, disenchantment, doubt, not to mention physical, psychological and emotional weariness, are not only part and parcel of the pathological phenomena of living under and struggling against contemporary capitalism (and other axis of evil members such as patriarchy and colonialism), but arguably belong to the rank and file experiences, indeed are perhaps a necessary (pre-)condition and at the same time inextinguishable element of the process of revolution itself. And while the official, monumental Vladimir Ilyich Lenin presented to us for decades was one of God-like superhuman strength and perseverance – buff, bold and beautiful – an image that undoubtedly and fortunately inspired and may still inspire millions of us across the world to pick up and reimagine our hammers, sickles and smartphones, it may just be that a more demonumentalised image of him could offer similar use-value for those of us – most of us? – facing the occasional difficulty to create another day of struggle. I am talking about the sick, exhausted, defeated, tormented, frail and dying lenin[8] so vividly described to us by his long-time companions Nadezhda Krupskaya, Alexandra Kollontai and Angelica Balabanoff – yes, all of them female,

---

5 See, for example, Serge's novels *The Case of Comrade Tulayev*, *Midnight in the Century* and *Unforgiving Years*.

6 In the English-speaking world, the work of Angolan writer and former anti-colonial guerrilla Pepetela has not yet received the attention it deserves. Regarding the question of political disillusionment his 1992 novel *A Geração da Utopia* remains a literary event. For the Portuguese-language reader, the 2017 edition with a preface by fellow Angolan writer Ondjaki is especially recommended.

7 "Haunting can be seen as intrinsically resistant to the contraction and homogenization of time and space. It happens when a place is stained by time, or when a particular place becomes the site for an encounter with broken time." (Fischer 2012: 19)

8 As viscerally portrayed by Ursina Lardi in Milo Rau's 2017 play, LENIN. See the interview with Ursina in Chapter 14.

I wonder why. What comes to mind are the images of the bedridden lenin plagued by frequent and intense headaches in the difficult years before the revolution, the grieving, "shrunk" lenin at Inessa Armand's funeral at the height of the Civil War[9] and, of course, the isolated, supervised, silen(t)ced and suicidal lenin withering away in his dacha – like Hölderlin in his tower[10] – on the outskirts of Moscow in the final days of his life.

It might be pushing it too far to hypothesise that lenin was battling with mental health during his long years of struggle, but from all we know and admire about his capacity of analysing concretely the concrete conditions around him, it may not be overly blasphemous to presume that an intellectually lonely, physically ailing, emotionally suffering and existentially imploding lenin, hanging on to a life of revolution in constantly adverse circumstances, must have at least occasionally questioned his own dialectical condition: What is to be done, Ильич? The political therapy that emerged from this speculative self-questioning was not a pre-historical version of today's neoliberal self-optimisation, but a politics of endurance composed of: grudging self-care, in the form of his oft-cited restorative walks in the countryside; comradely love – being among workers and especially sharing his life with powerful women, for example Maria Alexandrowna, Nadezhda Konstantinovna and Inessa Fyodorovna; compulsive (letter) writing, including the surely not always justified but unquestionably liberating taking-it-all-out-on-others; and an unceasing epistemic curiosity – how many books did he read again during his multiple exiles? – all of which, taken together, resulted in a renewed capacity and desire to revive the struggle through the strategic application of his power for positive hallucinations in action, i.e. his uncanny ability to see what is not there (yet) followed by the mobilisation of all his physical and mental energies to turn singular vision into collective reality – the right to disillusionment and "beginning from the beginning"[11] included.

The bedridden lenin went on to boldly pronounce his *April Theses* and then made sure that the locomotive of history reached its destination, at least temporarily, for the first time. The grieving lenin eventually recovered his life force and did not hesitate to "descend from [a] height that no one before him ha[d] reached," stunning friends and foes alike with the announcement of a New Economic Policy that kept the locomotive going when everyone's fuel was running low. The silen(t)ced Lenin, finally, provided a rude awakening from beyond the grave, in the form of his belatedly released "testament," to all those who had since betrayed his legacy by embalming him into an infallible icon adorning the country's train stations while the locomotive went sputtering on until finally crashing into

---

9 See Deutscher 1976: 121.
10 For a Marxist (re-)claiming of the contested legacy of German poet Hölderlin, celebrating his 250th anniversary in 2020, see Weiss 2011.
11 See Žižek's "How to Begin from the Beginning" for a contemporary engagement with Lenin's "Notes of a Publicist."

the abyss in 1991.

It is this Comeback Lenin who, in today's parlance, knew and came to accept that "there is a time for depression, [a]nd we shouldn't underestimate its cognitive potential;"[12] this vanguard-cum-rearguard Lenin[13] who had to learn the hard way that "Little Annoyances Should Not Stand in the Way of a Big Pleasure;"[14] this Sisyphean Lenin, who understood that the revolutionary personality is forged, nourished and sustained in the ebbs and flows between the drowning disillusionments of the nadir and the intoxicating heights of the summit – it is this Lenin of whom we may wish to think not only with forbearance, for all he did and did not do, but with whom we may also want to be in critical solidarity for all his awkward rock-climbing and free-falling done not only in his but in all our names. For it is the lessons we can still learn from his attempts to create a more just and beautiful world, free of exploitation and alienation, that are arguably the most potent antidote to the heart- and mind-numbing, politically immobilising consumer temptations with which the "ruling ontology"[15] desires to bewitch us. One of these lessons, perhaps the most encouraging one, is that there is always an alternative track worth believing in and struggling for: yesterday, today, tomorrow. #goodriddancetina.[16]

In my experience, the Lenin monuments in Kyrgyzstan, in the year of the old man's 150th anniversary, despite or even because of their beautiful decrepitude, continue to exude and echo precisely this (haunting) Leninist spirit. They implore those of us born after to hear the terrible news and pass the time given to us on earth struggling against and beyond the dark times we live in, all the while never forgetting that those in power sit safer without us.[17] Paraphrasing Mark Fisher, yes, we can choose to regard these icons as that which (in actuality) is no longer, but which is still effective as a virtuality: our (anti-)communist compulsion to repeat via Soviet nostalgia and Left-wing USSR-phobia. More importantly, however, we can also choose to view them as quite literally standing in for that which (in actuality) has not yet happened, but which is already effective in the virtual – an attractor, an anticipation potentially shaping current and future actions.[18]

---

12 Berardi 2008: 10.
13 For a recent theorisation about the importance of the rearguard in political struggle, see Santos 2014.
14 Lenin 1977: 366.
15 Fisher 2009: 43.
16 The acronym TINA stands for "There is no Alternative" (to free-market capitalism, liberal democracy and human rights), a logic associated with the radical neoliberal restructuring of the world, led by former British Prime Minister Margaret Thatcher and former US president Ronald Reagan in the early 1980s. Since the end of actually existing socialism, TINA and its ideological evil twin, "The End of History," as declared by US neocon Francis Fukuyama, have been incessantly promoted as the horizon of human possibilities by the world's political, economic, cultural and ideological elites, but not without resistance.
17 This sentence is a paraphrasing of Bertolt Brecht's poem "To Those Born After." Please see new translation on page 313-315.
18 "Provisionally, then, we can distinguish two directions in hauntology. The first refers to that which is (in actuality is) no longer, but which is still effective as a virtuality (the traumatic "compulsion to repeat," a structure that repeats, a fatal pattern). The second refers to that which (in actuality) has not yet happened,

Introduction

This attractor, for many of us, continues to be a variant of the communist horizon,[19] lying far in the distance, but clearly visible, though we ourselves, just like Lenin and his poetic disciple Bertolt Brecht, may ultimately fail to reach it. Nonetheless, the seeming impossibility of our task – after all, we know that we do not make history under self-selected circumstances – has never stopped us from wagering that a world in which wo/man is helper to wo/man will one day emerge from the flood in which many of us (will) have gone under. And while we have yet to prove Marx wrong that history repeats itself the first time as tragedy and the second time as farce, chances are that next time round we will create something much more just, democratic, beautiful and joyful than what all hitherto existing attempts – our attempts – have accomplished. #spectreofcommunism. #lenin150.

So that's it. Socialism or Barbarism 2.0. Our response is obvious: no alternative, but to fight. Fight with despair, fight with outrage, fight with hope, fight with joy, fight with commitment, fight with groove. Fight in whatever way comes most natural to each and every one of us. But fight we must. Individually and together. Full of communist desire,[20] and for the communist necessity.[21] From all I have come to know about them in the process of composing *Lenin150 (Samizdat)*, the comrade-authors in this book are all powerful and amazing fellow fighters on our multiple paths to the communist horizon. As such, I am confident that their texts and their compelling, and in some cases absolutely urgent, appropriations of Lenin will be of considerable use-value for our struggles ahead.

¡ *La lucha continúa* !
¡ *Venceremos y Encantaremos* !

References

Adamczak, Bini (2021), *Yesterday's Tomorrow: On the Loneliness of Communist Specters and the Reconstruction of the Future*. Cambridge: MIT Press.

Ahmed, Sara (2017), *Living a Feminist Life*. Durham: Duke University Press.

Berardi, Franco "Bifo" (2008), *Félix Guattari: Thought, Friendship and Visionary Cartography*. London: Palgrave Macmillan.

Brecht, Bertolt (2020), "To Those Born After." Translation: Patrick Anderson.

---

but which is already effective in the virtual (an attractor, an anticipation shaping current behaviour)." (Fisher 2012: 19)

19 The expression "communist horizon" was frequently invoked by former Bolivian vice-president Álvaro García Linera in the first few years of the (2006-2019 & 2020-) led by Evo Morales Ayma. See Dean 2012 for a crucial engagement with the communist horizon.

20 See Adamczak 2021 for a beautifully harrowing engagement with our past communist failures and the need for the reconstruction of our individual and collective communist desire(s).

21 See Moufawad-Paul 2020 for a polemical but/and forceful distinction between the communist possibility and the communist necessity.

Cummings, Sally N. (2013), "Leaving Lenin: Elites, official ideology and monuments in the Kyrgyz Republic," *The Journal of Nationalism and Ethnicity*, 41, 606-621.
Dean, Jodi (2012), *The Communist Horizon*. London: Verso.
Deutscher, Tamara (ed.) (1976), *Not By Politics Alone – The Other Lenin*. Westport: Lawrence Hill and Company.
Fisher, Mark (2009), *Capitalist Realism*. London: Zero Books.
Fisher, Mark (2012), "What Is Hauntology?," *Film Quarterly*, 66(1), 16-24.
Hall, Stuart (1987), "Gramsci and Us," *Marxism Today*.
Lenin, V.I. (1977), *Collected Works Vol. 7*. Moscow: Progress Publishers.
Loginov, Vladlen (2019), *Vladimir Lenin: How to Become a Leader*. London: Glagoslav Publications.
Moufawad-Paul, J. (2020), *The Communist Necessity (2nd Edition)*. Montreal: Kersplebedeb.
Pepetela (2017), *A Geração da Utopia*. Alfragide: Leya/Livros RTP.
Santos, Boaventura de (2014), *Epistemologies of the South: Justice against Epistemicide*. Boulder: Paradigm Publisher.
Serge, Victor (2008), *Unforgiving Years*. New York: NYRB Classics.
Serge, Victor (2011), *The Case of Comrade Tulayev*. New York: NYRB Classics.
Serge, Victor (2014), *Midnight in the Century*. New York: NYRB Classics.
Traverso, Enzo (2016), *Left-Wing Melancholia: Marxism, History, and Memory*. New York: Columbia University Press.
Weiss, Peter (2011), *Hölderlin: A Play in Two Acts*. Kolkata: Seagull Books.
Žižek, Slavoj (2009), "How to Begin from the Beginning," *New Left Review*, 57, 43-55.

1. V.I. Lenin – On His Fiftieth Birthday (1920)[1]

Leon Trotsky

Lenin's internationalism needs no recommendation. It is best characterised by Lenin's irreconcilable break, in the first days of the world war, with that counterfeit internationalism which reigned in the Second International. The official leaders of "Socialism" used the parliamentary tribune to reconcile the interests of the fatherland with the interests of mankind by way of abstract arguments in the spirit of the old cosmopolites. In practice this led, as we know, to the support of the predatory fatherland by the proletarian forces.

Lenin's internationalism is in no sense a formula for verbally reconciling nationalism with internationalism. It is a formula for international revolutionary action. The world's territory in the clutches of the so-called civilised section of mankind is regarded as a unified arena where a gigantic struggle occurs, whose component elements are constituted by the individual peoples and their respective classes. No single major issue can be kept restricted within a national framework. Visible and invisible threads connect such an issue with dozens of events in all corners of the world. In the evaluation of international factors and forces Lenin is freer than anyone else from national prejudices.

Marx concluded that the philosophers had sufficiently interpreted the world and that the real task was to change it. But he, the pioneering genius, did not live to see it done. The transformation of the old world is now in full swing and Lenin is the foremost worker on this job. His internationalism is a practical appraisal plus a practical intervention into the march of historical events on a world scale and with worldwide aims. Russia and her fate is only a single element in this titanic historical struggle upon whose outcome hinges the fate of mankind.

Lenin's internationalism needs no recommendation. But at the same time Lenin himself is profoundly national. His roots are deep in modern Russian history, he draws it up into himself, gives it its highest expression, and precisely in this way attains the highest levels of international action and world influence.

At first glance the characterisation of Lenin as a "national" figure may seem surprising, but, in essence, this follows as a matter of course. To be able to lead such a revolution, without parallel in the history of peoples, as Russia is now living through, it is obviously necessary to have an indissoluble, organic bond with the main forces of the people's life, a bond which springs from the deepest roots.

Lenin personifies the Russian proletariat, a young class, which

---

[1] Source: https://www.marxists.org/archive/trotsky/1920/04/lenin.html.

politically is scarcely older than Lenin himself, but a class which is profoundly national, for recapitulated in it is the entire past development of Russia, in it lies Russia's entire future, with it the Russian nation rises or falls. Freedom from routine and banality, freedom from imposture and convention, resoluteness of thought, audacity in action – an audacity which never turns into foolhardiness – this is what characterises the Russian working class, and with it also Lenin.

The nature of the Russian proletariat, which has made it today the most important force of the world revolution, had been prepared beforehand by the entire course of Russian national history: the barbaric cruelty of the Tsarist autocracy, the insignificance of the privileged classes, the feverish growth of capitalism fed by the lees of the world stock-market, the escheated character of the Russian bourgeoisie, their decadent ideology, their shoddy politics. Our "Third Estate" knew neither a Reformation nor a great revolution of their own and could never have known them. Therefore the revolutionary tasks of the Russian proletariat assumed a more all-embracing character. Our past history knows no Luther, no Thomas Münzer, no Mirabeau, no Danton, no Robespierre. Exactly for that reason the Russian proletariat has its Lenin. What was lost in way of tradition has been won in the sweep of the revolution.

Lenin mirrors the working class, not only in its proletarian present but also in its peasant past, still so recent. This most indisputable leader of the proletariat not only outwardly resembles a peasant, but there is something inwardly in him strongly smacking of a peasant. Facing the Smolny stands the statue of the other great figure of the world proletariat: Karl Marx, on a stone pedestal in a black frock coat. Assuredly, this is a trifle, but it is impossible even to imagine Lenin putting on a black frock coat. Some portraits of Marx show him wearing a dress shirt against whose broad expanse something resembling a monocle dangles.

That Marx was not inclined to foppery is quite clear to all who have an inkling of the spirit of Marx. But Marx was born and grew up on a different national-cultural soil, lived in a different atmosphere, as did also the leading personalities of the German working class, whose roots reach back not to a peasant village, but to the corporation guilds and the complex city culture of the middle ages.

Marx's very style, rich and beautiful, in which strength and flexibility, wrath and irony, severity and refinement are combined, also contains the literary and aesthetic accumulations of the entire German socio-political literature since the days of the Reformation and even before. Lenin's literary and oratorical style is awesomely simple, utilitarian, ascetic, as is his whole make-up. But in this mighty asceticism there is not a trace of a moralistic attitude. There is no principle here, no elaborated system and, of course, no posturing; it is simply the outward expression of inward conservation of strength for action. It is a peasant's practical proficiency but on a colossal scale.

The entire Marx is contained in the *Communist Manifesto* in the foreword to his *Critique*, in *Capital*. Even if he had not been the founder of the First International, he would always have remained what he is today. Lenin, on the other hand, is contained entirely in revolutionary action. His scientific works are only a preparation for action. If he never published a single book in the past, he would forever enter into history just as he enters it now: the leader of the proletarian revolution, the founder of the Third International.

A clear, scientific system – the materialistic dialectic – is necessary for action on such a historical scale as devolved upon Lenin; it is necessary but not sufficient. Needed here in addition is that irrevealable creative power we call intuition: the ability to judge events correctly on the wing, to separate the essential and important from the husks and incidentals, to fill in mentally the missing parts of the picture, to draw to conclusion the thoughts of others and above all those of the enemy, to connect all this into a unified whole and to deal a blow the moment that the "formula" for this blow comes to mind. This is the intuition for action. In one of its aspects it merges with what we call shrewdness.

When Lenin, screwing up his left eye, listens over the radio to a parliamentary speech of one of the imperialist makers of destiny or goes over the text of the latest diplomatic note, a mixture of bloodthirsty duplicity and polished hypocrisy, he resembles a very wise *muzhik* whom words cannot cajole nor sugary phrases ensnare. This is the peasant shrewdness elevated to genius, armed with the last word of scientific thought.

The young Russian proletariat was able to accomplish what it has only by pulling behind itself, by its roots, the heavy mass of the peasantry. This was prepared for by our whole national past. But precisely because the proletariat has come to power through the course of events, our revolution has been able suddenly and drastically to overcome the national narrowness and provincial benightedness of Russia's past history. Soviet Russia has become not only the haven for the Communist International, but also the living embodiment of its program and methods.

By paths, unknown and as yet unexplored by science, by which the human personality is moulded, Lenin has assimilated from the national milieu everything he needed for the greatest revolutionary action in the history of humanity. Exactly because the socialist revolution, which has long had its international theoretical expression, found for the first time in Lenin its national embodiment, Lenin became, in the full and true sense of the word, the revolutionary leader of the world proletariat. And that is how his fiftieth birthday found him.

2. Lenin, Founder of the Modern Meaning of the Word 'Politics'

Alain Badiou

To this day, the word 'politics' is predominantly used to signify matters related to the exercise of authority, whether it be the ways in which power is won, the management of public affairs, the various levels of that management (national, provincial, municipal, etc.), or the existence of political parties and the regulated practice of an opposition that also lays claim to power. All of these can be synthesised into a constitutional framework, as is the case in all 'Western' imperial powers. Of course, this includes the decisive question of the army, the police and the judiciary. Even an institutionalised form of trade unionism can be part of this definition. The most consistent result of this orientation to the word 'politics' is the existence, in various forms, of a range of professional politicians and specialised administrations, including of course the police and the military, which together form the backbone of the state apparatus. In summary, the definition would then be as follows: politics is the range of processes that concern the control and management of the state apparatus. This definition seems applicable to all of the forms that states have assumed since their appearance, three or four thousand years ago, from the imperial monarchies of China and Egypt, to modern 'democratic' states.

With regard to this age-old definition, it is only very recently, with the French Revolution, followed by the various critical orientations constituted by the communist, socialist and anarchist currents that began to appear in the first half of the 19th century, that the word 'politics' has assumed, in a way that remains subordinate and somewhat marginalised to this day, another meaning: politics defined as a division between populations with differing views as to its objective. Is that objective the least possible mismanagement of the existing order? Or is it the complete transformation of that order with a view to higher justice? In a sense, in this definition, *politics becomes a non-consensual discussion of politics itself.* It no longer signifies merely the distinction between a majority party and an opposition concerning the intricacies of the state – a peaceful divergence of views based on tacit agreement about society and its institutions; rather, inherent in this definition is major, irreconcilable discord amongst populations with regard to both societal goals and the means to achieve them. As a result, the political landscape is defined by the antagonism of two opposing paths. In this sense, the existence of politics must always presuppose the existence of at least two political viewpoints between which there can be no synthesis. It is in order to elucidate this point that we refer to Lenin's political thought here.

Let us take as an example a specific circumstance in which the Leninist conception of politics is clear. Let us go back in time to the spring of 1917 in Russia. In February of that year, a mass movement overthrew the Tsarist regime. Lenin writes what he thinks of the situation and what should be done about it so that the politics of the revolution, of which he is one of the organisers, becomes a historical reality and begins to exist, as such, throughout the whole country – and perhaps, he thinks, the whole of Europe.

The content of Lenin's thought, what it prescribes, is the transformation of one revolution into another, through the confrontation – imposed on all of the actors involved – of the two meanings of the word 'politics.' The February Revolution, which is still ongoing, aims only to change the form of the state; 'politics' hereby assumes the first of its two possible meanings: it is a question of replacing the monarchical mode of domination, which has now become obsolete, with the modern, 'democratic' parliamentary model adopted by the great imperialist powers, notably England and France. By contrast, Lenin's position consists in dividing the revolutionary process, proposing that it continue everywhere, but according to a completely different vision, inspired by the second meaning of the word 'politics': the aim of all political action must be to transform the organisation of society in its entirety, shattering the economic oligarchy and entrusting production, both industrial and agricultural, no longer to the private ownership of the few, but to the management of all those who work.

This revolution within the revolution, this division of politics into two antagonistic politics, including the meaning of the word itself, would gain substance through the turbulent upheavals that were to follow: seizure of power, civil war, blockade, foreign intervention. It was this process itself that created the *political project* ("œuvre politique") – commonly referred to as the 'Russian Revolution' – a project whose empirical finiteness is obvious, since it can be considered to have been completed in 1929, at the time of Stalin's launch of the first five-year plan.

The general idea of politics in its second sense was able to prevail because it was present, consciously and voluntarily, in what is important to call a *political consciousness*. First in Lenin (we will see how), then in the majority of the Bolshevik party, and finally, in the early autumn of 1917, in the majority of the organs of the masses, the popular organs that emerged from the February Revolution – called in Russian 'soviets' – and especially the most important of them, the soviet of the capital, Petrograd.

In effect, Lenin presented a summary of this political consciousness in the general programme that he began to circulate within the Party from April 1917, in order to provoke discussion throughout the country, and particularly among the soviets. Here, it is immediately visible that, in Lenin's eyes, the soviet was the predominant forum in which to promote the struggle, not between two variants of the same conception of politics, but between two opposite conceptions of politics itself.

Lenin set forth the action he deemed it necessary to take in Russia's specific situation, in view of both the world war, which was still ongoing, and the February Revolution, whose bourgeois, democratic and parliamentary principles – 'politics' in the first sense of the word – continued to dominate opinion. This led to Lenin's 'theses,' – ten theses, which at the time came to be known, communicated and commented upon throughout the world under the name of the *April Theses*. The content of these theses was like a handbook, in the Russian context, of political possibility: 'politics' in the second sense – the truly modern sense – of the word.

Thesis 1: Russia must find a way out of the war. The war has nothing to do with the Russian people, who can do no more than sacrifice their lives to it, because, according to Lenin, the war is "a predatory imperialist war owing to the capitalist nature of this government," namely, the so-called democratic government that emerged from the February Revolution. In 1917, this was a thesis of truly global significance: a systematic refusal to participate in wars of conquest, colonial wars, predatory wars between imperialist powers, and a categorical rejection of chauvinism and militant nationalism.

Thesis 2: Lenin's second thesis characterises the overall situation in Russia: *The specific feature of the present situation in Russia is that the country is passing from the first stage of the revolution – which ... placed power in the hands of bourgeoisie – to its second stage, which must place power in the hands of the proletariat and the poorest sections of the peasants.* Politics in the second sense must therefore prevail, amongst the populace, over politics in the first sense. This thesis remains, to this day, a kind of general prescription for the exit from politics in its first sense, enclosed in a finite system with the state at its centre, and for the movement towards politics in its second sense, where 'power' is understood as the egalitarian action of the popular masses and their organisations.

Thesis 3: No support for the provisional government. This thesis also has a general scope: one should not, for reasons of circumstances (e.g. war) agree to support the old political regime in any form whatsoever. Revolutionary politics must create its own independence, both mental and practical, from the dominant state. Or, in other words: always remember that the two meanings of the word 'politics' create an antagonistic contradiction in public opinion.

Thesis 4: This thesis recommends lucidity. It must be recognised, Lenin insists, that our orientation is a minority one, especially in the popular assemblies, in the soviets. Political action must therefore be a permanent labour of discussion, of explanation, of deploying among the masses, within the soviets, what Mao would later call "contradictions among the people" – so as to create peacefully, from within the movement, a new orientation, a rallying towards the second meaning of the word 'politics.' I quote Lenin: "Our task is ... to present [to the masses] a patient, systematic and persistent explanation of the errors of their tactics, an explanation especially adapted to [their] practical needs. As long as we are in the minority, we carry on the work of criticising and exposing errors and at the same time we preach the necessity of transferring the entire state power to the Soviets of the Workers' Deputies, so that the people may overcome their mistakes through experience."

Lenin's statement describes the political action required to find a way out of the endlessly repeating paradigm that has dominated human society since the Neolithic revolution, namely the triumph of the trinity of 'family, private property, and state.' The departure from this paradigm paves the way to an unprecedented power – no longer that of a separate state, but that of the workers' and peasants' assemblies. We must, therefore, writes Lenin, create *not a parliamentary republic … but a republic of Soviets of Workers,' Agricultural Labourers' and Peasants' throughout the country, from top to bottom*. According to Thesis 5, this completely new republic requires the abolition of the police, the army and the bureaucracy. The salaries of all officials, who would henceforth be elected and dismissible, should not exceed the average wage of a competent worker.

Theses 6 to 8 constitute the general programme of a revolution without precedent since the existence of states, which have always been at the service of a dominant oligarchy. They concern the overcoming of capitalism, the modern – and doubtless final – manifestation of this form, which has lasted several millennia.

The first step is to dismantle what remains of the feudal order, namely the landed estates. Thus: *Nationalisation of all lands in the country, the land to be disposed of by the local of Soviets of Agricultural Labourers' and Peasants' Deputies*.

Next, the financial might of capital is broken: *The immediate union of all banks in the country into a single national bank, and the institution of control over it by the Soviet of Workers' Deputies*. More generally: *Our immediate task … [is] to bring social production and the distribution of products at once under the control of the Soviet of Workers' Deputies*. Clearly, these statements lend definitive meaning to Marx's declaration in the *Manifesto of the Communist Party*: "The theory of Communists may be summed up in the single sentence: Abolition of private property." But what Marx foresaw as a long-range historical programme, becomes, in the movement of the Russian Revolution, "our immediate task."

Theses 9 and 10 concern political organisation, the need for the immediate renewal of the Party program. Most significant is the proposal to change its name; officially it had been known as the Russian Social Democratic Labour Party, henceforth it would be called the Communist Party. For it was communism itself – the pooling of common resources, the empowerment of the commons, and thus the end of the multimillennial reign of private ownership of the means of production – which is, from the Russian revolution onwards, the "immediate" task. Following this, it would obviously be necessary to create an international communist movement – a movement truly situated in the epoch of victorious revolutions, the epoch of communism as the immediate task.

All this, Lenin insists, must be explained and discussed with infinite patience, in the soviets, among the masses, and not imposed through violence of any kind. He stresses this point at length at the end of the *April Theses*: *I write, announce and elaborately explain ... [that] our task is to present a patient, systematic and persistent explanation.* The methods of political action advocated by Lenin were founded in patience and persistence, at the very moment when the transition from a paradigm of classical bourgeois revolution to a completely new paradigm, one that involved the total upheaval of the organisation of society, was of paramount importance. Indeed, the fact that this general orientation, set forth by Lenin in April, would become by early October the majority position held in the major Workers' Soviets, notably the Petrograd Soviet, would enable the situation to shift in the direction of a victorious communist ascendance.

On these bases, and through tremendous trials brought about by the specific circumstances in Russia, there is in effect, from October 17, the first victory, in the whole future of humanity, of a revolution which goes beyond millennia of our historical existence, an existence dominated until that time by the rule of private property, the protection of inequality by the state, and the unlimited hereditary transmission of accumulated wealth. In other words, the first lasting victory of politics in the second sense of the word: a revolution to establish a new kind of power, whose stated aim is the destruction of the very old, very ancient social structure that claims to be 'modern' – the capitalist and bourgeois society, the covert dictatorship of those who own the financial means of production and trade, of their heirs and state accomplices. A revolution that paves the way to the foundation of a new modernity. The common name for this absolute political innovation, for the true existence of politics in the second sense of the word, has been – and in my opinion remains – 'communism.'

This name has been recognised by millions of people the world over, people of all backgrounds, from the popular masses of workers and peasants to intellectuals and artists, who have greeted it with an enthusiasm commensurate with the antithesis it represents to the devastating failures of the previous century. Now, Lenin was able to declare, for the first time in the history of humankind, that the epoch of victorious revolutions had arrived. He was able to say this in the name of the political project ("œuvre politique") known as the 'Russian Revolution,' a term applicable not only to the events of the 1917, but to the decade or so between 1917 and 1929. Today, it is this political project that, faithful to Lenin's thought, we must revive, through popular movements and struggles that display the historical possibility of victory.

Translated from the original French by Patrick Anderson

Lenin150 (Samizdat)

3. Lenin Does Not Mean Leninism

Elvira Concheiro Bórquez

Given that he was one of the leading figures of a highly complex revolutionary process that, in the words of US-American journalist John Reed,[1] "shook the world," surely Lenin would not be surprised by the enormous volume of words that have been written about him, especially as he was himself so apt to engage in vitriolic polemics. Yet it is obvious that in so much that has been said about Lenin there exists a political intention, resulting in a certain construction of him to which a number of political groups continue to lay claim, and which in effect prevents an understanding of the continued relevance of his work. It is therefore necessary, first of all, that we distinguish and separate Lenin from all of the political and ideological constructions that have been made of him, one case in point being so-called Marxist-Leninism. The latter, which at first sight appears to be the simple unity of the works of Marx with those of Lenin, is in fact an official state ideology that went beyond its own borders and has its own particular history, to which we will now turn our attention.

At a moment when, according to Lenin, the difficulties faced by Soviet power demanded its democratic re-making and a search for new ways of moving the country forward, his death at the age of fifty-three in January 1924 unleashed fierce disagreement among the leadership of the Bolsheviks, which was soon to become a fratricidal struggle that would end in the supremacy of Stalin and the reconfiguration of the Bolshevik project.

The differences among the leaders, even while Lenin was still alive, concerned the various complex problems that beset the new Soviet power, among them the question as to the most effective way to transform the economy and the thorny issue of nationalities, which Marxists debated incessantly. Furthermore, as Lenin himself had foreseen, the varying levels of capacity among the members of the Bolshevik leadership contributed to a scenario of intense in-fighting: Bukharin's and Pyatakov's youth; the lack of prestige for which Zinoviev and Kamenev, arguably Lenin's closest allies, had to atone as a result of their mistakes during the decisive moments of the insurrection; as well as Trotsky's and Stalin's control of the army and the party, respectively, making them the two most powerful members within the government, which led to the most entrenched and vicious struggle for power of all. It was in this situation, in which nobody had stood out definitively as Lenin's legitimate successor, that each laid claim to Lenin's intellectual authority, presenting himself as Lenin's rightful heir, both politically and intellectually.

Meanwhile, the grieving population, exhausted by these endless titanic

---

[1] Based on his testimony as a journalist working in Russia in 1917, John Reed wrote an extraordinary account of the revolution, entitled *Ten Days That Shook the World* (e.g. Penguin Classic, 2007).

battles, was seemingly indifferent to the question of Lenin's replacement. Through drawn-out and elaborate acts of mourning, they elevated Lenin to the position of the most important person in (their) history, in the process obliging his family to accept the embalming of his body, which remains on display at the Red Square in Moscow to this day.[2] In the years before his death, Lenin attempted to combat many of the tendencies that would inform the events of 1924. In his final works he advocated for numerous reforms and issued a series of stern warnings, some of which can be found in what is known as his "Testament."[3] In spite of these efforts, he was no longer effectively able to alter the course of what was to come, resulting in the bitter history in which Lenin's body and words were utilised in the authoritarian construction of Soviet power headed by Stalin, who proved adept at combining the idealisation of the party led by him with the cult of Lenin, symbolised by the proliferation of monuments to Lenin throughout the Soviet Union and in other socialist countries. This process was accompanied by the dissemination of a narrow body of teaching, codifying Lenin's work in accordance with the demands of the new authoritarian power imposed by Stalin.[4] In his famous texts *The Foundations of Leninism* (1924) and *Concerning Questions of Leninism* (1926), Stalin managed to create a Lenin of universal value, owing largely to the fact that Lenin – according to Stalin – had rescued Marxism from being "suppressed" by the Second International and had developed it "further under the new conditions of capitalism and of the class struggle of the proletariat." For Stalin, Lenin "completes Marx" by advancing three "theories" – of the party, of imperialism, and of the dictatorship of the proletariat[5] – which, slyly, were of particular importance to Stalin's project of power and which consequently obtained universal status over and above any other attempts, such as those made by Bukharin and Zinoviev, to systematise Lenin's thought.

In Stalin's version of Lenin, the latter's qualities were the result of a highly powerful party, created by Lenin himself, and composed of people "made of a special stuff": "We Communists are people of a special mould," he said in a speech following the death of Lenin.[6] Stalin was able to exploit this duplexity between leader and party organisation in order to promote his own leadership so that, in the final instance, the work of Lenin was deemed valuable because it was the expression of the work of the party. In this way, and always in the name of the party, Stalin gradually moulded an image of Lenin to his liking. In parallel, and increasingly at one with the State, the party organisation was converted into an efficient instrument in the hands of a new power, which increasingly distanced itself from the transforma-

---

2 See Ingerflom 1999. For the video of Lenin's funeral, see https://www.youtube.com/watch?v=oStHN2xwWeE.
3 See Lenin 1977a: 593-611. For an account of Lenin's activities and positions in his final years, see Lewin 1973.
4 See Gerratana 1977.
5 Stalin 1953: 71f.
6 Ibid: 47.

tive nature of the revolution in order to become a powerful dictatorship, ostensibly represented by the party, but ultimately led by its General Secretary: Stalin. It is this systematisation of the thought and works of Lenin, narrowly boxed into supposedly generally applicable theories, which came to be known as Marxism-Leninism, and to which was soon added, in an expression of utter delirium, Stalinism.

In summary, what we are talking about here is an ideological state discourse that utilised both the works of Marx and Lenin as a way of promoting a highly elaborate process of self-legitimisation, which over the course of large parts of the 20th century became the dominant current of Marxism, leading to the creation of a series of strong biases with regard to Lenin, evident even among other ideological currents, and repeated until this day, all the while establishing the one general way of understanding Lenin.

In contrast to the very narrow formulations of Stalin, Vladimir Ilyich's Marxist way of thinking was in fact extremely adaptable and anti-dogmatic, an issue that Lenin himself explicitly discussed in order to address the distortions of Marxism already in evidence during his lifetime:

> Our doctrine – said Engels, referring to himself and his famous friend – is not a dogma, but a guide to action. This classical statement stresses with remarkable force and expressiveness that aspect of Marxism which is very often lost sight of. And by losing sight of it, we turn Marxism into something one-sided, distorted and lifeless; we deprive it of its life blood; we undermine its basic theoretical foundations – dialectics, the doctrine of historical development, all-embracing and full of contradictions; we undermine its connection with the definite practical tasks of the epoch, which may change with every new turn of history.[7]

Surely, this was Lenin's response to the prevailing positivist monotony at the time, which, as expressed by the majority of European Social-Democracy, impoverished Marxist theory through the application of schematic and narrow interpretations, without novel and timely theorisations of its own and therefore destined to become no more than mechanical repetition. By contrast, Lenin's insistence on rigorous and specific problematisation based on an analysis of concrete reality continues to be a highly ingenious approach, which derives knowledge through action, and produces knowledge by actively participating in the struggle for social transformation.

---

7 Lenin 1977b: 39.

As Lenin insisted time and again:

> Marxism requires of us a strictly exact and objectively verifiable analysis of the relations of classes and of the concrete features peculiar to each historical situation.[8]

It is in the search for the neuralgic point in every moment – the initial isolation in order to understand it, followed immediately by its connection to the totality of social existence – that the creative capacity of Leninian, not Leninist, Marxism resides. For the Bolshevik leader, the commitment to social transformation is the reason why the work of Marx has at its core the analysis of real, not imaginary, processes of a continuously moving and changing quality; a perspective that demands that we observe these processes in a specific, detailed and concrete manner.

Departing from this epistemological perspective, Lenin developed a great capacity to capture the political moment and to define with extreme precision what was to be done, which action to take. In reality, it was this capacity that allowed him to identify the revolutionary opportunity, undetected by others, which presented itself with the re-emergence of the Soviets in Russia in early 1917, as a result of which he launched a political initiative that surprised even his closest allies. The same can be said about the 1905-06 revolution, in which he was convinced that the unpredictability of the situation required an abrupt change in how to confront, moment by moment, the counter-revolutionary forces, first via an armed uprising, then by boycotting the electoral process promoted by the Tsar, and finally by participating in the call for the establishment of the State Duma, the new legislative assembly. A third moment was, of course, Lenin's well-documented opposition to WWI, a war waged with the consent of the majority of workers' parties in Europe at the time.

In short, this quality of Lenin's can be called, in the words of E. Sereni, his understanding of "the dialectical unity between the continuity and discontinuity of historical time."[9] Through this capacity, Lenin was able to take and wield the political initiative at the right moment, and to imbue it with an appropriate rhythm that allowed the prevailing course of events to be modified. Moreover, this quality enabled Lenin to sustain a revolutionary praxis that was not only built on solid foundations but was also politically effective. It is here that the immense value of his works resides.

Translated from the original Spanish by Hjalm(ar) Jorge Joffre-Eichhorn

---

8 Lenin 1974: 43.
9 See Sereni and Luporini 1978.

References

Gerratana, Valentino (1977), "Sobre las relaciones entre leninismo y estalinismo," *Materiales*, 4, 67-96.

Ingerflom, Claudio Sergio, and Tamar Kondratieva (1999), "Por qué debate Rusia en torno al cuerpo de Lenin?," *Prohistoria*, 3, 81-110.

Lenin, V.I. (1974), *Collected Works Vol. 24*. Moscow: Progress Publishers.

Lenin, V.I. (1977a), *Collected Works Vol. 36*. Moscow: Progress Publishers.

Lenin, V.I. (1977b), *Collected Works Vol. 17*. Moscow: Progress Publishers.

Lewin, Moshe (1973), *Lenin's Last Struggle*. London: Wildwood House.

Reed, John (2007), *Ten Days That Shook The World*. London: Penguin Classics.

Sereni, Emilio, and Cesare Luporini (1973), *El concepto de "formación económico-social"*. Buenos Aires: Pasado y Presente.

Stalin, Joseph (1953), *Collected Works Vol. 6*. Moscow: Progress Publishers.

4. Learning from Lenin – and Doing It Differently

Michael Brie

At the end of the 1980s, after a century of hot and cold wars, the people of Europe, especially in the east and south-east of the continent, had a dream: to come together under one roof as peoples and nations, living collectively in societies with a dynamic economy, a robust welfare state, a democracy in which power rests with the citizens, in peace and with permeable borders. In the three decades since, however, Europe appears to have moved in precisely the opposite direction: wars in the southern and south-eastern neighbouring states of North Africa, the Near and Middle East; unresolved conflicts in Ukraine, the Caucasus. The United Kingdom has left the EU. The continent is divided along economic lines, while societies are increasingly fragmented. Walls are being put up. From the Right, liberal democracy is being called into question. Terror is omnipresent. The ecological catastrophe has become undeniable. Natural systems are being destroyed at great speed.

The Left is jointly responsible for this. Social democratic, green, and even communist parties have implemented neoliberal policies as partners in coalition governments or have failed to offer an effective alternative in opposition. Many citizens feel disappointed, betrayed even, by this failure of the Left – a failure to uphold its role as the protector of social well-being, democracy, the environment and peace. At best, it is simply waging defensive battles.

But the tide is beginning to turn. The global balance of power is rapidly shifting. The 'Fridays for Future' movement has propelled ecological transformation to the top of the political agenda. This could prove to be a concrete opportunity to question the system from the Left in a new way. With the rise of the People's Republic of China, a new model of development has emerged that can challenge the West on an even playing field. Meanwhile, the New Right continues to work towards rupturing the bond between capitalism and liberal democracy while bolstering proto-fascist trends; Trump and Bolsonaro are two of its most repugnant proponents. Migration has brought global social issues from the periphery back to the centre. The threat of war is once again real in the West. The ruling classes can no longer simply carry on with business as usual as citizens increasingly demand a new approach. Nevertheless, persuasive and politically feasible solutions remain elusive – programmatically, strategically and organisationally. The question is: What is to be done when almost nothing can be done – but there is still so much to do?

April 22 of this year marks the 150th anniversary of the birth of Vladimir I. Lenin. As controversial as he remains as a politician, there is no doubt that he was one of a handful of people who determined the fate of the 20th century. Without him, world history would have taken a different course. Equally undisputed is that he was truly a guiding spirit of the Left, a declared communist and Marxist. Through Bolshevism, he breathed new meaning into both of these terms. In times of paralysis and a potential new offensive by the Left, there are very good reasons to seek inspiration from Lenin, the most influential Leftist politician of the 20th century. This inspiration is two-fold: On the one hand, one can learn from Lenin which tasks the Left needs to embrace if it is to be strategically effective in any meaningful sense. On the other hand, one can and must learn what absolutely must be done *differently*, given that Lenin's legacy has also contributed to the weakness of today's Left. The Soviet state he created in 1917/18 failed thirty years ago, due in part to the inherent defects, never overcome, of this state and the ideas on which it was founded. Below are eight concrete proposals as to what should be done *differently* – eight direct challenges to the European Left.[1]

First: Lenin began with an explicit 'no' to World War I. Not only was he one of the most resolute opponents of the war, but unequivocally qualified it as an imperialist war – irrespective of the nuances. For a short time, he supported the call for a united Europe, but soon came to see this as a distraction from the tasks at hand and declared the Civil War of the Slaves against the War of the Slaveowners, as he put it. Or as Karl Liebknecht declared: Not *Burgfriede* but *Burgkrieg*![2] But what is the explicit 'no' of the European Left? What is its convincing 'no' today? Greta Thunberg's "How dare you!" is such a 'no,' as are the boats rescuing refugees in the Mediterranean after the EU abandoned its mission there.

Second: Lenin spent the first long months of World War I in the libraries of Berne, Switzerland, where he read Hegel! He began a phase of intense philosophical reflection. His political statements of that time comprise thirty pages; more was not possible given his state of almost complete isolation. His article on Marx for the Russian Encyclopaedia *Granat* is fifty pages long. In contrast, his annotations on *Science of Logic*, Hegel's most abstract work, run to 150 pages. Lenin related his experiences to Hegel's dialectics of development and practice; he trained his thinking in contradictions, under the conditions of the ruptures and leaps of abruptly unfolding events. He was convinced that truth is always concrete. This was how he prepared for the unpredictable. Nothing in Hegel's work is more materialistic than his idealistic dialectics, he wrote. On what philosophical basis is the European Left

---
1 There are several works from my immediate environment that positively supported the text that follows in terms of strategic solutions for the contemporary Left in Europe. These include analyses by the Institute for Social Analysis of the Rosa Luxemburg Foundation (2011), Klein 2013 and Candeias 2019. See also Brie 2014 and, more specifically on Lenin, Brie 2017.
2 The term *Burgfriede*, derived from a medieval German practice of imposing a state of truce within the jurisdiction of a castle, was applied to the approach adopted by the Social Democratic Party of Germany not to oppose government policy during World War I. Liebknecht refused to adhere to this, and was the only member of the Reichstag to vote against extending war loans, under the slogan *Burgkrieg, nicht Burgfriede!* The former term, Burgkrieg, is a play on the German word *Bürgerkrieg*, meaning 'civil war.' [Translator's note].

preparing for a completely new global situation? The very idea that such an approach is indispensable seems totally foreign to it.

Third: After his initial shock at the politics of the German Social Democrats and other parties of the Second International, Lenin developed his own alternative narrative. It was intended to explain how this betrayal of the decisions of the International of 1912 could have come to pass. Lenin's aim was to clarify why a new 'we' – a new, communist International, was needed, why it must put socialist revolution in Europe on the agenda and how that could be achieved. By contrast, the idea of a common narrative is alien to both the German and European Left, bordering on fairy tale. But how can we unite, today, that which is disparate and separated if not through narrative (and thereby in an organising and practical way)? The 'we' must be created. An abstract commonality of interests is not enough, because many obstacles stand in the way of that which we have in common. The pride and desire in belonging to a new 'subjectivity,' a new 'we,' must be actively created. Without a narrative, the battle is lost before it begins. Could it be possible to form a new narrative from the idea of radical socio-ecological transformation – with global, as well as local and regional dimensions?

Fourth: In his years of exile in Switzerland during the First World War, Lenin wrote *Imperialism, the Highest Stage of Capitalism*. In the work, Lenin cites over a thousand sources, with excerpts comprising 900 pages. He was aided by a number of colleagues. What interested Lenin was not a comprehensive analytical explanation of the nature of imperialism, but its significance for strategic intervention by the Left. He saw Kautsky's ultra-imperialism as only an abstract possibility; in concrete terms, things would be completely different. Lenin, looking for points of weakness in this incredibly robust international system, turned his attention to the inequality of development, inner-imperialist contradictions, the conflict between the leading imperialist nations and their colonies and semi-colonies. He investigated the national and agrarian questions, as well as those elements that had given rise to imperialism and war and which thus pointed to the possibility of a new economic order. Above all, he understood that there can be no 'purely socialist' revolution. In order to bring about substantial change, inimically heterogeneous processes must be effectively combined: national and social struggles, struggles for radical democracy with an attendant transformation of property rights. According to Lenin, identifying which concrete question was the most central could not be achieved abstractly, only concretely and practically. Taken together, these thoughts reflect an incisive analysis of society. To what extent is today's European Left equipped with such practically relevant analyses – which, instead of focusing on what is not possible, address what *is* possible, here and now? Where is the modern Left's concrete utopia, as envisaged by Ernst Bloch, or its real utopias, in the words of Erik O. Wright?

Fifth: Following the February Revolution of 1917, Lenin, in just a few weeks, sacrificed the holiest cow of Russian social democracy, namely the doctrine of the two phases of revolution: bourgeois revolution as precursor to socialist revolution. Trotsky had already done this in 1905/6. Imperialism and the war, Lenin said, had created the objective and now also the subjective conditions for a socialist revolution, first in Russia, then in Germany and Europe. In his *April Theses* he placed this revolution firmly on the agenda. What concept of revolution, reform, transformation does the European Left have? Surely it is not enough simply to repeat the mantra that, if humankind is to survive, capitalism cannot be the last word in our history – while not having any concrete vision of how such a radical shift should actually occur! Could the concept of a double transformation from within and beyond capitalism contribute meaningfully to such a vision?

Sixth: At the same time, Lenin developed an understanding of 'epoch' as a time to take action. "What to do?" and "Who will do it?" had always been central questions of the Left in its objective to transform society. Now, Lenin brought such considerations into the foreground once again: a focus not on general evolutionary tendencies, but on their intersection with concrete opportunities for action. His analyses were aimed at specific scenarios. With regard to the agricultural question, either the Prussian or the US-American approach could be adopted; national questions too provided scope for alternatives. In this way, he could 'experiment' with various possibilities and remain flexible in the face of unexpected eventualities. The European Left, however, is often driven by an either/or, right-or-wrong mentality. Individual possibilities are set up in opposition to each other and thereby made absolute. This divides and paralyses us. We need scenarios that do justice to the openness of the situation and at the same time realistically reflect the concrete possibilities.

Seventh: The Bible, Proverb 29.18, states: "Where there is no vision, the people perish." What is needed is a liberating, emancipatory, utopian visualisation of 'another world.' In the summer months of 1917, Lenin composed *The State and Revolution*. What is most astonishing about this work is that here Lenin confronts the contradictions of a new socialist order. The new socialist state must have elements of the bourgeois state, so that the workers as "members of society" could enforce the principle of merit against themselves in their capacity as private individuals. In other words, repression not only against the ruling classes of the old society! What Lenin lacked was the understanding that politics concerns not only the exercise of power, but is also a space for dialogue, for self-understanding, which must guarantee the freedom of those who think differently – epitomised in his now infamous assertion that "there is no freedom and no democracy where there is […] violence." But what is the vision of the European Left? How is it preparing for the contradictions created by its own politics? In particular, the need to deal with the consequences of participation in government always seems to catch the Left completely off guard. There is talk of neo-socialism, a socialism relevant to the 21st Century, that can address modern ecological, social and democratic issues, and the question of peace, from a new perspective. There is discussion of infrastructure socialism, which focuses on the communist foundations of a good society – education, health, ecology, transport, housing, etc. The common goods of a free society have been privatised or destroyed by neoliberalism. And in some cases, they must be created for the very first time in the face of globalisation and digitalisation. In order that everyone can have access to the goods of a free life, a radical transformation is needed that would make these common goods available for this purpose.

Eighth: All of these questions lead to what could be called entry projects ("Einstiegsprojekte"). Lenin did not dream these up on his own, as one often reads, but based them on the demands of the soldiers, the workers, the peasants, the representatives of oppressed peoples of Russia. "All power to the Soviets" and "overthrow of the provisional government," "immediate peace without preconditions," "workers' self-government," "the right to self-determination" are prominent examples. As the Menshevik Internationalist and gifted chronicler Nikolai Sukhanov wrote, Lenin's speech struck like lightning upon his arrival in Petrograd in April 1917: "Suddenly, before the eyes of all of us, completely swallowed up by the routine drudgery of the revolution, there was presented a bright, blinding, exotic beacon, obliterating everything we 'lived by.' Lenin's voice, heard straight from the train, was a 'voice from outside.' There had broken in upon us in the revolution a note that was not, to be sure, a contradiction, but that was novel, harsh, and somewhat deafening." The alternative to war and oppression became very concrete and seemed feasible. But what entry projects does the European Left have? Which of its projects are rooted in the mass consciousness? How can it be ensured that the vision for a new European order, a new era of peace, a new welfare state, a new kind of mobility, for fundamental constitutional reform and a new energy system will simultaneously drive the necessary socio-ecological transformation?

What the eight elements of Lenin's strategic platform described above have in common is an orientation towards antagonism, towards irreconcilable opposition, either/or, the exclusion of a middle way, the state of emergency, which, in the long term, has proven to be a fatal restriction and weakness. The 'no' was absolute, the philosophical conception was directed at the amplification and intensification of contradictions and focused exclusively on the leap. The narrative was centred on the absolute rupture with social democracy. The analysis excluded any capacity for reform on the part of capitalism and imperialism; the scenarios practically admitted only the barbarity of war on the one hand, and socialist civil war against the capitalist slaveowners on the other. The emancipatory vision promised the deprivation of all and any democratic rights, including the right to freedom, to those who resist; and the central project was the 'proletarian power' exercised by the Bolshevik Party, a power that mercilessly oppressed its opponents. Each of the elements of Lenin's strategy was designed from the extremes. The strategy of the extremes and of civil war had proved its strength, under the conditions of the situation in Russia and World War I, on the road to power in 1917. After October 25, 1917, everything would depend on how that power was used. But that is a different story.

Today's European Left cannot and should not copy Lenin. It must find a fundamentally new way. But it can derive inspiration from Lenin, in the form of the eight propositions outlined above. Without a concrete 'no,' without a dialectical philosophy of praxis, without a narrative of its own, without a strategic analysis of society, without an understanding of 'epoch' and a focus on possible scenarios, without an emancipatory vision taking into account inherent contradictions, and without entry projects arrived at through consensus, the paralysis of the Left in Europe today will persist. The Left will not be able to oppose the rise of the Right and the dogged survival instincts of the ruling bloc. It will find itself unprepared for a new crisis. It will not be able to seize the opportunities of an open situation. Therefore, let us learn from Lenin in order to bring about – in a new way – radical, transformational and emancipatory social change.

Translated from the original German by Patrick Anderson

References

Bloch, Ernst (1985), *The Principle of Hope*. Boston: MIT Press.

Brie, Michael (ed.) (2014), *Futuring: Perspektiven der Transformation im Kapitalismus über ihn hinaus*. Münster: Westfälisches Dampfboot.

Brie, Michael (2018), *Rediscovering Lenin. Dialectics of Revolution and Metaphysics of Domination*. London: Palgrave Macmillan.

Candeias, Mario (2019), *Linkspartei, was nun? Drei Vorschläge für eine Strategiediskussion*. Berlin: Rosa-Luxemburg-Stiftung.

Institut für Gesellschaftsanalyse (2011), *Organische Krise des Finanzmarkt-Kapitalismus: Szenarien, Konflikte, konkurrierende Projekte*. Berlin: Rosa-Luxemburg-Stiftung.

Klein, Dieter (2013), *Das Morgen tanzt im Heute. Transformation im Kapitalismus und über ihn hinaus*. Hamburg: VSA.

Sukhanov, Nikolai (1984), *The Russian Revolution 1917*. Princeton: Princeton University Press.

Wright, Erik Olin (2017), *Envisioning Real Utopias*. London: Verso.

5. Lenin from Latin America – Towards a Reactivation of the Marxism of Political Organisation and Strategy

Mauricio Sandoval Cordero

Confronting reactivation: Welcome to interesting times

We are currently going through a civilisational crisis threatened by a possible collapse on a global scale,[1] with varying socio-economic consequences in different parts of the world, further impacted by the ongoing health and climate crises as a result of the COVID-19 pandemic and the large-scale devastation repeatedly caused by hurricanes, flooding, droughts etc. At the time of writing, the overall situation in Latin America is one of intense socio-political effervescence marked by a series of acute conflicts in places like Bolivia, with the return to power of the *Movimiento al Socialismo* (MAS) a year after having been deposed by a coup d'etat; Chile, where a popular uprising and the demand for the re-writing of the dictatorial constitution of the Pinochet times is challenging the status quo; and countries like Columbia, Peru, Brazil, Guatemala and Costa Rica, among others, which have witnessed confrontations between repressive state forces and the popular masses.

This tumultuous scenario of class struggle allows for the affirmation that we live in what Slavoj Žižek calls "interesting times," that is, situations of crisis that simultaneously open up new opportunities for much-needed political intervention. Yet, it is not just any type of intervention we need, but one that effectively engages with the particular historical moment we live in. In order to do this, we believe that the time has come to reactivate[2] and bring (in)to the 21st century the best that the history of the internally diverse Left has to offer, and especially the legacy of two realms of revolutionary theoretical and practical production, that of K. Marx and V.I. Lenin.

To start off, it is important to emphasise that the exercise of reactivation is by no means easy. First and foremost, it implies the need to confront the historic sedimentation of defeats suffered in the 20th century, which provide for a general situation of short-term impossibility: the breakdown of actually existing socialism in the former Eastern Bloc and the defeat of the Left in many other parts of the world, all of which led to the disappearance of a horizon of global transformation that found its most condensed expression in the advent of the so-called "end of history" in the 1990s.

On the other hand, in Latin America, we were reminded as early as 1994 that history had in fact not ended, when the *Ejército Zapatista de Liberación Nacional* (EZLN) rose up in arms in the south of Mexico explicitly denouncing neoliberal capitalist globalisation. In the years after, a number

---

1 See Vega 2019.
2 As suggested by the edited volume *Lenin Reloaded: Toward a Politics of Truth* (2007). Editor's note: The book was published in Spanish as *Lenin reactivado: Hacia una política de la verdad* (2010).

of socio-political conflicts, revolts and mobilisations began to inflame and repoliticise the region, eventually resulting in the emergence and consolidation of political forces that made up the first "wave" of progressive and Left governments in the 21st century, in countries like Venezuela, Bolivia, Argentina, Brazil and Ecuador.[3]

This first wave lasted for approximately 15 years and allowed for a series of crucial experiences full of advances and setbacks, but finally interrupted by a conservative reaction emboldened by the rise of a new, global extreme Right and a reinvigorated imperialism, leading to right-wing governments in Honduras, Brazil and Argentina,[4] though the situation in the latter was reversed when Alberto Fernández and Cristina Fernández de Kirchner won the general elections in 2019.

By and large, the political changes of the past few years imply that Left forces in Latin America have passed from a situation of being on the offensive to one of once again having to resist, a scenario that provides for the heightened possibility of a sense of paralysis, defeatism and "left-wing melancholia" emerging among large parts of the militant and popular sectors. Following Enzo Traverso, this development is to be avoided and combatted, because this type of melancholia prevents us from connecting and responding to the political present,[5] with serious consequences for theoretical and political action.

Therefore, we intend to contribute to the politico-intellectual engagement with this issue and how to confront it by proposing the following two urgent ways of intervention:

1. "Unthinking"[6] Marx and Lenin by understanding them not as distinctly defined and closed political and theoretical bodies of work, but rather as spaces for intervention, i.e. as critical projects under construction, which develop with every new work aimed at continuing their legacy. This responds to the so-called crisis of Marxism of the 1980s, when it was affirmed that Marxist theoretical production was no longer able to adequately analyse the present.[7]

2. Thinking Marxism-Leninism "in reverse,"[8] i.e. the adoption of a radically different perspective to that provided by the Soviet manuals of historical and dialectical materialism and the official ideology developed and propagated by the Soviet state. In short, we do not need a dead and mystified Marx and Lenin,[9] but figures that are alive, haunting

---

3 See García Linera 2017.
4 Ibid.
5 See Traverso 2019.
6 Following the contribution made by George García's (2018) engagement with the theoretical work of unthinking Marxism by Immanuel Wallerstein as well as the proposition made by Bolívar Echeverría to understand Marx as a theoretical and political project under construction.
7 See Ortega 2019.
8 Here we follow the proposal made by Bruno Bosteels (2018) to think Marx in reverse, based on the theoretical works of Oscar del Barco.
9 See Concheiro 2016.

us like spectres to remind us that it is possible to make the revolution and to enhance people's power everywhere.

Based on these two premises we can formulate a perspective[10] that responds to the times we live in, taking as its starting point the singular multiplicity of Latin America, and aiming to contribute to theoretical and political debates and battles of global relevance, since it is possible for Latin America to project itself as a political space of a universal character, which at different moments generated the most advanced transformations – that is, those with the most revolutionary potential – as in the case of the Cuban or Bolivarian Revolutions, both of which continue to resist despite the intense onslaught waged against them by the forces of counter-revolution.

Now, what most interests us among the different possible theoretical ways of engaging with the above premises is addressing the issue of political organisation and strategy, as one of the main challenges we face is the currently prevalent anti-organisational and "unstrategic" common sense[11] partially inherited from the disappearance and/or radical change of approach adopted by many Left organisations in Europe, Latin America and the world in general.[12]

What is needed, therefore, is a re-engagement with the question of political organisation and strategy aiming at the emergence of new Left waves of revolutionary transformation. Who better to support us in this task than the political leader and thinker par excellence and one of the monumental protagonists continuing the work of Marx: V.I. Lenin?

Lenin: The return of strategic perspective and political organisation

The type of reactivation we propose consists in the thinking of politics as a strategic art, as formulated by the French Marxist Daniel Bensaïd, one of the forerunners of the ongoing development of Marxist theorisations about the political in the wake of the difficult defeats suffered over the course of the 20th century.[13] In this sense, we depart from Bensaïd, but what is of particular interest to us is to integrate the contributions made by Lenin as a crucial "nucleus of political desire," in order to re-think the organisation and strategy of revolutionary transformation.

At its core, this conception of politics as a strategic art[14] implies the

---

10 This perspective should be seen as part of the renewed interest in the theoretical practice of Latin American Marxisms, promoted by the experiences of the revolutionary first wave of the 21st century. By way of example, we mention the numerous Marxist working groups of the *Consejo Latinoamericano de Ciencias Sociales* (CLACSO); the series of seminars and publications, *Pensando el mundo desde Bolivia*, supported by the Vice Presidency of the Plurinational State of Bolivia; and the *Premio Libertador al Pensamiento Crítico*, an award given by the Bolivarian Revolution for the most outstanding theoretical production of Marxist and/or critical thought in the region.
11 See Jameson 2010.
12 See Catanzaro and De Gori 2019.
13 See Bensaïd 2017.
14 It is worth remembering that on the political Left there exists an ample tradition of politics as a strategic

reactivation of the thinking and exercising of the power of transformation – whether as part of an immediate, radical or a more gradual temporality – and its direct or indirect link to the structure and system of the state. This involves a reinterrogation of the old debate about the revolutionary subject, which for us centres around the question of the different forms of political organisation (the party, the movement, the collective), the different concrete processes of political practice (direct action, parliamentarianism and institutional administration, armed struggle, communal and sectorial organisation, etc.) and the creation of political power via institutional sedimentation.[15]

The different possibilities to create organisational forms and strategic routes depend on the concrete political conditions as well as the corresponding expanding or contracting margins of potentiality. What is important to recognise is that each organisational form is in itself capable of organising the popular masses and therefore no one organisational form is a priori better than another. Besides, in each strategic coordinate one can discern and prioritise the most adequate and relevant options in order to achieve one's political objectives, granted that it is understood that these are neither exclusive nor excluding of one another, that is to say, that they are not absolute options, but that they can be changed. Also, the strategic coordinates must be conceived of by the political organisations themselves and should be operationalised in concrete and innovative propositions for all existing social spheres, with the aim of materialising these in coherent political programs.

Finally, every organisational form and strategic route must be rooted in actually existing historical experiences, thereby transmitting and projecting the people's desires for collective transformation and providing guidance and direction to those sectors and movements in a state of political confusion.[16]

Having established the basic parameters of what we are dealing with, what is needed now is to think politics as a strategic art deeply informed by the organising of political desires[17] in the action of theoretical production, i.e. utilising Lenin as a "nucleus of desire" that allows us to (re-)think organisation and strategy in order to intervene in concrete political situations. This nucleus consists of the following contributions made by Lenin:

- **Political contingency:** One of the most germane ways to understand Lenin's theoretical production is to recognise that he thought the issue of politics based on an understanding of the contingency of any political action, without guarantees or teleologies, but always in the direction of the Communist horizon.[18] Embracing contingency is in clear contrast

---

art, starting with Marx and of course with Lenin himself, both of whom referred to the art of insurrection (see Lenin 1917b).
15 See Sandoval 2020.
16 See Dean 2017 and Garo 2019.
17 What Bini Adamczak (2017) calls the "desire for another world that is possible."
18 See Dean 2013.

to the orthodox Marxist-Leninist philosophy of history that affirmed the inevitability of historical progress and World Socialist Revolution. What interests us, however, is to reclaim a Lenin audacious enough to understand that each and every moment in time and space requires its own particular response, thereby allowing for a precise political analysis and the subsequent opportunity to intervene correctly in different political situations, always subject to the possibility of winning or losing, and all the while continuing the revolutionary Communist struggle through leaps, leaps, leaps. In sum, the first lesson for the reactivation of Marxism starting from Lenin is the permanent creation of strategic routes towards the Communist horizon.

- **Political analysis:** With the exception of people like Antonio Gramsci, Hồ Chí Minh, Fidel Castro, Che Guevara and a few others, 20th-century Marxism and Left culture(s) witnessed few examples where a great political leader was also an intellectual giant. This was precisely the case of V.I. Lenin, who – from the margins of the world system – engaged with Revolution both on the theoretical and practical level. He did so thanks to developing his intellectual capacities in the heat of socio-political struggle, listening to the people and diagnosing concretely the different forms of domination and exploitation present in Imperial Russia on the national level, but also by linking these to the global situation via his critique of imperialism and colonialism. What is key to point out here is that Lenin's capacity to connect with the people and to translate this encounter analytically is based on his relating directly to the political actions of the proletariat and other popular sectors in their concrete historical context. Therefore, the second lesson for the reactivation of Marxism starting from Lenin is that without theoretical practice one cannot influence political practice and vice-versa.

- **Time and political conjuncture:** Another contribution made by V.I. Lenin is the importance given to understanding and taking advantage of the times of politics, in accordance with the existing power relations. What can be highlighted here is the relevance of engaging with moments of crisis by determining the "weakest link," the central political conflict, and taking advantage of the ensuing opportunities based on the composition of the different political forces (government, political parties, movements, etc.), the correct identification of the political moment (of advancement, retreat, stagnation, etc.) and the struggle for the administration and change of institutionality in a revolutionary direction. The third lesson for the reactivation of Marxism starting from Lenin is hence that political organisations must adapt their tactics and strategies in accordance with the political pulse of each specific context, thereby avoiding the dogmatism and sectarianism that has historically beset the global Left. This approach also provides us with a much-needed theoretical orientation about what is at stake in situations in which revolutionary forces find themselves either fighting for or exercising power, as for Lenin the concrete experiences of struggle and (being involved in) the running of the state constitute a qualitative leap in all processes of transformation. This orientation is of great importance as such theoretical reflections are relatively rare on the Left.[19]

- **Organisation and militancy:** V.I. Lenin was undoubtedly a master of political organisation and revolutionary practice, a recognition that is very important in an overall scenario where Left common sense(s) have increasingly moved towards "folk politics"[20] (especially in the Anglo-Saxon world) and "autonomism"[21] (in many parts of Europe and Latin America). Both currents postulate that political parties and state power constitute forms of domination and co-optation of social movements and are hence non-desirable. We therefore reiterate our esteem for organisation and militancy revolving around three central issues: First, the capacity to connect with and unite militant sensibilities and popular movements via dynamic political organisations;[22] second, the possibility of institutions such as parties, unions or cooperatives that produce types of collective political power with the capacity to create situations that resemble what Lenin called "dual power;"[23] and third, the need to resuscitate the question of the revolutionary power of the state as a not-to-be neglected area of political struggle, given that it offers the possibility of great institutional reach that can afford security and better living conditions for the majority of the people and which can also serve as a dynamising engine for the popular movements and organisations.[24] Here we have the fourth lesson for the reactivation of Marxism starting from Lenin: the importance of organising our desire to struggle collectively with the aim of creating an institutional struc-

---

19 Of course, the various revolutionary projects from the Paris Commune, the USSR and the Socialist countries of Eastern Europe to China, Vietnam and Cuba carried out numerous critical reflections about their experiences running the state in the direction of socialist transformation. Nonetheless, these reflections often remained within the boundaries of the local without larger international repercussions, and today, due to the hegemony of the Western liberal democracies, they have largely been forgotten. Also, the recent experiences in Latin America made by the first wave of progressive governments in the 21st century have had great difficulties in producing theoretical reflections that account for the achievements and challenges faced in the political transformation of the state. Some notable exceptions include Rauber (2012, 2017), Harnecker (2013), Cadahia (2019) and García Linera & Errejón (2019).
20 For a critique of "folk politics", see *Inventing the Future: Postcapitalism and a World Without Work* (Srnicek and Williams 2017), one of the pioneering works of the so-called "accelerationist" current of the Left.
21 A critical debate about "autonomism" can be found in Díaz and Romano (2018).
22 One interesting example of thinking about this question is the experience of the so-called party-movements ("partido-movimiento") as in the case of the *Movimiento al Socialismo* (MAS) in Bolivia, and in a similar vein the experience of the Spanish left party *Podemos* with the so-called citizen circles ("círculos ciudadanos"). While both of these examples can serve as starting points for the rethinking of organisational forms, they also provide crucial lessons regarding the limitations of such forms.
23 According to Lenin (1917a) a situation of dual power arises when the power of the bourgeois state is opposed by the alternative power created by a revolutionary organisation.
24 See Cortés and Tzeiman 2017.

ture that allows for the planning and carrying out of revolutionary transformations informed by the approach adopted by Lenin – without recipes and equipped with both imagination and realism in order to widen the horizons of possibility and thereby intensify our powers of intervention and political decision-making. Furthermore, in Lenin we find the value of the most crucial aspects of political organisation: comradeship combined with militant practice, consisting of the desire to struggle collectively and the creation of social bonds of a Socialist character, thereby confronting the ongoing processes of the colonising of modern subjectivity in the form of a liberal individualist sociability.[25]

In summary, each of these four lessons make up the nucleus of political desire called Lenin, which today presents itself to us as the best way to reactivate Marxism, as well as the desire to make possible the impossible, that is, to make the revolution.

Lenin from Latin America: The example of René Zavaleta Mercado

Finally, it is time to anchor the above exercise of reactivation in the concrete political translation V.I. Lenin has received within Latin America, i.e. our aim is to situate Lenin as an important theoretical nucleus of and moment in Latin American politics.[26] In order to do this, we must refer to those intellectual-militants[27] who carried out their theoretical production based on and together with the nucleus of political desire called Lenin, and in particular the case of René Zavaleta Mercado (1937-1984),[28] who in our mind represents the most creative and prolific moment of this constellation.

---

25 See Selci 2018 and Dean 2019.
26 See Ortega 2017.
27 Following Ortega (2018) and without claims to completeness, we mention the work of Rodney Arismendi *Lenin, la revolución y América Latina* (1976) dealing with the relationship between the Latin American Communist parties and the Comintern throughout the 20th century; Roberto Fernández Retamar's "Notas sobre Martí, Lenin y la revolución anticolonial" (1970) about the experiences of the Cuban Revolution; the work of Tomás Moulian describing the revolutionary experience of the *Unidad Popular* government in Chile "Acerca de la lectura de los textos de Lenin: una investigación introductoria" (1972) and *Cuestiones de teoría política marxista: una crítica de Lenin* (1980) and Roque Dalton's *Un libro rojo para Lenin* (1973) written in the heat of the Salvadorian struggle and the internationalisation of the revolutionary Left in Central America and the Caribbean. Martha Harnecker's *La revolución social: Lenin y América Latina* (1986) also engages with the Centralamerican conflicts while the *Obras Completas* (2011-2015) of René Zavaleta and Álvaro García Linera's *Las condiciones de la revolución socialista en Bolivia (a propósito de obreros, aymaras y Lenin)* (1988) analyse different moments of the Bolivian revolution. Finally, there is Atilio Borón and his "Actualidad del ¿Qué hacer?" (2004) written in the midst of the emergence of the first wave of progressive governments in Latin America at the start of the 21st century.
28 For a deeper engagement with the thinking of Zavaleta, see the edited volumes of Giller and Ouviña (2016b, 2018).

Zavaleta Mercado pertained to the group of exiled Latin American intellectuals living in Mexico in the 1970s and 80s, who during the exercise of living with and thinking themselves in exile, began engaging in the reactivation of Marxism in our region through the reading of the works of José Carlos Mariátegui (1894-1930).[29] However, in contrast to many of his comrades, Zavaleta thought this reactivation not only via Mariátegui but also through a re-reading of the writings of V.I. Lenin, thereby swimming against the tide of dominant perspectives towards Lenin at the time.[30]

In this sense, the work of Zavaleta is fully aligned with the nucleus of political desire called Lenin, as all four lessons mentioned above can also be found in his thinking:

- **Political contingency:** the thinking of Zavaleta is a thinking of contingency and singular multiplicity. For instance, his proposition that the different Latin American socio-economic formations are "motley formations," meaning that various modes of production converge in a single formation, thereby emphasising the heterogeneity and structural diversity of every country on the continent and the corresponding heterogeneous forms of resistance waged by the popular masses. For the Bolivian author, this implies the creation of adequate, always context-specific strategic responses.

- **Political analysis:** Zavaleta's work is the result of the influence of a number of revolutionary experiences in our region, especially the Bolivian National Revolution (1952-1964), the Unidad Popular government in Chile (1970-1973) and the Cuban Revolution (1959-ongoing). Engaging with these different experiences obliged him to learn from both their victories and defeats in order to be able to develop new theoretical inputs for the Bolivian and Latin American Left. For this he developed a creative, complex and robust analytical apparatus that includes concepts such as the apparent state, motley formations, the State of 52, irradiation, dual power, social equation, primordial form and the constitutive moment, among many others.[31]

- **Time and political conjuncture**: In Zavaleta we encounter a perspective of temporal multiplicity and the need to think and take action in accordance with the prevailing circumstances: from the concrete situation for the concrete situation.[32] This is how he thought the revolutionary processes, based on a perspective both strategic and tactical, identifying the potentialities and limitations of the different organisational and governmental experiences to then organise and project the diverse popular desires for change.

---

29 See Giller 2018.
30 See Concheiro 2016.
31 See Giller and Ouviña 2016a.
32 See Concheiro 2016.

- **Organisation and militancy:** What we find in Zavaleta is fundamentally a type of theoretical practice vis-à-vis the question of the proletarian organisation of miners in Bolivia, of the different organisational methods of Chilean workers and of the attempts to promote popular power in Cuba. In short, Zavaleta re-engages the challenge of Left political organising, in particular concerning the importance of thinking those types of organisation directed at the creation of "dual power" as a distinguishing trait of every revolutionary process.[33]

In conclusion, Zavaleta Mercado is one clear example[34] of how Latin American Marxism has been reactivated via the nucleus of political desire called Lenin, perpetually informed by an irreverence towards any type of dogmatism and the search for a Latin American Marxism in the tradition of the *amauta*[35] José Carlos Mariátegui: a fruitful and creatively situated analysis of the relationship between the concrete political problems of our highly diverse region and the theoretical output produced by the various Marxisms, allowing us to affirm that there indeed exists a Marxist way of thinking specific to and from Latin America and the Caribbean.[36] It is from within these coordinates provided by Zavaleta that we desire to continue the process of reactivating V.I. Lenin, audacious political leader and thinker, militant of the revolution and unwavering comrade of the people of the Global South.

Translated from the original Spanish by Hjalm(ar) Jorge Joffre-Eichhorn

References

Adamczak, Bini (2017), *Comunismo para todxs: Breve historia de cómo, al final, cambiarán las cosas.* Madrid: Akal.

Arismendi, Rodney (1976), *Lenin, la revolución y América Latina.* México: Grijalbo.

Bensaïd, Daniel (2017), *Estrategia y partido.* Barcelona: Sylone Editorial.

Borón, Atilio (2004), "Actualidad del ¿Qué hacer?," *in* V.I. Lenin *¿Qué hacer?.* Buenos Aires: Ediciones Luxemburgo.

Bosteels, Bruno (2018), "El otro Marx. Filosofía y teoría crítica," *in* Mabel Moraña (ed.), *Sujeto, decolonización, transmodernidad. Debates filosóficos latinoamericanos.* Madrid: Iberoamericana.

Budgen, Sebastian, Kouvelakis, Stathis and Slavoj Žižek (eds.) (2010), *Lenin reactivado: Hacia una política de la verdad.* Madrid: Akal.

---

33 Ibid.
34 The ongoing influence of Zavaleta could be witnessed in the political leadership and theoretical practice of Álvaro García Linera while serving as Vice President of the so-called Process of Change ("Proceso de Cambio") in Bolivia between 2006 and 2019.
35 *Amauta* is a Quechua term that means wise person or teacher, and that also has been used to name José Carlos Mariátegui.
36 See Martínez-Heredia 2010.

Cadahia, Luciana (2019), *El círculo mágico del Estado: populismo, feminismo y antagonismo*. Madrid: Lengua de Trapo.

Catanzaro, Gisela and Esteban De Gori (2019), "Las dificultades del imaginario revolucionario. Entrevista a Eduardo Grüner," *Revista Sociedad*, 38, 107-110.

Concheiro, Elvira (2016), "El análisis concreto de situaciones concretas: Lenin en la obra de René Zavaleta," in Diego Giller and Hernán Ouviña (comps.), *René Zavaleta Mercado. Pensamiento crítico y marxismo abigarrado*. Buenos Aires: Quimantú.

Cortés, Martín and Andrés Tzeiman (2017), "Discutir el Estado: dilemas estratégicos a la luz de los procesos políticos latinoamericanos," *Theomai. Estudios críticos sobre Sociedad y Desarrollo*, 35, 202-219.

Dalton, Roque (1973/1986), *Un libro rojo para Lenin*. Managua: Nueva Nicaragua.

Dean, Jodi (2013), *El horizonte comunista*. Barcelona: Bellaterra.

Dean, Jodi (2017), *Multitudes y partido*. Navarra: Katakrak.

Dean, Jodi (2019), *Comrade. An Essay on Political Belonging*. London: Verso.

Díaz, Ibán and Silvina María Romano (2018), *Antipolíticas: neoliberalismo, realismo de izquierda y autonomismo en América Latina*. Buenos Aires: Luxemburg.

Fernández-Retamar, Roberto (1970), "Notas sobre Martí, Lenin y la revolución anticolonial," *Casa de las Américas*, 59.

García, George (2018), "Impensar a Marx" (book chapter, unpublished). San José.

García Linera, Álvaro and Íñigo Errejón (2020), *Qué horizonte: Hegemonía, Estado y revolución democrática*. Madrid: Lengua de Trapo.

García Linera, Álvaro (1988), *Las condiciones de la revolución socialista en Bolivia (a propósito de obreros, aymaras y Lenin)*. La Paz: Ofensiva Roja.

García Linera, Álvaro (2017) "¿Fin de ciclo progresista o proceso por oleadas revolucionarias?," in Emir Sader (coord.), *Las vías abiertas de América Latina: siete ensayos en busca de una respuesta: ¿fin de ciclo o repliegue temporal?* Caracas: CELAG/BANDES.

Garo, Isabelle (2019), *Communisme et stratégie*. Paris: Éditions Amsterdam.

Giller, Diego and Hernán Ouviña (2016a), "René Zavaleta Mercado, un imprescindible," in Diego Giller and Hernán Ouviña (comps.), *René Zavaleta Mercado. Pensamiento crítico y marxismo abigarrado*, Buenos Aires: Quimantú.

Giller, Diego and Hernán Ouviña (comps.) (2016b), *René Zavaleta Mercado. Pensamiento crítico y marxismo abigarrado*. Buenos Aires: Quimantú.

Giller, Diego and Hernán Ouviña (eds.) (2018), *Reinventar a los clásicos. Las aventuras de René Zavaleta Mercado en los marxismos latinoamericanos*. Leiden: Almenara.

Giller, Diego (2018), *7 ensayos sobre socialismo y nación (incursiones mariateguianas)*. Buenos Aires: Caterva.
Harnecker, Martha (1986), *La revolución social: Lenin y América Latina*. Managua: Nueva Nicaragua.
Harnecker, Martha (2013), *Un mundo a construir (nuevos caminos)*. Barcelona: El Viejo Topo.
Jameson, Fredric (2010), "Lenin y el revisionismo," *in* Sebastian Budgen, Stathis Kouvelakis and Slavoj Žižek (eds.) *Lenin reactivado: Hacia una política de la verdad*, Madrid: Akal.
Lenin, V.I. (1917a), "El doble poder," *in* V. Lenin, *Obras selectas/Vladimir Ilich Lenin (Tomo dos: 1917/1923)*. Buenos Aires: Ediciones IPS
Lenin, V.I. (1917b), "El marxismo y la insurrección. Carta al Comité Central del POSDR (B)," *in* V. Lenin, *Obras selectas/Vladimir Ilich Lenin (Tomo dos: 1917/1923)*. Buenos Aires: Ediciones IPS.
Martínez-Heredia, Fernando (2010), *El ejercicio de pensar*. La Habana: Editorial de Ciencias Sociales/Instituto Cubano de Investigación Cultural Juan Marinello.
Moulian, Tomás (1972), "Acerca de la lectura de los textos de Lenin: una investigación introductoria," *Cuadernos de la Realidad Nacional*, 13.
Moulian, Tomás (1980), *Cuestiones de teoría política marxista: una crítica de Lenin*. Santiago de Chile: Flacso.
Ortega, Jaime (2017), "Órbitas de un pensamiento: Lenin y el marxismo en América Latina," *Latinoamérica*, 65, 227-255.
Rauber, Isabel (2012), *Revoluciones desde abajo: gobiernos populares y cambio social en Latinoamérica*. Buenos Aires: Peña Lillo/Ediciones Continente.
Rauber, Isabel (2017), *Refundar la política: desafíos para una nueva izquierda latinoamericana*. Buenos Aires: Peña Lillo/Ediciones Continente
Sandoval, Mauricio (2020), "El momento republicano y la urgencia de lo nacional-popular [online]," Flacso Costa Rica. Available at: https://flacso.or.cr/noticias/el-momento-republicano-y-la-urgencia-de-lo-nacional-popular/
Selci, Damián (2018), *Teoría de la militancia: organización y poder popular*. Buenos Aires: Cuarenta Ríos.
Srnicek, Nick and Alex Williams (2017), *Inventar el futuro. Poscapitalismo y un mundo sin trabajo*. Barcelona: Malpaso.
Traverso, Enzo (2019), *Melancolía de izquierda: después de las utopías*. Barcelona: Galaxia Gutenberg.
Vega, Renán (2019), *El capitaloceno: crisis civilizatoria, imperialismo ecológico y límites naturales*. Bogotá: Teoría & Praxis.
Zavaleta, René (2011-2015), *René Zavaleta Mercado: Obra Completa*. La Paz: Plural Editores.
Žižek, Slavoj (2012), *¡Bienvenidos a tiempos interesantes!* Navarra: Txalaparta.

6. Peace! Land! Bread! We are not going to die of Coronavirus, we are going to die of hunger!

Vashna Jagarnath

On 16 April 1917, Lenin made his return to Russia after a ten-year exile. The country he returned to was very different from the one he had left in 1907. After centuries of oppressive autocracy, and several unsuccessful attempts to overthrow the state, Russia was now on the cusp of revolutionary change led by the renowned Bolshevik leader.

Following the 1905 revolution, Tsar Nicholas II had consented to the establishment of the Duma, an assembly with advisory functions; but the ruling class continued with business as usual, and very little authority was actually conceded. In general terms, the regime was marked by a distinct lack of concern for, or understanding of, the plight of the majority of Russians. Despite the ultimately limited gains of 1905, there were important shifts in the general political atmosphere. One such example was the 'Days of Freedom,' a period of six weeks between 17 October and December 1905, which saw an unprecedented opening of Russian society after years of repression. There was a flourishing of revolutionary newspapers, books and pamphlets, while countless meetings were held across the country as people exercised their newly won freedom of assembly. Over four hundred gatherings and meetings were carried out in Moscow alone during this period; sixty-seven trade unions were established in Moscow and fifty-eight in St. Petersburg.

Lenin, writing years later, noted that it was "in this awakening of tremendous masses of the people to political consciousness and revolutionary struggle that the historic significance of January 22, 1905 lies."[1] In the growing, organised power of the proletariat, expressed most potently through the tactic of the mass strike, Lenin discerned a fundamental transformation of Russian society:

> The Russian revolution was also a proletarian revolution, not only in the sense that the proletariat was the leading force, the vanguard of the movement, but also in the sense that a specifically proletarian weapon of struggle – the strike – was the principal means of bringing the masses into motion and the most characteristic phenomenon in the wave-like rise of decisive events. The Russian revolution was the first, though certainly not the last, great revolution in history in which the mass political strike played an extraordinarily important part.[2]

---
1 Lenin 1977a: 237.
2 Ibid: 239.

This burgeoning labour movement had a massive impact on the newly established "soviets," the councils set up to organise workers both on the factory floor and in their communities, which now included around eight thousand workers. For the next ten years, the soviets would play a vital role in organising workers' power within the context of a repressive state. In the years prior to 1905, there had been many attempts to challenge the tyranny of the Russian nobility, including experimental communes like the one led by Leo Tolstoy, intelligentsia-led movements such as the *Narodniks*[3] who went to the countryside to organise the peasants, and various smaller groups of radicals.[4,5] The soviets, however, were the first form of organisation that was able to build sustained organisational counter-power from below.

When, in the years that followed, state repression of political activity began to reverse the limited gains of 1905, opposition to the state shifted into the realm of political violence, most notably in the form of the assassination of members of the state bureaucracy and the police. It was in this wave of political dissent, led by the working classes, that the Bolsheviks, under Lenin's leadership, placed their hope for the emancipation of Russia:

> The proletariat can generate fighting energy a hundred times greater than in ordinary, peaceful times. It shows that up to 1905 mankind did not yet know what a great, what a tremendous exertion of effort the proletariat is, and will be, capable of in a fight for really great aims, and one waged in a really revolutionary manner![6]

Peace! Land! Bread! – Russia 1917

In August 1914, Russia was dragged into the inferno that was World War I. In contrast to the German Social-Democrats, who voted in support of the war, Lenin, with others, was vociferous in his opposition, emphasising that it would be the working classes and the poor who would pay with their lives for a war waged by and for the benefit of bourgeois elites.[7] Lenin's prophecy was correct: some ten million Russian peasants were forced to fight, more than one-and-a-half million were killed, and around four million suffered serious injuries. By late 1916, widespread strikes and food riots broke out all over Russia as popular opposition to the war increased.

Meanwhile, the Romanovs, entranced by their fortune-telling mystic Rasputin, were seemingly oblivious to the revolution that was about to destroy their world. Nicholas II even commissioned Peter Carl Fabergé to

---

3 Lenin 1977b: 213-216.
4 See Hill 1982.
5 Lenin's brother, Aleksander Ulyanov, was a member of one of these radical groups, the *Narodnaya Volya*, a militant arm of the Narodniks. He was eventually charged with attempting to assassinate the emperor and executed in 1887.
6 Lenin 1977a: 236-253.
7 Lenin 1974a: 15-19.

create a Fabergé Easter egg, the Karelian Birch egg, for his mother Empress Maria Feodorovna; this little trinket cost 12,500 roubles, about 52 times more than the monthly wage an unskilled Russian labourer earned in 1916. These lavish bejewelled eggs had been produced for the Tsars and their families since 1885 to celebrate the death and rebirth of their Christian god during Easter. However, in 1917 there was no rebirth – only the death of the Romanov dynasty. Tsar Nicholas never got the chance to present the commissioned egg to the dowager empress. Following the February Revolution, on March 15 he was forced to abdicate his throne.[8]

On hearing the news of the Tsar's abdication, Lenin ended his exile in Switzerland and found passage back to Russia via a dangerous route through Germany. Arriving at the Finland station in Petrograd in mid-April, Lenin immediately spoke to the large crowd waiting to receive him on the platform with the beginnings of what would become his *April Theses*. Later that evening, he addressed the revolutionary guard of honour:

> The people need peace; the people need bread; the people need land. And they give you war, hunger, no bread – leave the landlords still on the land...[9]

Thus, the slogan that would become the war cry of the Bolshevik revolution was born: "Peace! Land! Bread!" In that moment, Lenin not only captured the stark reality lived by most Russians but was also able to express the ideology of socialism in concrete terms understood by ordinary people. It was a clear statement of truth that summed up the damnable living conditions of the Russian people: broken and wounded soldiers, who were by now fleeing from the battlefields *en masse*; peasants toiling on the estates of the nobility; and urban workers starving in the cities due to food shortages. Within six months of arriving at the Finland station, Lenin and the Bolsheviks took power and ushered in the world's first socialist state.

Peace! Land! Bread! – South Africa 2020

Just over a century later, on the opposite side of the world, at the southernmost tip of the African continent, in South Africa, the cry of "Peace! Land! Bread!" remains as relevant as ever. Over the past twenty years, despite the arrival of the democratic dispensation of 1994, the ever-present threat of state violence continues unabated. Currently, a mere three thousand five-hundred South Africans own more of the country's wealth than the bottom thirty-two million.[10] Hunger and poverty are prevalent, with over seventy percent of the population suffering food insecurity. Seventy-two percent of the land still remains in the hands of nine percent of the population.

---

8 Jagarnath 2014.
9 See Crankshaw 1954.
10 See Webster 2020.

According to World Bank statistics on income inequality, South Africa is ranked as the most unequal country in the world.[11] While the end of Apartheid brought opportunities and a far more integrated society for the elites and middle classes, most South Africans still endure severe economic exploitation and exclusion as well as everyday racism and patriarchy.

Then came the coronavirus. In March 2020, the South African government, led by President Cyril Ramaphosa, declared a state of National Disaster to deal with the global outbreak of COVID-19. The measures instituted included a national lockdown, which involved the complete shutdown of the economy, the closure of land, air and sea borders, the banning of non-essential travel and the general confinement of people to their homes. In addition, the South African National Defence Force was deployed to assist with various aspects of the National Disaster.

In general terms, the South African state deserves praise for its effective response to the pandemic, with its key decisions based on science and medical research rather than fearmongering, conspiracy and fake news. At the same time, however, the conditions created by the lockdown have brought the deeply unequal nature of the South Africa economy into sharp focus.[12] In a country with an unemployment rate of almost thirty percent, millions of people eke out a precarious living in the informal sector. Many of these people have no savings and live in shacks without access to refrigeration. With no daily income there is no food. This has been compounded by the closing of schools, resulting in nine million children who depend on school meals currently missing out on a daily meal.

To make matters worse, there has been a dramatic rise in basic food costs. In the space of a month, prices have more than doubled in many cases. According to the Pietermaritzburg Economic Justice and Dignity Group, cooking oil has risen by 4%, rice by 8%, sugar beans by 9%, brown bread by 14% and spinach, butternut, potatoes, carrots and onions all by more than 25%. In other words, the COVID-19 pandemic has worsened a long-standing food crisis in which one in four South Africans lives in hunger. As a result, we are now witnessing daily food grabs, riots, and protests across the country amongst the most desperate in society. Bread!

While many go hungry others are being rendered homeless. Since the advent of the pandemic, the state has violently evicted shack-dwellers across South Africa.[13] Despite a declaration by the national government that no evictions would take place during the lockdown, impoverished and working-class people continue to be forcibly displaced. Members of the social movement Abahlali baseMjondolo, the largest and best organised popular movement to have emerged after Apartheid, have been particularly targeted. Their land occupations have come under repeated state attack with live ammunition

---

11 See Beaubien 2018.
12 See Valodia and Francis 2020.
13 See Abahlali baseMjondolo 2020.

being frequently used against unarmed people. In South Africa the housing question is, fundamentally, a question of access to urban land. It is also a question of the need for the state to recognise land occupations and the self-made structures erected on them, and to provide essential services such as water and electricity. At the time of writing, more than four million South Africans live in informal homes, often with very little access to basic services. For example, in a settlement called Marikana in the Western Cape there are fifty communal water taps for sixty thousand families. This is unacceptable. Land![14]

Finally, state violence has always been a feature of modern South Africa, from the era of colonialism, through Apartheid and continuing into today's post-Apartheid times. While there have been moments when the violence of the South African state against poor black people were thrust into the elite public sphere, such as the infamous Marikana Massacre in 2012,[15] it largely passes without attention. In fact, deadly state violence against working class and impoverished black people has been normalised to the point that it seldom makes the news. This is also true of the violent repression of popular protests, evictions, and the torture and assassination of grassroots militants.[16] Today, under the cover of the coronavirus lockdown, this violence has increased sharply. Peace!

What Is to Be Done? – Lessons from Lenin

As lockdown measures increase around the world, it is the workers, peasants and unemployed who face the worst consequences, from India[17] and Nigeria,[18] to Colombia.[19] It is in this context that we can continue to learn from Lenin, especially in the Global South. Here in South Africa, his slogan of "Peace, Land and Bread" is epitomised by the daily struggle for survival of impoverished people and the working class. Currently, organisations such as the National Union of Metal Workers of South Africa (NUMSA), the largest and most militant trade union, and others like Abahlali baseMjondolo, United Front and the Socialist Revolutionary Workers Party are together struggling against the exploitation and oppression imposed by globalised capitalism.

As the COVID-19 pandemic brings social tensions to a head, the call for peace is not, as in Lenin's day, to end a global war but to end state repression and violence against the poor and marginal. The call for bread, on the other hand, is ever more important as an increasing number of South Africans go hungry while the rich stock up and hibernate in their high-walled mansions. Finally, the need for land is evident in the ongoing occupation of urban areas in the face of extraordinary state violence aimed at protecting its commodification.

---

14 See SERI 2019.
15 See Pithouse n.d.
16 See Ashraf Hendricks 2020.
17 See Human Rights Watch 2020a.
18 See Human Rights Watch 2020b.
19 See Human Rights Watch 2020c.

In these difficult times we need to organise ourselves, find new ways to mobilise and show solidarity in an era of social distancing. One response must be to look to the past and draw important lessons on how to agitate, organise and rally society. Lenin's lessons are crucial in this regard. First, the consolidation of the complex demands of society need to be translated into a clear message, as Lenin did in 1917 with "Peace! Land! Bread!" This is vital if any Left forces are to be able to harness the dissatisfaction and ferment brewing in South Africa for years. It is all the more important in a time when the organised power of ordinary people, and the liberatory power of popular politics, is drastically weakened not only by the state from above but also through a process of the NGO-isation of political activism. As prominent Marxist Tanzanian scholar Issa Shivji has noted:

> ...the transformation from a colonial subject society to a bourgeois society in Africa is incomplete, stunted and distorted. We have the continued domination of imperialism – reproduction of the colonial mode – in a different form, currently labelled globalisation or neoliberalism. Within this context, NGOs are neither a third sector, nor independent of the state. Rather, they are inextricably imbricated in the neoliberal offensive, which follows on the heels of the crisis of the national project. Unless there is awareness on the part of the NGOs of this fundamental moment in the struggle between imperialism and nationalism, they end up playing the role of ideological and organisational foot soldiers of imperialism.[20]

In South Africa, as in the rest of the continent, the NGO-sector has often effectively shifted the insurgent popular political power built from below into the realm of workshops, petitions and technical sets of demands on the state. This politics operates largely within a middle-class Left sphere and has no ability to rally the imagination of the working class and the most dispossessed in society behind a radically liberatory vision. While NGO-isation may be a mechanism used to dismantle the power of the most oppressed in society, it is not a new method. In 1917 in the *April Thesis*,[21] Lenin accurately exposed "petty bourgeois opportunist elements," who fear the mass organisation of the working class and tend to work towards the undoing of its power in favour of liberalism. We must urgently revisit this work in order for us to understand how, in the current situation, we can successfully identify and reject these opportunistic elements in our political and ideological activism in order to begin to ground ourselves in the true struggles faced by the working class and poor.

---

20 See Shivji 2007.
21 Lenin 1974b: 19-26.

A second lesson we can draw from Lenin for this moment is to recommit to our solidarity with the proletariat. This needs to be done despite the shrinking organised working class across the world and in South Africa. The proletariat of Russia from 1905 to 1917 was less than twenty percent of the population, yet its growing organisational power had an immense impact on the course of the revolution. Therefore, now more than ever, we cannot allow the strong organisations of the working class built over the past century to wither away. On the contrary, we need to reaffirm their power in today's South Africa. Given our current context, this is still possible, as we continue to have a strong, militant and radical organised working class in the form of NUMSA, as well as several other working-class formations such as the Congress of South African Trade Unions and the South African Federation of Trade Unions. If we are to take Lenin seriously and learn from his experience, we in South Africa must work towards reinforcing and building the power of the working class. Or in the words of Irvin Jim, the General Secretary of NUMSA: "Our task is to unite the working class across all of society."[22]

In conclusion, the Coronavirus has sharpened the contradictions of capital. In South Africa, where the majority of society is vulnerable and workers enjoy neither safety nor access to adequate healthcare, this pandemic could prove to be very deadly indeed. As a result, it is absolutely urgent that we build our solidarity and find new ways of resisting the inhumanity of capitalism. We can do this. We can organise, just as in various periods of history workers have organised themselves, often in far worse conditions than ours, to promote a better life for the majority of society. We as workers are the producers of society, and this includes the producing of new ways of activism. Often in history, moments of great devastation have ultimately led to great advancements for those at the receiving end of systematic oppression. This is our moment and it is now that we need to reinforce our commitment to the struggle for Peace, Land and Bread. Another world is possible, and it is up to us to make it!

---

22 See Jim 2014.

References

Abahlali baseMjondolo (2020), "Impunity for Attempted Murder." Accessed on 29.06.2020, at https://www.facebook.com/abahlalibasemjondolo/posts/3191725324191031?__tn__=K-R.

Beaubien, Jason (2018), "The Country With The World's Worst Inequality Is…," *npr*. Accessed on 29.06.2020, at https://www.npr.org/sections/goatsandsoda/2018/04/02/598864666/the-country-with-the-worlds-worst-inequality-is.

Crankshaw, Edward (1954), "When Lenin Returned," *The Atlantic*. Accessed on 29.06.2020, at https://www.theatlantic.com/magazine/archive/1954/10/when-lenin-returned/303867/.

Hendricks, Ashraf (2020), "City vs shack dwellers: Occupations and demolitions escalate in Cape Town," *Ground Up*. Accessed on 29.06.2020, at https://www.groundup.org.za/article/khayelitsha-shacks-demolished/.

Hill, Christopher (1982), *Lenin and the Russian Revolution*. Middlesex: Penguin Books.

Human Rights Watch (2020a), "India: COVID-19 Lockdown Puts Poor at Risk." Accessed on 29.06.2020, at https://www.hrw.org/news/2020/03/27/india-covid-19-lockdown-puts-poor-risk.

Human Rights Watch (2020b), "Nigeria: Protect Most Vulnerable in COVID-19 Response." Accessed on 29.06.2020, at https://www.hrw.org/news/2020/04/14/nigeria-protect-most-vulnerable-covid-19-response.

Human Rights Watch (2020c), "Armed Groups in Colombia Threaten Civilians Over COVID-19 Measures." Accessed on 29.06.2020, at https://www.hrw.org/news/2020/04/13/armed-groups-colombia-threaten-civilians-over-covid-19-measures.

Jagarnath, Vashna (2014), "Easter: A Moveable Feast," *The Con*. https://www.theconmag.co.za/2014/04/17/easter-a-moveable-feast/. This website is no longer up.

Jim, Irvin (2014), "United Front a weapon for the working class." Accessed on 29.06.2020, at https://www.youtube.com/watch?v=p5pdoXFTVgU.

Lenin, V.I. (1974a), *Collected Works Vol. 21*. Moscow: Progress Publishers.

Lenin, V.I. (1974b), *Collected Works Vol. 24*. Moscow: Progress Publishers.

Lenin, V.I. (1977a), *Collected Works Vol. 23*. Moscow: Progress Publishers.

Lenin, V.I. (1977b), *Collected Works Vol. 20*. Moscow: Progress Publishers.

Pithouse, Richard (n.d.), "Fidelity to the Durban Moment After Marikana?" Accessed on 29.06.2020, at https://www.sahistory.org.za/sites/default/files/Paper_Richard_Pithouse.pdf.

Shivji, Issa G. (2007), *Silences in NGO discourse: The role and future of NGOs in Africa*. Nairobi: Fahamu Books.

Socio-Economic Rights Institute of South Africa (2019), "Our Place to Belong." Accessed on 29.06.2020, at http://mile.org.za/QuickLinks/News/Sanitation%20Workshop24%20to%2025%20October%202019/Marikana%20Informal%20Settlement.pdf.

Valodia, Imraan, and David Francis (2020), "South Africa needs to mitigate the worst of its iequalities in tackling coronavirus," *The Conversation*. Accessed on 29.06.2020, at https://theconversation.com/south-africa-needs-to-mitigate-the-worst-of-its-inequalities-in-tackling-coronavirus-135564.

Webster, Dennis (2020), "SA's richest 3500 own more than the bottom 32 million," *New Frame*. Accessed on 29.06.2020, at https://www.newframe.com/sas-richest-3-500-own-more-than-the-bottom-32-million/.

7. Notes on "Left-Wing" Communism: An Infantile Disorder[1]

Atilio A. Boron

The Immediate Context

Lenin wrote this highly interesting essay in April 1920, on the eve of the Second Congress of the Communist International (Comintern). At that time Russia was immersed in a bloody civil war that the counter-revolutionary forces had started a few months after the October Revolution, which would eventually conclude with the triumph of the Red Army. The text was due to be presented at the Comintern congress convened in Moscow between July 19 and August 7, 1920, aiming to become an ideological guide for the rising international communist movement. Later this congress became known for Lenin's proposition (and imposition) of the "Twenty-one Conditions," officially the "Conditions of Admission to the Communist International," to be strictly adhered to by any revolutionary force that aspired to become part of the Third International and follow the trail of the Russian Revolution.

It is worth remembering that these conditions provoked fierce debates both inside and beyond Russia, as they effectively proposed the "Bolshevisation" of all social-democratic and workers' parties that wished to integrate into the Comintern, through the establishing of general guidelines as well as strategies and tactics with which the entire army of the world proletariat should comply. For many protagonists and commentators at the time, these impositions meant the creation of a type of communist "Vatican" that would be responsible for making decisions on the precise modes of struggle for the various "national detachments" of the communist movement, albeit subjecting them to what was most important internationally.

In reality, this translated into the subordination of all revolutionary parties to the line established by Moscow. Given that the struggle for a communist revolution was a global undertaking, Lenin was convinced that only strategy and tactics of an equally global scope, coupled with iron discipline, could achieve this. Hence, what was required was a guiding text that would allow for the correction of those political deviations deemed to put at risk the success of world revolution, which Lenin at some point thought to be a matter of a few weeks, therefore making it essential not to commit any mistakes that could frustrate this impending achievement.

According to Lenin, one of the principal mistakes was "Leftism," a dogmatic current within social-democracy, with intransigent politics vis-à-vis the building of political alliances and the completely fanciful assumption of a linear progression towards communism, capable of thwarting the efforts of the world proletariat. In order to fight against this current, Lenin

---

[1] A longer version of this text was originally published in V.I. Lenin, *La enfermedad infantil del izquierdismo en el comunismo.* Taffala Nafarroa: txalaparta (2020).

wrote *"Left-Wing" Communism: An Infantile Disorder*, valuable not only because it provides vital lessons from the particular process in revolutionary Russia but also because many of his recommendations are surprisingly valid in the current Latin American – and why not say it, European – context, where attitudes of "Leftism" have been one of the preferred weapons used, incited and promoted by both the political Right and US-imperialism in order to castigate and debilitate the ongoing revolutionary and emancipatory processes in the region over the past two decades.

Overall, we should not be surprised that the leader of the Russian revolution chose this particular topic. In general terms, "Leftism" is an ideological theory and practice that proposes the uncontrolled radicalisation of a revolutionary project without giving due consideration to the different objective and subjective conditions necessary for the success of the revolution. "Leftism" is a type of voluntarism taken to the extreme, based on a positivist, linear and anti-dialectic conception of revolution, akin to what Antonio Gramsci called "pedantic doctrinalism." According to this theoretical approach, the revolution is understood as a rigid and always rising process powered by the Promethean will of its leaders and/or its vanguard. In the case of revolutionary defeat or failure, "Leftists" will always find guilt in one place: the treason of its leaders. This "abstract revolutionism" ends up producing exactly the opposite of what it claims, and this is precisely the reason why Lenin committed himself so strongly to fight against it.

In other words, similar to almost all texts written by the Bolshevik leader, this is a text written in response to the urgent needs of the revolution, which in the middle of 1920 appeared to be coming to a halt in a Western Europe devastated by WWI, thereby severely damaging the Bolshevik leadership's expectations that the European proletariat would soon come to help their besieged Russian comrades. As the not uncontroversial work of Fernando Claudín has shown, however, these hopes of an imminent revolution in Europe were not based on a rigorous analysis of the changes imposed by the advent of the age of imperialism, the transformations of bourgeois society in Europe and the disparate meanings and value of peace in the old continent and in Soviet Russia.[2]

At this point, it is necessary to mention the extreme threats to survival faced by the fledgling and beleaguered Soviet republic due to the combined onslaught of the European and international Right, the so-called "democratic" powers of the West, more than a dozen foreign armies in total (e.g. USA, UK, France, Japan), who fought with unheard-of cruelty against a revolutionary Russian government[3] aided by great masses of peasants,

---

[2] There are obviously an enormous number of texts available that examine the different aspects of the "failure of the revolution in the West." In the Spanish language, we point out the work of Fernando Claudín (1980) for its direct link to the writings of Lenin.

[3] This type of conduct can be observed again today in the case of the systematic attacks against Cuba and Venezuela, carried out by US-imperialism and its allies. Of course, in fifth-generation warfare, or hybrid wars, the use of foreign troops is only one moment, generally the last, of a series of other, "softer" attacks, which include economic sanctions and blockades, diplomatic harassment, information warfare and others. Little over a century ago, however, the preferred form of warfare was the invasion and physical occupation

workers and soldiers, intent on conquering the heavens.

Even though the Red Army eventually prevailed, its victory was clouded by the multiple defeats suffered by communists in Western Europe: The German revolution was crushed and its two great leaders, Rosa Luxemburg and Karl Liebknecht, treacherously murdered; in Hungary, the brief Soviet experience led by Béla Kun was defeated, while in Poland the prospects of a Communist triumph depended entirely on a Soviet victory that ultimately failed to materialise. In France and Great Britain, the proletariat faithfully followed their "traitorous" political leadership, to use a misguided expression in common use at the time.[4] Finally, in Italy, numerous failed insurrections revealed, like a serpent's egg, the first glimpses of the rise of fascism. It was at this point in time that the Second Congress of the Communist International convened.

Alliances and the Question of "Compromises"

Lenin begins his text with an initial description of "Leftism," which he develops over the course of the book. His first use of the term refers to the petty bourgeoisie, which in the European context constitutes quite a numerous social class that tends to react with an "ultra-revolutionary mentality" vis-à-vis capitalist oppression and the rapid deterioration of their living conditions. However, he remarks that this reaction is characterised by volatility and a lack of perseverance. The "enraged petty bourgeois" has revolutionary whims that because of its lack of a "spirit of organisation, discipline and firmness" can quickly turn to apathy and submission to new political subjects that re-channel their anger in the opposite direction. This description, shared by other leaders of the Third International like Trotsky and Clara Zetkin, anticipates what Italian fascism would soon forcefully confirm.

These considerations about petty bourgeois mentality give rise to one of the central themes discussed by Lenin in his book: the problem of alliances and the "compromise" demanded for the advance of the revolutionary process. This presupposes the admission that revolutions are not merely events that simply happen when the objective and subjective conditions converge for their realisation, but rather long, complex and contradictory processes, during which it is impossible to progress without making compromises with powers that, even though they do not share the revolutionary project, may offer an opportunity to momentarily and for specific purposes join forces and make the process advance.[5]

---

of the enemy's territory. And yet, the Red Army imposed a resounding defeat on the invaders, albeit at the cost of large areas of cities and countryside destroyed and many human lives lost. Later the beasts of capitalism tried again in countries like China and Vietnam, then Cuba and Nicaragua, and in fact any government whose politics implied even the most modest challenge to US interests.

4 The accusation of betrayal was used every time one was unable to explain convincingly why the masses supported their leadership.

5 Although we will deal with this issue later in the text, it is worth emphasising already that this discussion is of the utmost transcendence for the current Latin American and Caribbean context, where many "Leftist" forces have persistently engaged in ferocious criticism of the various progressive and centre-left

Lenin gives the example of Karl Radek and Mikhail Bukharin, both of whom for a time opposed the Treaty of Brest-Litovsk, but later changed their positions. Lenin affirms that for them "the Treaty of Brest-Litovsk was a compromise with the imperialists, which was inexcusable on principle and harmful to the party of the revolutionary proletariat. It was indeed a compromise with the imperialists, but it was a compromise which, under the circumstances, *had to be made*."[6] He then goes on to provide the following example: "Imagine that your car is held up by armed bandits. You hand them over your money, passport, revolver and car. In return you are rid of the pleasant company of the bandits. That is unquestionably a compromise. '*Do ut des*' (I 'give' you money, firearms and a car 'so that you give' me the opportunity to get away from you with a whole skin). It would, however, be difficult to find a sane man who would declare such a compromise to be 'inadmissible on principle,' or who would call the compromiser an accomplice of the bandits (even though the bandits might use the car and the firearms for further robberies). Our compromise with the bandits of German imperialism was just that kind of compromise."[7] In other words, the compromise was imposed by the weight of concrete circumstances, i.e. due to the objectively existing balance of power at that moment and place in time.

Lenin concludes by saying: "to reject compromises 'on principle' [...] is childishness, which it is difficult even to consider seriously." Elsewhere in the book he describes as "absurd" the politics that "formulate[s] a recipe or general rule ('No compromises!') to suit all cases."[8] What is to be done then? The answer is that any revolutionary leadership worthy of the name must know how to distinguish between different types of compromise: there are those that express a politics of opportunism and treason of the revolution, but there also exist those that make possible an advance of the cause of the proletariat. Returning to his example, he recommends that "[o]ne must learn to distinguish between a man who has given up his money and fire-arms to bandits so as to lessen the evil they can do and to facilitate their capture and execution, and a man who gives his money and fire-arms to bandits so as to share in the loot."[9] In short, there are compromises and compromises. The Treaty of Brest-Litovsk had to be signed after all attempts to agree on a "peace to all nations" had gone awry and the revolution in Germany had failed. There was no alternative to signing this treaty.

In another passage of the book, Lenin applies his understanding of "compromise" to the scenario of a pre-revolutionary or pre-insurrectional situation, in which "[t]he more powerful enemy can be vanquished only by exerting the utmost effort, and by the most thorough, careful, atten-

---

governments of the early 21st century, precisely for their politics of "class reconciliation," which would inevitably thwart the revolutionary process.
6 Lenin 1974: 36.
7 Ibid: 39.
8 Ibid: 68.
9 Ibid: 38.

tive, skilful and obligatory use of any, even the smallest, rift between the enemies, any conflict of interests among the bourgeoisie of the various countries and among the various groups or types of bourgeoisie within the various countries, and also by taking advantage of any, even the smallest, opportunity of winning a mass ally, even though this ally is temporary, vacillating, unstable, unreliable and conditional. Those who do not understand this reveal a failure to understand even the smallest grain of Marxism, of modern scientific socialism *in general*."[10] He then reminds us that Marxism "is not a dogma, but a guide to action."[11]

In fact, the above quotation is so categorical and at the same time so eloquent that it precludes any additional comment. It synthesises in an exemplary manner how the Left should engage in politics in real life, absorbed in the mud of history or in the difficult and relentless "struggle of opposing Gods" as Max Weber, a contemporary of Lenin, called it. The recommendations of the Russian revolutionary are in direct opposition to the way the various "Leftisms" – whether a hundred years ago or today – conceive of "doing politics," that is to say, as if they were operating in an impeccable, platonic, Cartesian world of pure and bright ideas. In such a world, political processes and their protagonists vividly appear as participants in a polyphony of political forces and situations operating in a cosmos of immutable essences, in which one can only construct power by insisting over and over again on the immutability of dogma, and where any alliance, even if temporary and circumstantial, is considered heresy – the first step towards what will surely become unforgivable treason.

We find this type of attitude very frequently in organisations on the political Left, but reading Lenin and thinking with and from Lenin we can say, without fear of being wrong, that this type of "chatter" is anything but politics. It would be more appropriate to call it "messianic preaching," because there does not exist within it any intention to construct political power but rather only the desire to preach the Good News and thereby gain the fidelity and loyalty of a handful of converts passionately awaiting the advent of "Judgement Day;" and while they are waiting, everything else is nothing but treason. In other words, their "politics" produces an almost imperceptible, but inherently fateful passage from politics to religion, from the Hell of opposing Gods to a New Jerusalem, where, to put it in postmodern or Habermasian terms, politics is converted into a competition of discourses and texts, totally detached from the real world.

An Alliance between Equals?

The questions above defined the overall framework for the type of possible alliances that could be potentially beneficial for the popular classes. Now

---

10 Ibid: 70-71.
11 Ibid: 71.

we must ask: alliances with whom? Formally speaking, a revolutionary party can only ally itself with another Left force. Yet, such a constellation appears to be closer to a (temporary) reunification of the same political faction following a split in the past, rather than a true alliance, especially if the allies share the same Left ideas and propositions. The problem with this type of alliance is that if "they" and "we" also share the same lack of rootedness in society, what is brought together are two groups of little relevance, the sum of which produces an even larger irrelevance. Lenin speaks of this in his book when he affirms that "politics is more like algebra than arithmetic, and still more like higher than elementary mathematics."[12] Hence, one plus one does not automatically equal two but can sometimes be zero. The unity of two forces equal in essential matters can therefore debilitate both of them and lead to a worsening of the overall situation.

What is the reason then for such a serious and often repeated error? In our view, it has to do with ignoring one essential recommendation made by Lenin, namely that alliances can be strategic and long-lasting only in exceptional circumstances. In fact, the most effective alliances, the ones that advance the project of the popular classes, have proven to be the type of tactical, temporary and punctual alliances that allow the Left to disseminate its message while subjecting to its hegemony classes and social groups to which it is traditionally opposed. The notion that any alliance must necessarily be a strategic alliance, and that therefore a Left, socialist or communist party can only ally itself with those who share their aim to transcend capitalism or establish a new socialist society, is condemned to failure in advance, as has been clearly demonstrated by innumerable examples in contemporary Latin American history. Inspired by some of the evangelical, millennial sects, one could call these strategic alliances of the Left "Judgement Day alliances" that coalesce around the final attack aimed at burying a society that condemns the majority of people to poverty, social exclusion and humiliation, all the while causing irreparable damage to the environment.

The problem besetting this approach to alliances is obvious: the Judgement Day of capitalism is nowhere in sight. On the contrary, and regardless of whether we agree with Immanuel Wallerstein's hypothesis that capitalism does not have more than thirty years of life left, what is undeniable is that in political life one can neither forge alliances nor elaborate tactics of struggle for a duration of thirty or forty years. What is imperative is the "here and now," the Marxian *"hic Rhodus, hic salta"* based on the well-known Aesopian fable that demands immediate proof of what can easily be proven instead of seeking refuge in idle chatter or, as Che Guevara put it, "pseudorevolutionary mumbo jumbo." Given that we are not in Rhodes, and although we are aware of the gravity of the challenges that ail the capitalist mode of production and the exasperating contradictions it produces, the

---

12 Ibid: 102.

truth is that this scenario of dissolution and breakdown does not appear to be on the immediate political horizon. In fact, it is precisely this remoteness that allows for the kind of debates that have absolutely nothing to do with the urgencies of the current situation. In the case of the Argentinian Left, one poignant example is the seemingly interminable conflict about the correct interpretation of the October Revolution and the role played by Stalin and Trotsky, controversies that profoundly divide the very few forces on the Left, and that end up leading to the type of sectarianism and dogmatism that distances us even further from the popular masses, who contemplate these disputes with a mixture of sarcasm and indifference.

Another problem with the alliance among equals is that it does not correspond to the level of public consciousness, an issue brought up time and again by people like Marx and Engels, then Lenin and eventually Fidel. The crucial question is the following: To what extent are the popular classes – the proletariat and the growing sub-proletariat of Latin America – prepared to follow and extend their support to the propositions made by the radical Left? What is their actual level of consciousness, not the one which the proletariat *should* have in theory, but the one that exists in the contextual construction of the concrete conditions that affect the chronically unemployed, the landless peasants, displaced workers, youth without work and the enormous contingents of those permanently subjected to the informal economy and precarity?

It was Fidel who insisted on this issue during his famous visit to Salvador Allende's Chile in November 1971, when some radicalised sectors questioned Allende's policies for being merely "reformist" and demanded that Fidel take a position on whether what was happening in Chile was a revolution or not. His response to them was twofold: first, that revolutions are not events that fall from the sky, but complex and contradictory processes that unfold over time and that therefore to determine their direction and possible outcome is something that cannot be done beforehand or based on theory; and second, Fidel urged them to thoroughly ask themselves about the highest possible level of popular consciousness at that precise historic moment, and whether they truly believed that the masses were prepared to extend their militant support vis-à-vis a radicalisation of the political process led by Allende's Popular Unity (*Unidad Popular*), with all the suffering and conflict that this would entail. Returning to the case of contemporary Argentina, I dare to predict that this "alliance-reunification of equals" would not obtain more than 5% of popular support at best. The same maximum amount would agree with the idea of replacing capitalism with socialism. For the rest of the population such a proposition would appear nothing less than foolishness. A "popular front" alliance, on the other hand, aimed at uniting the various political forces opposed to neoliberalism and beginning to create a new common sense in favour of the anti-capitalist struggle, could possibly count on the support of 50% or more of the electorate.

In conclusion: If we have opted, for different reasons, for the long march through the institutions, discarding insurrection – whether peaceful or violent – then we must accept that this course entails the unavoidable need to convince the majority of the population to support this type of alliance. Or to put it in the words of Gramsci, before one can become the dominant class one has first to become the leading class, that is to say, capable of exercising "intellectual and moral leadership" over vast sectors of civil society. This, in turn, means conquering a popular majority among the victims of capitalism, the women and men who, according to Che, have been deliberately "uneducated" over the course of five centuries by the ever-changing ideological apparatuses of bourgeois society that have imposed an ideology, a common sense, according to which capitalism has become completely naturalised as the only possible form of organising the economic and social life of a nation while simultaneously discarding all other alternatives as either toxic anachronisms or the "utopian" projects of delusional social prophets, such as socialists and communists, totally lacking any sense of realism and, if put into practice, destined to subject society to an orgy of blood and violence.

As a matter of fact, contemporary Neoliberalism constructs its entire strategy of propaganda based on an idea that evokes certain basic Christian principles: Capitalism is what it was, what it is and what it always will be. History has no alternatives. To break with this creed, so profoundly rooted in our societies, requires more than beautiful words. Therefore, if an alliance discards insurrection and at the same time does not deploy a strategy to conquer majority support, or at least the support of a substantial section of the population, in the framework of what Lenin called "legal forms of struggle," it is condemned to die out like a candle without oxygen and to vegetate until eventually becoming a political nonentity. There have been many such experiences throughout history.

Alliances with Others

Having explored the obstacles posed by an "alliance among equals," let us now interrogate the possibilities and necessary conditions for an alliance with political forces that do not share the same strategic vision of abolishing capitalism and creating a new type of society. As mentioned before, this option is anathema to the "Leftists" and has been labelled by the most dogmatic political sectors as mere opportunism and inadmissible treason of the socialist project – the reason why Lenin wrote his book in the first place. Needless to say, these types of alliances have given rise to the most scandalous political compromises, full of despicable acts perpetrated in the name of political "realism." Nevertheless, if a revolutionary force is determined to advance its project and finds itself in a situation of being in the minority, it cannot but walk a stretch of the way with political forces with which it can only be in partial, tactical and temporary agreement, with an exclusive focus on the current moment. An example of this was the Fidel-led 26th of July Movement in Cuba, which allied with a number of political forces that under no circumstances intended to construct a new, post-capitalist order. In fact, not until the Bay of Pigs Invasion of 1961 did Fidel declare the Cuban revolution to be socialist in nature. Up to that point, a series of alliances had been made and unmade according to the needs of the guerrillas in the mountains and the protest movements in the cities. The objective of these tactical alliances was to strengthen the popular resistance, promote socialist consciousness and improve popular organisation, thereby gradually shifting the balance of power in favour of the popular camp and against the tyranny of the US-backed dictator Fulgencio Batista. A similar lesson can be drawn from the history of the Russian Revolution, particularly the period between February and October 1917, when Lenin himself said that the decisive criterion for forging an alliance was whether it would expand or diminish the protagonism of the soviets of workers, peasants and soldiers. If their cause was advanced even by an inch, Lenin said, the alliance was useful and should be forged. Once this advance was made, everything else would have to be redefined, and the need would arise for new friends to walk with, thereby counteracting the new enemies of the revolution in the making.

In an illuminating passage of the book, Lenin says something about the forging of alliances that deserves to be reproduced in full, because it buries once and for all any argument in favour of the type of political solipsism that urges us to take action "without compromises":

> Prior to the downfall of tsarism, the Russian revolutionary Social-Democrats made repeated use of the services of the bourgeois liberals, i.e., they concluded numerous practical compromises with the latter. In 1901-02, even prior to the appearance of Bolshevism, the old editorial board of *Iskra* (consisting of Plekhanov, Axelrod, Zasulich, Martov, Potresov and myself) concluded (not for long, it is true) a formal political alliance with Struve, the political leader of bourgeois liberalism, while at the same time being able to wage an unremitting and most merciless ideological and political struggle against bourgeois liberalism and against the slightest manifestation of its influence in the working-class movement. The Bolsheviks have always adhered to this policy. Since 1905 they have systematically advocated an alliance between the working class and the peasantry, against the liberal bourgeoisie and tsarism, never, however, refusing to support the bourgeoisie against tsarism (for instance, during second rounds of elections, or during second ballots) and never ceasing their relentless ideological and political struggle against the Socialist-Revolutionaries,

the bourgeois-revolutionary peasant party, exposing them as petty-bourgeois democrats who have falsely described themselves as socialists. During the Duma elections of 1907, the Bolsheviks entered briefly into a formal political bloc with the Socialist-Revolutionaries. Between 1903 and 1912, there were periods of several years in which we were formally united with the Mensheviks in a single Social-Democratic Party, but we never stopped our ideological and political struggle against them as opportunists and vehicles of bourgeois influence on the proletariat.[13] During the war, we concluded certain compromises with the Kautskyites, with the Left Mensheviks (Martov), and with a section of the Socialist-Revolutionaries (Chernov and Natanson) [...].[14]

Later in the text Lenin continues his reasoning, asserting: "At the very moment of the October Revolution, we entered into an informal but very important (and very successful) political bloc with the petty-bourgeois peasantry by adopting the Socialist-Revolutionary agrarian programme in its entirety, without a single alteration – i.e., we effected an undeniable compromise in order to prove to the peasants that we wanted, not to 'steam-roller' them but to reach agreement with them."[15]

Lenin's observations are of irrefutable forcefulness. Even at the pinnacle of revolutionary frenzy and despite the fact that the plebeian power of soldiers and workers were the backbone of massive public mobilisation, Lenin and the leadership of the Revolution did not hesitate to forge a tactical alliance, informal but effective, with a sector of the Social Revolutionaries (a party with ample support among the Russian peasantry), and even incorporated, for a time, their agrarian programme as their own governmental policy. For our Leftist Latin Americans this would, of course, have constituted an act of unforgivable treason, worthy of all kinds of reproaches and denunciations. Not so for the leader of the October Revolution, however. In short, we should no longer dwell on this particular issue. The success of Lenin's approach condemns "Leftism" to an absolutely unsustainable position, full of sterility to advance the revolutionary cause.

Classes and the Construction of a New Society

Over the course of the text, Lenin expresses his concern about the repeated "mistakes" committed by the parties of the proletariat. First, he emphasises that despite the triumph of the Revolution "[w]e in Russia are making

---

13 It is worth remembering that Trotsky became a member of the Bolsheviks only in September of 1917. Before that, he flirted with the Mensheviks and/or played the role of mediator between the two main factions of the Russian Social Democratic Labour Party. He finally accepted a position of leadership offered to him by Lenin just before the outbreak of the Revolution.
14 Ibid: 71-72.
15 Ibid: 72.

the first steps in the transition from capitalism to socialism or the lower stage of communism. Classes still remain, and will remain everywhere for years after the proletariat's conquest of power."[16] This reflection is of the utmost importance because it directly confronts the theorisations, or rather the simplistic ideological discourses of "Leftism" that presuppose that with the conquest of power by the revolutionary forces classes and class struggle will disappear from the political agenda. In concrete terms, this means that even if the social basis of the resistance to the revolutionary process has not totally disappeared, it has at least been considerably weakened, and hence what is inferred is that if the revolution does not advance in double time, the responsibility can only lie with the treacherous leadership, the supposed vanguard. It goes without saying that Lenin provides a much more refined analysis when he affirms that "[t]he abolition of classes means, not merely ousting the landowners and the capitalists -- that is something we accomplished with comparative ease; it also means abolishing the small commodity producers, and they cannot be ousted, or crushed; *we must learn to live* with them."[17]

Regarding the former, it is obvious that Lenin's affirmation has acquired new life as a result of recent experiences with financial, industrial and agribusiness capitalism, which are today infinitely stronger than their counterparts in the time of the Russian revolution. Whereas the latter could be ousted "with comparative ease," the current strength of the capitalist class, equipped with immense, diversified and efficient mechanisms of power that can be wielded at any time to frustrate, abort and topple any revolutionary project, suggests that "abolishing" them will not be as simple, but they must at least be neutralised.

With regards to the petty bourgeoisie, Lenin acknowledges its vastness in terms of numbers and that consequently, as the recent history of various Latin American countries has confirmed, "we must learn to live with them," as it is impossible to drive them out or eradicate them precisely because they are profoundly rooted in our societies. According to Lenin, this is the case because "capitalism would not be capitalism if the proletariat *pur sang* were not surrounded by a large number of exceedingly motley intermediate types between the proletarian and the semi-proletarian, between the semi-proletarian and the small peasant, between the small peasant and the middle peasant, and so on, and if the proletariat itself were not divided into more developed and less developed strata, if it were not divided according to territorial origin, trade, sometimes according to religion, and so on."[18]

So what is to be done with these intermediate sectors? Lenin's answer is straightforward and highly relevant to the current context: they are to be enticed and eventually incorporated into a new historic bloc: "[...] they

---

16 Ibid: 44.
17 Ibid.
18 Ibid: 74.

can (and must) be transformed and re-educated only by means of very prolonged, slow, and cautious organisational work." The Revolution must, over the course of a long and tenacious struggle, vanquish "the forces and traditions of the old society [...] The force of habit in millions and tens of millions [...] a most formidable force"[19] opposed to the construction of a new society of free men and women.

Undoubtedly, Lenin's words reveal an indispensable task of enormous proportions, which must not be postponed, lest the triumph of the revolution be put in danger. Hence, the "function of the proletarian vanguard which consists in training, educating, enlightening and drawing into the new life the most backward strata and masses of the working class and the peasantry."[20] That is why Lenin rejects vehemently "the pompous, very learned, and frightfully revolutionary disquisitions of the German Lefts to the effect that Communists cannot and should not work in reactionary trade unions, that it is permissible to turn down such work, that it is necessary to withdraw from the trade unions and create a brand-new and immaculate 'Workers' Union' invented by very pleasant (and, probably, for the most part very youthful) Communists, etc., etc."[21] On the contrary, given the previous analysis of deeply rooted petty bourgeois sentiments and traditions, which have equally taken root in working class conscience, the task of political education is absolutely essential. This reactionary spirit is simply a reality and, therefore, whoever wants to engage in politics must learn how to deal and work with it, how to educate its proponents and win them over to the cause of the proletariat. To disregard this task is one of the most serious errors that a political vanguard can commit, which is why Lenin affirms so decisively that one "must be capable of any sacrifice, of overcoming the greatest obstacles, in order to carry on agitation and propaganda systematically, perseveringly, persistently and patiently in those institutions, societies and associations – even the most reactionary -- in which proletarian or semi-proletarian masses are to be found [...] The task devolving on Communists is to convince the backward elements, to work among them, and not to fence themselves off from them with artificial and childishly 'Left' slogans."[22]

This conviction leads Lenin to make the following categorical assertion: "From all this follows the necessity, the absolute necessity, for the Communist Party, the vanguard of the proletariat, its class-conscious section, to resort to changes of tactics, to conciliation and compromises

---

19 Ibid: 44.
20 Ibid: 51.
21 Ibid: 49.
22 Ibid: 54. Concerning the political education of the masses, the words of Rosa Luxemburg are also highly pertinent. In her speech to the Founding Congress of the Communist Party of Germany, she said: "Marxists of Kautsky's school still believe in the existence of those vanished days. To educate the proletarian masses socialistically meant to deliver lectures to them, to circulate leaflets and pamphlets among them. No, the school of the socialist proletariat doesn't need all this. The workers will learn in the school of action." (Luxemburg 1918)

with the various groups of proletarians, with the various parties of the workers and small masters. It is entirely a matter of knowing how to apply these tactics in order to raise – not lower – the general level of proletarian class-consciousness, revolutionary spirit, and ability to fight and win."[23] Note that to resort to such manœuvres, agreements and compromises with a heterogeneous conglomerate of classes and fractions of classes with the aim of raising their general level of consciousness, attracting the most backward sectors and establishing intellectual and moral leadership is what Gramsci, following in Lenin's footsteps, established to be a necessary prior condition for the communist revolution to triumph. In other words, compromises of all types will be needed, but these must be always guided by a compass that indicates the correct revolutionary path in order to raise the level of consciousness of the most backward masses so that they can fully comprehend the situation imposed on them by capitalism, the need to abolish it and to create a new society.

Final Comments

What characterises an exceptional book such as this one is the great difficulty one experiences in even temporarily concluding the exercise of learning that its content inspires. In fact, Lenin opens up perspectives from the most diverse angles, all of which provide us with instruments of analysis to understand social reality. Consequently, we thought it appropriate to include in this final section some comments about topics that constitute important elements for the theoretical education of all revolutionaries, past or present.

First, concerning the importance of certain "small differences" or the comparison between different political protagonists or forces, Lenin says that "[t]he differences between the Churchills and the Lloyd Georges [...] on the one hand, and between the Hendersons and the Lloyd Georges on the other, are quite minor and unimportant from the standpoint of pure (i.e., abstract) communism, i.e., communism that has not yet matured to the stage of practical political action by the masses. However, from the standpoint of this practical action by the masses, these differences are most important." (94-95).[24] This comment is of great significance for many of the countries in our region where Trotskyite and "Leftist" critics of governments such as the ones of Cristina Fernández de Kirchner, Nicolás Maduro (and before that Hugo Chávez), Evo Morales, Rafael Correa and in the past Salvador Allende, expressed that in certain electoral scenarios – for example the one in 2015 between Daniel Scioli and Mauricio Macri in Argentina – they did not care which of the two alternatives would win since they basically stood for the same thing, an attitude which was repeated in 2019 in the elec-

---

23 Ibid: 74.
24 Ibid: 94-95.

tion between Alberto Fernández and Mauricio Macri. While this, following Lenin's astute remarks, might be true in the terrain of abstract Marxist theory, given that both are "bourgeois politicians," in the multifaceted world of concrete politics their actual differences are of tremendous importance. The lack of a capacity for differentiation exhibited by these "Leftist" groups is therefore an expression of a fatal deficit in their theoretical education and a profound ignorance of the dialectical nature of historical change. All they could see in Scioli was the bourgeois politician, without understanding that he was merely the figurehead of a complex network of social and political forces that would never have consented to or collaborated with the type of deeply destructive politics that president Macri would finally impose on the poor Argentinian people. In fact, they ended up adopting the bourgeois approach to history, which emphasises that "history is made by great men," thereby effectively ignoring the lessons of historic materialism.[25]

Second, with regard to doctrinairism, i.e. the lack of differentiation between the abstract analysis of capitalism as a mode of production, on the one hand, and the capitalist state and general politics in their mundane concretion, on the other, Lenin writes: "It is now essential that Communists of every country should quite consciously take into account both the fundamental objectives of the struggle against opportunism and 'Left' doctrinairism, and the concrete features which this struggle assumes and must inevitably assume in each country, in conformity with the specific character of its economics, politics, culture, and national composition (Ireland, etc.), its colonies, religious divisions, and so on and so forth."[26] This is in line with his well-known aphorism that Marxism is not a dogma, but a guide to action and that, even if it is very important to coordinate anti-capitalist struggle internationally, it is equally important to consider the "concrete features that this struggle assumes," something that is frequently not done. There is simply nothing more anti-Leninist and anti-Marxist than to insist on "a single model" or a "single path" to socialism and communism. Every national situation demands a detailed study and understanding of its defining features, not ignoring the international scenario, but also not giving up on the creation of one's own path towards the pursuit of a revolutionary process. This requires the identification of the principle contradictions in their historic concretion (and not only in theory), the definition of allies and enemies, the organisation and education of the masses, and the transition from the terrain of a discourse contaminated with "pedantic doctrinairism" to action.

---

25 In the case of Venezuela, it is worth remembering that some members of the Argentinian Trotskyite groups together with the most recalcitrant and proimperialist sectors of the Venezuelan Right participated in protests against the "dictatorship" of Maduro outside the Venezuelan embassy in Buenos Aires. For these crazy people there is no difference between Nicolás Maduro and Juan Guaidó. Apparently, the fact that one of them is a working-class leader proposed by Chávez and the other is a puppet remote-controlled by Trump does not matter. All of this in the name of Leon Trotsky who, if he were alive, would have certainly shot some of his self-proclaimed followers without pity.
26 Ibid: 91.

In line with the aforementioned point, Lenin adds that international coordination of the various struggles and "the unity of the international tactics of the communist working-class movement [demand], not the elimination of variety of the suppression of national distinctions (which is a pipe dream at present), but an application of the fundamental principles of communism (Soviet power and the dictatorship of the proletariat), which will correctly modify these principles in certain particulars, correctly adapt and apply them to national and national-state distinctions."[27] This in turn requires that we "seek out, investigate, predict, and grasp that which is nationally specific and nationally distinctive."[28]

Third and last, what is the remedy in the fight against the "infantile disorder" of Left-wing communism? Here, Lenin for once expressed himself in overtly optimistic terms, affirming at the end of the book that "[world] revolution is developing in scope and depth with such splendid rapidity, with such a wonderful variety of changing forms, with such an instructive practical refutation of all doctrinairism, that there is every reason to hope for a rapid and complete recovery of the international communist movement from the infantile disorder of 'Left-wing' communism."[29] This did in fact not happen. First of all, because world revolution was aborted and the great Russian Revolution had to embark on its own on a path laid with traps and aggressions of all kinds, eventually leading to its deformation, then its paralysis and finally its slow, inexorable death, so presciently predicted by Che Guevara in his *Apuntes Críticos a la Economía Política*;[30] and second, because the tendency towards "pedantic doctrinairism" managed to persist before, during and after the Revolution and even after the demise of the socialist camp. Clearly, the proliferation of groups adhering to such tendencies results from multiple causes, among them certain psychosocial factors such as the habit of confusing desires with reality; impatience transformed into a dogmatic and theoretical argument; blind obstinacy converted into the supreme expression of everything revolutionary; rivalry among different Left groups claiming to be the most revolutionary or trying to avoid being labelled as "reformists" or "opportunists"; and finally the enormous difficulties posed by beginning and sustaining a revolutionary, anti-capitalist project in the actuality of contemporary capitalism. The cases of Cuba and Venezuela are instructive in this regard, with many on the Left accusing their respective governments of being "accommodating" of imperialism and of not wanting to radicalise the revolutionary project, thereby totally disregarding the combination of economic war, media terrorism, constant cyberattacks and diplomatic pressure, in short, the whole arsenal of contemporary hybrid wars launched against these two countries.

---

27 Ibid: 92.
28 Ibid.
29 Ibid: 104.
30 Editor's note: The text was published in *Critical Notes on Political Economy: A Revolutionary Humanist Approach to Marxist Economics* (Ocean Press, 2015).

In summary, Left-wing communism is a tendency that has proven to be difficult to eradicate and that, unfortunately, in some cases continues to intervene in the everyday reality of our countries, effectively aiding the imperialist cause. To attack the Bolivarian government "from the Left," as various political groups inside and outside Venezuela insist on doing, is what most suits President Trump in his aim to bring down *Chavismo*. The same applies to Cuba. Once again it was Fidel who knew early on that the most significant problem faced by the revolutionaries of *Nuestra América*[31] was that the Right learned faster than the Left. We will, therefore, have to work very hard on the ideological front to eliminate at last this political current, "Leftism," which often ends up being the main obstacle to our emancipatory projects. In other words, the "the battle of ideas" is absolutely crucial right now; we must wage this battle not only against the Right, imperialism and its acolytes, but also from within the Left, putting an end to the calamity that motivated Lenin to write this remarkable book, which undoubtedly will continue to be an instrument of great utility for the theoretical education of the new and upcoming generations of anti-capitalist and anti-imperialist fighters.

Translated from the original Spanish by Hjalm(ar) Jorge Joffre-Eichhorn

References

Claudín, Fernando (1980), *La crisis del movimiento comunista. De la Komintern al Kominform*. Madrid: Ruedo Ibérico.

Guevara, Ernesto Che (2015), *Critical Notes on Political Economy: A Revolutionary Humanist Approach to Marxist Economics*. Melbourne: Ocean Press.

Lenin, V.I. (1974), *Collected Works Vol. 21*. Moscow: Progress Publishers.

Luxemburg, Rosa (1918), "Our Program and the Political Situation," *Marxist Internet Archive*. Accessed on 29.06.2020, at https://www.marxists.org/archive/luxemburg/1918/12/31.htm.

---

[31] Editor's note: *Nuestra América*, Our America, is an important text written by Cuban poet and politician José Martí in 1891. His eloquent insistence on the need for a genuinely independent and sovereign Latin American subcontinent, free of colonial and imperialist interference, has since become a rallying call of the Latin American Left.

8. Dead Russians on the Wall – Growing up Leninist in Thatcher's England[1]

Owen Hatherley

The shelves and walls of the houses I grew up in were full of dead Russians. My parents divorced when I was four, but their separate households each had the signs. A constant of my Dad's various flats was a black bust of V.I. Lenin, always given pride of place on the bookcase. In the house in Eastleigh, Hants, where I lived with my Mum, brother and sister in the late 1980s and early 1990s, there was a poster in the entrance hallway of an ageing, fork-bearded Leon Trotsky reading the American publication *The Militant*, a photograph that was very popular with the British Trotskyist organisation that bore the same name. In the living rooms of both were Trotsky's books – among those I remember being a permanent backdrop were *The Revolution Betrayed*, *Problems of Everyday Life*, *The Third International After Lenin*, *My Life*, the huge *History of the Russian Revolution* (most of my Mum's copies of these are now on my bookshelf). Lenin could be found on the bookshelves too – *The State and Revolution*, that anarchic book that ends with an appendix saying that participating in revolution is more interesting than writing about it. There were many more exegeses and glosses, which, because of the 'tendency' my parents belonged to, included some names – Peter Taaffe, Ted Grant, Alan Woods, none of whom could actually read Russian, but who could explain to you *Lenin and Trotsky – What they Really Stood For* – and excluded others from other 'tendencies,' despite their seemingly similar politics, such as Victor Serge, or Isaac Deutscher, who actually knew Russian.

This must sound senseless, I'm sure, to a Russian audience. Imagine that in the period I'm talking about, roughly from the late 1980s, when I first became aware my parents' politics were 'different,' to the late 1990s, when I left home, that people in the south of England genuinely believed that the Bolshevik October revolution was the most important and heroic event in human history. *And* that it could be repeated. Imagine what you were doing at the same time, and your own reflection on that period, and the absurdity that just at the point where it was being buried in the place where it actually happened, people in the West thought it would rise again. But then, my parents also supported the forces that apparently killed off the state that spoke in 1917's name. There were Solzhenitsyn books on the shelves too. My Dad had a book called *Cry Hungary*, full of photos of the Hungarian insurgents of 1956, looking dashing and dour in long coats and quiffs. I have a vague recollection of a *Solidarność* mug in my Dad's small flat, along with the black Lenin bust. These people thought that the USSR's

---

[1] A version of this piece was originally published in Russian in the autuum 2017 issue of the journal *Neprikosnovenniy Zapas*.

death would clear Lenin's name. And all of this was somehow connected to things happening in Britain, in the present, like the Poll Tax or the 'degeneration' of the Labour Party. Here, I'm going to try and explain how this did, in a very strange way, make some kind of sense for those involved.

It is conventional, now, for people brought up in a far-left milieu to write books about their strange and absurd parents. Some of those who have done so, such as David Aaronovitch, were extremely well connected to the leadership of the Communist Party of Great Britain, others, such as the Liverpudlian comedian Alexei Sayle, less so. Curiously, the Trotskyist movement, the Protestants of Leninism, as it were, has not faced the same, although comedians like Mark Steel or John O'Farrell have touched on their prior allegiances in autobiographical works. The two are, however, closely linked, both in their remarkably similar organisational practices – a total fidelity to the party structures advocated in the Russian Social Democratic Labour Party for operating in a police state in the 1900s – in their skewed ideas about their own history and uniqueness, and also, in the extreme dedication, discipline and altruism of a great many of their rank and file members.

They were also linked in my own family. At my maternal grandparents' house – both of them primary school teachers – the children's books were downstairs, but upstairs were the political books. *The Socialist Sixth of the World, New China – Friend or Foe*, the *Little Lenin Library*, and if you dug hard enough into the dusty shelves, a couple of volumes from the *Little Stalin Library* too – *Foundations of Leninism, Anarchism or Socialism?* My divorced parents' respective bookshelves were groaning with books about the crimes of Stalin, and the martyrdom of Trotsky to the assassins of the NKVD, the Interior Ministry of the USSR, so I knew that Stalin was very bad indeed. But there were never arguments about him at the dinner table. In my 20s, I asked them about it. "We just didn't believe what we read in the press." They dropped out of active work in the Communist Party of Great Britain (CPGB) in the mid-1950s, when they started having children, which just happened to coincide with the Secret Speech and the suppression of Budapest. They remained members until the early 1980s, when they moved to Cumbria, where there was no local branch (they joined Labour, which was then further left anyway).

So I could write one of those 'my silly family' articles. 'My family, who denied the Gulag and/or denied Kronstadt,' depending on which part of it we're talking about. I've got the material, right down to my childhood confusion at the resemblance between the late Trotsky on the poster in the hallway and Colonel Sanders, responsible for the 'secret recipe; for truly finger-lickin'-chicken. I won't, and that's because I think that where they were – Britain, in the second half of the 20th century – my parents and the organisations they were part of were a force for good.

I am sure that there are some, but I suspect very few people in the

West ever joined a Communist Party because of a commitment to blast furnaces, dams, nuclear power stations, prefabricated housing, show trials, famines, purges, or even bureaucratically administered command economies. They did so because they hated capitalism, and they considered a Communist Party, rather than a Labour Party or a Social Democratic Party, to be the shortest and most plausible route to its destruction. In many other non-Communist countries, this was also a ticket to a mass movement of the working classes – France, Italy, Spain and Portugal, Finland, Chile, Indonesia, India. But not Britain, where the CPGB remained a marginal, if sometimes influential group for most of its history; joining it involved a leap of faith, a belief based on very little evidence that this minor party would at some point enjoy some sort of sudden spurt of growth and popularity that would lead to it becoming a 'real' party, like Labour was. That isn't to say it was the thing that half-remembered Orwell and books by repentant journalists and comedians would have you believe – a group of Hampstead intellectuals longing to stamp their boots all over the 'human face.' There are a handful of places where the CPGB became a real force – the Vale of Leven and the Fife coalfield in Scotland, the Rhondda Valley in Wales, the inner East End of London, and for all their obvious differences, they shared something. They were cut off, by geography, by language or by trade, from the rest of the country; they suffered intense poverty and exploitation; and they had especially closely interknit communities. Yet many industries whose workers conventionally voted Labour consistently elected Communists as shop stewards and officials. One of these places was the vast industrial estate at Park Royal in West London, where my paternal grandfather, a sheet-metal worker, acquired a respect for Communism and a framed picture of Stalin.

Neither of my parents set out to join far-left sects. Instead, both of them joined the Labour Party in the middle seventies, when it came to power amid a strike wave, with a manifesto promising 'an irreversible shift of power' in favour of the working class, via workers' control of industry, expanded co-operatives and an expansion of the welfare state Labour had established in 1945 with the money Washington threw at western Europe to steer it from Moscow's orbit. My parents met in the Labour Party Young Socialists, which just happened then to be effectively controlled by a group called the Revolutionary Socialist League, a Liverpool-based Trotskyist group which produced, and was generally known by the name of, a newspaper, *Militant*. They had grown out of the British branch of Trotsky's Fourth International, which of course like all British Trotskyism could be ultimately traced to a split from the Communist Party of Great Britain. After a year or two in Labour my parents were recruited into the 'RSL' (Revolutionary Socialist League), which officially did not exist, but which came to have an important role in the left of Labour for the next ten years. This is a reflection, if nothing else, of surrender to the dominance of Labour in the British socialist movement – if you can't beat them, join them, and then organise from within. Some have argued that the aim of this was parasitic, to eventually take over and eat the host; I have no doubt that at the top of the organisation, that was true. But in the rank and file, being a member of Militant just meant what its name implied – militancy, in the factory and on the streets. Their most adroit piece of propaganda was refusing, when elected as Labour councillors or MPs, to receive more than the average wage of their constituents, with the rest of the money put back into the Party, a gesture both of solidarity and a particularly British puritanism.

My father, who is today a middle manager at a company in Basingstoke, worked for over 20 years as a sheet metal worker, like his father. He became a shop steward in his first job, at the shipyards in Gosport, just outside Portsmouth. His precursor in the job proclaimed at a meeting, "Don't vote for him, he's a Communist," to which, my Dad claims, a voice from the audience replied, "At least he's not a cunt like you." In his next job, in Bicc Vero, a Southampton-based company that made machine tools, where he world work for over 30 years, he rose to the position of trade union convener. He regularly brought the workforce out on strike, winning them better pay and conditions. So far, so social democratic, you might say. Indeed, this sort of ameliorative politics would seem to contrast with the maximalist demands that Militant made repeatedly at Labour conferences, where a Scouse-accented man would always shout that Labour must immediately nationalise the top 200 companies, abolish the House of Lords, and abolish the Monarchy.

Militant's greatest influence within Labour was not, naturally, in my hometown, Southampton, a largely working-class city but still in the softer, more diversified economy of the south, but in Liverpool, the larger but much poorer Atlantic port in the north. There, they managed to take control of the city council, where they embarked upon a programme of refusing to set a legal budget, so that they could do exactly the things that Labour councils used to do, before Thatcherite policies on fiscal restraint and municipal neutering made them impossible. In fact, at this distance, it's Militant's similarity rather than difference with mainstream social democracy that is striking – they wanted better working conditions (no fancy stuff about workplace democracy), more council houses (no modernist or communal experiments); they wanted apprenticeships for unemployed young people (no 'refusal of work' or 'right to be lazy' here). It's no wonder that Gregory Elliott called them, after they were expelled *en masse* from Labour and transformed first into Militant Labour and then the Socialist Party, "Labourism in exile." The theory was 1917 redux, the practice was 1945. This makes it hard to connect theory, which rests on the sacred texts and on the creation of ruthless cadre organisations to build for insurrection, and practice, which rests on saving the local youth centre and the local municipal care home. However, this insistence on working in day-to-day struggle has always rested on good Leninist principle. As we could learn from *Left-Wing Communism – An Infantile Disorder,* if you want to help the 'masses' and win their sympathy and support, you should not fear difficulties, or pinpricks, chicanery, insults and persecution from the reformists who are their actual nominal leaders. No: you "must absolutely *work wherever the masses are to be found.*"

Whereas my father's activism was workplace-based – and it was this which eventually got him promoted off the shop floor – what I remember of my mother's activism was community-based. The political action of the Thatcher years that I remember best by far, was the huge, popular movement against the Poll Tax, a regressive flat municipal tax which set the same rate for landed aristocrats and single mums on council estates. It was eventually finished off – and Thatcher with it – by a huge campaign of non-payment, which was orchestrated by Militant through local Anti-Poll Tax Unions. Mum ran the branch in Eastleigh, the railway town just outside Southampton where we lived at the time, which meant, suddenly, that politics went from being the shared odd hobby of my estranged parents – something weird, like being a Jehovah's Witness, a trainspotter, or an enthusiast for experimental poetry – to being something that everyone on our street talked about. My friends' parents came to our house to the meetings, to learn how they could be defended and what their rights were if they decided to refuse to pay. My grandmother went to court for non-payment, and at the court I managed somehow to lock myself in the toilet for the duration of the trial.

In 1988, Militant capped all of this with a rally at Alexandra Palace in London, where LED lights spelled out their name, a giant banner of Trotsky stared out at the participants, and his grand-daughter came in from Mexico especially, a real, flesh-and-blood link with 1917, with the motherland. After this peak, Militant disappeared from political life in England (they had a longer run in Scotland until their leader, Tommy Sheridan, who had been jailed for Poll Tax non-payment, was caught in a sad and tedious sex scandal). In the 1990s, politics for Mum and her comrades seemed to shift from a practice into a faith, something that sustained her through poverty, through benefit cuts and unemployment, through poor health, through depression, through an eviction from her house. In this time, she even ended up temporarily in the leadership of Militant's successor party, spending a year on the Socialist Party's National Committee. For her, questioning the possibility (let alone desirability) of the Leninist model of party-building and revolution was and is an insult to 'ordinary working people' and their capacity for action and change. Faith doesn't need proof. Though, it's worth remembering a stopped clock tells the right time twice a day – when, after Jeremy Corbyn won 40% of the vote on a strongly Old Labour manifesto in 2017 and I expressed my shock and surprise, she ascribed my inaccuracy precisely to my lack of faith. What does Leninism and the figure of Lenin mean in all of this? On one level, it is an expression of uncompromising intractability, and of refusing to listen to what 'the enemy' says about your heroes. This is not useful if what you want to do is, say, have a historically accurate or convincing account of 20th century Russian history, but it is a useful philosophy in a more general sense – do not let *them* write *your* history.

I do not share my family's politics completely. I think they were wrong about a great deal – about what capitalism was and what it was becoming, about the changes within the workplace, about systems of ownership, about race, about housing, and obviously, about what the USSR actually was, in which wishful thinking or martyrology replaced any sort of historical science. But I think that in a more fundamental sense, they were right. I think that what they fought against was and is a poison that destroys human lives so routinely that we barely even notice. A few years ago, the Scottish Communist and shipyard shop steward Jimmy Reid died. He was a cause célèbre in the 1970s, through a shipyard occupation in Glasgow, and the last plausible attempt of the Communist Party of Great Britain to win a Parliamentary seat. The then-First Minister of Scotland, Alex Salmond, decided on Reid's death to print his most famous speech, made to Glasgow University in 1972, and distribute it in schools. He speaks about alienation, and gives "two examples from contemporary experience" to illustrate his point:

"Recently on television I saw an advert. The scene is a banquet. A gentleman is on his feet proposing a toast. His speech is full of phrases like 'this full-bodied specimen.' Sitting beside him is a young, buxom woman. The image she projects is not pompous but foolish. She is visibly preening herself, believing that she is the object of the bloke's eulogy. Then he concludes – 'and now I give...' then a brand name of what used to be described as Empire sherry. Then the laughter. Derisive and cruel laughter. The real point, of course, is this. In this charade, the viewers were obviously expected to identify not with the victim but with her tormentors. The other illustration is the widespread, implicit acceptance of the concept and term 'the rat race.' The picture it conjures up is one where we are scurrying around scrambling for position, trampling on others, back-stabbing, all in pursuit of personal success. Even genuinely intended, friendly advice can sometimes take the form of someone saying to you, 'Listen, you look after number one.' Or as they say in London, 'Bang the bell, Jack, I'm on the bus.' To the students I address this appeal. Reject these attitudes. Reject the values and false morality that underlie these attitudes. A rat race is for rats. We're not rats. We're human beings. Reject the insidious pressures in society that would blunt your critical faculties to all that is happening around you, that would caution silence in the face of injustice lest you jeopardise your chances of promotion and self-advancement. This is how it starts, and before you know where you are, you're a fully paid-up member of the rat-pack. The price is too high. It entails the loss of your dignity and human spirit."

Maybe this sounds like moralism, like liberalism, even like Christianity – he follows it by quoting from the Gospel, after all. But in its cadences, I recognise a voice which does not belong to the mainstream of politics, and which has only very sporadically been heard from the British Labour Party. Here, not just the consequences of a capitalist system but its entire underpinnings are the object of attack: "Profit is the sole criterion used by the establishment to evaluate economic activity. From the rat race to lame ducks. The vocabulary in vogue is a give-away. It's more reminiscent of a human menagerie than human society. In a self-described democracy, this is grotesque. 'Government by the people for the people' becomes meaningless unless it includes major economic decision-making by the people for the people. This is not simply an economic matter. In essence it is an ethical and moral question, for whoever takes the important economic decisions in society ipso facto determines the social priorities of that society." These are words to live by, whatever the 'rat race' decides to call itself. I will never be embarrassed by them.

9. Engels and Lenin in Latin America: Yesterday and Today

Marcos del Roio

Without a shadow of doubt, the year 2020 will be remembered in history as the year in which a virus haunted humanity, a virus that forced people to distance themselves from each other, to cover their faces and to communicate almost exclusively through modern screen technology. A closer look, however, suggests that social distancing is not such a new phenomenon after all. Rather, it has been in the making for quite some time, perhaps since the 1980s when what used to be collective subjects organised in a variety of political, economic and cultural institutions quickly disintegrated as technological innovation flourished and the hegemony of Capital increased. States became progressively more controlling and repressive, as hard-won social and economic rights were gradually eliminated and new social relationships based on an extreme form of individualism were promoted as without alternative. The result is an overall atmosphere of cultural regression in which the forces of obscurantism grow stronger and stronger. On the other hand, this year 2020, laying bare humanity's profound crisis, is also the year in which we remember the births of Friedrich Engels and Vladimir Lenin, 200 and 150 years ago, respectively. Could it be that they still have something to tell us in the current scenario, in which the very survival of humankind is at stake?

In this overall context, the role and contribution of Latin America is contradictory. The modern history of this vast and diverse region begins with the European invasion and occupation of the 16th century, which soon turned the continent into a kind of subaltern West, in which colonial domination, justified by Catholic ideology, was established over the various indigenous peoples and those imported from Africa by brute force. Over time, the occupation produced a series of heterogeneous socio-economic formations, in which both slavery and feudalism coexisted, leading to the creation of large amounts of wealth that to some extent served as the foundation for what became known as primitive accumulation in Europe.

These socio-economic formations have proven to be incredibly long-lasting and the eventual creation of different territorial nation states merely served as a way to internalise the same colonial domination. The departure of Spain and Portugal from the continent in the early 19th century gave rise to fierce struggles between regional oligarchies intent on continuing colonial exploitation. All the while, the voices of the long-subjected and in many cases almost exterminated indigenous peoples and the descendants of those brought over by the slave trade were heard only in times of overt rebellion. Other than that, exploitation and oppression continued unabated in these mimetic and fictitiously sovereign 'nation states,' revolving exclusively around the interests of the local oligarchies and reconfiguring subalternity along Indo-African-American lines, later to be complemented by mestizos and impoverished migrants.

With the advent of the imperialist phase of capitalism in the 1880s, a new form of profit generation and exploitation of labour began to take hold in several countries on the continent. Meanwhile in Europe, the main points of debate regarding the notion of imperialism revolved around its usefulness (for the imperialist countries) and its alleged ethical validity vis-à-vis the underdeveloped countries about to be further exploited in the guise of an ever-so benevolent civilising mission. Imperialism was also intensely debated in the socialist movement with a number of different positions emerging among leading intellectuals. It was Lenin, however, who in his 1916 *Imperialism, the Highest Stage of Capitalism* developed a definition that is undoubtedly valid to this day.

For Lenin, imperialism was not merely a political choice made by governments, but a phase of capitalist development in which the contradictions of capital circulation were aggravated by the formation of a financial oligarchy that would soon become the dominant class in the most advanced capitalist countries, the increased concentration and centralisation of capital in the form of monopolies, and a growing competition for a share of the world market, which implied the exportation of capital. In turn, in Latin America, the importation of capital signalled the beginning of the development of capitalism, albeit in highly unequal ways. A local bourgeoisie started to form and with it the first seeds of a proletariat. The latter consisted largely of people who had come over from those backward parts of Europe, in which access to land was highly restricted and capitalist development was slow. It was hence on the back of these migrants that capitalism began to spread on the continent, and it was they who initiated the first struggles of resistance against exploitation.

Of course, in 1916 Lenin was only known among Marxist-Socialist groups in Europe and was not yet recognised as the great theorist and strategist of revolutionary politics he was. But this was about to change dramatically. Just a few years later the name Lenin resounded across the entire world, including in large parts of Latin America. It is via the name of Lenin that Marxism, a specific type of Marxism, started to spread across the continent. Which Marxism? A Marxism that, upon increased dissemination, adapts itself to the new environment and hence diversifies. In other words, a Marxism that is always determined by the social and cultural conditions it encounters, which is where Friedrich Engels enters the scene.

After his death in 1895, Engels' name was generally coupled with that of Marx as if the two of them had produced one single and inseparable body of work. Yet, although they collaborated closely with each other throughout their lifetimes, it is important to remember that they were in fact two separate writers with different, specific research and study interests. In the twelve years that Engels survived Marx he developed a type of Marxism arguably more his own than that of his friend, and if one takes a closer look at some of their works it is possible to identify various aspects in which they differ, particularly in the realm of dialectics. Roughly stated, Marx established a new dialectics, which negated the dialectics of Hegel; Engels, on the other hand, only discarded the more idealist elements of Hegel's argument.

This Engelsian Marxism, which was adopted and promoted by Karl Kautsky, soon became the basis for the type of Marxism that was developing in Russia, a Marxism in which Engels provided the philosophical and political foundations "translated" by Plekhanov and eventually leading to the formation of the Engels-Plekhanov-Kautsky-Lenin axis. Later, Lenin would break with both Plekhanov and Kautsky, but the link with Engels remained solid, whether in his *Materialism and Empirio-criticism* (1909) or in *The State and Revolution* (1917).[1]

In Latin America, the names of Marx and Engels became known to a small minority of people from about the 1880s. However, their works were generally received together with the various positivist and rationalist schools of thought so favoured by the European bourgeoisie, while the first continental socialists read them through a reformist lens due to the apparent backwardness of local capitalism and the infinitesimal size of the industrial proletariat. After all, in accordance with some interpretations of Marxism, in a scenario of capitalist underdevelopment and in the absence of a large industrial proletariat, revolution was unthinkable, and what remained was to somewhat improve workers' living conditions and their political representation.

At the time of the October Revolution carried out in the midst of inter-imperialist war, a series of worker-led uprisings, rebellions and revolutions sprang up on all continents, including in *Nuestra América*. Mexico, Argentina, Chile and Brazil all witnessed mass strikes, demonstrations and confrontations with the oligarchical states. Although all of these movements were eventually defeated, a space opened up in which a certain type of Marxism, i.e. the one that resulted from the theory and practice of the Bolsheviks, as well as the works of Lenin, became more popular. After all, Lenin was the first theorist-militant of the workers' movement to call explicitly for the emancipation of colonised peoples.

Apart from the lesson that the struggle for the liberation of labour was linked to the struggle for national liberation, Lenin also demonstrated the importance of disciplined political organising in the form of the revolutionary party. Moreover, Lenin's insistence on the creation of an international organisation, the Communist International, which, in the spirit of active solidarity, would stimulate and support the struggles of subaltern classes on all continents, contributed greatly to the foundation of numerous communist parties in different countries in Latin America, such as Argentina, Uruguay, Chile, Brazil, Mexico and Cuba in the first wave (1918-1925), and a few

---

1 It was the 25-year young Lenin who, after the death of Engels, published an obituary in which he acknowledged the immense merit of Engels for the revolutionary struggle as embodied by the proletariat. See Lenin 1972: 15-27.

years later in Andean countries such as Peru and Ecuador.

These communist parties were evidently neither the only nor the most powerful organisations that argued for a renewal of the nation state on the basis of a different economic matrix. They did, however, play an important subordinate role in the transformation of the continent towards a type of capitalist development that ultimately ended up reproducing and renewing the colonial matrix and the existing oligarchical power structures. While these parties strove hard to express the demands of the subaltern groups, their chief shortcomings lay in their limited understanding of the realities they aimed to transform as well as their insufficient knowledge of the works of Marx, Engels and Lenin, often reduced to dogmatic formulas and therefore subject to a certain stagnation. In a sense, the type of Marxism that reached Latin America was an ideology founded by Engels, re-founded by Lenin, congealed by Stalin and from the beginning hybridised by positivism.

Over the years, the political implications of these shortcomings became increasingly evident and from the 1960s onward there was a search for theoretical renewal and a simultaneous diversification of organisations that conceived themselves as Marxist. All these groups were defeated in subsequent decades in the form of multiple, well-coordinated military dictatorships that tried to ensure that the ongoing bourgeois revolution, led by the strong, developmentalist state, would not become a popular-democratic one. In the 1980s, once the dictatorships had fulfilled their historic role, the moment had come for the establishment of liberal-bourgeois democracies in conjunction with the promotion of an ultra-individualist neoliberal sociability opposed to any form of collective organisation. The dominant classes now aimed at consolidating their power through the adulation of the first person singular, the "I" as proprietor, entrepreneur and self-made wo/man, all the while preserving the façade that democracy and social rights existed for everyone.

In this context, Brazil was arguably the last country on the continent to adopt the neoliberal model. For a time, the national bourgeoisie was still looking for other approaches, and the strength of the democratic movement was expressed through the foundation of the Brazilian Workers' Party, the *Partido dos Trabalhadores* (PT) in 1980, the emergence of powerful trade unions such as the *Central Única dos Trabalhadores* (CUT) in 1983 and the formation of the *Movimento dos Trabalhadores Sem Terra* (MST), the Landless Workers' Movement, in 1984. Paradoxically, rather than a new beginning, these political developments would ultimately mark the end of an era. Indeed, the PT government of 2003-2016 was perhaps the final example/ experience of a historical period in which the Fordist working class played the role of vanguard, even if strongly influenced by an ultimately liberal type of corporatist syndicalism in line with the Washington Consensus.

In general terms, the organic crisis of the communist parties and of

Marxist ideology left the subaltern classes largely unarmed.[2] The ideological victory of neoliberal Capital demanded the demolition of the main institutions of the workers' movement – trade unions and the party – as well as their symbology. The latter included the systematic victimisation of the figures of Lenin and Marx, especially after the victory of reaction in Eastern Europe, when they began to be presented as the main culprits for all that went wrong in the important historical experience of creating the first workers' state. The ultimate result was the attempt to chart a new beginning for the Latin American Left along multiple, generally non-Marxist paths, including the definite shedding of the long-held belief in a democratic revolution with the strong participation of a supposedly progressive national bourgeoisie, leading to a type of autonomous, potentially more just capitalism.

These new paths have become generically known as "social movements," but in reality, they represent fragments of different popular struggles for land, housing, the environment, sexual and reproductive rights, the rights of indigenous people and the descendants of slaves. What is generally left aside by these movements, however, is the only struggle capable of unifying all these diverse fragments, that is to say, the fundamental struggle against Capital. Hence, with very few exceptions the majority of these social struggles do not go beyond a mere rights-based approach, thereby ultimately staying within the ideological horizon of the liberal-democratic, bourgeois world, occasional references to "socialism" notwithstanding.

One of the most visible expressions of this new type of opposition in the era of neoliberalism was the emergence of the *Ejército Zapatista de Liberación Nacional* (EZLN) in Mexico: a movement of indigenous Mayan people demanding self-determination within the Mexican state as well as the right to land and the right to live according to their ancestral communal and cultural values. Similar struggles went on throughout the Andean region, especially in Ecuador, Bolivia, Chile and Venezuela, and to a lesser degree in Colombia and Peru. The example of the government of Evo Morales in Bolivia stands out particularly, with its promotion of the ideology-cosmology of *Buen Vivir* or *suma qamaña*, and the strong focus placed on respect for indigenous traditions.

The most promising social movement, however, and one with a truly universal character, has arguably been the women's movement. The recent huge feminist demonstrations in countries like Argentina, Chile, Mexico and Brazil and the increased participation of women in public life has enormous transformative potential in our still brutally machista Latin American societies. *Ni una menos:* Not one [woman] less.

Nevertheless, as mentioned above, many of these movements are ideologically limited in the sense that they continue to yield to neoliberal, postmodern philosophy with its conception of a fragmented world made

---

2 It is important to point out that this vacuum was to some extent filled by the progressive Catholicism of "Liberation Theology."

up of infinite singularities. This Left postmodernism is characterized by its demands for 'affirmative action' and state support for certain social groups, but without any appeal to a much-needed universality.

Then again, it must be said that in times of an increasingly barbaric neoliberal capitalism, there has in fact been a renewed engagement with and understanding of the works of Marx and many of the important people that followed in his trail. Original research and publications have multiplied, and a number of committed and serious scholars have emerged in different places across the continent. Yet the majority of intellectuals find themselves disconnected from the popular movements, while the latter often ignore and occasionally even scorn the knowledge generated by the former, especially when it fails to materialise in concrete action. Hence, it is precisely from action that we must start, that is to say, from the accumulated experience and common sense of those struggling for change as opposed to the common sense of those who either naturalise the existence of exploitation and/or mythologise it as the result of the actions of some god. In other words, it is necessary to know and learn from our past struggles for the liberation of enslaved workers and serfs, women and indigenous people. There simply can be no future without this type of memory as well as the respect for the vast cultural reservoir that formed the backbone of these struggles.

So what does it really mean to remember Engels and Lenin, people who lived in such vastly different times and spaces from ours? In the case of Engels, author of a large and important body of work branching out into multiple, at times highly promising, epistemological realms, it was particularly his role as an effective founder of Marxism as the ideology of the working class, his sustained efforts to promote this ideology and his insistence on the systematic education of the workers – a long and arduous task given the power of Capital and the type of state that sustained it – which are perhaps his most important contributions. It was also Engels who in his 1884 *The Origin of the Family, Private Property and the State*, affirmed that the emancipation of labour went hand-in-hand with the emancipation of women, at a time when the woman question was at best an embryonic matter in the international socialist movement.[3]

Concerning Lenin, among the most salient elements of Engels he preserved was the need for disciplined organising, the importance of education and the necessity of systematic and patient study. The result was a series of innovations such as the need for a concrete analysis of a concrete situation as the basis for social transformation and the necessity of an effective operating organ for a revolutionary politics in the form of the party. Furthermore, while the October Revolution demonstrated that with the help of the soviets the masses were capable of self-organisation and self-government, Lenin understood that what was needed was a veritable cultural revolution to

---

3 Editor's note: Another notable book published just a few years before was August Bebel's *Woman and Socialism* (1879). See Ghodsee 2020 for a recent acknowledgement of its importance.

prepare the transition to socialism.[4]

In sum, the occasion of the 200th anniversary of the birth of Engels and the 150th anniversary of Lenin's coming into the world presents us with an opportunity to re-valorise the enormous scientific and practical political contributions of these two men: contributions that provoked and/or supported the struggle of millions of women and men who in the midst of indescribable suffering dedicated themselves to the task of Revolution, daring to fight for the construction of a new world and a new humanity. The failures were many, but the hope that informed their struggle is still well and truly alive.

The current crisis of Capital, threatening the very survival of humanity, is giving new life to the works of these two (and many other) giants of the struggle for freedom. Today, reading Engels and Lenin is once again becoming indispensable in order to nourish our everyday fight against barbarism. At the same time, they teach us the need for organisation, discipline and the joining of forces, as well as the importance of studying, learning and engaging in ideological battle, all of which are simultaneously a struggle for truth and human emancipation. Therefore, in the context of Latin America, there can be no doubt that these two great revolutionaries still have a lot to tell us if the great masses of people are to one day overcome the combined legacy of a genocidal colonialism and the outrageous exploitation perpetrated by a predatory capitalism. Indisputably, the only way to do so is to recreate and re-embark on the path towards socialism.

Translated from the original Brazilian Portuguese
by Hjalm(ar) Jorge Joffre-Eichhorn

References

Bebel, August (1879), *Woman and Socialism.* Marxist Internet Archive. Accessed on 29.11.2020, at https://www.marxists.org/archive/bebel/1879/woman-socialism/index.htm.

Engels, Friedrich (2010), *The Origin of the Family, Private Property and the State.* London: Penguin Classics.

Ghodsee, Kristen R. (2020), "Socialists Have Long Fought for Women's Liberation," *Jacobin.* Accessed on 29.11.2020, at https://jacobinmag.com/2020/02/socialism-feminism-august-bebel-germany-social-democratic-party/.

Gramsci, Antonio (2011), *Prison Notebooks Volume 1-3.* New York: Columbia University Press.

Lenin, V.I. (1972), *Collected Works Vol. 2.* Moscow: Progress Publishers.

---

4 A few years after the death of Lenin it was Antonio Gramsci who, in his *Prison Notebooks*, further developed some of the most intriguing issues dealt with by Engels and Marx. Incidentally, 2021 marks the 130th anniversary of Gramsci's birth.

10. A Note on Lenin and the Dialectic

Kevin B. Anderson

One place where Lenin stands out as a singular figure – compared to the 'classical' revolutionary Marxists Leon Trotsky and Rosa Luxemburg, or even Friedrich Engels, let alone to less revolutionary ones like Karl Kautsky – is in his deep engagement with, and incorporation into his overall theory of, Hegel and dialectics. As I argued twenty-five years ago in my *Lenin, Hegel, and Western Marxism*, those *Hegel Notebooks* of 1914-15, and the related essays and fragments on dialectics, constituted the philosophical foundation for Lenin's post-1914 theoretical work, helping to shape that work into a body of creative, revolutionary theory and practice. In fact, they mark a real breakthrough in Lenin's thinking, nudging Marxism away from the crude materialism in which it had fallen after Marx's death in 1883.

In the main part of these *Notebooks*, his abstract of Hegel's *Science of Logic*, Lenin attacked not only abstract idealism, but also vulgar or crude materialism at several key points. Moreover, he tied crude materialism to the best-known Russian Marxist theorist and his erstwhile philosophical mentor, Georgy Plekhanov: "Plekhanov criticises Kantianism... more from a vulgar-materialistic standpoint than from a dialectical-materialistic one."[1] These attacks reached their apex in the best-known passage from the *Notebooks*: "Aphorism: It is impossible completely to understand Marx's *Capital*, and especially its first chapter, without having thoroughly studied and understood the whole of Hegel's *Logic*. Consequently, none of the Marxists for the past half century have understood Marx!!"[2] This statement has frequently been interpreted – correctly in my view – as a self-critique and as an expression of a break with his earlier perspectives, especially with the Marxism of the Second International. In particular, these kinds of formulations amounted to a move away from the crude, mechanical materialism of his *Materialism and Empirio-Criticism* of 1908. In the *Hegel Notebooks*, Lenin also developed and worked with dialectical concepts like self-conscious subjectivity, consciousness as both reflective of society and constitutive of social action, contradiction, and transformation into opposition. In addition to the *Notebooks*, Lenin wrote essays and gave speeches referring to dialectics after the 1917 revolution. Most notably, in a 1922 programmatic article, "On the Significance of Militant Materialism," Lenin called upon Marxists of the new Soviet Russia and their international comrades to carry out "a systematic study of Hegelian dialectics from a materialist standpoint." In the same sentence, he connected this to another dialectical turn that had formed a part of his new analysis of imperialism and what he construed as its negation, movements for national liberation, "the awakening to life and struggle

---
1 Lenin 1961a: 178.
2 Ibid: 180.

of the new classes in the East (Japan, India, and China), i.e., the hundreds of millions of people who form the greater part of the world population."[3] Lenin ended this ground-breaking essay with a call for the formation of a "kind of 'Society of Materialist Friends of Hegelian Dialectics'."[4]

In *Lenin, Hegel and Western Marxism*, I not only emphasised Lenin's originality and his radical departure from mechanical and even Engelsian materialism after 1914, but I also took up the notion of a certain ambivalence in his legacy on dialectics. First, I noted his public mentions, even after 1914, of Plekhanov as an important source in Marxist philosophy and his republication without comment of *Materialism and Empirio-Criticism* in 1920. Since his characterisation in the *Hegel Notebooks* of Plekhanov as a vulgar materialist remained private, the newness of the critique of crude materialism that he had developed during his study of Hegel and dialectics was seriously obscured. Nonetheless, acute Marxist thinkers, beginning with Georg Lukács in *History and Class Consciousness*, were able to catch some of what Lenin had developed on the dialectic and to use it to good effect. A second problem was that even in his private *Hegel Notebooks*, Lenin was so excited to find that the supposedly totally abstract Hegel had embraced the practical idea toward the end of the *Science of Logic* that he gave short shrift to Hegel on the theoretical idea.

However, I concluded that it was more important to stress the new perspectives Lenin had developed in 1914-15 and after, as it still offered us a pathway within Marxism to move decisively beyond the kind of crude materialism that has so often plagued the tradition. Here, an important issue was the resonance of Lenin as a thinker and a revolutionary practitioner whose impact ranged far beyond the circles of academic and cultural Marxism to which Hegelian Marxism has been so often confined. In this way, Lenin gave revolutionary dialectics a circle of adherents that was far wider than either academia or even the intellectual sphere as such.

Besides the moment of Lukács, another moment at which Lenin's writings on Hegel decisively influenced the creative development of Marxism was in the U.S. after the Second World War with the Johnson-Forest Tendency (1941-55). This small but intellectually active faction within Trotskyism was led by C.L.R. James, Raya Dunayevskaya and Grace Lee Boggs. Eager to extend their state-capitalist analysis of Stalin's Russia and to theorise the relationship of race and class in the U.S. versus the reigning class reductionism, they also began to separate themselves from the Leninist concept of the vanguard party while exploring the young Marx and particularly Lenin's *Hegel Notebooks*, which Dunayevskaya had translated without being able to find a publisher. This was the first time that a group of Marxist thinkers had made Lenin's *Hegel Notebooks* their point of departure. During this period, James published in mimeographed form

---
3 Lenin 1961b: 233.
4 Ibid: 234.

his *Notes on Dialectics: Hegel-Marx-Lenin* (1948), which stressed issues in Lenin and Hegel like breaks and leaps rather than evolutionary gradualness, spontaneity versus top-down revolutionary movements, and self-movement by conscious human subjects.

It was not entirely surprising that James (an Afro-Caribbean), Dunayevskaya (a Russian-American), and Lee (a Chinese-American) drew their dialectical inspiration more from Lenin, a thinker originating in the borderland between Europe and Asia, rather than Central European Hegelians like Marcuse, whom they did study a bit, or Lukács, whom they did not take up very much. Of course, they were also Trotskyists and thus Leninists in politics, but none of the other leading Trotskyists of the time – or Trotsky himself – had much interest in dialectics, let alone in Hegel. More orthodox Trotskyists tended toward mechanical materialism, and most of the intellectuals drawn to Trotskyism in the U.S. laced their Marxism with a dose of pragmatism, as seen in the writings of the virulently anti-Hegelian Marxist philosopher Sidney Hook.

In dozens of unpublished letters in 1949-51, the three Marxists of the Johnson-Forest Tendency took up subjectivity, the idealist element in dialectics, and dialectical versus mechanical materialism, with Nikolai Bukharin seen as the prime exemplar of the latter among revolutionary thinkers. Their discussion saw philosophy as linked to Marxist politics and economics. Thus, a point they made while theorising about Lenin, one not found in Lukács or Marcuse, was the notion that his post-1914 books *Imperialism, the Highest Stage of Capitalism* and *State and Revolution* were grounded in the *Hegel Notebooks*.

The first published discussion in English of Lenin and Hegel came after the breakup of the Johnson-Forest Tendency, with Dunayevskaya's *Marxism and Freedom* (1958). It included an analysis of the 1914-15 *Notebooks* as a nodal point in dialectical thought as well as the first translation into English of the Notebooks in the appendix. In a chapter on Lenin and Hegel in relation to the betrayal of revolutionary Marxism by the Second International at the outbreak of the First World War in 1914, Dunayevskaya explored how Lenin's first theoretical response was to re-examine his philosophical foundations with a deep study of Hegel's *Science of Logic*. She extolled his new dialectical insights into issues like self-movement, the revolutionary character of dialectical idealism, and the cul-de-sac of vulgar materialism, with the latter including Lenin's own earlier writings on philosophy like *Materialism and Empirio-Criticism*. In interpreting anew Lenin's theory of imperialism, she saw his concepts of the aristocracy of labour and of national liberation as outgrowths of his Hegel studies, with particular focus on his writings on the 1916 Easter Uprising in Ireland. She also viewed *State and Revolution* as the product of "Hegelian-Marxian" insights.[5]

---

5 Dunayeskaya 1958: 191.

Besides his writings on Hegel and the dialectic proper, a second core aspect of Lenin's thought that has important resonance today was his new dialectical theory of imperialism and of the whole era of monopoly capitalism. At one level, imperialism and monopoly constituted a new and more hegemonic form of capitalism with global reach, but this second stage of capitalism (after its first competitive phase) also evidenced new contradictions that pointed toward resistance, instability, and revolution. These theoretical notions, it can be demonstrated, particularly in Lenin's 1916 article on the Easter Uprising in Ireland, owed something to the *Hegel Notebooks*. These new contradictions inside monopoly capitalism – and the imperialism that flowed out of this stage of capitalism – manifested themselves especially in the flowering of national liberation movements, which were often located in predominantly agrarian societies, rooted in the peasantries of Asia, Africa, the Middle East, and Latin America. Lenin argued that Marxists had to support these movements unreservedly and forcefully. Moreover, he held that national liberation movements could under certain circumstances step off ahead of the working classes in the fight for a global revolution against capital.

In a related context, Lenin also theorised the relationship of the working classes to oppressed racial and national minorities within large nations, arguing for their cultural and linguistic autonomy, or if ultimately desired, the right to secede and form a separate nation state. To be sure, Lenin's formulations on ethnicity and nation had serious limitations in practice, since in Soviet Russia these policies were often cancelled out by an overweening and centralised one-party state. However, enough remained of this legacy, at least as a cultural heritage, for Vladimir Putin to have declared, as late as 2016, that Lenin had left a "time bomb" sitting under the Russian state due to a nationalities policy "based on total equality along with the right of each to secede".[6] In this way, Putin blamed Lenin for helping to engender the collapse of the USSR and for Ukraine's efforts to break away from the Russian sphere of influence.

Be that as it may in terms of events inside Russia, the impact of Lenin's concept of national liberation was even greater on a global level. Thus, in the years after 1917, Lenin's theory of imperialism and national liberation – and the practices of the early USSR at junctures like the 1920 Baku Congress of the Peoples of the East – helped make Marxism a truly international movement of both ideas and action, allowing it to deeply penetrate the Global South for the first time.

A third aspect of Lenin's thought that is most salient today was his attempt – with great insight and originality – in *State and Revolution* and related writings to return Marxism to its founder's opposition not only to the rule of capital but also that of the state. In dialectical fashion likely linked

---

6 See Mandraud 2016.

to the *Hegel Notebooks*, Lenin theorised the centralised modern capitalist state as a structure that engendered negation on the part of grassroots democratic opposition from below. For him, this meant the Paris Commune of 1871 and the Russian soviets or councils of workers, peasants, sailors, and soldiers that first emerged in 1905 and then even more strongly in 1917. On the one hand, this theorisation on Lenin's helped put a dent in statist Marxism. But on the other hand, Lenin's own ambivalence, both theoretically and in practice after 1917, vitiated much of what he had achieved in this sphere. Here Luxemburg's critique of the lack of real democracy in the one-party state Lenin and Trotsky established holds up better today than Lenin's practice after 1917 concerning the state.

Two more areas of Lenin's thought, both of them problematic, should also be mentioned. First, Lenin clung to the concept of the vanguard party to lead, first developed in 1902 in *What Is To Be Done?* under the strong influence of Karl Kautsky. Although he modified the concept greatly in 1905 and 1917 under the impact of mass creativity from below, he never rejected it. This concept has hampered Marxism ever since, and in certain cases has supported the movement towards single-party authoritarian states after the revolution, including in many national revolutions whose leaders modelled their organisational structures on Leninist concepts. Second, Lenin wrote and said almost nothing original on gender and the family. To be sure, he affirmed women's emancipation and in practice Soviet Russia was the first country to recognise many forms of women's rights, including legalised state-funded abortion. At the same time, Lenin neglected gender and the family in his writings and made no original theoretical contribution in this sphere.

Looking back 150 years after his birth, I would argue that Lenin is someone we would be remiss to ignore, with regard to both the original and the more dubious aspects of his theoretical legacy. Despite some problematic facets of his theory and practice, we as twenty-first century Marxists narrow our horizons if we dismiss his profound insights on issues like Hegel and dialectics, or imperialism and national liberation, or the state and revolution. Lenin's theory and practice needs to be approached dialectically, as we examine his contradictions while also appreciating and developing further his important insights for today.

References

Dunayevskaya, Raya (1958), *Marxism and Freedom*. New York: Bookman Associates.
Lenin, V.I. (1961a), *Collected Works Vol. 38*. Moscow: Progress Publishers.
Lenin, V.I. (1961b), *Collected Works Vol. 33*. Moscow: Progress Publishers.
Mandraud, Isabelle (2016), "Une 'bombe à retardement' nommé Lénine," *Le Monde*. Accessed on 29.06.2020, at https://www.lemonde.fr/international/article/2016/02/03/une-bombe-a-retardement-nommee-lenine_4858507_3210.html.

11. Lenin and Non-Antagonistic Contradictions

Roland Boer

The category of non-antagonistic contradictions arose from the practical experience of constructing socialism, initially in the Soviet Union in the 1930s, and then in China, especially through the impetus of Mao Zedong and later in the context of the socialist project of 'Reform and Opening-up' led by Deng Xiaoping. Can earlier evidence of this significant theoretical and practical development be found? To answer this question, the following commences with the notion of antagonistic contradictions in the works of Marx, Engels and Lenin. Then, we will look at the beginnings of a theory of non-antagonistic contradictions in Lenin in the years after 1917. Finally, I deal with the seeds sown by Lenin's thinking, some of which would bear fruits only considerably later.

From Antagonistic Contradictions ...

A crucial distinction is our starting point: before and after a communist revolution. As Lenin and Mao observed, while gaining power through proletarian revolution is readily achievable, constructing socialism once in power is infinitely more difficult. Although there are many dimensions to this distinction, here my concern is with the implications for contradiction analysis. Before a revolution, Marxist analysis focuses on the rise of antagonistic contradictions. As Marx famously stated in his preface to *A Critique of Political Economy*: "The bourgeois relations of production are the last antagonistic form [*letzte antagonistische Form*] of the social process of production – antagonistic not in the sense of individual antagonism but of an antagonism that emanates from the individuals' social conditions of existence – but the productive forces developing within bourgeois society create also the material conditions for a solution of this antagonism [*die materiellen Bedingungen zur Lösung dieses Antagonismus*]."[1,2] Marx refers here to the process leading up to a proletarian revolution, in which antagonism reaches its apex between and within the forces and relations of production. He concludes his statement with the observation that once a proletarian revolution has arrived, the "prehistory of human society accordingly closes with this social formation."[3]

Closer to the revolutionary moment and the reality of proletarian power is Lenin's extraordinary rediscovery of the ruptural dialectic of revolutionary action. Lenin had already engaged in periods of extensive study of Hegel from 1894, when we find the emergence of a dual tendency, one

---
1 Marx 1859b: 101, and Marx 1859a: 263-64.
2 In his revised summation of the entire process in *Socialism: Utopian and Scientific*, Engels would make the point even more clearly (Engels 1880b: 579-80, and Engels 1880a: 324-25).
3 Marx 1859b: 101, and Marx 1859a: 264.

moving in a more mechanistic and the other in a more ruptural direction.[4] It is not my task here to analyse this complex and even dialectical relationship between the two tendencies, since I have done so elsewhere.[5] Instead, my focus is on Lenin's retreat in 1914 to the library in Berne, Switzerland, in order to understand why the Second International had failed to unite workers across borders and oppose the recently declared imperialist war. His study ranged across many sources, but the key lay in rediscovering[6] the ruptural dimension of Hegel's dialectic, which he read in a Marxist framework.[7] Lenin realised that there had been an overemphasis on the objective historical process, according to which one had to allow and even enable the bourgeois revolution (1905 in Russia) to achieve maturity before a proletarian revolution could arise: only when the objective contradictions of capitalism had unfolded over the long term and risen to a crescendo would a revolutionary party be able to seize the moment. This reading of Marxist dialectics was particularly noticeable in Plekhanov's works,[8] which influenced not a few Mensheviks and even some Bolsheviks. For Lenin, however, such an approach implied capitulation to the given conditions, and the diminution of Marxist analysis to a mere seeking to understand the objective conditions.

While this concern with analysing objective conditions is of course necessary, it is also one-sided, in that it casts aside the subjective dimension of changing the world: understanding requires a necessary process of abstraction, during which it is realised that the subject is an integral part of the world being studied; subjective and objective factors are thus intimately entwined.[9] One is inescapably part of the world, just as the world is part of one's consciousness. However, this also entails that one is not merely determined by objective conditions but can act to change them. "Consciousness," writes Lenin, "not only reflects the objective world, but creates it [...] i.e., that the world does not satisfy man and man decides to change it by his activity."[10] It follows that revolutionary practice is not merely concerned with the seizure of power but is even more importantly focused on the transformation of the objective world, of economics, society and culture. If human activity is able to create for itself an objective picture of the world, then such activity also "changes external actuality, abolishes its determinateness." How is this achieved? By the revolutionary agent's conscious

---

4 Lenin 1984a, and Lenin 1994b.
5 See Boer 2015.
6 Contra Anderson 1995: 23-25.
7 Lenin 1914b, and Lenin 1914a.
8 See especially Plekhanov 1907.
9 Note especially: "The abstraction of matter, of a law of nature, the abstraction of value, etc., in short, all scientific (correct, serious, not absurd) abstractions reflect nature more deeply, truly and *completely;*" "The formation of (abstract) notions and operations with them already includes the idea, conviction, consciousness of the law-governed character to the world ... the first and simplest formation of notions (judgements, syllogisms, etc.) already denotes man's ever deeper cognition of the objective connection of the world." (Lenin 1914b: 152-53, 160-61, and Lenin 1914a: 171, 178-79)
10 Lenin 1914b: 194-195, and Lenin 1914a: 212-213.

act, which can abolish the socio-economic foundations of the world as they are known and recreate them in a new way. Or, in Hegelian terms, such a socialist world can be made "as being in and for itself," as "objectively true."[11] More concretely, this means that a communist party can intervene in the apparently objective course of history and create it anew. In Russia, this meant seizing leadership of the process of the bourgeois revolution and turning it towards proletarian revolution.

Lenin began advocating these insights in his extraordinary *Letters from Afar* and the *April Theses*,[12] which would – in the face of initial opposition even within the Bolshevik Party – lead in only a few years to the October Revolution. In terms of contradiction analysis leading up to a revolution, this approach necessitated not only a thoroughly dialectical understanding of object and subject in epistemology (through abstraction and engagement), but also an active campaign to exacerbate the objective contradictions through subjective revolutionary intervention. Further, it was the key to Lenin's idea of the "weakest link" in the capitalist chain, through which a relatively undeveloped country would actually become the first where a communist revolution could succeed. In light of these momentous (re-) discoveries, it is no wonder Lenin exclaimed:

> It is impossible completely to understand Marx's *Capital*, and especially its first chapter, without having thoroughly studied and understood the whole of Hegel's Logic. Consequently, half a century later none of the Marxists understood Marx!![13]

... to Non-Antagonistic Contradictions

Thus far, my concern has been with contradiction analysis leading up to a communist revolution, when contradictions intensify to the point of extreme antagonism, in terms of the forces and relations of production and of class conflict. But what happens after a successful revolution, when the arduous process of constructing socialism begins? A late and brief guide is provided by Lenin in a marginal note to his reading of Bukharin's *The Economics of the Transition Period*.[14] Lenin writes: "Antagonism and contradiction are not at all the same thing. Under socialism, the first will disappear, the second will remain."[15] Although written in 1920, the notes on Bukharin were first published only in 1929. The timing was happenstance, but they would have profound repercussions into the 1930s and beyond, when the category of non-antagonistic contradictions began to be elaborated.

---

11 Lenin 1914b: 198-99, and Lenin 1914a: 217-18.
12 See Lenin 1917c, Lenin 1917a, Lenin 1917b, and Lenin 1917d.
13 Lenin 1914b: 162, and Lenin 1914a: 180.
14 See Bukharin 1920a, and Bukharin 1920b.
15 Lenin 1920: 391.

Apart from this observation, Lenin had relatively little to say on contradictions under socialism, not least because of the relatively brief years he had left – under very difficult circumstances – after the October Revolution.[16] However, there is a brief fascinating reflection on the role of trade unions during the transition period, in which Lenin identifies a number of contradictions: between persuasion-education and coercion; between protecting workers' interests and wielding state power – through the 'dictatorship of the proletariat' – for the construction of socialism; between adapting to the masses and seeking to lift the masses out of prejudice and backwardness. Are these contradictions a passing phase, especially in the context of the New Economic Policy? They are no accident, observes Lenin, for they "will persist for several decades ... as long as survivals of capitalism and small production remain, contradictions between them and the young shoots of socialism are inevitable throughout the social system."[17] Clearly, Lenin saw such contradictions as a long-term reality during the initial stage of the construction of socialism – the persistent relics of a capitalist mode of production and its attendant social forms, which would be overcome only with the advent of communism itself.[18]

Contradictions after Lenin

Obviously, these initial observations concerning non-antagonistic contradictions by Lenin are somewhat sparse. Overworked by the immense tasks of restoring even the basics of economic and social life after the October Revolution, dealing with the pressures and destruction caused by the Civil War, and beset by ill health resulting from a series of strokes only a few years into the construction of socialism, he had precious little time to think through the implications.

The task would fall to his successors, particularly during the immensely creative period of the 1930s, as the results of the socialist offensive – breakneck industrialisation and the collectivisation of agriculture – became clear. In this context, we begin to see the idea of non-antagonistic contradictions arising in response to three practical realities: the flowering of minority nationalities under the world's first comprehensive set of 'preferential policies' for such minorities; the development of class relations among workers and collective farmers; and, most importantly, the continuation in a very new

---

16 A letter to Gorky on 16 November, 1909, observes in a lapidary manner: "Believe me, the philosopher Hegel was right: life proceeds by contradictions, and living contradictions are so much richer, more varied and deeper in content than they may seem at first sight to a man's mind." (Lenin 1909a: 219, and Lenin 1909b: 403). And at the 10th congress of R.C.P. (B.) in 1921, Lenin spoke not only of managing the contradiction between workers and peasants, but also of "smoothing out" the antagonisms among the peasantry (Lenin 1921b: 59-60, and Lenin 1921a: 215-16).

17 Lenin 1921b: 349-50, and Lenin 1921a: 382-83.

18 This assumption was of course due to Marx's brief reflections concerning what he called an initial stage of communism, in which 'bourgeois right' would continue for some time, and Lenin's detailed exegesis of this text in terms of the stages of socialism and communism (Marx 1875b: 13-15, and Marx 1875a: 85-87; Lenin 1917a: 86-102, and Lenin 1917e: 464-479).

context of contradictions between the forces and relations of production.

In this situation, we begin to see the clear development of a greater understanding of non-antagonistic contradictions. For example, in *A Textbook of Marxist Philosophy* from the 1930s, we find the following explanation in reference to the above-mentioned observation by Lenin concerning antagonism and contradiction:

> If in developed socialism there were no contradictions – contradictions between productive forces and relations in production, between production and demand, no contradictions in the development of technique, etc. – then the development of socialism would be impossible, then instead of movement we would have stagnation. Only in virtue of the internal contradictions of the socialist order can there be development from one phase to another and higher order.[19]

At about the same time, a very long entry was published in the first edition of the *Bolshaya Sovetskaya Entsiklopediya*, which provides not only a careful survey of the history of dialectics, but also of the nature of dialectical materialism and the development of non-antagonistic contradictions under socialism.[20]

It was precisely this material, along with a flurry of translated works by Marx, Engels, Lenin and others, that Mao Zedong and his comrades would study during the immensely creative period in Yan'an in 1935-1937.[21] This was the period after the Long March and just before the Anti-Japanese War began in earnest: a time for in-depth study, late night discussion groups, lectures and writings that would eventually provide the basis for the New China. It would lead not only to the initial lectures by Mao Zedong on dialectical materialism, but above all to the foundational essay 'On Contradiction' and its follow-up after the Liberation of China, 'On the Correct Handling of Contradictions Among the People.'[22] The analysis of these developments is another task, but we can trace them to seeds first sown by Lenin. Indeed, these seeds can still invigorate our struggles today and tomorrow, whether in seeking the path to a proletarian revolution or in the arduous task of constructing socialism.

References

Ai Siqi (1936a), *Dazhong zhexue*. Shanghai: Dushu chubanshe.
Ai Siqi (1936b), *Sixiang fangfalun. 4th edition*. Shanghai: Shenghuo shudian.
Anderson, Kevin B. (1995), *Lenin, Hegel, and Western Marxism: A Critical*

---

19 Shirokov and Aizenberg 1937: 175.
20 See Mitin et al. 1935.
21 See Mitin 1936b and 1936a; Aizenberg, Tymianskii, and Shirokov 1932; Ai 1936a and 1936b; Li 1981.
22 Mao 1937a, Mao 1937b, and Mao 1957.

Study. Champaign: University of Illinois Press.
Boer, Roland (2015), "Between Ruptural and Vulgar Dialectics: Reassessing Lenin on Hegel," *International Critical Thought*, 5(1), 52–66.
Bukharin, Nikolai (1920a), Ėkonomika perekhodnogo perioda. Letchworth-Herts: Prideaux Press, 1980.
Bukharin, Nikolai (1920b), *The Politics and Economics of the Transition Period*. London: Routledge, 2003.
Engels, Friedrich (1880a), "Socialism: Utopian and Scientific." In *Marx and Engels Collected Works*, Vol. 24:281–325. Moscow: Progress Publishers, 1989.
Engels, Friedrich (1880b), "Socialisme utopique et socialisme scientifique." In *Marx-Engels Gesamtausgabe*, Vol. I.27:541–82. Berlin: Dietz, 1985.
Lenin, V. I. (1894a), "Čto takoe «druz'â naroda» i kak oni voûût protiv social-demokratov? (Otvet na stat'i «Russkogo Bogatstva» protiv marksistov). Vesna–leto 1894 g." In *Polnoe sobranie sochinenii*, Vol. 1:125-346. Moscow: Izdatel'stvo politicheskoi literatury, 1967.
Lenin, V. I. (1894b), "What the 'Friends of the People' Are and How They Fight the Social-Democrats (A Reply to Articles in *Russkoye Bogatstvo* Opposing the Marxists)." In *Collected Works*, Vol. 1:129-332. Moscow: Progress Publishers, 1960.
Lenin, V. I. (1909a), "A. M. Gor'komu. 3 (16) noiabriai 1909 g." In *Polnoe sobranie sochinenii*, Vol. 47:219–20. Moscow: Izdatel'stvo politicheskoi literatury, 1970.
Lenin, V. I. (1909b), "To Maxim Gorky, November 16, 1909." In *Collected Works*, Vol. 34:403–4. Moscow: Progress Publishers, 1966.
Lenin, V. I. (1914a), "Conspectus of Hegel's Book *The Science of Logic*." In *Collected Works*, Vol. 38:85–237. Moscow: Progress Publishers, 1968.
Lenin, V. I. (1914b), "Konspekt knigi Gegelia «Nauka Logiki»." In *Polnoe sobranie sochinenii*, Vol. 29:77–218. Moscow: Izdatel'stvo politicheskoi literatury, 1973.
Lenin, V. I. (1917a), "Letters from Afar." In *Collected Works*, Vol. 23:295–342. Moscow: Progress Publishers, 1964.
Lenin, V. I. (1917b), "O zadachakh proletariata v dannoĭ revoliutsii." In *Polnoe sobranie sochinenii*, Vol. 31:113–18. Moscow: Izdatel'stvo politicheskoi literatury, 1969.
Lenin, V. I. (1917c), "Pis'ma iz daleka." In *Polnoe sobranie sochinenii*, Vol. 31:9–59. Moscow: Izdatel'stvo politicheskoi literatury, 1969.
Lenin, V. I. (1917d), "The Tasks of the Proletariat in the Present Revolution: The April Theses." In *Collected Works*, Vol. 24:19–26. Moscow: Progress Publishers, 1964.
Lenin, V. I. (1920), "Zamechaniia na knigu N. I. Bukharina 'Ėkonomika perekhodnogo perioda'." In *Leninskii Sbornik*, Vol. 40:383–432. Moscow: Institute of Marxism-Leninism, 1985.

Lenin, V. I. (1921a), "Tenth Congress of the R.C.P.(B.), March 8-16, 1921." In *Collected Works*, Vol. 32:165–271. Moscow: Progress Publishers, 1965.

Lenin, V. I. (1921b), "X s"ezd RKP (b) 8–16 marta 1921 g." In *Polnoe sobranie sochinenii*, Vol. 43:1–127. Moscow: Izdatel'stvo politicheskoi literatury, 1970.

Li Da (1981), *Li Da wenji*. Vol. 2. Beijing: Renmin chubanshe.

Mao Zedong (1937a), "Bianzhengfa weiwu lun (jiangshou tigang)." In *Mao Zedong ji*, edited by Takeuchi Minoru, 6:265–305. Tokyo: Hokubasha, 1970-1972.

Mao Zedong (1937b), "Maodun lun (1937.08)." In *Mao Zedong xuanji*, Vol. 1:299–340. Beijing: Renmin chubanshe, 2009.

Mao Zedong (1957), "Guanyu zhengque chuli renmin neibu maodun de wenti (1957.02.27)." In *Mao Zedong wenji*, Vol. 7:204–44. Beijing: Renmin chubanshe, 2009.

Marx, Karl (1859a), *Marx and Engels Collected Works Vol. 29*. Moscow: Progress Publishers, 1987.

Marx, Karl (1859b), "Zur Kritik der Politischen Ökonomie." In *Marx-Engels Gesamtausgabe*, Vol. II.2: 95–245. Berlin: Dietz, 1980.

Mitin, M. (1936a), *Bianzhengweiwulun yu lishiweiwulun*. Translated by Ai Siqi and Zheng Yili. n. p.: Shangwu yinshuguan.

Mitin, M. (1936b), *Xin zhexue dagang*. Translated by Ai Siqi and Zheng Yili. Shanghai: Dushu Shenghuo chubanshe.

Mitin, M., V. Raltsevich, A. Saradzhev, G. Adamian, M. Konstantinov, A. Shcheglov, and B. Bykhovski (1935), "Dialekticheskii materializm." In *Bolshaia sovietskaia entsiklopediia*, Vol. 22:45–235. Moscow: Gosudarstvennyi institut «sovetskaia ėntsiklopediia».

Plekhanov, Georgy (1907), "Fundamental Problems of Marxism." In *Selected Philosophical Works*, Vol. 3:117-83. Moscow: Progress Publishers, 1974.

Shirokov, M., and A. Aizenberg (1932), *Bianzhengfa weiwulun jiaocheng*. Translated by Li Da and Lei Zhongjian. Shanghai: Bigengtang shudian.

Shirokov, M., and A. Aizenberg (1937), *A Textbook of Marxist Philosophy*. London: Victor Gollancz.

12. How Is Internationalism to Be Understood?
A Leninist Perspective on Identity Politics

Georgy Mamedov

To write a theoretical essay in "critical solidarity" with Vladimir Lenin proved to be a much more challenging task than I first imagined. From my initial idea of reflecting on Lenin as an anti-colonial thinker whose thought might be highly relevant to contemporary debate on class and identity politics, I found myself in a position of cultural and discursive resistance to serious engagement with Lenin as a thinker. This resistance originates in the specific post-Soviet context in which the figure of Lenin is hyper-mythologised. The fact that I had to write this text in English was helpful in providing some leverage for distancing myself from that mythologised image of the leader of the world proletariat. However, it still took a significant amount of time before I could arrive at a point in which I could set the right tone to my writing, neither too pathetic, nor too ironic. Faced with these difficulties, I decided to include in this piece a rather lengthy meta-reflection on Lenin's image in the post-Soviet context and only then proceed to the discussion of his dialectical approach to internationalism and its relevance for the understanding and potential mediation of the sharpened contradictions between class and identity politics. I hope this odd composition of my essay will not be misleading to the reader, but instead offer a heuristic perspective on Lenin and his theoretical legacy.

1.

The winter of 1993 in Dushanbe, capital of Tajikistan, was cold and bloody. The winter break for schools that year was extended to a month due to occasional fighting between the rival parties of the civil war (which lasted until 1997) and broken central heating. The teacher assigning reading to us, the third graders, noted, "There is a whole chapter on Lenin in the book. You can skip it, as it is redundant now." That section in the textbook included short stories about Lenin as a child and his interaction with children as a kind and supportive all-Soviet grandpa. I was a curious boy and did not follow the teacher's instruction. I don't remember most of those stories, but one of them, called *Barchuk (A Young Master)*, somehow stuck in my head. The story contrasted young Volodya Ulyanov, the self-sufficient, smart and fit gymnasium student, with his classmate, a lazy, dumb and fat son of a local magnate who could not even tie his shoelaces without the assistance of a servant. Class consciousness and self-discipline already characterised the leader of the world proletariat in his early boyhood.

Two years before my literary encounter with Volodya Ulyanov, in 1991, the monument to Vladimir Lenin in the central square of Dushanbe had been dismantled. A rally of nationalist and Islamist protesters took it down as a symbol of the corrupt communist regime and infidel Russian rule. I remember the tears of my Tajik history college professor, a grey-haired WW2 veteran, when he recalled how people had been jumping and peeing on the overthrown bronze body of Lenin. For him and many others, it was not just a monument being ruined, but their entire life collapsing as that statue fell apart.

I could keep filling pages of this essay with similar tragicomic anecdotes in which Lenin, or rather his image in different forms – from profile on a medal to a module office-size bust – would surface. But my point in telling these stories at the beginning of this text, which is meant to be a reflection on Lenin's revolutionary concept of internationalism and its relevance for the contemporary Left, is to show convincingly that in the post-Soviet context any serious discussion of Vladimir Lenin as a revolutionary thinker is complicated by his almost ghostly omnipresence in everyday life. At least for my generation of post-Soviet Leftists, Lenin was anything but a revolutionary thinker – an idol, a street, a kind grandpa, and even a mushroom.

If in the 1990s and early 2000s ruined Lenin statues and volumes of his *Collected Works* in dumpsters evoked sorrow and pain among many former Soviet citizens who saw in those images the ruins of their own lives and unfulfilled dreams, in the decade preceding the fall of the USSR, in the 1980s, a completely opposite sentiment towards Lenin, that is of mockery, was more common. In the 1980s Lenin was constantly caricatured in multiple urban legends and jokes that ordinary Soviet people, not dissidents and anti-communists, shared in their informal communication.

In the autumn of 1991, just a few months before the end of the Soviet Union, this culture of *stiob* (the Russian equivalent of an urban dictionary) reached official communication channels. The Leningrad television channel Five, which broadcast nationwide, aired its popular evening show *Pyatoe Koleso* (The Fifth Wheel) featuring avant-garde eccentric musician and performer Sergey Kurechin, who in the span of an hour tried to prove "scientifically" that Lenin was a mushroom. Departing from a quote in a letter from Lenin to Plekhanov, in which he mentioned that he had recently eaten a lot of mushrooms and felt very good, followed by smartly arranged photo and video footage, citations from various sources, and interviews with scientists and witnesses, Kurechin developed a convincing narrative that, due to many years of consuming hallucinogenic mushrooms, the personality of Lenin had been overtaken by that of a mushroom.

Despite being so obviously a prank, this televised hoax caused highly controversial reactions among the Soviet public. There were many who laughed, there were those who felt deeply insulted, but then there were also many who, even though they did not believe the statement was fully truthful, had their doubts. The latter reaction is unsurprising given that around the same time, the central Soviet television channels dedicated hours of airtime to shows featuring extrasensory healers asking viewers to place tap water near their television screens so that they could charge it with positive energy, which would turn it into a remedy against all manner of diseases. Millions of Soviet doctors, engineers and teachers actually did put the bottles of water near their TV sets.[1]

I focus on Kurechin's Lenin-mushroom hoax not only because it is an outstanding cultural artefact of the 1990s, which to a certain extent shaped the post-Soviet discourse on the figure of Lenin, but also because this prank subversively but precisely mirrored the late Soviet ideological practice that created that monstrous image of Lenin-model pupil-grandpa-mushroom in the first place. As Kurechin makes his ridiculous statement sound convincing by using actual quotations and references to documents, the late Soviet ideological canon too strove to justify its every political move as "truly socialist" by ritualistic references to Lenin's words and images.

"Return to Lenin's Norms" was the main motto of the de-Stalinisation campaign launched by Nikita Khrushchev after the CPSU Congress in 1956.[2] Practical realisation of that motto turned into the replacement of Stalin's monuments, portraits and quotes with those of Lenin. This Lenin-centred ideological canon also demanded that no political, scientific or educational text from astrophysics to cooking was published without referencing Lenin's works or involving Lenin's image in some way. It is in this late Soviet period of the 1960s-1980s that attempts to create from Lenin a sacred figure of socialism turned into the opposite, that is, a profane caricature of him suffused into everyday Soviet life.

In the post-Soviet period this caricatured image of Lenin persisted, but became even more diverse. Lenin remains a univocal hero to decaying old-school communists (though for this crowd Stalin often overshadows him); for the liberal-minded and conservative public alike he is an undoubted villain, albeit for different reasons: for liberals, Lenin is foremost a bloody murderer responsible for the Red Terror; Russian conservatives, on the other hand, hate the proletarian leader for his anti-Russian positions and the foundation of the USSR on confederative principles, guaranteeing the right of secession for all Soviet republics. Putin's comments on Lenin are very telling in this respect. Noting that he sincerely regretted the dissolution of the USSR, he held Lenin responsible for that dissolution because, "that right [to secession] was the delayed action mine planted under our statehood. This is what caused the country's eventual breakup."[3]

In summary, the representation and perception of Vladimir Lenin in the late Soviet and post-Soviet contexts, outlined above in a few rough brushstrokes, leaves almost no space for any serious critical engagement with

---
1 For a more detailed review of Kurechin's hoax, see Yurchak 2011.
2 Nikita Khrushchev denounced the personality cult and dictatorship of Joseph Stalin in his famous "Secret Speech" on the last day of the 20th Congress of the Communist Party of the Soviet Union held during the period 14-25 February, 1956.
3 See TASS 2016.

Lenin's theoretical legacy. It is therefore no wonder that substantial reflections on Lenin's thought and its relevance for the current political moment originate from outside of the Soviet and post-Soviet space, be it Althusser's *Lenin and Philosophy*, or a recent rediscovery of Lenin by Michael Brie, *Lenin neu entdecken*, for example. The Progressive Left in the post-Soviet space distance themselves from Lenin on all levels – symbolic, political and theoretical.

At the same time, the more caricatured the public image of Lenin, the more surprisingly solid, coherent and utterly radical his theoretical thought appears to a contemporary post-Soviet reader. The hyper-mythologised image of Lenin creates a unique epistemological opportunity for an estranged perception of the actual Lenin's thought and its actualisation in contemporary political theory and practice. In this essay I propose a reading of one of the later texts by Lenin – *"The Question of Nationalities or 'Autonomisation'"* – as an exercise that can shed light on one of the current issues of contemporary Marxist theory and politics, namely the split between class politics and the workers' movement on the one side, and identity politics and social movements on the other.

2.

In traditional Leftist politics, economic inequality and class oppression are considered as universal conditions, while different forms of bodily oppression based on gender, sexuality, race, disability or ethnicity are usually perceived as particular and specific. At the same time, socialist politics implies radical transformation of societal organisation in all its aspects. One of the greatest challenges Bolsheviks had to address after the October Revolution and consequent civil war was the issue of the social and cultural diversity of post-imperial Russian society with its attendant contradictions and conflicts. These contradictions included the gap between the urban and rural populations, patriarchal gender relations, questions of literacy, and many others. Arguably one of the most pressing issues, however, was the so-called "national question." The ultimate goal of post-revolutionary reconstruction was to transform the former Russian Empire into a multi-ethnic socialist federation, but in that very transformation Bolsheviks had to adhere to their own powerful pre-revolutionary slogan – *Za pravo natsii na samoopredelenie* – celebrating the right of nations to self-determination; and identify the ways in which the autonomy of national minorities would be strictly observed.

Lenin wrote *The Question of Nationalities* in response to what is known as the Georgian incident,[4] during which the principal differences in approaching

---

4 In February 1921, with the outbreak of popular uprisings against the Menshevik government in Georgia, the Red Army invaded to provide assistance. The extent and popularity of the uprising, however, had been exaggerated and it took the Red Army ten days of heavy fighting to enter Tiflis, the Georgian capital. Trotsky, head of the Red Army at the time, had not ordered or even been informed of the invasion of

the "national question" between Lenin and Stalin, at the time the Commissar of Nationalities, became apparent. *The Question of Nationalities*, along with other letters to the 12th Congress of the Communist Party of the Soviet Union that Lenin wrote in 1922-1923, and which constitute his final written works, often referred to as Lenin's *Testament*, remained unpublished until 1956. Their publication marked the public launch of the de-Stalinisation campaign and was aimed at proving that Lenin and Stalin had held conflicting views on the development of the Soviet state, and that the direction of Soviet policies after Lenin's death was a deviation from socialist principles.

The Question of Nationalities, along with Lenin's other works such as *The Right of Nations to Self-Determination* (1914) and *Critical Remarks on the National Question* (1913), have been well studied in the context of Soviet nationalities policies. However, I propose a reading of this text outside of these two dominant contexts, the one of personal conflict between Lenin and Stalin, and the other of actually existing Soviet nationalities policies. My point here is to consider this text not historically, but theoretically, as a piece of writing that exemplifies Lenin's thinking, or in Althusserian terms, Lenin's philosophical practice, applied to the contradiction between working class solidarity and historically accumulated divisions within the multi-ethnic and multicultural population of the former Russian empire.

The first thing that impresses the reader of Lenin's letter is its emotionally charged language. In an unadulterated manner, he points out that in the process of forming national autonomies, non-Russian minorities should be protected from that "true Russian man, the Great-Russian chauvinist, in substance a rascal and a tyrant, such as the typical Russian bureaucrat is. There is no doubt that the infinitesimal percentage of Soviet and sovietised workers will drown in that tide of chauvinistic Great-Russian riffraff like a fly in milk."[5] He also makes it clear that the three leading Bolsheviks, Ordzhonikidze, Dzerzhinsky and Stalin, representing Moscow in negotiations with the Georgian comrades over autonomisation in the Caucasus, acted in those negotiations exactly as the aforementioned Great-Russian chauvinist. The peculiarity of this accusation is that none of those three was ethnic Russian. However, Lenin remarks that "it is common knowledge that people of other nationalities who have become Russified overdo this Russian frame of mind."[6]

Such straightforward language demonstrates, on the one hand, the polemical character of inner-party debate still common for the Bolsheviks in the early 1920s, and on the other, Lenin's uncompromising anti-Imperialist, and let us be clear here, anti-Russian, position on the "national question." However, he also insists that the purpose of his address is not to clear

---

Georgia, which was mainly instigated and carried out by Stalin (General Secretary) and Ordzhonikidze (Chief commissar of the Revolutionary War Council of the Caucasus). (See Marxist Internet Archive)
5 Lenin 1974: 606.
6 Ibid.

the air about that particular incident, but to reflect on the question of principle, that is of *"how is internationalism to be understood?"*

Although somewhat brief and unrefined, given its epistolary genre, *The Question of Nationalities* nevertheless exemplifies what Althusser defined as Lenin's particular philosophical practice, that is of drawing a clear dividing-line between an idealist and dogmatic understanding of phenomena on one hand, and a materialist and dialectical one on the other. In *The Question of Nationalities* Lenin draws precisely such a dividing-line between an abstract internationalism that does not go beyond the declaration of equality, and a proletarian internationalism that acknowledges and addresses concrete contradictions of interethnic relations inherited from the Russian imperial past.

One such concrete contradiction is a tendency to Russification of the Soviet apparatus in national republics, which Lenin radically opposes. He insists on the primary use of the national languages in the Soviet republics and urges against their replacement by the Russian language under whatsoever logical and rational excuses of efficiency, coordination and centralisation. Lenin suggests that there must be a strict code on this matter and "only the nationals living in the republic in question can draw it up at all successfully."[7]

However, even the representation of national minorities in the state apparatus and the guaranteeing of the "freedom to secede from the union" may turn into a "mere scrap of paper" and remain nothing more than a formal declaration of equality. In Lenin's view, proletarian internationalism in a post-Imperial context should be based, first of all, on an acknowledgement of the historical inequality, damage and violence that characterise relations between the so-called great, or rather oppressor, nations, and the smaller, oppressed nations. In other words, a formal declaration of equality or even an appeal to the universal character of class oppression that Russian and non-Russian workers share would not make up for that historically accumulated violence and damage.

What would then? Here Lenin makes the radically dialectical and, I argue, highly contemporarily relevant, proposition that the only way to repair injustice towards the oppressed nations is in the inequality of the oppressor nation: "That is why internationalism on the part of oppressors or 'great' nations, as they are called (though they are great only in their violence, only great as bullies), must consist not only in the observance of the formal equality of nations but even in an inequality of the oppressor nation, the great nation, that must make up for the inequality which obtains in actual practice."[8]

Hence, according to Lenin, proletarian internationalism is based on the non-assimilation of minorities and the inequality of the oppressor nation.

---

7 Ibid: 610.
8 Ibid: 608.

These are the positions of principle for him in the polemic over the "national question" with Stalin and Co. In the *Question of Nationalities* Lenin does not elaborate on the practicalities of his vision of national equality. Nonetheless, the actual Soviet nationalities policy put in place after his death would be carried out under the motto "For the Leninist Nationalities Policy," and according to some historians reflected Lenin's distinction between the oppressor and oppressed nations and could be characterised overall as a policy of "affirmative action" towards national minorities.[9] However, as mentioned above, my intention here is to emphasise the dialectical power of Lenin's understanding of internationalism and deliberately avoid discussion of actual Soviet policies as the only and ultimate practical solution to his theoretical propositions.

By drawing a clear dividing-line between formalistically and dialectically understood national equality in *The Question of Nationalities*, Lenin exercises what Michael Brie defined as a "solidary mediation of contradictions."[10] Lenin developed this non-antagonistic approach to contradictions in the 1920s, confronted by the actual challenges of post-revolutionary reconstruction. Instead of the dogmatic sacrifice of particular experiences for the sake of universal unity (which finally won out in the actual Soviet nationalities policy in the late 1930s), Lenin called for the acknowledgement of the existing contradictions between the former coloniser and the colonised; their mediation through strictly observed non-assimilatory national autonomy (the priority of national languages, the right of secession) and a much more radical measure of "de-privileging" the oppressor nation.

It is exactly this Leninist dialectical "solidary mediation of contradictions," I would argue, that might be highly relevant for the contemporary theorisation and a practical rendering of the split between class politics and the workers' movement on one side, and identity politics and social movements on the other.

3.

In order to shift from history to the current moment, let me reformulate Lenin's question of principle "how is internationalism to be understood?" to its more contemporary version, that is *how is revolutionary identity politics to be understood?*

The very formulation "revolutionary identity politics" may sound blasphemous to a hardcore Marxist ear. Yet, I want to make a Leninist argument here that there can and should be a revolutionary identity politics. First, I agree with the growing discontent and sharp criticism of the neoliberal politics of recognition and representation (often reduced to mere tokenism)

---

9 The campaign against Great Russian chauvinism in the early 1930s is one example of how the "inequality of the oppressor nations" was put into practice in the Soviet nationalities policy. For more details, see Martin 2001.
10 Brie 2017: 113.

that has dominated the agenda of various emancipatory movements in the last thirty years.[11] Nevertheless, I do not think that the retreat to a politics that prioritises the universality of class struggle over the particularity of struggles against various forms of bodily oppression is the only solution. In fact, I think that it is the wrong solution. Capitalist exploitation exhibits not only a universal character, which forces an absolute majority to sell their labour to capital, but also a particular character: for women, homosexuals, transgender, people of different ethnic groups, disabled people and people with mental health issues, it creates specific conditions of exclusion and exploitation.

The rapid unfolding of the current global public health, social and economic crises triggered by the Coronavirus pandemic has laid bare this dialectical, simultaneously universal and particular, character of the capitalist condition. The damaging effects of the global spread of the microscopic virus and colossal human efforts to stop it are distributed unevenly among different populations. The most vulnerable to the infection are those with a weakened immune system among whom are the elderly, HIV-positive, and those struggling with cancer, cardiovascular disease and other chronic medical conditions. Let us be clear here, this is not just a biological, but a social condition determined by access to and the quality of different healthcare systems. In the United States, the number of African Americans among those infected is disproportionally high compared to the general population. Imposed, but seemingly absolutely necessary, measures of self-isolation and quarantine have an extraordinary impact on women as caretakers of children and the elderly. Further, the pandemic has triggered a spike in domestic violence against women and children all over the world.[12] Millions of precarious workers making ends meet on daily wages face the real threat of malnutrition and hunger. One can add homeless, incarcerated and institutionalised populations to those for whom this crisis might have fatal effects. In short, we experience universal conditions in very particular ways.

What we need, therefore, is not an antagonistic, either/or solution that prioritises one side of the contradiction over the other – either universal over particular (class struggle), or particular over universal (identity politics in its current neoliberal version) – but a non-antagonistic, dialectical solution, one that will simultaneously address universal oppression based on class and particular forms of bodily oppression. Rethinking identity politics, by drawing a dividing-line between identity politics as we now know it and the revolutionary identity politics that is to come, should be an integral part of that dialectical solution.

In drawing such a dividing-line, one question to reflect on is whether Leninist principles of proletarian internationalism, non-assimilation and

---

11 For example, see Aruza, Bhattacharya & Fraser 2019.
12 See Taub 2020.

inequality of the oppressor, are actually applicable to a wider range of identities and therefore should form part of our understanding of revolutionary identity politics. My short answer is a definitive 'yes,' but let us explore it in greater detail.

In the 1970s, during the debates over the "woman question" and the heteronormativity of Marxist politics of the time, Marxist feminists and queer socialists put forward arguments similar to the ones made by Lenin in *The Question of Nationalities.*

Let us begin with the principle of non-assimilation. Lenin formulates this principle in terms of a strict observance of national autonomy as a sort of vaccine against relapses of Great Russian chauvinism within the Soviet apparatus. Radical queer theory of the 1970s proposed the non-assimilation principle not as a protective measure against the leftovers of past social structures but as a principle of revolutionary social transformation. Queer Marxists saw heteronormative assimilation of queer bodies and sexualities within the matrix of the nuclear family as the frontline between revolutionary and reformist politics of identity. Non-assimilation was the decisive feature of what they themselves defined as the "struggle for sexual self-determination."[13]

The British Gay Left Collective, in their 1977 manifesto *Why Marxism?*, denounced the reformism of the mainstream gay liberation movement as "Liberation, Capitalist-style,"[14] referring to the fact that Western capitalism accepts and normalises some expressions of homosexuality but only within the confines of a patriarchal and familial framework. Marxism attracted queer activists as an organised political platform that would allow them to link their particular struggle for freedom of sexual expression to the wider political struggle against class exploitation, patriarchy and racism: "As a revolutionary politics Marxism provides a framework for an analysis of the ways in which the exploited and oppressed can struggle against capitalism and its attendant oppressions. The precondition for economic and social change then is the winning of political power from the dominant classes; the employment of this new power to begin the destruction of old attitudes and ideas; the creation of new forms of relationships."[15]

Gay Left Collective argued, however, that to be able to realise such a revolutionary social transformation, Marxist politics must acknowledge that the exploited position of the worker is not only determined by class structure but is also a result of social relations that are "initially inculcated through the family and reinforced through bourgeois ideology."[16] Unsurprisingly, their more traditional comrades met the anticipations and hopes of gay and lesbian socialists with indifference and, at times, hostility. They

---

13 Mitchell 2018: 104.
14 Ibid: 99.
15 Ibid.
16 Ibid: 101.

regarded cautions against heteronormative assimilation and calls for the creation of new forms of relationship as "petit bourgeois." The party line, so to say, insisted that social relations would naturally transform in the post-revolutionary situation. Therefore, any concerns beyond the narrowly understood class struggle were unnecessary distractions.

The stubborn economism of traditional Marxist politics, which prioritised the economy as the motor of historical change over political, cultural and ideological aspects of the anti-capitalist struggle, thus contributed to the establishment of the hegemonic position of neoliberal and assimilatory identity politics versus a revolutionary one. Instead of equal participation in the struggle for universal equality, the former offers queer subjects an equal part in the universal misery of national citizenship, heteronormative marriage and nationalist and imperialist politics (military service, etc.). The political horizon of the queer communist struggle for sexual self-determination therefore radically differs from neoliberal identity politics whose aim is to normalise heterogeneous sexualities, genders, or any other identities. Normalisation is achieved through assimilation that stresses similarity and simultaneously smooths out differences: homosexuals do not differ in any way from heterosexuals because they also value love and family and wish to raise children.

The radicality of the queer Marxist concept of non-assimilation is in its emphasis on particularity and difference, which challenges the established political thought that anticipates identity as the basis of collective action. However, as the Gay Left Collective argued, "the transition to socialism will not obviate the need for an autonomous gay movement or feminist movement; they will in fact be more essential, for in the struggle to determine the form of a new society, the activity of the oppressed groups and identities will be decisive."[17]

American Marxist and feminist Heidi Hartmann, in her powerful essay *The Unhappy Marriage of Marxism and Feminism*, echoed the British queer socialists in stating that "a struggle to establish socialism must be a struggle in which groups with different interests form an alliance,"[18] and these groups should have their own "organisations and power base."[19] However, in her reflection on the inability of traditional Marxism to come up with an adequate solution to the "woman question," Hartmann also echoes Lenin's principle of the inequality of the oppressor.

Hartmann convincingly argues that the vast majority of Marxist texts emphasised the oppressive position of women in relation to the economic system while ignoring the subordinate position of women to men. Traditional Marxist thought, as mentioned above, anticipated that the oppression of women would naturally (or we might say, magically) wither away as the

---

17 Ibid: 104.
18 Hartmann in Sargent 1981: 32.
19 Ibid.

result of economic transformation; and therefore did not have to be specifically addressed. However, Hartmann insisted that the patriarchal oppression of women by men, including working class women by working class men, had a material basis and was reinforced by solidarity among men that exceeded class lines. Due to the hierarchical structure of patriarchy, in which particular people (women) fill particular places (the ones of subordination and dependency), "men exercise their control in receiving personal service work from women, in not having to do housework or rear children, in having access to women's bodies for sex, and in feeling powerful and being powerful." [20]

The power of Hartmann's analysis lies in stressing the material, and not just symbolical, or superstructural for that matter, character of the patriarchal oppression of women by men. Addressing this form of oppression requires materialist measures. Measures that *de-privilege* the oppressor in terms of his access to such material resources as the time spared from reproductive labour, higher wages, and unconditional access to women's bodies. In other words, we can understand the inequality of the oppressor as a policy of reparations and redistribution of material resources that radically shifts our understanding of identity politics from a merely representational to a political-economic register.

In summary, the emancipatory project put forward by the queer and feminist Marxist movements of the 1970s rejects both the economism of traditional Marxist understanding of the class struggle, and identity politics based on the assimilation and normalisation of differences within the confinements of existing oppressive structures. In addition, the experience of the actually existing socialist regimes showed that economic transformation on its own does not lead to the transformation of social relations unless material and ideological structures that reproduce these relations are radically challenged. At the same time, the current crisis of so-called "progressive neoliberalism" shows that the mere celebration of diversity and multiculturalism without a radical transformation of economic structures leads to revitalised right-wing nationalism, military imperialism and patriarchal reaction spanning the entire world.

4.

As I started writing this essay, I struggled with the post-Soviet mythologised image of Lenin. I wanted to move away from Lenin-monument (or mushroom) to Lenin-thinker. As I finish this piece, I am resisting another feeling, a strong temptation to end my reflections with a radical revolutionary slogan inspired by the juxtaposition of Lenin's writing and the radical queer and feminist vibe of the 1970s. Something like, "Towards a Leninist Queer Feminist Identity Politics." But would that not be the replacement of one myth with another? Do we actually need to "make Lenin great again"?

---

20 Ibid: 18.

In the current moment of global crisis in which all previously mediated contradictions are exacerbated to an unprecedented degree, it may be high time for a Marxist to become a Leninist again. Part of this "return to Lenin's norms" might be the fascinating rediscovery of radical theory of the past, including that of Lenin himself. But the most important lesson a revolutionary Marxist can draw from Lenin's theoretical and practical experience is that no theory of the past, however radical and uncompromising, contains a blueprint for action in the current circumstances. Current contradictions demand current solutions. To be a Leninist, therefore, is to face these pressing contradictions not with dogmatic inebriety, even if it is dressed in catchy slogans, but with dialectic sobriety.

References

Althusser, Luis (1971), *Lenin and Philosophy and Other Essays*. New York: Monthly Review Press.

Aruza, Cinzia, Bhattacharya, Tithi, and Nancy Fraser (2019), *Feminism for the 99 Percent. A Manifesto.* London: Verso.

Brie, Michael (2017), *Otkryt' Lenina snova. Dialektika revolutsii vs. Metafisika gospodstva.* Moscow: Rosa Luxemburg Stiftung.

Hartmann, Heidi (1981), "The Unhappy Marriage of Marxism and Feminism: Towards a more Progressive Union," *in* Lydia Sargent (ed.), *Women and Revolution*. Montreal: Black Rose Books, 1-42.

Lenin, V.I. (1977), *Collected Works Vol. 36*. Moscow: Progress Publishers.

Martin, Terry (2001), *The Affirmative Action Empire: Nations and Nationalism in the Soviet Union, 1923-1939.* Ithaca: Cornell University Press.

Marxist Internet Archive (n.d.), "Georgian Affair 1921." Accessed on 29.06.2020, at https://www.marxists.org/glossary/events/g/e.htm#georgian-incident.

Mitchell, Pam (ed.) (2018), *Pink Triangles. Radical Perspective on Gay Liberation.* London: Verso.

TASS (2016), "Putin explains his remarks about Vladimir Lenin." Accessed on 29.06.2020, at https://tass.com/politics/852069.

Taub, Amanda (2020), "A New Covid-19 Crisis: Domestic Abuse Rises Worldwide," *New York Times.* Accessed on 29.06.2020, at https://www.nytimes.com/2020/04/06/world/coronavirus-domestic-violence.html.

Yurchak, Alexei (2011), "A Parasite from Outer Space: How Sergei Kurekhin Proved That Lenin Was a Mushroom," *Slavic Review*, 70(2), 307-333.

13. Lenin's Desire:
Reminiscences of Lenin and the Desire of the Comrade

Jodi Dean

From a bourgeois perspective, that is to say, from the perspective of commodified romance, marketised intimacy, and capitalist familialism, Nadezhda Krupskaya's *Reminiscences of Lenin* is a strange duck. Krupskaya was Lenin's wife, yet she doesn't describe how they fell in love. Instead, the two have discussions and take walks. She shares with him the details of her work teaching in an adult education school and producing and distributing agitational leaflets. There is no endearing marriage proposal. While both are in exile in Siberia, Krupskaya registers as Lenin's fiancé in order to be transferred to his village. It's not clear when they get married. Writing this off as the nonconformity of *fin de siècle* Russian *émigré* is too easy, an attempt to slide romance in through the backdoor. Something more uncanny, more machinic is at work: where we want to see sex, we find organisation. Again, this only appears strange if one's perspective is bourgeois.

From a communist perspective, the desire that suffuses, shapes, and enforms the text is familiar. The collective intimacy of comrades replaces the romantic intimacy of the couple; the two are two of many. Absorption in the political struggle for the Party, for the emancipation of the working class, for the revolution, and for socialism remakes familial relations. Krupskaya reports that Vladimir Ilyich loved his mother a great deal: "'She has tremendous will-power,' he told me once."[1] About her own mother, Krupskaya writes, "In March my mother died. She had been a close comrade, who had helped in all our work. In Russia, during police raids, she would hide all illegal materials. She took parcels and messages to comrades in prison. She had lived with us in Siberia and abroad, entertained the comrades who came to see us, made special vests with illegal literature sewn up in them, written the 'skeletons' for invisible-ink letters, etc. The comrades loved her."[2] These descriptions seem impersonal. They could apply to anyone, any comrade dedicated to living the struggle. And this is the point: communist desire involves intimacy of a new kind, one where love attaches not to some unique and irreplaceable trait or person but to a model that can be emulated, that must be copied and reproduced if the revolution is to succeed. The comrades love Krupskaya's mother for her discipline and dedication. Krupskaya loves her mother like a comrade. Collective desire for collectivity produces a closeness all the more intense for its exceeding of the merely personal.

Krupskaya's reports on Lenin's mother and her own are also striking in that the mothers are figured in terms that describe Lenin's and Krupskaya's own desires – tremendous will-power, detailed help in all the work,

---
1 Krupskaya 2018: 51.
2 Ibid: 303-304.

the love of comrades. What Krupskaya sees in their mothers is how she sees Vladimir Ilyich and herself, how she sees both of their aspirations for the Party. She says explicitly that Vladimir Ilyich inherited his mother's "strength of mind."[3] And much of the book details her own organisational work and close connections with comrades. The identification is clear.

What's not so clear is its direction. Is Krupskaya a comrade because her mother was a comrade or is her mother a comrade because of Krupskaya? Frankly speaking, for much of the book it appears as if Krupskaya and Lenin are dragging the poor woman all over Europe as they spend their time in exile moving from city to city. Likewise, is Lenin's mother depicted as having a strong will because of how Lenin's own will is imagined or does he like imagining himself this way because it lets him carry something with him of his mother? Does their desire shape how they imagine their mothers, does how they imagine their mothers shape their desire, or does the comradely desire of communists reshape it all?

These unanswerable questions illuminate another knot of desire, the entanglement of Lenin, class, and Party. They point to the mutual constitution of subject and Other, their dialectical interrelation and dependence on an organisational infrastructure. And they open a path into communist desire as a collective desire for collectivity and the Party as its necessary material support.

The Dialectic of Desire

One of Lacan's most well-known slogans is "desire is the desire of the Other." Bruce Fink renders it as *"the subject is caused by the Other's desire."*[4] The basic idea is that the subject isn't natural, given, or primary. The subject emerges dialectically through engagement with the Other, with an order of language and meaning exterior to it and in and through which the subject comes to be.

Lacan specifies alienation and separation as the processes through which the subject is constituted.[5] Alienation involves submission to signification and language, the Other. In order to be, the subject has to be in language. But language is inadequate: you can't say everything you want; it's hard to put things in words. The very medium that makes the subject possible, makes it lacking; something of the subject exceeds the form that structures it even as this excess would not be "of the subject" without the form or structure, without the language, that makes it possible. So the subject emerges as deprived (a Freudian name for this deprivation is "castration"). By itself, the process of alienation doesn't produce a subject. It produces the place of the subject, the site that the subject may come to occupy, the necessary condition for a subject. Subjectivity requires an additional second process, separation. Separation involves a confrontation with the Other, more specifically, with the desire of the Other, which means the lack in the Other. In separation, the subject recog-

---
3 Ibid: 52.
4 Fink 1996: 78 (italics in original).
5 Lacan 1998: 206-215.

nises that the Other, too, is lacking. It tries to fill this lack, to make its lack overlap with the lack in the Other. The subject tries to make itself the object of the Other's desire, to be what the Other wants, even when, especially when, it doesn't know and can't be sure what the Other wants. The subject's desire takes shape as the desire of the Other even as it will never, or rarely, be able fully to occupy that position. Separation, then, is an effect of the gap between the two lacks, the failed superimposition of the lack in the subject with the lack in the Other.

Rather than staying within the domain of language, Fink illustrates alienation and separation with the classic psychoanalytic figures of mother and child. He writes:

> If, then, alienation consists in the subject's causation by the Other's desire which preceded his or her birth, by some desire not of the subject's own making, separation consists in the attempt by the alienated subject to come to grips with that Other's desire as it manifests itself in the subject's world. As a child tries to fathom its mother's desire – which is ever in motion, desire being essentially desire for something else – the child is forced to come to terms with the fact that it is not her sole interest (in most cases at least), not her be-all and end all. There is rarely, if ever, a total mother-child unity, whereby the child can fulfil all of the mother's wants in life, and vice versa...a child is often obliged to await its mother's return, not only because of the demands of reality (she must procure food and other necessities for her child, not to mention the money with which to buy them), but also because of her own priorities and desires which do not involve her child. The child's unsuccessful attempt to perfectly complement its mother leads to an expulsion of the subject from the position of wanting-to-be and yet failing-to-be the Other's sole object of desire.[6]

We might also illustrate the same point with respect to the university. The university precedes any specific students. Entering students receive a number, an identification card, a designator of their place. The students try to figure out their place in the university. Who are they for, what is wanted of them? They will feel made to conform to expectations and practices not their own in order to recognise themselves as the students they are told that they are. Even as they try to fathom what is demanded of them and to meet these demands, a gap will remain that they will struggle to symbolise, represent, negotiate.

---

6 Fink 1996: 78.

The familial and academic examples help make sense of the dialectic of desire because the positions within them are relatively fixed. We expect the child and the student to be in the position of the subject struggling to emerge, the mother and university to supply the supportive yet demanding and engulfing presence against which this struggle unfolds. But what if the positions of subject and Other are not so clear? What if they are more unstable, co-constitutive, reversible? What if the Other is caused by the subject?

What Do Workers Want?

Krupskaya's *Reminiscences of Lenin* is an account of the emergence of Bolshevism, a story of party building. Lenin is as much a product of revolutionary working-class struggle as he is a leader of it. Krupskaya writes, "Leaders are formed in and grow out of the struggle from which they draw their strength."[7] She presents the process of formation as the never-ceasing problem of organisation. The dynamic throughout the book involves passionate engagement, intense absorption in the details of workers' lives, the mechanisms of communication linked to creating and distributing the all-Russia newspaper, the infrastructures of organisational practice. Accompanying these concerns are periods of exhaustion, over-extension, "frayed nerves," and the necessity of stepping back, heading to the mountains, and enjoying nature – what today's activists would call self-care. To recall Lenin is to recall him in becoming, in the context of the formation of class, party, revolution, and socialist society.

Krupskaya details Lenin's commitment to the fight against oppression and exploitation: "his whole life was bound up with that cause." Lenin was "devoted to the cause of the proletariat, the cause of the working people, and took their interests just as closely to heart."[8] She highlights his emphases on "establishing close contact with the masses, getting closer to them, learning to be the vehicle of their finest aspirations, learning how to win their confidence and rally them behind us."[9] Lenin's faith in the "creative power" and "historic mission" of the proletariat grew out of his "profound knowledge and thorough study of the facts of life."[10] As Krupskaya explains, "His work among the St. Petersburg proletariat has helped to identify this faith in the power of the working class with real life people."[11] Lenin's faith manifests in his particular gift in knowing how to read workers' letters. Where others might detect barely literate confusion, Lenin finds "inexhaustible energy, a readiness to fight to the victorious end."[12] He had a sense for "the moods of

---

7 Krupskaya 2018: 7.
8 Ibid.
9 Ibid: 26.
10 Ibid: 108.
11 Ibid.
12 Ibid: 109.

the working class at a given moment."¹³ He "knew and understood what the masses wanted,"¹⁴ Krupskaya tells us.

Solving the organisational problem, figuring out how to channel and direct political work, consumes Lenin. He works out organisational questions incessantly, sleeplessly. How can bodies, political associations, that do not yet fully exist, that are still being formed, be coordinated, practically and ideologically? Krupskaya writes that "[i]t was Vladimir Ilyich's passionate desire to create a united, solid party, merging into one all the detached groups whose attitude to the party was based on personal sympathies or antipathies. He dreamt of a party in which there would be no artificial barriers, national ones included."¹⁵ Among the squabbling emigres, party work is frustrating, often undermined by perpetual interpersonal conflict. In the hard years spent abroad following the defeats of 1905, the bickering intensifies, sometimes channelled into principled questions of materialism and tactical questions of legal and illegal work, sometimes dragged down into the "ugly scum" of scandal.¹⁶ Lenin tries to keep personal grievances at bay and remain focused on the cause at hand. The effort wears on his nerves.

After 1914, and in line with the revolutionary spirit of the Russian proletariat, Lenin treats the outbreak of war as the opening to revolution. After the February revolution, although still stuck in Switzerland, he attends to the concrete details of revolutionary struggle. He proposes a new militia of armed men and women. They will serve as sanitary inspectors, arrange for the distribution of bread and milk to children, and address housing questions by commandeering palaces. Lenin knows full well that these distributive measures are not socialist. But active work in militias will provide the practical education necessary for socialism. Yes, the situation calls for insurrection and Lenin waged a relentless struggle with comrades in his own party over the insurrectionary moment. Yet he was preoccupied with the practical infrastructure crucial to success. Krupskaya quotes Lenin's *Letters from Afar*: "On the order of the day is the task of *organisation*, but certainly not in the stereotyped sense of working only on stereotyped organisations, but in the sense of drawing unprecedentedly broad masses of the oppressed classes into an organisation and of making this organisation itself take over military, state and national-economic functions."¹⁷ What mattered most was meeting the concrete needs of the masses by organising them in a new way.¹⁸

Lenin's focus on organisation intensifies after the success of the October revolution. He is wholly occupied "with the problem of remodelling the entire machinery of government, reorganising the masses along new lines,

---

13 Ibid: 113.
14 Ibid: 111-112.
15 Ibid: 84.
16 Ibid: 208.
17 Ibid: 339.
18 Ibid: 340.

weaving anew the whole social fabric.[19] Building socialism is a matter of organisation. How can workers' lives be arranged for the better? What is the best way to organise consumers' cooperatives? How can the Soviet government make sure that children receive the milk they need? What are the mechanisms for getting workers into better apartments? What sort of accounting mechanisms does all this require? And, most important of all, how can this work be organised so that it be the work of the masses themselves?[20]

Organising Desire

Who is the subject of *Reminiscences of Lenin*? If it is Lenin, then the proletariat is the Other. Lenin's desire is the desire of the proletariat. The workers' movement precedes him – there are Marx and Engels, the Paris Commune, Chernyshevksy and *Narodnaya Volya*; there is a strong and growing German Social Democratic Party and rising discontent in Russia. The needs and desires of the masses precede Lenin and he finds himself in them, finds his own desire in theirs. Lenin as subject is constituted through his engagement with the proletariat. He tries to determine what – to *be* what – they want; he can read their letters like no one else can. He attends to every little detail of their stories, lives, experiences, and reports. He recognises, moreover, that the workers' needs are vast, that he cannot meet them. And he endeavours to create ways for them to do it themselves. What does the proletariat lack? Organisation. There in the overlap of two lacks, two desires, the Party appears, the organisational form of Lenin's separation from the proletariat.

But what if the proletariat is the subject and Lenin is the Other? Krupskaya's *Reminiscences* tells the story of collective work and the building of collectivity; it's a communist story less preoccupied with individuals than it is with common struggle for universal ends. The possibility that the proletariat is the subject is not far-fetched when we acknowledge the division between the working class understood as an empirical designator of social position and/or role in production and the proletariat as a universal revolutionary subject. As empirical designator, working class refers to an object given in capitalist relations. As revolutionary subject, proletariat points to an effervescence, a momentary heterogeneous unity that may or may not emerge. In the Marxist tradition, proletariat is a category associated with class consciousness and the moment when the class acts in-itself and for-itself. In the proletariat, universality becomes agential.

The Communist Manifesto outlines such a process of becoming: individual workers react to oppressive conditions by destroying means of production; these activities spread regionally and across different sectors of work; unions are formed and then a party as collective awareness of the political nature of the struggle radicalises and intensifies the workers' move-

---

19 Ibid: 373.
20 Ibid: 428.

ment. Over the course of its movement, the proletariat produces new leaders, organisations, and forms of struggle – the very story of *Reminiscences*. Through these, the workers come to see themselves as a class, and as a class with power. Leaders represent the workers' power back to them. Krupskaya tells us that Lenin learned to be a vehicle for the masses' "finest aspirations" – not for all of them. Leaders offer up slogans as demands, and as possible expressions of desire; is this what you demand now? When leaders get it wrong, no one follows and they cease to be leaders, or perhaps they never were. The working class as a class doesn't know what it wants, doesn't have a collective desire, until this desire is given back to them – Peace? Bread? Land? Nothing less than the overthrow of the state? All power to the Soviets? That the class doesn't know what it wants is another way of saying that its desire has not yet been given expression. The Other is the site where this occurs. Naming the desire brings it into being as the desire of a subject.

If alienation is the process whereby a place in language is opened for the subject, then we have a psychoanalytic explanation for Lenin's insistence on an all-Russia newspaper. Yes, of course, for tactical reasons of party building. But the paper could only be a good tactic for party building if it brings to expression something of workers' desire. Prior to its alienation in language, the subject isn't there; it has no being. The subject – the Russian proletariat – is an effect of the place made for it, even as it necessarily exceeds this place.

With regard to the Party: the class is not coterminous with the Party. The class needs the Party as a political form, a form for political struggle against the conditions that produce the class, even as the very fact of the Party marks the separation of the subject from the Other, the proletariat from Lenin. Why? Because the Party provides the material infrastructure that supports the proletariat as a political subject. Lenin can't do this alone. Producing, supporting, steering the proletariat requires a practical instantiation, a new form of organisation or apparatus of proletarian desire. The all-Russia newspaper – its authors, editors, and printers, and the elaborate secret network for distributing it in Russia and then supporting the comrades who get caught and arrested – was a condition for communicating with the masses, for organising workers, for generating a shared understanding of the situation. This work not only brought together previously disparate groupings of socialists and revolutionaries; it not only communicated ideas to workers; it also served as a means for building and strengthening the party organisation. Again, the Party is situated at the site of the overlap of two lacks.

Lenin's desire throughout Krupskaya's *Reminiscences* is expressed as a desire for organisation. It's not simply his desire for a Party capable of expressing and guiding the desire of the proletariat, not simply his desire for something more than small, squabbling friendship groups, something more than reading circles or intellectuals and committeemen, something more than an underground network or an electoral grouping. Something more – every little detail – is what has to be organised for socialism to be built. Organisation expresses the desire of the proletariat because it is through organisation – the reorganisation of life – that the proletariat builds socialism. Organisation is what enables the people to direct their lives; it's the way they direct them, how they get things done. Collective work produces collective desire or, organisation is the way communist desire is collectivised.

Invisible Ink

Krupskaya relates an "amusing adventure" she had while trying to meet up with Lenin in Europe after her exile came to an end. It's a story of desire and organisation. Thinking that Lenin was in Prague living under the assumed name Modráĉek, she sends him a telegram to meet her at the train. Lenin doesn't show up. After a long wait, Krupskaya gives up and goes to the address of a large tenement building. She knocks on the door of the fourth-floor apartment. A woman answers and Krupskaya says, "Herr Modráĉek. Herr Modráĉek." A workman comes to the door and identifies himself as Modráĉek. Krupskaya, bewildered, responds, "No, it's my husband." At first puzzled, the worker concludes that Krupskaya "must be the wife of Herr Rittmeyer. He lives in Munich, but sent books and letters" through him, Herr Modráĉek.[21] Krupskaya spends the whole day with Modráĉek sharing notes about the movement. She then goes to Munich. The first flat she goes to ends up being a beer-house. She approaches the barkeep, asks for Herr Rittmeyer, and gets the answer, "That's me." Krupskaya responds, "No, it's my husband." Herr Rittmeyer's wife comes in and says, "Ah, it must be Herr Meyer's wife. He is expecting his wife from Siberia." So she takes Krupskaya through the building and into a flat where Lenin is sitting with his sister and Martov. Krupskaya is massively angry and immediately begins to yell at Vladimir Ilyich: "Damn it all, couldn't you write and tell me where you were?" Lenin says that he had written and that he had been at the station three times a day. "How did you get here?" he asks. Krupskaya ends the story: "As we afterwards learned, the Zemstvo man to whom the book with the address had been sent had kept the book to read."[22]

Communist desire: organised associations, assumed names, a chain of connections and a worker's desire as the site of excess and lack. The book arrived at its destination, and so did Krupskaya. Her story is about getting there.

---

21 Ibid: 52-53.
22 Ibid: 53.

References

Fink, Bruce (1996), "The Subject and the Other's Desire," *in* Richard Feldstein, Bruce Fink, and Maire Jaanus (eds.), *Reading Seminar I and II: Lacan's Return to Freud*. New York: State University of New York Press, 76-97.

Lacan, Jacques, and Jacques-Alain Miller (eds.) (1998), *The Four Fundamental Concepts of Psychoanalysis, The Seminar of Jacques of Lacan Book XI*. New York: Norton.

Krupskaya, Nadezhda K. (2018), *Reminiscences of Lenin*. Chicago: Haymarket Books.

Poetic Interlude

My song

My song – you might ask: Who was it sung for?
For whom did my heart beat with such emotion?
And to whom does the nightingale pour out
Day and night these my dithyrambs?

I don't sing for gold or glory,
I don't sing out of greed or envy,
I sing of working people, and
My heart is enveloped in the flames of song.

1930

The Bolshevik march moves on

The falcon's wings beat more slowly now
And sorrow's kettles boil ever faster
The labouring poor are grieving
For the loss that all are feeling.

"My heart is hurting with such pain
I don't know with whom I'll share it!"
It's like a prank life played on us,
The telegram that fell on us
And caused sad voices to be heard
Last night on all sides around us.

Automobile transport and trams,
They all stood still in dead silence.
The factory hooter sounded
Sadly and the train engines cried
Just as unrestrained and loud
When the tragic news burst on us.

The people were crying, grieving,
Trying to comfort each other,
As the labouring poor went out
Into the streets to say goodbye.

And how could the labouring poor
Not mourn the one who gave them freedom?

Black is the colour of flags hung
Out all around our neighbourhood,
As working people are grieving,
Their world now sunk low in darkness
While enemies loudly rejoice
And clap their hands in happiness.
A poisonous fog from Moscow
Has fallen on us, and sad sounds
Of weeping heard in Ala-Too.
Our grief is like a heavy sigh.
Our pain rattles and hisses like
An engine motor out of sync.

He went pale, his nostrils narrow
With pain that sorely racked the brow
Of our friend of the working man
Who had just lost the prize of life.
His blood was boiling, churning hard
And pain shot through his noble heart...

What bitter tears we shed that day
We said farewell to our Father!
But now seven years have gone by
To get over the pain and grief.
The working poor are on the march,
The Bolshevik hero's voice is
Heard echoing from shore to shore,
Not tolerating any talk
Of 'orphans,' he walks forward and
Allows no humiliation.

The news of freedom has fallen
On hired labourers like a swarm,
The working poor are overjoyed.
Our villages rejoice, shaking off
The dust of outworn traditions.
New machinery in the fields,
A blue flame burns in the workshop
And the motors roar into life,
As the factory hooter sounds
And the desert lands have turned green
Irrigated by new canals.
The Bolshevik march moves forward.
The bells ring out in joyful sound.
Each day we make a further step
Preparing socialism's ground.
We have destroyed the wealthy class
And labour rules on every side,

Lenin150 (Samizdat)

The speed of changes Bolshevism
Brings sends scoundrels running scared.
Our land flowering, sweet smelling
As the labourer is honoured
And the cuckoo calls day and night,
A melody of joy. Meanwhile
The capitalist is crying
Bitterly, cold and coughing blood,
And in the sky Lenin's flag flies
Brightly, happily and boldly.
The enemies of yesterday
Are disgraced, no longer laughing.
Our wings are spread widely now and
The sons of labour have space now,
The population is growing
And leaving the old ways behind.
New factories and plants appear,
And motors roar, whirring as they
Bring Lenin's commandments to life
And bring new order to our land
As cuckoos and nightingales sing
Filling our gardens with sweet sound.

Even if Lenin dies, life shows
That we can step up and take his place,
There are lots of good people in
The ranks of former hired labourers,
And some as fast as a racehorse
Outpacing camels, socialism
And the Bolshevik march moves on,
The path set by Marx and Lenin.
The nightingale sings class struggle,
This pen – a racehorse in his hands.

1931

To N.K. Krupskaya

She spent all her life working for the people
And we honour all her good qualities.
She closed her eyes and went away for ever
But the results of her work are forever.

The hand of cunning death beckons us all, and
Only rests when we are laid in the black earth.
But those who struggled for the good of people
Will never die, they will burn like candles.

Without tiring, she climbed up the stony pass
And with Lenin were victorious in war.
Not fearing curses, she was as determined
As the loyal daughter of a *baatyr*.[1]

She devoted the best years of her life to
Freedom and the happiness of her people,
Always a friend and comrade in arms to our
Father and forever respected Lenin.

Grieving, our whole country bids you farewell and
Writes another sad page in our history.
Fearless daughter of a warrior people,
We honour your work and say a thousand thanks!

1939

Translated from the original Kyrgyz into Russian by Aisuluu Kokoyeva, and from Russian into English by Charles Buxton

---

1 Editor's note: The Kyrgyz word *baatyr* is the approximate equivalent of the English "hero." In Soviet times, it was given to people who contributed significantly to the Communist cause.

Joomart Bokonbaev (1910-1944), Kyrgyz revolutionary poet, playwright, journalist and intellectual. Bokonbaev's biography is typical for many Soviet Kyrgyz intellectuals of the 1920s-1930s. Born to a poor family in a rural area of southern Kyrgyzstan, he spent a few years in a boarding home, trained as a teacher in Osh and later in Frunze (now Bishkek). Later, he continued his professional education in Moscow. Bokonbaev studied at the Communist Institute of Journalism in 1933-1935. His first poem – *To the poor who obtained the land* – was published in 1927 in the Osh district newspaper. His first book of poetry, *The Beginning of Labour*, was published in 1933. In his poems Bokonbaev masterfully blends the Kyrgyz lyrical tradition of *akyns* (folk singers) and Manas epic singers with an acute sense of modern life and revolutionary sharpness. He often turns to the metaphor of the pen as sword, emphasising the class motivation of his poetic labours. In his early lyrics Bokonbaev almost exclusively features people of labour – peasants and workers – as builders of a new life, and strives to document the rapidly changing social reality of post-Revolutionary Kyrgyzstan. In his later poems and plays, he turns to historical, philosophical and lyrical themes as well.

Bokonbaev also dedicated a number of his poems to Vladimir Lenin, most notably, "The Bolshevik march moves on" and "The Spirit of Lenin." Celebration of Lenin in poetry and song was common in Soviet culture after 1924. In Central Asia both professional poets and *akyns* wrote numerous homages to the leader of the world proletariat. In 1934, Dziga Vertov produced an agitation film featuring the gains of the Cultural Revolution in Central Asia entitled "Three Songs About Lenin" which referred to this widespread cultural practice.

Bokonbaev's short creative life of 17 years coincided with the two major historical periods in early Soviet Kyrgyz history – the Cultural Revolution and the Second World War. In 1941 Bokonbaev joined the Red Army as a volunteer. At the front, he served as the editor of the division newspaper. In the 1940s, Bokonbaev wrote poems celebrating the heroism of the Kyrgyz men and women fighting in WW2. He died in 1944 in a car accident, aged 34.

For this publication we selected three poems by Bokonbaev translated into English by Charles Buxton with the help of Aisuluu Kokoyeva. His poetic manifesto "My song" (1930); the militant communist hymn "The Bolshevik march moves on" (1931), written on the occasion of the seventh anniversary of Lenin's death; and an homage to Lenin's wife and communist "warrior" Nadezhda Krupskaya (1939).

Georgy Mamedov

Translators' notes

Aisuluu Kokoyeva: In a sense, the poems of Joomart Bokonbaev are representative of a whole generation of builders of socialism in the Kirghiz (A)SSR: poets like Aaly Tokombaev (1904-1988), Kasym Tynystanov (1901-1938), Alykul Osmonov (1915-1950), Zhusup Turusbekov (1910-1944) and others who wrote about the bad times before the arrival of Soviet power, and how the latter gave a future to the poor, and especially the peasantry. Literary activities were strong at the time. Writers and poets wrote in Kyrgyz and were actively translated into Russian so that their words could be propagated throughout the Soviet Union.

The content of their poems was generally in line with Socialist Realism (supervision of the intelligentsia included): first, an Ode to Lenin, to the Soviet Union, to the Party, to the Motherland, and only then words about love, philosophical ideas or about oneself. At the same time, what stands out is how these authors genuinely believed that everything would be fine; that by the year 2000 we would all live under communism: "I don't sing for the sake of red gold, I don't sing for the sake of a fat herd," wrote Bokonbaev, and I am sure he believed it.

Overall, Bokonbaev is like a role model for us. His work and service to literature are an example of a true patriot. The poet went to war, fought against fascism, sang about peace. He understood that a lot of work was needed for his people to achieve true quality of life. And to help make this happen he fulfilled his filial, poetic duty. His contemporaries called him "our Pushkin." The imagery, depth and sincerity of his poetry, his effort to collect the works of the akyn (oral epic) singer Toktogul Satylganov are great contributions to the literature of Kyrgyzstan and those who study it.

In short, in these times of complex political events and the ambivalent impacts of globalisation – for a nation like ours – Joomart's work gives us strength. In the context of the threat of radical Islamisation, one cannot fail to mention his reflecting on the fate of girls and young women, his celebration of the equality between sexes. So how can one imagine the future of the Kyrgyz nation without him? Joomart is one of those poets who, living in our hearts, entered our flesh and blood. Therefore, it is important for us and for our future, to view his work like a pure spring and continue to draw energy from it.

Charlie Buxton: For me this was a great chance to learn a bit more about Kyrgyz poets in the early Soviet era. Working from Aisuluu's careful translation from Kyrgyz into Russian, I tried to maintain line length (i.e. number of syllables) and rhythm, while not attempting to keep the rhymes. I also carried the sense over the line ending more than in the original. This worked best in the "Bolshevik March" with its highly compressed images and sense. The translation stimulated me to make a short research of early Kyrgyz poets (and poetesses) which it would be good to translate and disseminate more widely. Most of them wrote in Kyrgyz originally but they were translated into Russian and I realised what a huge amount of work was done in the Soviet period to encourage these new literary movements.

14. Playing Lenin –
A Conversation with Ursina Lardi on Lenin and Theatre

The following is an interview with Ursina Lardi, who portrayed Lenin in Milo Rau's 2017 play, *LENIN*. The setting of the play: "In 1917 Russia is shaken by the October Revolution. Just a few years later, socialism has been implemented. Lenin, the ringleader of the revolution, is in a dacha near Moscow battling physical and mental decay. Surrounded by a depleted inner circle, cut off from the Central Committee, he fights to retain his political influence. His companion Trotsky, cultural politician Lunacharsky and others who visit Lenin's dacha conjure up recollections of the brief moment in history when everything seemed possible. But Lenin's failing body and weakened spirit mean the "greatest mind of the 20th century" is on his own. Meanwhile, scheming to become his successor, his opponent Stalin is already waiting in the wings. In *"LENIN"* Milo Rau and the *Schaubühne* Ensemble look via Lenin's brain to what is arguably the most momentous revolution in the history of humankind: in a society caught between awakening and apathy, revolutionary longing and reactionary opposition – a labyrinth of hope and fear, of political ideals and the collective experience of violence." [1]

Hjalmar Jorge Joffre-Eichhorn (HJJE): Ursina, thank you for taking the time to speak to me about your interpretation of Vladimir Ilyich Ulyanov in Milo Rau's play, *LENIN*. Let's jump right in. What did you find most tempting about taking on the role?

Ursina Lardi (UL): The impossibility of the task. Ultimately, you can only fail in such a role. And along the way, you might be fortunate enough to create the odd moment of beauty.

HJJE: How did you prepare for the role? After all, there is no shortage of material and stereotypical imagery…

UL: In order to avoid unnecessary battles with stereotypes, I read Lenin's own words and not what had been written about him – his speeches, annotations, essays, letters and so on. But then in rehearsal, I put all of that to one side and concentrate on what I can bring to the role, how I can bring this person to life. To do that, I focus on concrete, real-life things, for example what it must feel like when nobody understands you because you can no longer speak clearly after suffering a stroke, or I deal with the insult, caused by being given a wheelchair before you actually need it.

---

1 Rau 2017.

HJJE: Lenin as he is conceived in the play goes through a vast range of emotions: he is funny, dying, evil, solidary, forgetful, helplessly aggressive, speechless, fragile, despairing, isolated, the list goes on… In short, not an icon, but an extremely contradictory and somehow even *"verfremdet"* (estranged) creature. What were your greatest artistic challenges in playing the role?

UL: That list of emotions is pretty much exactly what a role needs in order for it to interest me! The challenge is to embody these seeming contradictions in a believable way. That is possible in acting, it is actually a kind of realism. In a human being, in a character, there is usually much more space than we imagine. I experienced that too in my work with Milo on *"Mitleid. Die Geschichte des Maschinengewehrs"* ["Compassion. The History of the Machine Gun."]. There we worked with the verbatim statements of a dozen people, and it was not difficult to combine them all into one character.

HJJE: We asked all of the contributors to our book to write their text with as much joy as possible, free from neoliberal pressures. What did you find most joyful in the role and the performances?

UL: My favourite moment is when the doctor calmly and precisely lists the consequences of Lenin's stroke. Step by step I relate to, I embody, each one of these realities. So then, what at first might seem very technical, suddenly gains depth, magnitude, and we realise what we are witnessing – the decline of a human being in time lapse. At that point, it is no longer only about Lenin, but about us all. It is for moments like these that I chose this profession.

HJJE: In the fourth scene, we see a conversation between Lenin and the People's Commissar for Education of the RSFSR, Anatoly Lunacharsky, in which Lenin asks: "How would you play Lenin?" The Commissar replies, "To play Lenin as a human being would already be a mistake, I think." How did you ultimately play Lenin? And if you were to play him again, what might you do differently?

UL: Krupskaya, Lenin's wife, responds to the Commissar: "But why? Why would he not be a human being?" – I begin the play without any optical modifications, no makeup, in casual clothes. Then, step by step, using costumes and masks, a transformation takes place in front of the audience. In a sense, I perform the iconisation of Lenin on myself, which is an act of physical violence. As with Lenin in life, over the course of the evening I lose, one after the other, the things that make me who I am. I cannot imagine playing Lenin again. I have never played a character or acted in the same play twice. But if I were to do it, I would change everything, of course.

HJJE: A main theme in the play is the critical scrutiny, in the context of the contemporary struggles of the 21st century, of the embalming of Lenin's body and thought. Heiner Müller even went so far as to suggest stealing Lenin's body from his mausoleum-prison, in order to finally set him free again. Based on your intensive examination of the man, Lenin, what would you say are the facets of his thought and action that we should, on the 150th anniversary of his birth, set free, revive or elaborate?

UL: "As long as one single human being is in bondage, oppression has not been eliminated! If the whole world is not free, then our freedom is not worth a damn." I would say we can work towards this simple, global maxim for quite some time yet.

Translated from the original German by Patrick Anderson

References
Rau, Milo (2017), *LENIN*. Berlin: Verbrecher Verlag.

15. What Lenin Teaches Us About Witchcraft[1]

Oxana Timofeeva

Oh I believe in miracles
Oh I believe in a better world for me and you
The Ramones

In the 1990s, right after the collapse of the USSR, the Russian tabloid press launched an extensive series of exposés on leaders from the state socialist past. Much of this attention fell on Lenin: as the founder of the state, he became a privileged target of all sorts of attacks. Historians and journalists competed to reveal unknown, weird, or unpleasant facts in Lenin's biography. This genre is still alive, and seems to replace – or simply invert – an old Communist legacy: everyone who, like me, was born in the Soviet Union, can still recollect a number of stories from Lenin's life. Among them are stories of: Lenin deceiving the police officer who came for a home inspection, Lenin writing secret messages to his comrades from prison, Lenin inviting a stoveman for a cup of tea, Lenin meeting a beautiful red fox in the forest.

In these Soviet legends, the leader was always portrayed as positive and gentle, whereas post-Soviet texts represent him as a negative or extremely ambiguous figure. One recent essay of this latter kind suggests that Lenin's ancestors came from Western Europe, more specifically from Germany,[2] and that someone in Lenin's family line, perhaps the leader's great-grandmother, was defamed for using black magic and witchcraft, and was burned at the stake by the Inquisition.

Given the number of people massacred for this 'crime' from the fifteenth to the seventeenth centuries, this story might very well be true. My goal, however, is not to investigate the historical veracity of this claim and determine whether Lenin was indeed a descendant of this enigmatic woman. Rather, the very idea that the revolutionary leader could have had an ancestor who was a witch, sorcerer, or magician is intriguing to me: the superpowers which, as a Soviet child, I imagined he possessed could have been inherited from someone who fell victim to the genocide committed under the banner of Christianity amidst the rise of capitalist modernity.

This coincidence does not seem random. In *Caliban and the Witch: Women, the Body and Primitive Accumulation,* Silvia Federici brilliantly explains capitalism's birth from the spirit of the Inquisition. Federici presents

---

1 A version of this article originally appeared in e-flux journal #100 (May 2019; https://www.e-flux.com/journal/100/268602/what-lenin-teaches-us-about-witchcraft/).
2 Editor's note: The accusation that Lenin was a "German agent" dates from at least his return to Russia in the famed "sealed train" from Switzerland, in April 1917. On the occasion of the 100th anniversary of the October Revolution, this tedious charge was once again brought up in the bourgeois press, ever so concerned with disinterested historical accuracy.

the figure of the witch "as the embodiment of a world of female subjects that capitalism had to destroy: the heretic, the healer, the disobedient wife, the woman who dared to live alone, the obeah woman who poisoned the master's food and inspired the slaves to revolt."[3]

Behind the witch hunt, she uncovers a joint effort by the Church and the State to establish mechanisms of gendered control of bodies that immanently resisted newly instituted regimes of productive and reproductive work. "No one yet has determined what the body can do,"[4] said Spinoza in his 1677 *Ethics*. However, the nascent capitalist system determined what the body must do: it must work. According to Federici, in the transition from feudalism to capitalism the multiple powers of the body were transformed into a calculable and controllable work-power. This transformation required the destruction of the conception of the body "as a receptacle of magical powers that had prevailed in the medieval world,"[5] in which the lines between Christian religion, magic, and the remains of paganism were still unclear. Precapitalist bodies felt themselves connected to nature and the stars in various ways: the *Malleus Maleficarum* (the Hammer of Witches) arrived in 1487 to sever these ties. As Federici puts it: "The body had to die so that labour-power could live."[6]

The death of the body meant cutting off any magical potential that did not fit into the scenarios of capitalist development. The 'age of reason' chased out magic, queer, female, and animistic lifestyles, just as, in Foucault's analysis, it excluded madness.

Foucault showed how madness was targeted by police measures, which criminalised it along with other forms of workless life. Federici adheres to this Foucauldian approach of uncovering the genealogy of power, placing greater emphasis on it than conventional Marxist and feminist analyses. She states that witches do not work either; they are engaged in alternative activities, and this is their main crime against the bourgeois order:

> A variety of practices were designed to appropriate the secrets of nature and bend its powers to the human will. From palmistry to divination, from the use of charms to sympathetic healing, magic opened a vast number of possibilities. There was magic designed to win card games, to play unknown instruments, to become invisible, to win somebody's love, to gain immunity in war, to make children sleep ... Eradicating these practices was a necessary condition for the capitalist rationalisation of work, since magic appeared as an illicit form of power and an instrument to obtain what one wanted without work, that is, a refusal of work in action [...] Equally incompatible with

---

[3] Federici 2014: 11.
[4] Editor's note: For a version of this quote, please see Descartes, Spinoza & Leibniz 1960: 226.
[5] Ibid: 141.
[6] Ibid.

the capitalist work-discipline was the conception of the cosmos that attributed special powers to the individual: the magnetic look, the power to make oneself invisible, to leave one's body, to chain the will of others by magical incantations [...] The incompatibility of magic with the capitalist work-discipline and the requirement of social control is one of the reasons why a campaign of terror was launched against it by the State.[7]

The capitalist conception of the world implies that all the body can do is work, and it is only through work that the needs of that body can be satisfied. "Capitalist ethics, a pitiful parody on Christian ethics, strikes with its anathema the flesh of the labourer; its ideal is to reduce the producer to the smallest number of needs, to suppress his joys and his passions and to condemn him to play the part of a machine turning out work without respite and without thanks,"[8] wrote Paul Lafargue.

However, this has not always been the condition of our bodily existence. There was a time when the body was conceived as an intersection of cosmic forces and a part of the natural whole in which everything is related to every other thing. Federici again: "At the basis of magic there was an animistic conception of nature that did not admit to any separation between nature and spirit, and thus imagined a cosmos as a *living organism*, populated by occult forces, where every element was in 'sympathetic' relation with the rest."[9]

A miracle might have violated the laws of nature, but it did not violate the whole of magical being and thinking. At a certain point, this became impossible. Under capitalism not only did the economic system change, but also, as Federico Campagna claims in *Technic and Magic*, the very composition of the world, its metaphysical presuppositions:

> The character of our contemporary existential experience points towards a certain type of ordering of our world, and of ourselves within it. This ordering is superficially social/economic/etc., but in fact derives from a set of fundamental metaphysical axioms. These axioms combine together in an overall system, which is the reality-system of our age. A reality-system shapes the world in a certain way, and endows it with a particular destiny: it is the cosmological form that defines a historical age. At the same time, however, it is also a cosmogonic force: its metaphysical settings and parameters actually create the world.[10]

---

7 Ibid: 142-143.
8 See Lafargue 1883.
9 Federici 2014: 141-142.
10 Campagna 2018: 5.

Campagna differentiates between two great reality-systems or "cosmogonic forces:" he calls them "technic" and "magic." From this perspective, one can say that the age of reason – or the age of capitalism, whose advent, according to Federici, coincides with the emergence of witch hunts and the eradication of alterity – is defined by the metaphysical parameters of the "technic:" representation, abstraction, separation, etc. Within these cosmological conditions, miracles are "technically impossible" (they might be possible in an alternative reality-system). The first constitutive principle of "magic," on the other hand, is the presence of the "ineffable" dimension of existence, "which cannot be captured by descriptive language, and which escapes all attempts to put it to 'work' – either in the economic series of production, or in those of citizenship, technology, science, social roles and so on."[11]

Magic introduces, according to Campagna, a sort of therapy for the pathologies of our existence in the technic reality-system, such as the foreclosure of the future and the general feeling that we are incapable of building an emancipatory project that would fundamentally change the direction of history. A therapeutic injection of magic, suggests Campagna, is key to overcoming this situation.

I would like to respond to this call with my own theory of witchcraft – well, not really a theory, but rather brief notes towards a theory that might then be fleshed out by anyone. These notes are conditioned by my personal experience of being a child who was so scared of the dark that the only way to overcome the horror was to let myself be fully absorbed by this darkness, to identify with it. I'm sure I'm not the only child who has used this tactic to deal with her fear of the dark. When I realised that the source of my fear was not outside of me, but within, I felt ecstatic. I thought I could become a magician if I learned to be more attentive to the darkness that was a part of me.

A child might feel the desire to become a magician when the world, which at first seemed to be so loving and gentle, ceases to comply with her every need, and instead starts to live a life of its own. The child's mother, who just a moment ago was reading her a fairy tale, must now leave for work; left alone in her cradle, the child helplessly waves her hands, trying and failing to call her mother back. At a certain point, it turns out that the desires of the child are not the one and only law for her parents, who sometimes have to obey other laws – laws that are indifferent to the desires of the child. This experience is catastrophic, but at the same time a necessary and constitutive rupture between the world and the subject. Beginning in early childhood, we gradually realise that when it comes to the world and the subject, things can go terribly wrong. Everyone has their own way of dealing with this existential mess.

---

11 Ibid: 10.

I want to propose two paradigmatic strategies that people use to negotiate the competing demands of desire and the law: religion and magic. Religion helps one conform to the world, subordinating desire to a codified law. Magic, by contrast, invites one to make the world conform to one's own desires, subordinating the law to the subject's arbitrary rule. Accordingly, our culture knows at least two types of spiritual practices; these can be illustrated by the two different paths that a child who wants to become a magician might take. In one, the child turns to religion, establishing a relation of exchange with God and expecting the latter to grant her wishes. In the other, the child establishes a relation of exchange with the Devil instead; she gives him her soul, and in return he gives her the ability to become a master magician and grant any wish herself.

The child who becomes a magician is ready to make an inhuman effort to force the world to conform to her desires. She becomes a witch out of injury, resentment, weakness, despair, melancholy, envy, jealousy, loneliness, the irreversibility of death, or poverty. (When I was poor, I wanted to use sorcery to obtain five hundred rubles so that I could buy a sweater.) She also becomes a magician out of boredom, just to avoid being a philistine.[12] The main source of her magic force is her firm belief in herself, which she perhaps acquires at precisely her worst moments of loss and catastrophe. She desperately wants, at any cost, to do what others cannot – awaken the dead, bring a lost loved one back to life, enact revenge, turn back time and redeem a fatal error committed in the past. A person who becomes a magician has learned that something is fundamentally wrong – the world is unjust, and this order of things can, in fact, be changed miraculously. A magician challenges the order of things dictated by God and nature. If the essential injustice of this reality –the domination of the rich over the poor, the strong over the weak, the living over the dead – is a law, she wants to transgress this law and impose her own will in its place.

A witch needs certain skills and superpowers that exceed those of ordinary humans, in order to grant her own wishes or those of others. This requires the witch to interrupt the order of things, transgress the law, and break through the inertia of so-called normal life. Witchcraft starts at the limit of the possible, where the competence of ordinary people ends. It is forbidden because the very fact of being a witch violates natural and social law, which allocates a place and time to everyone and everything. There are cracks and holes in reality that witches plug up with their own bodies. Witches are thus alien. They belong, in part, to another world in which the

---

12 Editor's note: Famously, "Philistine" was one of Lenin's most widely used polysemic insults. In the 45 volumes of his English-language Collective Works, numerous variations of the expression are used a staggering 700+ times. Among some of the more well-known victims of Lenin's vitriol were Eduard Bernstein, Rudolf Hilferding, Friedrich Adler, Ernst Mach, John Maynard Keynes, Sidney and Beatrice Webb, Oswald Spengler, Pierre-Joseph Proudhon, Peter Struve, Julius Martov, Victor Chernov, Irakli Tsereteli, Philipp Scheidemann, Otto Bauer, Nikolai Sukhanov, Alexander Bogdanov, Clara Zetkin, Leon Trotsky, and, with particular delight, his erstwhile mentors Georgy Plekhanov and Karl Kautsky.

law is not applicable. But they also belong intimately to this world, which they try to change or fix; they therefore still depend on the laws which they suspend. Deleuze and Guattari write that "sorcerers have always held the anomalous position, at the edge of the fields or woods. They haunt the fringes. They are at the borderline of the village, or between villages."[13]

But sorcerers do not only exist at the border: as anomalous beings, they are the border itself. In other words, the borderline passes through their bodies. In Deleuze and Guattari's framework, this borderline runs between two multiplicities, or two packs.[14] The anomalous individual belongs to neither of these packs, but instead enters into secret alliances: "The important thing is their affinity with alliance, with the pact, which gives them a status opposed to that of filiation. The relation with the anomalous is the one of alliance. The sorcerer has a relation of alliance with the demon as the power of the anomalous."[15] However, the border between two multiplicities is not the only border where witches can be found. I would like to complement Deleuze and Guattari's schematic with three additional kinds of borders, which I first outlined some time ago: 1) the border between something and a similar thing; 2) between something and a different thing; 3) between something and nothing.[16]

I am particularly interested in the third border, where we face the ultimate edge of the world. Locating the witch at this border can help us understand how miracles work. If we consider the 'real' world as a unity of things (okay, you can call it a multiplicity, but still, within its border it functions as a kind of unity), the witch definitely breaks up this unity in a freaky way, while also being part of it. On the one hand, the witch secures this unity by using her body to fill in the holes in being. On the other hand, she breaks it – behind her back there is either another world, whose agency she represents, or there is nothingness. It is said that witches do not have a back. I think that having no back means precisely that there is nothingness behind the witch. This is why it's so difficult to hunt her. The moment she turns her back to you, she disappears.

As Federici shows, the persecution of witches was an instance of gendered violence on a massive scale. The victims were overwhelmingly women. However, I would like to differentiate between real victims of the Inquisition who were accused of witchcraft, and the witch more generally, or the magician, or the sorcerer – the border figure, whose body is neither male nor female,

---

13 Deleuze & Guattari 1987: 246.
14 Editor's note: See Deleuze & Guattari "Memories of a Sorcerer, I:" "A becoming-animal always involves a pack, a band, a population, a peopling, in short, a multiplicity. We sorcerers have always known that [...] We do not wish to say that certain animals live in packs. We want nothing to do with ridiculous evolutionary classifications à la Lorenz, according to which there are inferior packs and superior societies. What we are saying is that every animal is fundamentally a band, a pack. That it has pack modes, rather than characteristics, even if further distinctions within these modes are called for. It is at this point that the human being encounters the animal. We do not become animal without a fascination for the pack, for multiplicity. A fascination for the outside?" (Deleuze & Guattari 1987: 239-240)
15 Ibid.
16 See Timofeeva 2013.

neither animal nor human, neither young nor old, neither alive nor dead. In my view, this figure is perfectly queer. Think about witches in fairy tales. Baba Yaga, the witch from Russian folklore, is a ferocious old woman who, by all appearances, exists on the border between life and death. It is said that her nose "grows into the roof," which means that the wooden hut where she lives (at the edge of the forest) is as small as a coffin. Witches can transform into birds, frogs, snakes, and so forth – they can be anything, but the 'real' world always remains intolerable to them. Between something that is and something that is not – that is, nothing – their bodies bear within them that active part of nonbeing that we call desire. Seeing a naked woman flying on a broom during the night, an ordinary human being might think that a witch's desire is sexual. But it is more than that. A witch's desire is ontological: it must be strong enough to transform something that is not into something that is, nonbeing into being (to trigger rain, to raise the dead). Such a transformation is a miracle.

Let's return to Lenin and his great-grandmother the witch, who inspires me infinitely. Among the many things that Lenin surely inherited from her was his insistence that miracles are possible. It is possible to make something out of nothing – that is, to transform something that is not into something that is, to bring something into being from nonbeing. As noted by Ronald Boer – who, in his study *Lenin, Religion, and Theology*, sees in the notion of the miracle "a crucial dimension of Lenin's approach to revolution"[17] – Lenin used to say that intelligent people do not believe in miracles that happen all of a sudden. At the same time, he developed an alternative conception of the miracle, insisting that people can perform them if they are enthusiastic enough, if they are driven and capable of making a supreme effort.

"Every man and every woman is a star,"[18] said Aleister Crowley. In Lenin's sense, every man and every woman is a miracle man and a miracle woman. There is something demonic in this: as Lenin sees it, miracles do not simply happen, nor can they be ascribed to God or to some other supreme being; they are performed by real people themselves. Lenin famously said that "a revolution is a miracle."[19]

In his writings and speeches, Lenin clearly appreciates the miraculous aspect of great human endeavours – such as political struggle and hard work for the sake of socialist revolution. For Lenin, the radical breakthrough that is revolution is a "miracle." In Badiou's terminology, this kind of breakthrough is called an "event." But in Lenin's framework, "miracle" is the better word since it describes something that transpires precisely when that thing seems most impossible. People create miracles in a desperate attempt to overcome the state of impotence they face in a given situation. We never know in advance, we risk everything, and only then, retroactively, can we discern a miraculous dimension to our efforts. In 1917, Lenin wrote:

17 Boer 2013: 141.
18 Crowley 2018: 6.
19 Lenin 1973: 153.

> There are no miracles in nature or history, but every abrupt turn in history, and this applies to every revolution, presents such a wealth of content, unfolds such unexpected and specific combinations of forms of struggle and alignment of forces of the contestants, that to the lay mind there is much that must appear miraculous.[20]

A dozen years prior, in 1905, he stated in "Two Tactics of Social-Democracy in the Democratic Revolution":

> Revolutions are the locomotives of history, said Marx. Revolutions are the festivals of the oppressed and the exploited. At no other time are the masses of the people in a position to come forward so actively as creators of a new social order as at a time of revolution. At such times the people are capable of performing miracles, if judged by the narrow, philistine scale of gradual progress.[21]

According to Boer, "Lenin's overt usage of miracle lays its emphasis on human energy, effort and enthusiasm [...] Yet it requires stupendous moments for such miracles to occur, moments that evoke almost superhuman effort from those who did [not] know they could do so."[22]

I would like to highlight Boer's use of the word "superhuman." There is a clearly Nietzschean aspect to Lenin's politics: the human, the all-too-human being, is the subject who overcomes. Desperation can move mountains – we all know this, but we rarely dare. In Boer's interpretation, a key part of Lenin's equating of revolution with miracle is the tension between organisation and spontaneity, between the so-called vanguard party and the spontaneity of the people. Organisation and spontaneity are two terms in dialectical opposition, and what appears miraculous is their synthesis. That is where political magic begins, and the political technic ends.

We must make a crucial distinction between Lenin's magic and the magic of the lonely child with whom I began. The novelty of Lenin's magic is that miracles are brought about by collectivities of people rather than by individuals. In a materialist sense, the condition of possibility for Lenin's miracle is collectivity itself. The superpowers of the magicians of revolution come from solidarity and comradeship. In my view, this solidarity and comradeship has something in common with witchcraft. Witchcraft transforms and renders impersonal the body of the witch, who is otherwise individualised, scrutinised, and punished by the witch hunt. Solidarity and comradeship, as forms of person-to-person attachment, also do away with individual identity. They are different from friendship and love, where the unique identities of the people involved is fundamental. In solidarity

---
20 Lenin 1974: 297.
21 Lenin 1977: 113.
22 Boer 2013: 139.

and comradeship, identity vanishes: I love this particular person, but my comrades are treated anonymously and equally regardless of who they are.

Lenin and other so-called professional revolutionaries worked underground. This was called *konspiratsiia*. According to Lars Lih, in Lenin's historical context *konspiratsiia* referred to "all the practical rules of conduct needed to elude the police," or the "fine art of not getting arrested."[23] One should not confuse konspiratsiia with 'conspiracy.' As Lih explains, the logic of konspiratsiia is precisely the opposite of conspiracy: "A conspiracy means keeping information and knowledge within the small group, so that it can go and knock off somebody or lead a palace coup. *Konspiratsiia* is the opposite – it is about getting knowledge and ideas out to as many people as possible."[24] Lih paraphrases a passage from *What Is to Be Done?* that describes a concrete example of *konspiratsiia*:

> Although a strike might not be secret to anybody in the town where it happens, people across the country might not know about it, so our task is to get that word out and let everybody know about it. But in order to do that we need people organising professionally in underground conditions in order to get the report, write it up, send it off to Geneva, where the paper is printed, and then smuggle it back into Russia again for distributing. This demands the logic of *konspiratsiia* – empirically worked-out rules for not getting arrested.[25]

Sometimes people forget that 'Lenin' was the underground nickname of a person actually named Vladimir Ulyanov. Bolsheviks in *konspiratsiia* lived faked social lives under fake names, constantly changing their passports, families, appearances, and even genders. What connected them was that they were all comrades. In her theory of the comrade, Jodi Dean suggests four theses that "articulate a generic political component activated through divisive fidelity to the emancipatory egalitarian struggle for communism:"[26]

1. 'Comrade' names a relation characterised by sameness, equality, and solidarity. For communists, this sameness, equality, and solidarity is utopian, cutting through the determinations of capitalist society.
2. Anyone but not everyone can be a comrade.
3. The Individual (as a locus of identity) is the 'other' of the comrade.
4. The relation between comrades is mediated by fidelity to a truth. Practices of comradeship materialize this fidelity, building its truth into the world.[27]

---

23 Lih 2011: 67.
24 Lih 2010.
25 Ibid.
26 Dean 2017.
27 Ibid.

According to Dean, "a comrade is one of many fighting on the same side."[28] I want to complement Dean's theory by detailing some metamorphic and miraculous moments of comradeship.[29] Comrades are replaceable. This aspect of the masquerade makes politics a theatre, but a very special one, similar to Artaud's theatre of cruelty; here, ancient masks return, as they present a show, a ritual of direct and instant communication. The mask is more important than the face behind it (if there is one) – it directly communicates affect. We must understand that we live in a society in which individualism is recognised as a supreme value. Everyone is required to have an identity: we are identical in that we all have to be clearly identifiable. Comradeship, in the sense that I am trying to develop here, transgresses this rule: it breaks with identitarian ideology, it is destructive of the individual, autonomous person. In his conception of theatre, Artaud attacks classical Western theatre – where actors represent characters and so on – and instead advocates a "superior notion of the theatre," which he compares to a plague, a contagion:

> Like the plague, theatre is a crisis resolved either by death or cure. The plague is a superior disease because it is an absolute crisis after which there is nothing left except death or drastic purification. In the same way, theatre is a disease because it is a final balance that cannot be obtained without destruction. It urges the mind on to delirium which intensifies its energy. And finally from a human viewpoint we can see that the effect of the theatre is as beneficial as the plague, impelling us to see ourselves as we are, making the masks fall and divulging our world's lies, aimlessness, meanness and even two-facedness. It shakes off stifling material dullness which even overcomes the senses' clearest testimony, and collectively reveals their dark powers and hidden strength to men, urging them to take a nobler, more heroic stand in the face of destiny than they would have assumed without it. And the question we must now ask ourselves is to know whether in this world that is slipping away, committing suicide without realising it, a nucleus of men can be found to impress this higher idea of theatre on the world, to bring to all of us a natural, occult equivalent of the dogma we no longer believe.[30]

Similarly, in comradeship, there is no individual, but only a set of appearances that run from one figure to another. The only stable thing between

---
28 Ibid.
29 Editor's note: For a more in-depth theorisation of the notion of the comrade, see Dean's *Comrade: An Essay On Political Belonging* (2019).
30 Artaud 2010: 21-22.

comrades is the essence of their solidarity: the shared cause. The comrade is someone on whose neck you can place your own head, someone to whom you can give one of your own hands if she has none at the decisive moment when the enemy attacks. Friendship and love cannot sustain such disturbing acts of fellowship – they are too innocent, too kind, too human. As we showed above, the emergence of witch hunts coincides historically with the birth of humanism in its classical sense. Comradeship transcends the borders of this humanism, placing it in the same category as sorcery, with its secret alliances, communication with beasts, and of course, breathtaking naked night flights.

Comradeship is not an easy thing: along with sorcery, it can evoke forces that an individual cannot control. These forces can be destructive, as in Goethe's story of "The Sorcerer's Apprentice" (1797) who, when his old master leaves, initiates a powerful magical process that he cannot stop because he does not know how. Georges Bataille links this figure to art: "The 'sorcerer's apprentice,' first of all, does not encounter demands that are any different from those he would encounter on the difficult road of art."[31]

Indeed, art is closely linked to both witchcraft and comradeship. Let me refer to the works of my comrade Nikolay Oleynikov, of the group *Chto Delat*, who paints weird, monstrous collective bodies that shatter the continuity of nature and portray strange interspecies alliances. At his 2015 installation *Oslobodenje: The Burlesque Museum*, held in Tito's bunker in the mountains near Sarajevo, a canvas in a modest wooden frame depicted a big Courbet-like vagina, from which emerged a realistic brown bullhead with a yellow tag in its ear. In another canvas (*Romantic Collection*, 2013), a penis ended in a mad dog's head, which barked while its entire body was being masturbated. In other canvases, a person's face was replaced with an animal's head, with a flower, with something or someone else. "Who are all these characters?" I asked Nikolay. "They are folks," he replied. These motley folks gathered together transgender dancers, bulls, philosophers, horses, cats and dogs, girls, wolves, roses, fingers, spirits and ghosts, vampires, and other living, dead, and of course undead creatures. Brecht, Lenin, Gramsci, and Hegel rose from their graves and took their places among a utopian group of 'folks.'

In this impersonal multiplicity, there is no one. What does this 'no one' mean? It means a structural impossibility for 'one' to be. A comrade is never alone – not in the trivial sense that there is always someone else around, but in the more radical sense that you are always many. You are Legion. This is how you succeed in "the fine art of not getting arrested," persecuted, or burned alive by the inquisitors of your age. When you are many, you turn your back to the police officer and disappear. Comradeship creates a shield against the witch hunters who will try to catch us one by one, but who will

---

31 Bataille 1986: 233.

never destroy the whole set of alliances that make up the Great Sorcery International.

References

Artaud, Antonin (2013), *The Theatre and its Double*. London: Alma Classics.

Bataille, Georges (1986), *Visions of Excess: Selected Writings 1927-1939*. Minneapolis: University of Minnesota Press.

Boer, Roland (2013), *Lenin, Religion and Theology*. New York: Palgrave Macmillan.

Campagna, Federico (2018), *Technic and Magic*. London: Bloomsbury.

Crowley, Aleister (2018), *The Aleister Crowley Collection*. Los Angeles: Enhanced Media Publishing.

Dean, Jodi (2019), *Comrade: An Essay On Political Belonging*. London: Verso.

Dean, Jodi (2017), "Four Theses On The Comrade," *e-flux #86*. Accessed on 23.10.2020, at https://www.e-flux.com/journal/86/160585/four-theses-on-the-comrade/.

Descartes, René, Spinoza, Benedict de, and Gottfried Wilhelm Freiherr von Leibniz (1960), *The Rationalists*. New York: Dolphin Books.

Deleuze, Gilles and Felix Guattari (1987), *A Thousand Plateaus. Capitalism and Schizophrenia*. Minneapolis: University of Minnesota Press.

Federici, Silvia (2014), *Caliban and the Witch: Women, the Body and Primitive Accumulation*. New York: Autonomedia.

Lafargue, Paul (1883), *The Right To Be Lazy*. Marxist Internet Archive. Accessed on 25.10.2020, at https://www.marxists.org/archive/lafargue/1883/lazy/index.htm.

Lenin, V.I. (1973), *Collected Works Vol. 32*. Moscow: Progress Publishers.

Lenin, V.I. (1974), *Collected Works Vol. 23*. Moscow: Progress Publishers.

Lenin, V.I. (1977), *Collected Works Vol. 9*. Moscow: Progress Publishers.

Lih, Lars T. (2010), "Scotching the myths about Lenin's 'What is to be done'," *Links – International Journal of Socialist Renewal*. Accessed on 23.10.2020, at http://links.org.au/node/1953.

Lih, Lars T. (2011), *Lenin*. London: Reaktion Books.

Timofeeva, Oxana (2013), "Imagine There's No Void," *Filozofski vestnik*, 34(2), 163-175.

16. Lenin, the Revolution, and the Uncertainties of Communism in the Works of Platonov

Tora Lane

To seek in the words of Andrei Platonov an understanding of the importance of Lenin – as a thinker of politics, of Marxism, or even of the Russian revolution – is like peering into the substance of the sun to discover its actual meaning: its radiating force cannot be explained merely by the movement of its atoms or by its minimal constituents, but must be understood through the experience of the light and warmth it provides. In a similar vein, Lenin's significance as a historical figure, or rather as a historical fact synonymous with the fact of the revolution, is revealed in Platonov's novels through the godlike aura that Lenin seemed to exude for the Russian people who adhered to the cause of the revolution, as the oracular leader of its movement and founding father of the Soviet state. Indeed, there is almost something Christ-like about Platonov's Lenin as portrayed through their minds, perhaps most prominently in the novel *Chevengur*, which deals with the theme of the first years of the revolution. Here, the revolution appears above all as a Second Coming – without god or religion, but with a higher principle of life: the principle of the truth of socialism. In its name, Lenin embodies socialism as a promise "like the sun [that] will ascend higher in the summer," as one of the characters in *Chevengur* exclaims.[1] In Platonov's works, the reassuring suggestive notion that "Lenin is with us" – as the cover of the book declares – is at least as important as Lenin's theories of the revolution or his historical deeds. This is not to say, however, that communism and Lenin are all sun, light and warmth in Platonov's writings, nor that he merely confirms the monumentalised image of the nascent official Leninist cult; rather, Platonov portrays the contradictory importance of Lenin through the minds and deeds of the people who believed in him. It is through their perspectives that Lenin simultaneously becomes the leader of a historical process and an ideology that runs amok in its implementation, and consequently forms a surface on which the hopes, desires and enthusiasms that the ideology evoked in them can be reflected or projected.

Andrei Platonov (1899-1951) was a unique chronicler of the Russian revolution and of post-revolutionary society precisely because of his peculiar internal or immanent perspective of recounting the revolution always through the understanding of its everyday protagonists. In a sense, one could say that the Soviet Russian writer offered a phenomenological reading of the revolution in his literary works. This is not to say that Platonov was a phenomenologist, rather to suggest that his understanding or rendering of the importance of Lenin and of the revolution (and of Lenin *as* the revolution)

---
1 Platonov 1978: 98.

cannot be understood solely through the historical facts or its/his teachings or ideology, but instead must be retrieved through the minds and lived experiences of the protagonists of the revolution – ordinary people – interpreting it/him in their own lives and deeds. What Platonov 'actually' thought about Lenin as a historical person and his politics of the revolution is difficult to tell, since that would imply the possibility of a transcendental point of reference, whereas Platonov remained faithful to the Marxist idea that society can only be understood from within the concrete situation and the immanent perspective of the people. This does not imply a blind or thoughtless subordination to party dictate, rather an extreme form of immanent critique, which became increasingly evident over the course of his works.

In *The Foundation Pit*, for example, Platonov tells the story of laying the foundation of a future house for all proletarians, a task which instead turns into the digging of a mass grave. Conceptually, this can be read as an anti-utopian critique of the project of building Soviet society (*Sovetskii stroi*): the novel ends with a postscript in which Platonov indeed expressed concern about the revolutionary cause gone wrong or becoming lost in the post-revolutionary world.[2]

Yet what most marks Platonov's writings is his paradoxical vision, wherein the impact of the revolution, and the course of its political development, is depicted out of, and from within, the people's own experience – *as if* this experience were being communicated through their own consciousness and language. Communism, ideology and the state do not appear as solely abstract categories; the party and its slogans are almost always represented through concrete people, be it the voice of a party functionary, a revolutionary fighter or a proletarian worker. At the same time, the atrocities committed in the name of Lenin, of the revolution and/or of communism, are rendered in naïve style through the beliefs of those who took part in the revolutionary struggle – without any comment from a critical onlooker. Thus, for instance, the 'proletarian' citizens of *Chevengur* literally set out to liquidate the bourgeoisie through mass murder in accordance with the dogma that the bourgeois class must be eliminated for communism to be achieved. While no one condemns this development, it results in a fundamental sense of alienation, as the protagonists are faced with the disastrous consequences of their deeds – the grotesque conclusion of their own appropriation of the political language.

Lenin's revolutionary politics thus acquires a very specific meaning in Platonov's literary treatment of it, a meaning that is contingent upon and yet transcends the political theories on which it is based. The revolution is portrayed as an historically given fact through the very event of the

---

[2] An orphan girl, Nastya, is buried in the grave and the writer comments: "The author may have been mistaken to portray in the form of a little girl's death the end of the socialist generation, but this mistake occurred only as a result of excessive alarm on behalf of something beloved, whose loss is tantamount to the destruction not only of all the past, but also of all the future." (Platonov 2009: 150)

Bolshevik seizure of power and the proclamation of the Soviet state, and yet in the political language through which it is taught and spread – in the form of Marxist dogma, Lenin's theses, Soviet propaganda, but very rarely in the form of theory as such – the revolution is not a given, but something constantly in the making. Moreover, this 'something' is engulfed by uncertainty as to how it is to be interpreted, understood and implemented. In this way, Platonov exposes a double bind in the idea that the revolution had already taken place and yet was to be implemented through the people, who did not fully understand the meaning of the ideological dictates and yet somehow willed them. In a way, this is consistent with and conveys the consequences of the Bolshevik idea that the revolution was to be led by a vanguard of professional revolutionaries and subsequently spread amongst the people in the form of spontaneity-consciousness dialectics.

But Platonov also depicts the revolution and Lenin's framing of it in a language that is not the master of its own meaning, and yet is full of meaning. In other words, while it was vital that the revolution be disseminated through the appeal of Lenin's ideological directives, thereby teaching the masses its political meaning, this did not mean that the masses, on an existential level, understood or even experienced the revolution as intended, nor that the revolution was simply ideological and false. In fact, Platonov portrays Lenin as a leader who eschews any prescription as to how the meaning of his teachings should be actually interpreted and yet, precisely because of this, becomes the loadstar of the revolution in terms of both its inspirational promise and its dismal implementation. Platonov thus reveals how the directive enters a space of ideological uncertainty, a difference with regards to itself, which is not to be understood as the reason for its failure, but rather points to its real political impact in the form of people's contradictory understanding and application of it.

This is perhaps most notable in *Chevengur*, a novel consisting of a compilation of several shorter stories woven together through the destiny of the young Sasha Dvanov who – accompanied by Kopenkin, a fervent admirer of Rosa Luxemburg, and his horse Proletarian Strength – wanders through rural Russia in his fight for the revolutionary cause. A central story depicts the foundation and building of the city of Chevengur, a place where, in the words of one of its inhabitants, communism already exists; here the protagonists make a halt. It soon becomes evident, however, that what this 'communism' precisely is/means, to what kind of phenomenon the word relates in actuality, is unclear to its inhabitants. There is only a general sense that communism refers to a society that is concerned with the people, the poor and the downtrodden, and that it is meant to bring happiness. The characters, we are told, wait for Lenin to come, "as a guest here in Communism, so that there in Chevengur he could embrace all the sufferers of the earth and put an end to the movement of unhappiness in life."[3] The expression "in Communism" is symptomatic of the idiomatic slips through which Platonov renders the people's appropriation, or rather their domesticising translation, of abstract political terms into colloquial Russian diction: the word "Communism" is used here as a proper noun to denote a place, rather than a political idea or structure. It indicates not only a concretisation of the term, but also a typical way of establishing a sense of familiarity that is characteristic of people's language. Furthermore, no one in the city knows how the "Communism" they have proclaimed can be achieved, because no one really knows the actual meaning of the word. A large part of the novel is based, therefore, on this opposition between the idea that communism is realised in the city of Chevengur and the fact that all its protagonists are searching for its precise meaning. One character, "the Jap," exclaims that "it's not clear if we have communism fixed here or not. I ought to go see comrade Lenin, so that he could formulate the whole truth for me!"[4] Another, Chepurnyi, knows "all Lenin's teachings word by word,"[5] and yet he cannot make any connections or sense out of his memories and thoughts, and therefore all that he remembers "constituted no useful ideas whatsoever." The awkwardly naïve and inconspicuous use of language to convey what is not correctly understood is very funny, and yet, at the same time, utterly serious as a portrayal of the workings of the revolution as a quest for its true meaning, not only through the characters' search for it but also in the novel itself.

In his investigation of the importance of Lenin in and beyond his teachings and actual political strategies, Platonov's treatment has something in common with Slavoj Žižek's conclusion in *Repeating Lenin*: "As a result, *repeating* Lenin does not mean a *return* to Lenin – to repeat Lenin is to accept that 'Lenin is dead,' that his particular solution failed, even failed monstrously, but that there was a utopian spark in it worth saving."[6] In the works of Platonov too, Lenin stands for the utopian spark of the revolution and the imperative of communism, yet in their interpretation of this utopian spark, Žižek and Platonov differ. The former goes on to spell out this spark in capital letters: "LENIN WAS NOT AFRAID TO SUCCEED," meaning that he was not afraid to lead the revolution in spite of its uncertainties as an "open situation." For Žižek, therefore, Lenin must be repeated not as a lesson that can be derived from the history of communism in the Soviet Union and the Eastern Bloc, but as a readiness to enter an uncertain historical situation through the multiple doors that were opened by the revolution. In a way, repeating Lenin is thus also to unlearn Lenin, since he did not actually treat the revolution in terms of openness, but was driven by a belief in the necessity of the dialectical laws of history, combined with a conviction that the

---

3 Platonov 1978: 227.
4 Ibid: 184.
5 Ibid: 178.
6 Žižek 2002: 310.

situation in Russia called for an overtaking of power, a "violent revolution" as he argued in *State and Revolution*. In other words, Lenin was not afraid to succeed, but he appears not to have been afraid to fail either. The Bolshevik revolution thus emerges as the pure success of communism, albeit without clear ideas about its implementation. To a certain extent, we can infer from this a crucial aspect of Leninism: the insistence on the utter necessity of the revolution *per se,* as the only way means of achieving the triumph of socialism. It is the revolution as an actual event that enabled the factual possibility of socialism/communism as an entirely different state and world order, dictated or at least somehow mediated in and through the people who created it.

Yet the necessity of the revolution is nevertheless intimately linked with the openness or rather the uncertainty of the "utopian spark" of Lenin as an historical character and/or in the minds of the people. To understand this utopian spark, we must examine the relationship between his failed ideology and his "utopian energy."[7] As I have sought to demonstrate, if we are to believe Platonov, Lenin first and foremost denotes the very fact of the Russian revolution and the possibility of communism on earth in the minds of the people, but what that actually means, what communism actually *is*, remains a question for the people themselves to understand and interpret. Platonov conveys this through a peculiar language, which the Nobel laureate Joseph Brodsky, who was important in canonising Platonov as one of the foremost Soviet writers and was influential in framing the reception of his works outside of the USSR, characterised as revealing "a self-destructive eschatological element in the language itself"[8] and in particular of the "revolutionary eschatology"[9] of Soviet newspeak. Thus, Brodsky placed Platonov on the side of writers who were actively critical of the totalitarian dictate of the Soviet leader.[10]

In other words, according to Brodsky, Platonov would seem to concur with Hannah Arendt's critique of totalitarianism, which for her is the consequence of a strong leader's dictatorial manipulations of the masses with the purpose of the political formation of the people in order to target their existential experience of life itself.[11] Platonov's insistence on the misunderstandings and uncertainty of the revolutionary eschatology, however, shows how he diverges from Arendt's critique of totalitarianism. To begin with, he reveals a paradoxical situation in which the people's existential experience of life is dictated by the revolution in an uncertain way. Moreover, he understands the ideology of the revolution as containing a quest for the truth of the

---

7 A term used by Stefan Jonsson in Lane 2017: 40.
8 Brodsky 1986: 287.
9 Ibid: 283.
10 In the same text, Brodsky concedes that "this willingness, not to say abandon, with which he went for newspeak, indicates, it would seem, his sharing of some beliefs in the promises the new society was so generous with." (Ibid: 288)
11 Hannah Arendt even argued that only through the suppression of experience itself could the totalitarian state be effectuated (Arendt 1968: 22).

existential experience of the people and their interpretation of the political language, with all of their mistakes. The realisation of communism on earth as a form of Second Coming is at the same time a return to the people themselves. As one of the inhabitants of *Chevengur* states: "Even Lenin does not have to know that about communism, because it's a job for the whole proletariat all at once, and not just one by one. You ought not to get used to being smarter than the proletariat."[12] This is to say that for the people the truth of the revolution does not have to be a given, not even Lenin has to know it, because its truth lies in its utopian realisation by everyone, by "the whole proletariat at once."[13]

Platonov thus seeks a meaning in the experience of the people, while remaining faithful to the idea that the realisation of the revolution depends on their consciousness. This consciousness, however, is not communal in a political sense: the world made common is called upon as a political dictate, but it creates itself through the contradictory experiences of the people that it hailed as the revolutionary force. What the people in Chevengur are looking for in the communist utopia is themselves as people, albeit a process lived as a nameless experience, exemplified by the orphan Dvanov who carries the surname of the family that took care of him because no one remembers the name of his own family, and who throughout the novel searches for a name for himself and for what he carries inside of him:

> No matter how much he read and thought, some kind of hollow place always remained ever within him, an emptiness through which an undescribed and untold world passed like a startled wind. At seventeen Dvanov still had no armour over his heart, neither belief in God nor any other intellectual. He did not give a stranger's name to the nameless life which opened before him. However, he did not want that world to remain untitled; he only waited to hear its own proper name, instead of a purposely conceived appellation.[14]

For Dvanov, the revolution means the possibility to retrieve this "undescribed and untold world," the world of the nobodies who, according to the International, were to become the all: "We are nothing, let us be all." The revolution means the quest for this untold experience to receive its proper name, to take part in universal culture, but not to be found or named as a purely subjective experience. Rather, socialism denotes for Platonov the quest for an existential sense of commonality, or the insight that existential commonality is the condition for the experience of sense. It is in this utopian

---
12 Platonov 1978: 237.
13 Ibid: 222.
14 Ibid: 43.

vein that Platonov develops a modernist prose and language, breaking with established forms of narrative and normative language in classical realist Russian in order to convey the untold experience of the people in their immanence. To retrieve this name is a promise of socialism as provided precisely by the utopian spark of the failure of Lenin.

To conclude, Leninism sometimes stands for the success of certain tactics that led to the proletarian people's revolution in Russia 1917. In Platonov's assessment, however, Lenin's revolution does not mean the realisation of communism as an actual reality, but rather as the presence of the utopian spark in the failure of ideology to do or be precisely what it says: as such, the revolution appears as a forgotten dream, or "a memory of the future." In this sense, Lenin represents the fact that, after the revolution, the Russian people became driven by the beautiful idea of communism as something that is at once made present through the revolution and as something that is yet to come. The revolution as a dream becomes a loadstar in the abysmal darkness of its own implementation, which points, if we are to believe Platonov, not to the similarities of the terrifying consequences of totalitarian ideology, but precisely to its differences. Ideology works not through its dictates, but through its misunderstandings, which is to say that Lenin and the revolution did not signify the realisation of communism but a memory of the future, in terms of the realised possibility of seeking the shared truth of the world, and the truth of the world as shared. Without socialism, this may be forgotten.

References
Arendt, Hannah (1968), *Totalitarianism. Part Three of the Origins of Totalitarianism.* New York: Harcourt, Inc.
Brodsky, Joseph (1986), *Less than One: Selected Essays.* New York: Farrar, Straus, Giroux.
Jonsson, Stefan (2017), "Subalternernas utopi," *in* Tora Lane (ed.), *Läsningar av Platonov.* Stockholm: Ersatz.
Platonov, Andrei (1978), *Chevengur.* Ann Arbor: Ardis Publishers.
Platonov, Andrei (2009), *The Foundation Pit.* New York: New York Review Books.
Žižek, Slavoj (2002), *Revolution at the Gates. V.I. Lenin: A Selection of Writings from February to October 1917.* London: Verso.

17. Eleven Theses on Lenin in the Corona Era

Thomas Rudhof-Seibert

When I gladly accepted the offer to contribute to this book, the Coronavirus was not yet on the map. As I write now (20.03.2020), it seems the world is talking about almost nothing else. Although, with the exception of Slavoj Žižek,[1] nobody has yet made the connection to Lenin, there are obvious links to the decisive thinker behind the question, "What is to be done?" In fact, we might just be witnessing a "Lenin moment":[2] suddenly many things seem possible that were previously considered impossible. This not only concerns the coercive measures employed by the media and the police to isolate millions of people, and the suspension of basic rights. Nor does it only concern solidarity, in which individuals assume responsibility towards themselves and, without exception, towards all others (see XI.5 below). Rather, the impossibility that has suddenly become possibility concerns the entire process of capitalist globalisation, i.e. the prevailing dynamic of the last five decades and, at the same time, the whole of postcolonial modernity. It thus concerns the transformation of the world in its entirety, which for decades has been considered impossible. Tomorrow, it seems, the free circulation of capital, goods and services around the globe might come to an end, as the movement of people, which has always been regulated, is abruptly and completely curtailed, every one of us being detained in our current location. It is also clear, however, that the closure of national borders in itself necessitates binding global rules, and it is equally clear that nation states, as the creditors of a near-paralysed global economy, could be called upon from all sides to nationalise production to a significant extent. It is therefore hardly remarkable that the neoliberal dogma of "austerity" – with its compulsory balancing of state budgets – is no longer worth the paper on which, only yesterday, it was prescribed for all eternity, on whatever dubious grounds and with whatever sinister intentions. If everything can so suddenly become completely different from before, and given that the post-Corona world will no longer be the same, the Left must, in all urgency, turn once more towards Lenin: "What is to be done?" This is less about concrete instructions than about what one could call the spirit of Leninist thought and action: the resolve to engage with history in the purest sense of the word, namely with the possibility of a revolutionary rupture of fundamental and thereby world-historical significance.

---

1 See Žižek 2020. Žižek writes not of Lenin himself, but of a "Lenin moment."
2 Porcaro 2013: 89.

I.

Let us then investigate the "Lenin moment." The term signifies not only a specific historical moment, but a way of thinking and acting that is characterised by extreme openness to even the most inconspicuous changes in the given situation. It found its ideal-typical expression in the Bolshevik revolutionary leader and is therefore encapsulated by his *nom de guerre*: "Lenin therefore is a continuous *movement of rupture* in the face of convictions, of political lines and of organisational forms, which, having matured in a preceding situation, tend by inertia to repeat their problems and solutions and therefore remain prisoners of the old class relations. This is the fundamental core of the concept of party (and therefore of communist politics) in Lenin: [...] the idea of a politics that continuously shifts the more simple and direct reactions of the movements and *of the party itself,* raising them to a level at which it is possible to understand the reciprocal relations among all the classes and between all the classes and the state and *therefore* to understand the *continuous change* of these relations – for a communist goal, which [...] is always itself subject to incessant redefinition."[3]

I.1

To promote revolutionary self-empowerment with an orientation towards the sudden dawning of the "eve of revolution," in 1902 Lenin wrote *What is to be done?*[4] The book differentiates between three conflicting modes of thought and action with regard to the revolution:

I.2

truly revolutionary, "social democratic" thought and action, which according to current language usage, based on the schism of the Second and the foundation of the Third International, is called communist;

I.3

the simultaneously "economistic" and "opportunistic" limitation of revolutionary activity to a purely trade-unionist sphere and rationale, which in today's language is called social democratic or socialist thought and action;

I.4

the abstract negation of economism through "revolutionary" thought and action, which perpetually imagines itself on the "eve of the revolution," wants to bring on the dawn via force ("terrorism") and thereby also falls prey to opportunism; we refer to this today rather as anarchism, in the sense of an existentially driven voluntarism.

---

3 Ibid: 135.
4 Lenin 1977: 304.

II.

What is to be done? remains relevant to this day because the triad of social democrats (communists), opportunists (social democrats) and revolutionists (anarchists) is not only to be found in early 20th century Russia. It was, and is, also found in all social struggles of capitalist modernity and in all emancipatory movements, including in locations where the terms themselves are not used. Thus understood, anarchist, social democratic and communist tendencies existed and exist not only in the workers' movement, but also in the youth, student and women's movements, in the anti-colonial and anti-racist movements, in all broadly anti-normalist movements, as well as in the ecological and even the democratic movements. Socialism, anarchism and communism thus signify the structural differences in all emancipatory action and thereby form the three elementary answers to the question, "What is to be done?" Those seeking illumination of this should read (not only for this reason) Emile Zola's great novel *Germinal*, which personalises the inner conflicts of a miners' uprising in the 1860s in the form of three protagonists, whose position can be understood as typically social democratic ("economic-opportunistic"), typically communist ("social democratic") and typically anarchistic ("revolutionary"). If, in what follows, I at first focus on Lenin, it must be noted that the structural character of the triad of emancipatory action has an intrinsic quality, including tendencies criticised by Lenin, to which we will turn our attention in due course.[5]

II.2

The error of both social democracy and anarchism lies, according to Lenin, in their "bowing to spontaneity."[6] This orientation is economistic and opportunistic, he argues, because it takes its cue from spontaneously emergent, on the whole economically driven social struggles, to which it seeks to "lend a political character"[7] based on their inherent nature, i.e. justified by their own logic and dynamics. For Lenin, however, such an orientation "degrades" a clearly universalistic politics to the level of executing what can always and only be a particularistic calculation of interests.[8] Lenin ascribes to economism a fundamental misinterpretation of Marx's central discovery, which was indeed not intended to be understood in terms of tactics. To illustrate this point, Lenin cites the opportunist newspaper *Rabocheye Dyelo*, which states in an apparently classical Marxist manner: "What Social-Democrat does not know that according to the theories of Marx and Engels the economic interests of certain classes play a decisive role in history, and, *consequently*, that particularly the proletariat's struggle

---

5 I make this reservation with thanks to Karin Zennig, who, as the first reader and comrade of this text, rightly insisted on an early clarification.
6 Ibid: 378 and 12 further instances.
7 Ibid: 401 and 18 further instances.
8 Ibid: 365 and ten other instances.

for its economic interests must also be of paramount importance in its class development and struggle for emancipation?" (Lenin's emphasis).

II.3

Lenin immediately presents his fundamental objection to this: "The word 'consequently' is completely irrelevant. The fact that economic interests play a decisive role *does not in the least imply* that the economic (i.e. trade union) struggle is of prime importance; for the most essential, the 'decisive' interests of classes can be satisfied *only by* radical *political* changes in general. In particular the fundamental economic interests of the proletariat can be satisfied only by a political revolution that replaces the dictatorship of the bourgeoisie by the dictatorship of the proletariat."[9] Whereas economic struggle arises spontaneously, political struggle comes about only by means of a conscious decision by those who struggle towards a universal project that transcends even their own immediate interests. Between spontaneity and consciousness, and thus between economy and politics, there lies a gaping, existential discontinuity; as a result, economic struggle cannot, in and of itself, be given a "political character." This is precisely the error made by both opportunists and revolutionists, who differ "only" in the choice of means (legality vs. illegality) with which they seek to politicise spontaneous struggle driven by narrow self-interest.

III.

Having formulated the polemic in this manner, Lenin arrives at his central thesis: that the consciousness necessary for leading the political struggle can only be brought to the proletariat "from without," through a tightly centralised organisation, initially consisting primarily of intellectuals, which must thereby act as a vanguard always one step ahead of the working classes.[10] The centrality of this thesis is clearly demonstrated by the fact that it is, to this day, the first point of reference for all objections made against Lenin. The majority of these objections, however, are undermined by a misunderstanding of the discontinuity that Lenin not only claimed but insisted upon between economics and politics, between spontaneity and consciousness. Contrary to what is generally assumed, this discontinuity must not be understood categorically, but specifically[11] – as is evident from the passage in which Lenin clarifies what he means by "from without," which we cite here in its entirety:

---

9 Ibid: 390-391.
10 Ibid: 375, 384, 422.
11 Nor, incidentally, should it be tied to the different types of existence of workers and intellectuals, nor to the divergence between looser and tighter forms of organising – which Lenin explicitly refers to tactically and not strategically, and which are to be abolished as soon as possible by alignment with the rules of German Social-Democracy. Cf. Ibid: 478f.

Class political consciousness can be brought to the workers *only from without*, that is, only from outside the economic struggle, from outside the sphere of relations between workers and employers. The sphere from which alone it is possible to obtain this knowledge is the sphere of relationships of all classes and strata to the state and the government, the sphere of interrelations between *all* classes. For that reason, the reply to the question as to what must be done to bring political knowledge to the workers cannot merely be the answer with which, in the majority of cases, the practical workers, especially those inclined towards Economism, mostly content themselves, namely: 'To go among the workers.' To bring political consciousness to the workers the Social Democrats must *go among all classes of the population*; they must dispatch units of their army *in all directions*.[12] (Lenin's emphasis)

IV.

There follow five passages in which Lenin indicates the actual tasks that the communists must carry out when, with regard to the "sphere of relationships of *all* classes and strata with the state and the government" and the "interrelations between all classes," they resolutely "go among all classes" and "dispatch units of their army in all directions."

IV.1

In the first passage, Lenin describes the political struggle, which is superior to all economic (i.e. particularistic) struggles, as an "all-round political struggle," that is, a universal struggle waged in consciousness of this universality.[13]

IV.2

In the second passage, Lenin qualifies the "all-round" communist struggle in the words of a worker as a struggle in which all the "sections of the people" will learn "how to live and how to die." As this existential demand for right action makes clear, the struggle is not only a political but an ethical one, and in the same sentence Lenin defines it as primarily a struggle for "publicity"[14] – i.e. a struggle that must be waged through public discourse. Lenin's use of the term "publicity" should not be reduced to the example he cites (newspapers) but understood as referring to the leading role that

---
12 Ibid: 422.
13 Ibid: 428.
14 Ibid: 477. Lenin uses the term "publicity" five times and, tellingly, ascribes to the ecomomists a "fear of publicity." Ibid: 364 and 478.

theory – i.e. discourse, reflection, debate, and thus education – plays in the relationship between theory and practice. Even in its most tangible praxis, the communist project is also an educational project; it is, in the words of Alain Badiou, a "politics of truth."[15]

IV.3

The third passage separates once again the political struggle, the "all-round" struggle carried out in all classes, from "the economic struggle against the employers and against the government," in that Lenin prescribes to the communists the task of "actively intervening in every 'liberal' issue and of determining *[their] own*, Social-Democratic [= communist] attitude towards this question." (Lenin's emphasis)[16] I will return to this point in IV.6 below.

IV.4

The fourth passage is found in a footnote at the end of the entire book and summarises the communist struggle in light of its explicitly universal goal, which according to Lenin, is "to transform radically the conditions of life of the whole of mankind." The universality of this goal corresponds to Lenin's admonition in the same sentence that the communists must not "be 'perturbed' by the question of the duration of the work."[17] This should be understood not only as a reference to the length of time needed to prepare the ground for revolution, but also to the utter suddenness with which it can arrive.

IV.5

Let us then get to the heart of the specific discontinuity between economistic and political struggle, as well as between spontaneity and consciousness. This discontinuity should *not* be conceived of as two sides: economism and spontaneity on one side, politics and consciousness on the other; unorganised struggling workers on one side, while on the other, organised professional revolutionary intellectuals, who move among the workers to bring consciousness and politics to them. Rather, the discontinuity between economism and politics, or spontaneity and consciousness, is intrinsic to the nature of spontaneity and consciousness *per se*. Those who spontaneously follow their particularistic, generally economic interests, and align their political affiliation accordingly, will change little or nothing in the consciousness that has informed them from the very beginning. S/he sets out, fights, wins or loses, achieves or does not achieve that which s/he desires. S/he is, at best, wiser as a result, but has not yet become someone else. If, however, the workers spontaneously pursuing their particularistic interests

---

15 For example, Badiou 2005.
16 Ibid: 436.
17 Ibid: 514.

in the struggle are to become communists, they must no longer be beholden to the spontaneity of their immediate interests, rather they must consciously pursue the universal interest in order to "to transform radically the conditions of life of the whole of mankind." They must therefore conduct their political struggle resolutely, over a longer period and in all directions and all classes of society. To do so, however, they must extend their consciousness, originally fixed on the calculation of their own economic interests, to a new, completely different consciousness: one that is at the same time moral and political. This, then, will be a consciousness that has learned "how to live and how to die," and how to lead this living and dying with regard to itself and all of humanity. Yet this consciousness of how one "should" live and die can only be adequate to its all-encompassing, radically universalistic task if it does so spontaneously, if those waging the struggle do not only – and this is ultimately the decisive point! – change their inherent consciousness, but also their inherent spontaneity. As an existential example of this anticipated change in both consciousness and spontaneity, and thus of existence itself, Lenin can then cite his own professional-revolutionary existence. The term "professional revolutionaries" does not only mean professionalism in a technical-pragmatic sense, but a specifically adopted vocation – a "profession" in the purest sense (from the French *profession*, vow, calling, position, from Latin *professio*, public avowal, public declaration of name, property, or trade, to Latin *profiteri*, *professus sum*, to declare, confess, acknowledge openly, publicly and voluntarily; in Lenin's case, therefore, the term expressly points to the essential "publicity" of political action, despite tactically unavoidable clandestinity).[18] In an appropriately existential passage he condenses his "professional" universalism into the assertion that "the 'economic struggle against the employers and the government' can *never* satisfy revolutionaries" and that the revolution itself therefore demands a "militant organisation" that "satisfies […] all revolutionary instincts and strivings."[19]

IV.6

The fifth passage, referred to previously in IV.3, clarifies the ultimate goal of the dissociation by the proletariat from its particular interests in favour of its "revolutionary instincts and strivings," i.e. in favour of both a different consciousness and spontaneity. In effect, this goal does not only concern the moral progress achieved in the transition from a particularistic-economistic to a universal-political position, but far more significantly, the existential denunciation of subjugation to the "dictatorship of the bourgeoisie" and the self-empowerment towards the "dictatorship of the proletariat" – a step in which Lenin explicitly identifies the "most essential," indeed the "decisive"

---

18 Cf. Jacques Derrida's enduringly authoritative essay, "The University Without Condition," in Derrida 2002: 202-237.
19 Ibid: 477.

interests of classes.[20] Concomitantly, however, this means that as long as the proletariat is driven by its narrow economic self-interest, it remains subject to the dictatorship of the bourgeoisie – even when engaged in the most fervent economic struggle.

V.

If one realises that the politicisation of proletarian consciousness and proletarian spontaneity, that is, of its entire existence, is the real point of Lenin, the actual communist point, then it becomes equally clear that the professional-revolutionary existence was and is also the precise condition of the 'Lenin moment,' that is, the condition of the extraordinary tactical agility of Lenin and the Bolsheviks. At the same time, conversely, one recognises the moment of truth in the accusation that Lenin's opponents repeatedly make against him, namely his "overestimation of ideology," which is in itself an "overestimation of the conscious element."[21] According to such criticism, this overestimation is the reason why the communists, as they pursue their all-round course in all directions, frequently depart from the "class point of view" – upheld by the economists as their most immanent task – and "obscure class antagonisms"[22] in the purely economic sense. Simultaneously, this overestimation of consciousness and ideology is at the root of the communists' failure to speak to the proletariat through its own economic interests, instead addressing it as the "vanguard fighter for democracy", i.e. through deeply "ideological" interests.[23] Lenin rejects these reproaches, rightly – and wrongly: he conceives the communist activity of the working classes explicitly with a view to the "the world-historic significance of the struggle for the emancipation of the proletariat," which, in his own words, however, is only revealed through an "ideological" interest whose aim is "to transform radically the conditions of life of the whole of mankind." Therefore, it can only reveal itself in the fullest sense when one exists spontaneously from one's conscious ideological choice – in and from one's own idea.[24] This point alone ultimately explains the concrete organisational-political question of founding a newspaper as the "collective organiser" of the search for the answer to the all-important question: "What type of organisation do we require?"[25] Both the newspaper and the organisation are the media of the true Leninist project of turning "workers' revolutionaries," with their spontaneous and conscious economic interests, who are thus radically subjected to the bourgeoisie, into radically de-subjugated "professional revolutionaries" on account of their spontaneous and conscious political interests: a deeply "ideological" project in which the

---

20 Ibid: 390f, Notes.
21 Ibid: 318f, 382, 386, 394, 395, 433.
22 Ibid: 434.
23 Ibid: 421-436.
24 Ibid: 514.
25 Ibid: 510-516.

path and the goal, the medium and the message, are to coincide.[26] Thus, Lenin was wrong only because he should have shrugged his shoulders when accused and simply said: "So fucking what?"

VI.

Let us now return from the year 1902 to the present day, as the world finds itself convulsed by the Corona pandemic, and can only be convulsed by the pandemic because it has found its "collective organiser" in the form of the electronic media (of course, Lenin would today, in concrete terms, no longer propose the creation of a newspaper, but strategic participation in precisely these media!). If this present, despite its obvious horror and unfathomable perilousness, appears to us, at least for the moment, to be open, then this has to do not only with the virus, but also with the fact that until recently the modern era seemed to us to be just the reverse, to be closed in on itself. Worse still: at the turn of the century, many observers even believed that we had arrived at the "end of history," that we had reached a time in which only incidental changes would now be possible to our irrevocable achievements.[27] Of course, there have been massive upheavals since then, from the 9/11 attacks to the 2015 European migrant crisis, but there has not been – and this is my point – since the epoch of May 68, a political project concerned with the whole world and the existence of humankind. That this was and still is so, owes much to Lenin again: but this time to the failure of the Bolshevik-led October Revolution in almost all of its immediate and later repercussions. While it is true that the "Lenin moment" did indeed lead to a glorious, ever memorable beginning, it is also true that it subsequently led to a literally bloody failure, over decades, and finally to a pitiful agony: perhaps the greatest broken promise in secular history. Here, this fiasco can only be discussed within the limits of the question as to the relevance of Lenin in the Corona era. If we concede that Lenin's criticism of economism and revolutionism was correct and has been confirmed by the ensuing history of both social democracy and anarchism, we must now also admit that his proposal for the politicisation of proletarian existence, through its professional revolutionary education under a tightly centralised vanguard leadership, has equally failed.

VI.1

Moreover, the full extent of the dilemma lies in the fact that the failure of all three strategic options (social democracy, anarchism and communism) applies not only to proletarian struggles in the narrower sense, but to all social struggles more broadly: they too have been unable to take the step from the calculation of their immediate interests to their "most essential" and "decisive"

---

26 Ibid: 472.
27 See Fukuyama 1992.

interest, or at least not in a sufficient way, and have therefore not achieved the common goal of "transform[ing] radically the conditions of life of the whole of mankind." If we nevertheless recognise Lenin's relevance to our time, this derives solely from the clarity with which he framed the question that still occupies us today: namely, that spontaneous social struggles must first become political struggles, in the purest sense of the word, if they are to fulfil the hopes that Lenin, and we ourselves, place in them.

VII.

Acknowledging Lenin's ongoing relevance also means rejecting the three post-Leninist alternative solutions to our problem that have emerged in the intervening period.

VII.1

The first alternative solution lies in simply abandoning the supposedly unattainable goal of "transform[ing] radically the conditions of life of the whole of mankind." It is not difficult to recognise how this will only lead to a renewal of economism, as we allow ourselves to be reduced from our "most essential" and "decisive" interests to our most immediate, largely economic particularistic interests – this time without even the sense of remorse that troubled the economists in Lenin's time. As Lenin's criticism made clear, however, this proposal is doomed from the start: in the structural capitalist crisis it cannot even achieve these starkly reduced interests. Worse still, as Lenin perceptively recognised, by limiting us to the purely economistic, it subjects us to the dictatorship of the bourgeoisie, whose foundation rests precisely on the reduction of our spontaneity and consciousness to the economic sphere. With regard to the Corona pandemic, this can be seen in the willingness with which entire societies, including significant segments of the Left, have submitted to a crisis management regime that threatens to reduce us to living beings whose sole interest is mere survival.

VII.2

This last point leads us to the second alternative solution, that of an anarchist self-assertion raised to an end in itself, whose only goal would be anti-bourgeois, i.e. pure anti-economic de-subjugation as such. It would follow the surrealist André Breton's 'revolver maxim,' which states:

> The simplest Surrealist act consists of dashing down the street, pistol in hand, and firing blindly, as fast as you can pull the trigger, into the crowd. Anyone who, at least once in his life, has not dreamed of thus putting an end to the petty system of debasement and cretinisation in effect has a well-defined place in that crowd with his belly at barrel level.[28]

---
28 Breton 1972: 125.

Regardless of the extent to which the "debasement" and "cretinisation" produced by the economism of the bourgeoisie might lead us to support such a proposition, its observance today could not be distinguished from fundamentalist terror of any origin, with which it under no circumstances wishes to be conflated.

VII.3

That leaves us with the third alternative solution to Lenin's problem: if the proletariat is not capable of politicising itself, then we replace it with another subject of history, or eliminate such a subject altogether. Whichever of the two options of "farewell to the working class"[29] one chooses, both lead in practice to either an economistic or a revolutionist position: one either eventually gives up on broader goals and demeans oneself to particularism, or one despairs in the dark glow of aimless anarchic self-assertion. In fact, what the proletariat has thus far been unable to accomplish can equally not be expected from a "global civil society," or from any "new social movements" regardless of their race or gender, nor yet from the "multitudes" – at all of whom this most far-reaching proposal for the replacement of the proletariat is aimed.[30]

VIII

It is perhaps no coincidence that a fourth proposal was developed by Jean-Paul Sartre directly after the nightmare of the Second World War, in the face of the Stalinist reversal of the revolution and, last but not least, on the "eve of the revolution" of May 1968: a proposal which, suffused by this historical *intermediacy*, seems to have fallen out of the passage of time. It is certainly no coincidence that, through this proposal, Sartre was able to free himself from the aimless anarchic self-assertion of his early existentialism. In order to present his proposal as reflectively as possible, I introduce it by means of the criticism made of it by Sartre's erstwhile companion, Maurice Merleau-Ponty: a criticism that relates to Sartre's first concrete composition in its immediate temporal context, rather than to his actual, more broadly historical point. The justified criticism of this first concrete proposal concerned Sartre's decision to toe the line of the Soviet Union and the *Parti communiste français*, despite his own objections to their specific policies: a decision that Sartre himself soon abandoned. The connection to Lenin lies in the actual point of the proposal and is at once evident in the extremely apposite term that Merleau-Ponty coined to describe it: "Ultrabolshevism," i.e. an immanent radicalisation of Lenin's Bolshevism.[31]

---

29 See Gorz 1997.
30 See the manifesto-like pamphlet by Hardt and Negri 2012.
31 Merleau-Ponty 1973: 95-201. The works of Sartre to which Merleau-Ponty refers are the essay *Materialism and Revolution* (in Sartre 1962) and the article series *The Communists and Peace* (Sartre 1968), originally published in 1952 in *Les Temps Modernes*. At the time, Sartre's later Marxist works had not yet been written.

VIII.1

In its actual point, Ultrabolshevism adheres to Marx and Lenin's conception of the proletariat as the immanent subjective negation of capitalist society. It does not, however, regard the proletariat as an empirical, social reality, much less an economically driven one, but rather as a universal-existential possibility of history and its politicisation. In his commitment to this possibility, Sartre is thus concerned with a politics that continues to aim at "transform[ing] radically the conditions of life of the whole of mankind" and, to this end – and herein lies its "Lenin moment" – seeks to transcend all particularistic interests, without exception. If I now outline this Ultrabolshevism in the words that Merleau-Ponty used to critique Sartre, in which he sought to remain true to Lenin, I also place my own emphasis on the philosophical-political realisation on which Merleau-Ponty, Sartre and Lenin all agree. According to this realisation, the historical facts themselves say "neither yes nor no" to the possibility, asserted by Lenin and Sartre, of the arrival of the revolutionary proletariat in history, thereby confirming it in its inescapable potentiality as such:

> It is [...] a question of [...] remaining faithful to what you think of capitalism and pursuing the consequences of this position. If capitalism overturns personal relationships by subjugating one class to another, if it even succeeds in depriving the oppressed class any hold on history, dispersing it through the democratic game, which allows for all opinions but not for the enterprise of *recreating humanity and beginning history anew*, and if you do not want to become the enemy of the proletariat and of mankind by opposing this enterprise – if, additionally, you hold with Sartre that the dialectic, aside from a few privileged moments, never was anything but a cover for violent action [...] – then what is there to do except to open a credit account (which cannot be precisely measured in advance) to the only party that claims kinship with the proletariat, all the while reserving only your right to inspect the account? In a history which is without reason, in the name of what would you proclaim that the communist enterprise is impossible? This reasoning takes into account only intentions, not what one prefers or chooses; it tells us *on what condition we will be irreproachable before the proletariat*, at least in the short run, but it does not tell us how our action will liberate the proletariat. Yet it is the liberation of the worker that you are pretending to pursue. If the facts say "neither yes nor no," if the regime the proletariat desires is equivocal, and if, being aware of that and knowing the liabilities of the system, you help

the proletariat establish such a regime, *it is because you are thinking less of the proletariat than of yourself.*[32] (My emphasis)

IX.

This "thinking of oneself," which in the undecidability of historical facts makes it at all possible for us to decide "on what condition we will be irreproachable before the proletariat," Sartre later identified as the concept of the "singular universal": the one who stands alone for herself and at the same time for all others, and thus does what she is and remains free to do under all circumstances, like each and every other, namely to give all others the example of her own action and thus to impose it on them insofar as they are of good will.[33] Although Sartre was thinking, in this regard, less of Lenin than of Kierkegaard, he nevertheless confirmed the truth in which Lenin and Kierkegaard, Marxism and existentialism coincide. In this way, he does exactly what Lenin demanded of communists in his time: he poses liberal questions, that is, questions about freedom, in a communist way, that is, as questions about equality, and thus refuses to separate the two questions that guide modernity (cf. IV.3 above). In a similar vein, the contemporary value of the party, as both Sartre and Lenin conceive of it, is revealed. For Sartre, the term 'party' evokes only the necessity that all those who, in thinking of themselves, think always also of all others and thereby become 'political,' must unite with one another in order to be able to take action together, both theoretically and practically. On this point, Marx spoke of the "party in the broad historical sense" and categorically separated this party from all concrete organisations, including the Communist League, which he himself co-founded and was the nucleus of all later social democratic and communist parties.[34] Sartre, then, placed this "party in the broad historical sense" under the further condition of a "right to inspect," to be practised in any case on one's own account, and thereby made it the subject of a "politics in the first person" to be freely exchanged with others.

IX.1

Such a "party in the broad historical sense" also alters, however, the relationship between social democracy, anarchism and communism. Given that they express structural tendencies of all social struggles, their contradiction must not be determined in favour of one tendency in particular. Instead, one must always re-evaluate this contradiction according to the situation, thereby dialectically emphasising the moment of truth in each tendency.

---

32 Merleau-Ponty, loc. cit.: 180.
33 Sartre 2008: 141-169.
34 See Marx 1860.

IX.2

The right of social democracy lies precisely in its realism, i.e. in the unfortunate yet undeniable understanding that, on the whole, "the people" fight only for their spontaneous interests, and that this narrow self-interest must therefore be taken into account strategically, that is to say, politically.

IX.3

If anarchism sets the antithesis to this, its "propaganda of the deed" rightly bears witness to the always and everywhere available possibility of de-subjugation, performed in the here-and-now and in the first person. In this way, it testifies to the fundamental primacy of possibility over all reality and realism, without which we would indeed be without any hope.

IX.4

The right of communism, however, then lies in insisting – against social democracy and against anarchism – on the dialectic, which as such is always also the dialectic of the possible and the necessary. If, in the contradiction of the three tendencies, it is thus rightly given prominence, then for this very reason it must not make itself into a party in the narrow historical sense, and certainly not into a state: the leading role of the communists must be exercised only indirectly, primarily through 'publicity,' i.e. through the dissemination of thought in the form of speaking and writing. This insight leads back from Lenin to Marx and Engels, for whom the primacy of the communists lay, tellingly, precisely in being "not a special party in relation to the other working-class parties," but championing in these parties the power of reflection on the "most essential," the "decisive" interest.[35]

X.

Philosophically, Sartre's Ultrabolshevism is based on an ultra-dialecticism that impels the original Leninist understanding against Hegel and Marx. As its "in-itself," it presupposes a *physis*, to which nature and the "practical inertia" moment of all social praxis belong.[36] This *physis* confronts the "for-itself" of an *antiphysis* that explicitly recognises its radical contingency and thus, borderline to all dialectics, its perhaps ultimate incommunicability, i.e. "uselessness."[37] Dialectically, the contradiction between the in-itself of *physis* and the for-itself of *antiphysis* remains, because the for-itself does not run away from the struggle for recognition and wagers everything on

---

35 Marx and Engels 2002: 234f and not to forget 257. For a detailed discussion of the structural contradictions of social democracy, anarchism and communism (in German), see Seibert 2017: 351-393.
36 Sartre first employs the conceptual pairing *physis-antiphysis* in *Materialism and Revolution*, where he states that he derived the terminology from Marxism (1950). "Practical inertia" is a key term in Sartre's *Critique of Dialectical Reason Vol. 1* (2004).
37 In the final sentence of *Being and Nothingness* Sartre calls man "a useless passion," which nonetheless cannot and must not lose itself. (Sartre 1993: 615)

the *possibility* of a transition from the "society of laws" to a "Kingdom of Ends": the irredeemable possibility of "classless society or the liberation of man."[38]

XI.

In the Corona crisis, Ultrabolshevism and ultra-dialectics are not entirely without strategic points of reference in empirical reality. If these points appear comparatively abstract, this only indicates that the whole world and the whole of human existence are on the line and just how high the stakes must therefore be.

XI.1

In the first point, the Corona Crisis presents itself as a palpable crisis of globalisation, which it situates just as palpably in the everyday life of each and every one of us. The virus infects the whole world and affects every dimension of our being-in-the-world: more generally, in the fear and anxiety of the world inherent in many emotions, very practically in the increasing daily upheavals that affect us simultaneously in the most diverse places of life: at home, on vacation, in the factory and office, in the supermarket, in front of suddenly closed doors, in the cancellation of a multitude of appointments and plans, and almost inevitably in the comprehensive communication of all events through the media. Today we can only imagine what it will mean in Lagos, Mexico City or Karachi.

XI.2

The second point translates the double corona/globalisation crisis directly into the capitalist crisis that encompasses them – both the long-standing capitalist crisis, as well as the one that will result from the interruption, if not the total disruption, of global manufacturing and supply chains.

XI.3

That this crisis is not only an economic but also a political one is demonstrated by the third reference point, namely the ambiguous return of state power and authority. This return of the state goes hand in hand with a macro-political weakening of all transnational or global governance, and a micro-political infiltration that interweaves everyday life and the state in a web of relationships and practices of solidarity, the former badly, the latter well, albeit thus far insufficient.

---

38 *Materialism and Revolution:* 234, 236. This extremely well-considered formulation connects St. Paul ("society of laws"), Kant ("Kingdom of Ends") and Marx ("classless society") through their shared conceptualisation of that which runs through all of history: "the liberation of man."

XI.4

This crisis is of course also political, in the purest sense of the word, and here at last the circle closes, in the equally immediately palpable re-opening of history. The fourth point conveys the breadth of this historical re-opening, by revealing that the corona, globalisation, capitalist and political crises are in fact an ecological crisis, connected on the one hand with the climate crisis, which is present everywhere, and on the other with the now plainly irrefutable knowledge that the out-of-control threat of this global virus is largely a consequence of capitalist agribusiness. If it is precisely here that the necessity, ultimately even the inevitability, of "transform[ing] radically the living conditions of all of mankind" is called for, Corona also reveals a deeper dimension, which is still far from being understood: that we are, and must be, *antiphysis* to the extent that the *physis* that surrounds and penetrates us is, and must always be, a hostile, life-threatening milieu in which we ourselves, conversely, exert the no less life-threatening effect of a virus: again, for better or worse, since the spirit, as Hegel already knew, has its "immediate existence " in the "skull."[39]

XI.5

Finally, the fifth point refers us to the two virtues without which we will be lost. These virtues are imposed on us by the sudden shut-down of the machinery of capital and labour that has been hit at full swing. On the one hand, it forces us into the mutuality of practical recognition, and on the other, it condemns us to solitude, to loneliness, at worst to abandonment. The Leninist quality herein will be a political conception of solidarity, understood as a universal obligation of all individuals to all others that thereby frees us from the arbitrariness of spontaneous empathies, sympathies and antipathies. Sartrean in this is the concept of the sudden condemnation to be-alone-for-oneself, which through the employment of quarantine is affirmed as a "condemnation to freedom": "Man is condemned to be free. Condemned, because he did not create himself, yet is nevertheless free, because once cast into the world, he is responsible for everything he does."[40]

XI.6

Drawing all of this together – and how could one not do so in such a time as this! – there remains a fundamental uncertainty that we are exposed to in the form of Corona, thanks to which history is being reopened: as in all of its epochs, history can always turn towards the better or the worse, and ultimately towards the best or the worst. The facts will say neither yes nor no

---

39 Hegel 2018: 192. See also Seibert 2007: 224-241 and 393-422, as well as the first footnote in the article by Žižek cited above.
40 Sartre 2007: 29.

on this score for some time to come, and as such we would be well advised to reflect on the question posed by Lenin and Sartre: what could it mean, today, to be "irreproachable" perhaps no longer only before the proletariat but before all humanity? Here, "humanity" and "proletariat" would be understood as the immanent subjective negation of existing reality, which, as a "perpetual dream of *antiphysis*," is still the possible "that becomes possible starting from us."[41] To test this perhaps useless passion, then, the "legitimacy of conversion" (ibid.) must still be claimed, which Lenin, like Sartre, locates not in economics but only in politics, as its first and last truth. One of the more hopeful tendencies of the Corona era is that this truth communicates itself even where the names Lenin and Sartre are not mentioned at all. The risk taken by this text of overestimating the Corona crisis, which cannot be ruled out today, thus only partially impacts the embrace of this truth, because the pure facts would then have said "neither yes nor no" once again. They would have shown yet again that philosophically, politically and ethically, they are not the only things that matter if we do not wish to fall into the trap of economism and opportunism. Thanks to Lenin.

Translated from the original German by Patrick Anderson

References

Badiou, Alain (2005), *Metapolitics*. London: Verso.
Breton, André (1972), *Manifestos of Surrealism*. Ann Arbor: The University of Michigan Press.
Derrida, Jacques (2002), *Without Alibi*. Stanford: Stanford University Press.
Fukuyama, Francis (1992), *The End of History and the Last Man*. New York: Free Press.
Gorz, André (1997), *Farewell to the Working Class*. London: Pluto Press.
Hardt, Michael, and Antonio Negri (2012), *Declaration*. Argo Navis Author Services.
Hegel, Georg Wilhelm Friedrich (2018), *Phenomenology of Spirit*. Cambridge: Cambridge University Press.
Lenin, V.I. (1977), *Collected Works Vol. 5*. Moscow: Progress Publishers.
Marx, Karl (1860), "Marx To Ferdinand Freiligrath." Accessed on 29.06.2020, at https://marxists.catbull.com/archive/marx/works/1860/letters/60_02_29.htm.
Marx, Karl, and Friedrich Engels (2002), *The Communist Manifesto*. London: Penguin Books.
Merleau-Ponty, Maurice (1973), *Adventures of the Dialectic*. Evanston: Northwestern University Press.

---

41 Sartre 1992: 6f.

Porcaro, Mimmo (2013), "Occupy Lenin," *The Socialist Register*, 49, 84-97.
Sartre, Jean-Paul (1950), *Materialismus und Revolution*. Stuttgart: Kohlhammer.
Sartre, Jean-Paul (1962), *Literary and Philosophical Essays*. New York: Collier Books.
Sartre, Jean-Paul (1968), *The Communists and Peace with a Reply to Claude Lefort*. New York: George Braziller.
Sartre, Jean-Paul (1992), *Notebook for an Ethics*. Chicago: University of Chicago Press.
Sartre, Jean-Paul (1993), *Being and Nothingness*. New York: Washington Square Press.
Sartre, Jean-Paul (2004), *Critique of Dialectical Reason Vol. 1*. London: Verso.
Sartre, Jean-Paul (2007), *Literary and Philosophical Essays*. New Haven: Yale University Press.
Sartre, Jean-Paul (2008), *Between Existentialism and Marxism*. London: Verso.
Seibert, Thomas (2017), *Zur Ökologie der Existenz. Freiheit, Gleichheit, Umwelt*. Hamburg: Laika Verlag.
Žižek, Slavoj (2020), "Das Ende der Welt, wie wir sie kennen," *Welt*. Accessed on 29.06.2020, at https://www.welt.de/kultur/plus206189063/Corona-Epidemie-Das-Ende-der-Welt-wie-wir-sie-kennen.html.
Zola, Emile (2004), *Germinal*. London: Penguin Classics.

18. On Revolutionary Prudence, or the Wisdom of Lenin

Matthieu Renault

For Liebknecht, 'prudence' did not mean kicking the revolution as soon as it begins to decline (even if temporarily) and adjusting oneself as soon as possible to a truncated constitution. No. By 'prudence' this veteran of the revolutionary movement meant that a proletarian leader must be the last to 'adjust' himself to the conditions created by the temporary defeats of the revolution; that he must not do so until long after the bourgeois poltroons and cowards have done so.[1]

The following is said to be the most reliable method of catching foxes. The fox that is being tracked is surrounded at a certain distance with a rope which is set at a little height from the snow-covered ground and to which are attached little red flags. Fearing this obviously artificial human device, the fox will emerge only if and where an opening is allowed in this fence of flags; and the hunter waits for it at this opening. One would think that prudence would be the most marked trait of an animal that is hunted by everybody. But it turns out that in this case, too, 'virtue unduly prolonged' is a fault. The fox is caught precisely because it is overly prudent.[2]

*P*reliminary note: This text was written in December 2019, in France, in the midst of a massive strike against the reform, which has become another term for destruction, of the pension system, and in the uncertainty of its outcome. Against such a backdrop, the considerations that follow may seem profoundly irrelevant, perhaps even futile, as they primarily concern that which occurs *after* the victorious insurrection, once the power is overthrown. It would be false to say that this, at the present moment, is *our* problem: the current struggle, as so many before it, imperative as they may be, are – whether we like it or not – *defensive* struggles, aimed at preserving the gains and conquests of past battles. While it is true that a whole series of individual *offensive* struggles converge there, or mature at their margins, we cannot deny the predominant refusal, guided by a sense of presentism constructed by political strategy, to consider that which comes 'after'; a refusal, therefore, to think of the revolution literally, as it designates less an event than a process, which does not end with the overthrow of power but actually begins with it. Of this ebb of the idea of revolution, the slogan written on walls that sprang up following recent protest movements –

---
1 Lenin 1972: 405.
2 Lenin 1973a: 207-208.

"Waiting for the revolution ..." – far from being a negation, is a symptom. We are nevertheless convinced of the pressing need to (re)imagine *the future in the present*, without submitting to the sirens of a revolutionary teleology that has caused so much damage, nor shying away from the formulation of "concrete utopias"[3] that are not ashamed to draw on examples from the past. In this context, we claim full responsibility for the *inconvenient untimeliness* of the meditations on Lenin set forth in this essay.

"Dear Prudence, won't you come out to play?" – these words, which open the second track of the Beatles' *White Album*, came back to mind like a refrain as the outline of the reflections that form the subject of this text was taking shape: a free association of words revealing connections all the more significant because they were unconscious. "Dear Prudence" was composed in March 1968, on the eve of the multiple protest movements that were to set the world ablaze. Certainly, the Beatles, then secluded at the Rishikesh Ashram in India to learn transcendental meditation, were far removed from such political concerns. The "Prudence" in the song does not refer to the commonly used noun signifying a quality of the foreseeing mind, calculating the consequences of its actions, but to a proper noun, that of Prudence Farrow. As fanciful as it was, however, one could not fail to hear in these words, from the Indian experience of the Beatles, an echo of the idea circulating at the time, according to which Gandhi was the archetype of a *phronimos* – the sage portrayed by Aristotle in the *Nicomachean Ethics*; "Gandhi, rather than Einstein or Bergson"[4] since the philosopher distinguished theoretical wisdom, *sophia*, in its Platonic sense, from practical wisdom, *phronesis* or 'prudence.' But the association of ideas did not stop there. At the beginning of "Dear Prudence," we hear the sound of an airplane engine from the end of the previous track, "Back in the U.S.S.R." What if this sequence was not pure coincidence? What if the Beatles had established a connection between Gandhi and Lenin, which they would have been neither the first nor the last to do?[5] It is obviously not the aim of this essay to seek to prove this eccentric hypothesis, but to test its heuristic value by examining to what extent Lenin could, in turn, be considered an embodiment of the Aristotelian *phronimos*.

Against Wisdom: Prudence as a Philosophy

There is no doubt that the statement above will make more than one reader smile. Wasn't Lenin by definition the anti-sage? Probably, but it should be noted that he adopted that position *deliberately* – one need only browse his writings to be assured of the fact. 'Wise' is part of the vast repertoire of names with which he disparaged his enemies; Lenin pursued a genuine *strategy of political insult* based on an idiosyncratic style combining

---

3 See Bloch 1976-1991.
4 René-Antoine Gauthier, cited in Aubenque 2004.
5 For example, see Balibar 2010: 305-321.

rigorous (counter-)argumentation and casual mockery. Lenin's purpose was doubtless to deride, above all, the false wisdom of the bourgeoisie, yet almost none of his other adversaries was spared the epithet: the populists (*narodniki*), the Kadets, Plekhanov and the Mensheviks, Bogdanov and the exponents of empirio-criticism (Mach and Avenarius), etc. According to Lenin, it was crucial to put an end to politics conceived of as the reign of self-proclaimed sages. "Every cook must learn to govern the state" – the phrase, while undoubtedly apocryphal, is faithful to the spirit of Lenin.[6] The latter does not reject all forms of wisdom. This is evidenced by his repeated use of popular proverbs, and the proverbial style with which he endeavoured to imbue his words. In this regard, one could apply *mutatis mutandis* to Lenin that which has been said of Aristotle, namely that the basis of his thought on *phronesis* "is not wise, but popular."[7] Contrary to common belief, Lenin attributes wisdom to the working masses – a wisdom produced *in and through* struggle: "It was the great creative spirit of the people, which had passed through the bitter experience of 1905 and had been made wise by it, that gave rise to this form of proletarian power."[8]

Let there be no illusions, these remarks will not suffice to convince the most sceptical, for whom such an appeal to popular wisdom was no more than a ruse intended to manipulate the feelings of the 'people' to win them over to the cause of Bolshevism. Was it not, moreover, because the moral virtue of *temperance* was singularly foreign to him that Lenin took pleasure in mocking the wisdom of his rivals? Following Plato, Aristotle, playing on Greek etymology, had indeed defined temperance (*sophrosyne*) as the "safeguard of prudence."[9] In Greek culture, it was set up in opposition to *hubris*, that is to say 'excessiveness,' which in itself constituted a crime. Are we not therefore condemned to agree with Stéphane Courtois, author in 2017 of *Lenin, the Inventor of Totalitarianism* – a book whose commercial success speaks volumes about the strength of liberal-reactionary thought, in direct proportion to its intellectual poverty – when he declares that "hubris of the will," rather than "declared Marxist rationality," was "one of Lenin's principal psychological drivers"?[10] More parenthetically, Iwona Barwicka-Tylek, emphasising "the natural instinct [of Europe] for truth" (*sic*) and recognising affinities between Lenin and the Aristotelian *phronimos* in terms of its usage in dialectical reasoning, set out to demonstrate that this proximity was only superficial, accusing the Bolshevik leader of having systematically ignored the difference between truth, the object of science or *sophia*, and opinion, the domain of dialectics, that is to say also of *phronesis*. This confusion, Barwicka-Tylek argues, has had devastating consequences for "political

---

6 Editor's note: In fact, a variation of this quote exists in Lenin 1974a: 493.
7 Aubenque 2004: 24.
8 Lenin 1974b: 90.
9 Aubenque 2004: 60.
10 Courtois 2017.

theory and practice."[11]

Let us attempt to reconsider things more prudently, by first recalling that, in Aristotle, prudence is a dianoetic, intellectual, and not moral, disposition. It is a virtue, bound to other virtues, or strictly speaking ethics, but which remains irreducible to them; *phronesis* for Aristotle is part of the 'opinionative' or 'calculative' part of the soul: there can be no *phronesis* without calculation. Now, are not those who accuse Lenin of all evils the first to assert, against him, that he was a first-rate "calculator"?[12] If *phronesis* is distinguished from *sophia*, it is nonetheless a form of knowledge; knowledge of contingent things, which may be otherwise than they are, and on which human action, political in particular, has for this reason taken hold. Practical wisdom is "variable depending on […] the circumstances."[13] This does not mean that it is concerned solely with the 'particular,' given that it involves the determination of 'rules' applicable in various circumstances. Prudence means, in short, a certain capacity to link, *situationally*, the particular and the universal. Lenin's motto "concrete analysis of the concrete situation" is the epitome of such a political imperative to articulate thought and action, theory and practice.

This concern runs through the immediately practical-political reading that Lenin made of Aristotle's *Metaphysics*, among other classics in the history of philosophy, following the outbreak of the First World War. Praising Aristotle for having revoked any "doubts of the reality of the outside world," he criticised him, however, for having become "confused" in the "dialectics of the universal and the particular."[14] If, from this point of view, Aristotelian philosophy was only an imperfect prefiguration of Hegelian dialectics, and took its start from an adequate understanding of the connection of the universal and the particular, the advantage nonetheless returned to Aristotle, against Hegel, in terms of the beginnings of materialism: "The idealist Hegel in cowardly fashion fought shy of the undermining of the *foundations* of idealism by Aristotle (in his criticism of Plato's ideas)."[15] In *Metaphysics*, Lenin discerned Aristotle's true politics. It was not a question for him of unduly raising opinions to the rank of truths, to better then subordinate political virtues to a dialectical materialism held up as science, but to *(re-)dialecticise* the relationships between *phronesis* and *sophia*. Lenin's famous phrase, "Without revolutionary theory, there can be no revolutionary movement" is well-known, but it is often forgotten that implicit in this statement is its corollary: "Without revolutionary movement, there can be no revolutionary theory." In this, Lenin was the most faithful heir to Marxist wisdom.

....
11 Barwicka-Tylek 2008: 321, 333.
12 Curzio Malaparte (2013) had already demonstrated this in a far more inspired yet deeply sarcastic way.
13 Aubenque 2004: 9.
14 Lenin 1976a: 363-372.
15 Ibid: 339.

Aristotle in Russia

Insofar as *phronesis* only makes sense in context, we must now re-examine the political thought-practice of Lenin according to the particularity of his times and places of formation and expression. Lenin's writings of the early years of the 20th century reveal that *circumstances*, namely the conditions of revolutionary activity under the censorship of the Tsarist Empire, had long taught him to be prudent. As Lars Lih has shown, the *konspiratsiia* claimed by Lenin is by no means synonymous with 'conspiracy,' but designates "all the practical rules of conduct needed to elude the police, even while preserving the threads connecting the [revolutionary] organisation to a larger community."[16] Lenin also called on the members of Russian social democracy to exercise the utmost circumspection in order to "weld [the] vanguard [of the proletariat] into a genuine political party, *absolutely* independent of all the other parties": "It is therefore incumbent upon us to exercise extreme caution in taking any step likely to cause confusion in clear-cut and definite Party relations."[17] The *vanguard party* model was thus the product *par excellence* of Lenin's political wisdom, which is scarcely debatable, unless one wishes to substitute for the word 'wisdom' that of 'madness.' The error of Marxism-Leninism, after Lenin's death, invariably consisted in conceiving such wisdom in terms of *sophia*, whereas for its author it was a matter of *phronesis*, that is to say, calculation, 'deliberation' in a particular geo-historical-political context. The vanguard party was a model, of course, but a contingent model, whose applicability to other times and other places was by no means guaranteed in advance.

This was affirmed by the Caribbean Marxist theorist C.L.R. James in 1963 when he wrote that "the theory and practice of the vanguard party" was by no means Lenin's "central doctrine": "It is not even a special doctrine. [...] Objective circumstances in Russia forced Lenin into a certain position."[18] It is probably not by chance that, at the same time, James deemed it absolutely necessary to insist on the prudence of the "last Lenin," to whom we will now turn our attention. After the great "leap forward" represented by the "overthrow of the bourgeoisie," Lenin tirelessly repeated that the construction of socialism in Russia would take decades, even centuries: "[...] it is an elementary business and a slow, careful business. [...] No great leaps in the development of industry and production, none at all."[19] In the aftermath of the Civil War, the two main tasks incumbent upon the Soviet government were "the reconstruction of the apparatus of government" and "the education of the almost illiterate peasantry," requiring party members to educate themselves: "learn, learn and learn again." In a "backward country" like Russia, patience and prudence were cardinal political virtues: "A backward

---

16 Lih 2011: 67.
17 Lenin 1977a: 281.
18 James in Grimshaw 1992: 327-330.
19 James in Austin 2009: 193-194.

country can easily begin [the international revolution] because its adversary has become rotten, because its bourgeoisie is not organised, but for it to continue demands of that country a hundred thousand times more circumspection, caution and endurance"[20] than in 'advanced' Western countries.

One of Lenin's last texts, whose title is derived from a proverb, succinctly symbolises this injunction to revolutionary prudence: "Better Fewer, But Better." The task of "improving [the] state apparatus," he insists, demands the "greatest caution, thoughtfulness and knowledge." As for the situation created by the imperialist war, it requires the "display [of] extreme caution so as to preserve our workers' government."[21] From the day the Bolsheviks had come to power, this *policy of prudence* was bound to be defined on a world scale: "The instability of the international situation" required "prudence, caution, self-control and presence of mind…"[22] If before the revolution, the Communist was expected to "give [his] life," the consolidation of the Soviet regime after 1917 had called him to "quite another task": "Now […] we must take all things into account, and each of you must learn to be prudent,"[23] that is to say to observe careful restraint, to cultivate one's *phronesis*. In his so-called "Testament" of 1923, Lenin wrote: "Comrade Stalin, having become Secretary-General, has unlimited authority concentrated in his hands, and I am not sure whether he will always be capable of using that authority with sufficient caution."[24] It was the first part of this assertion, along with the reference to Stalin's "brutality," that generally drew attention; but it may well be that it was the second part that truly encapsulated Lenin's primary charge against Stalin. If we agree that revolutionary prudence had become the fundamental political virtue for Lenin, there is no doubt that Stalin now represented the number-one danger.

Decolonial *Phronesis*

For Lenin, prudence, as an intellectual-practical disposition, was also an instrument of knowledge, the primary object of which must be the masses in their internal heterogeneity: "We must learn to approach the masses with particular patience and caution so as to be able to understand the distinctive features in the mentality of each stratum, calling, etc."[25] This warning was particularly valid for the peasantry, who made up the overwhelming majority of the population. In this matter, Lenin recommended that "[t]he greatest prudence should be exercised in introducing innovations, and the possibility of achieving what is being undertaken should be triple-checked."[26] This was all the more imperative in cases where, as in the above quotation,

---

20 Lenin 1974b: 291.
21 Lenin 1973a: 487-502.
22 Lenin 1974b: 365-381.
23 Lenin 1973a: 435-443.
24 Lenin 1977b: 595.
25 Lenin 1974c: 192.
26 Ibid: 339.

relating to Ukraine, the agrarian question was modulated and intensified by the national question and where "many centuries of oppression have given rise to nationalist tendencies" that manifested "among the backward sections of the population." With regard to these tendencies, it was necessary "to exercise the greatest caution" and to "oppose them with words of comradely explanation concerning the identity of interests of the working people" of all countries.[27] The situation was similar in the Caucasian republics, countries "of an even more pronounced peasant character than Russia," where it was necessary "to practise more moderation and caution, and show more readiness to make concessions to the petty bourgeoisie, intelligentsia, and particularly the peasantry."[28]

No doubt some will perceive in this an echo less of Aristotelian *phronesis* than of Machiavellian prudence commonly and reductively conceived of as the simple means of achieving one's ends. That would, however, be to disregard Lenin's determination to de(con)struct the Russian Empire and to combat the 'Great Russian' imperialist mentality (even amongst Communists), in other words to strive towards *de-imperialisation*, without which any attempt to create an international socialist union was doomed to fail. Lenin repeated time and again: the prudence exercised vis-à-vis national minorities must be proportional to the distrust *legitimately* felt by them vis-à-vis the Great Russian population, which is nothing other than a reaction to "Great Power chauvinism," an *effect* of the oppression that made the Russian Empire a vast "prison of peoples." It is therefore, writes Lenin in his *Draft Theses on National and Colonial Questions* for the Second Congress of the Communist International of 1920, "the duty of the class-conscious communist proletariat of all countries to regard with particular caution and attention the survival of national sentiments in the countries and among nationalities which have been oppressed the longest;"[29] hence the need to recognise the latter's right to self-determination, the right to found a state, and the duty of communists to know how to wait for the opportune moment, the *kairos*: "Experience has shown that this distrust wears off and disappears only very slowly, and that the more caution and patience displayed by the Great Russians, who have for so long been an oppressor nation, the more certainly this distrust will pass."[30]

This issue would prove to be crucial in the conflict over the so-called 'autonomisation' project of Transcaucasia in 1922, a prelude to the formation of the USSR; a conflict which revealed that, in Lenin's eyes, the glaring absence in Stalin of any virtue of prudence had first manifested itself in terms of the national question: "[...] in the present instance, as far as the Georgian nation is concerned, we have a typical case in which a genuinely

---

27 Lenin 1974d: 163-166.
28 Lenin 1973b: 316-318.
29 Lenin 1974c: 144-151.
30 Lenin 1974d: 291-297.

proletarian attitude makes profound caution, thoughtfulness and a readiness to compromise a matter of necessity for us. The Georgian [Stalin] who is neglectful of this aspect of the question [...] violates, in substance, the interests of class proletarian solidarity."[31] Far from being marginal, or addressing issues whose scope was limited to geopolitical concerns, Stalin's attitude towards the national minority from which he himself came belied the perils to which his impatience, his lack of prudence, would sooner or later expose the *entire* Soviet masses, in the centre as well as on the periphery.

That this insistence on prudence was a matter of principle for Lenin, who harboured a visceral hatred of chauvinism, in no way detracts from its deliberateness as a policy of immediate strategic importance. Let us not forget that it was first formulated in the context of a civil war in which the rallying to the Bolshevik cause of the 'nationalities' of the border regions of the (ex-)Empire, coveted by Western imperialism, was vital. It was in this context that Lenin exhorted the Military Council of the Caucasian Front to "display particular attention and caution in regard to the Georgian population,"[32] and to "display caution and maximum goodwill towards [... and d]o everything to demonstrate [...] our sympathy for the Muslims;"[33] Muslims of the Caucasus in this instance, but also Muslims from Central Asia, Turkestan, who had been conquered in the second half of the 19th Century and since subjected to outright colonial domination. In Turkestan, the 'national question' was synonymous with the 'agrarian question' and the 'colonial question': an entanglement symbolised by the *(imperialist) monoculture of cotton.*

In the summer of 1921, in a letter to Mikhail Tomsky, Lenin, intervening in an internal conflict among the Soviet authorities in Turkestan, insisted that "the Muslim poor should be treated with care and prudence, with a number of concessions."[34] In his eyes, Turkestan, the border area between Russia and the East, then under the yoke of the European imperialist powers, was a space where the conditions necessary to experience a fusion of the proletariat of the oppressive nations and the peasant masses of the oppressed nations were already met; it was a *laboratory of world revolution*, as he emphasised in another letter which synthesises the central tenets of his *decolonial policy*: "It is terribly important for all our *Weltpolitik* to win the confidence of the natives; to win it over and over again; *to prove* that we are *not* imperialists, that we shall *not* tolerate any *deviation* in that direction. This is a world-wide question, and that is no exaggeration. There you must be especially strict. It will have an effect on India and the East; it is no joke, it calls for exceptional caution."[35]

---

31 Lenin 1977b: 605-611.
32 Lenin 1973c: 479.
33 Lenin 1974d: 494.
34 Lenin 1976b: 246.
35 Ibid: 297-298.

Conclusion: The Dethroned Philosopher-King

Our journey through Lenin's work has, at last, brought us back to its point of departure: India. Let us wager that it was not by pure chance that, at the end of this itinerary, the 'last Lenin' makes a positive (albeit discreet) reference to that type of wisdom which had previously been the object of his derision: "It is possible and necessary to combine and *consolidate* the line of wisdom and prudence, maintaining the interests of our 'world politics' *throughout* the East."[36] The circle is complete, the link between "Back in the U.S.S.R" and "Dear Prudence" by the Beatles is revealed: Lenin's revolutionary prudence arrives, by strange detours, at Gandhi's *phronesis*. Such a connection would have remained unsuspected had we subscribed to the perspective of Jacques Derrida when he declared that "the U.S.S.R. is the name of a state individual, of an individual and singular State which gave itself, or pretended to give itself, a proper name without reference to any specific place or to any national past."[37] Citing for other reasons the Beatles' "Back in the U.S.S.R.," Derrida ignores the fact that the song's references to "Ukrainian girls" or even "that Georgia" reminds us that, in the 20th Century, no other political regime was more concerned with the future of 'nations' and the frontiers of their respective 'places' than the Soviet regime. It is not a question, however, of setting in opposition two visions conceived as intrinsically contradictory: on the one hand, the U.S.S.R. as a "common name," in Derrida's terms, on the other, the U.S.S.R. as an irreducible plurality of proper names. Because the challenge was precisely to articulate communism and national politics – in other words, the decline of the state and the *decline of empire*. If this combination never ceased to be synonymous with certain tensions, as if it were doomed to remain aporetic, it was for Lenin the terrain *par excellence* of a dialectic of the universal and the particular that lay at the very heart of *phronesis*.

By way of conclusion, we must attend to a final objection. Have we not insidiously overlooked, throughout our argument, the fact that, for Aristotle, the objective of *phronesis* was to determine "what is good and bad for mankind"? Now, does the history of communism not bear witness, at best to a serious lack of 'calculation,' at worst to a deliberate desire to disguise evil as good? Such retrospective judgments continue to flourish. Opposing them in no way implies denying the errors, absolving the crimes, or exempting Lenin from criticism, but only – and one is almost ashamed to have to say it – a refusal to situate 'Good' and 'Evil' somewhere in a sky of Intangible Ideas. This anti-idealist posture, 'anti-Platonic' in its mundane sense, was adhered to by Lenin himself, to whom the 'ideal' of the philosopher-king had always remained profoundly foreign: the attribution of power to the holders of knowledge, the dream of a "fusion of philosophy with the State"

---
36 Lenin 1976b: 246 to 247.
37 Derrida 1995: 17-18.

as it would be pursued by Stalin.[38] The essential discord between Lenin and Stalin thus ultimately boils down to the difference between *phronesis* and *sophia*. On this issue, Lenin's 'idealistic' denigrators, whether they like it or not, place themselves on the side of Stalin, sharing with him the same terrain, a battlefield that Lenin had long since deserted. Let them fight against windmills, while we give the last word to György Lukács who, in the 1967 postscript to *Lenin – A Study on the Unity of his Thought*, wrote:

> There has been an important change in human attitudes over the last centuries: the ideal of the Stoic-Epicurean 'sage' has had a very strong influence on our ethical, political and social opinions, well beyond the limits of academic philosophy. But this influence was equally an inner transformation: the active-practical element in this prototype has become far stronger than in ancient times. Lenin's permanent readiness is the latest and till now the highest and most important stage of this development. The fact that today, as manipulation absorbs practice and the 'end of ideology' absorbs theory, this ideal does not stand very high i n the eyes of the 'experts,' is merely an episode, measured against the march of world history. Beyond the significance of his actions and his writings, the figure of Lenin as the very embodiment of permanent readiness represents an ineradicable value – a new form of exemplary attitude to reality.[39]

Translated from the original French by Patrick Anderson

References
Aubenque, Pierre (2004), *La Prudence chez Aristote*. Paris: Gallimard, 2004.
Balibar, Étienne (2010), *Violence et civilité*. Paris: Galilée, 2010.
Barwicka-Tylek, Iwona (2008), "Intricacies of Practical Wisdom: or Why Aristotle Would Vote for Pericles Rather Than Lenin," *Krakowskie Studia z Historii Państwa i Prawa*, 11(3), 321-341.
Bloch, Ernst (1976-1991), *Le Principe espérance, 3 vol*. Paris: Gallimard.
Courtois, Stéphane (2017), *Lénine, l'inventeur du totalitarisme*. Paris: Perrin.
Derrida, Jacques (1995), *Moscou, aller-retour*. Paris: Editions de l'aube.
James, C.L.R. (1992), "Lenin and the Vanguard Party," in Anna Grimshaw (ed.), *The C.L.R. James Reader*. Cambridge: Blackwell Publishers, 327-330.

---
38 Labica 1984.
39 Lukács 2009: 97.

James, C.L.R. (2009), "Lenin and the Trade Union Debate in Russia, Part Two," *in* David Austin (ed.), *You Don't Play with Revolution. The Montreal Lectures of C.L.R. James*. Edinburgh: AK Press, 193-194.

Labica, Georges (1984), *Le Marxisme-léninisme (éléments pour une critique)*. Paris: Éditions Bruno Huisman.

Lenin, V.I. (1972), *Collected Works Vol. 11*. Moscow: Progress Publishers.

Lenin, V.I. (1973a), *Collected Works Vol. 33*. Moscow: Progress Publishers.

Lenin, V.I. (1973b), *Collected Works Vol. 32*. Moscow: Progress Publishers.

Lenin, V.I. (1973c), *Collected Works Vol. 35*. Moscow: Progress Publishers.

Lenin, V.I. (1974a), *Collected Works Vol. 25*. Moscow: Progress Publishers.

Lenin, V.I. (1974b), *Collected Works Vol. 27*. Moscow: Progress Publishers.

Lenin, V.I. (1974c), *Collected Works Vol. 31*. Moscow: Progress Publishers.

Lenin, V.I. (1974d), *Collected Works Vol. 30*. Moscow: Progress Publishers.

Lenin, V.I. (1976a), *Collected Works Vol. 38*. Moscow: Progress Publishers.

Lenin, V.I. (1976b), *Collected Works Vol. 45*. Moscow: Progress Publishers.

Lenin, V.I. (1977a), *Collected Works Vol. 9*. Moscow: Progress Publishers.

Lenin, V.I. (1977b), *Collected Works Vol. 36*. Moscow: Progress Publishers.

Lih, Lars T. (2011), *Lenin*. London: Reaktion Books.

Lukács, Georg (2009), *Lenin – A Study on the Unity of his Thought*. London: Verso.

Malaparte, Curzio (2013), *Le Bonhomme Lénine*. Paris: Grasset.

19. Lenin's 'Turn to the Masses' (1921-1923)

Michael Neocosmos

Don't be afraid of the people's initiative and independence. Put your faith in their revolutionary organisations [...] Lack of faith in the people, fear of their initiative and independence, trepidation before their revolutionary energy instead of all-round and unqualified support for it – this is where the S.R. and Menshevik leaders have sinned most of all.[1]

Politics must take precedence over economics. To argue otherwise is to forget the ABC of Marxism.[2]

At the end of the civil war, in the early 1920s, the dictatorship of the proletariat (socialism) in Russia was in grave danger. Not only was the country economically devastated by war and famine, but the Communist Party itself was faced with a political crisis most obviously apparent as several of its major leaders and theoreticians (notably Lenin, Trotsky and Bukharin) disagreed so vehemently that the danger of a split appeared to be a real possibility. Yet, arguably, and this was Lenin's view, the problem had much deeper roots than mere personal or theoretical disagreements. This crisis was formed by several interconnected elements: increasing evidence of state bureaucratic practices undermining socialism, the growth and greater independence of the administrative apparatus within the party and the consequent arrogant practices of party cadres towards the masses. As a result, there was clear evidence of a distancing of the party from the masses who were supposed to be the main beneficiaries of the transition, particularly given the appalling conditions they were facing in the post-civil war period. Finally, there appeared a threat to the worker-peasant alliance (or *smychka*) itself on which the 'dictatorship of the proletariat' ultimately depended. While the introduction of the *New Economic Policy* (NEP) helped to mitigate the threat to the *smychka* in particular by allowing trade in agricultural commodities, the fundamental problems remained. These were political and not economic or administrative, as Lenin never ceased to stress. During this period, Lenin developed extremely detailed arguments to counteract politics within the state apparatuses and the party itself that relied on bureaucratic coercive methods.

The 'dictatorship of the proletariat' (DOP), the term which, following Marx, Lenin and the Bolsheviks used as an equivalent for 'socialism,' the

---
1 Lenin 1974: 374.
2 Lenin 1973a: 83.

period of transition to communism, was in danger of losing support among the masses. It is crucially important to understand that for Lenin, the DOP meant not only dictatorship over a small bourgeoisie, its representatives, laws and practices, but that this should be combined with the broadest possible democracy for the people/masses who were the overwhelming majority. In this, Lenin closely followed Marx's statements in various political texts such as the *Civil War in France* and the Critique of the Gotha Programme.[3]

A brief review of Lenin's arguments in this specific context is extremely valuable as it enables us to acquire an understanding of the deeply democratic (in the proletarian and not the bourgeois sense) political position which Lenin saw as necessary to achieve the ultimate goal of a Communist society. It was Lenin's view that class struggle persists under socialism although it should today be apparent that 'class' is not the exclusive concept for understanding the contradictions inherent in such a transitory society. In particular, it does not sufficiently clarify the practices of the state itself. To call the state a "workers' state" as Trotsky did was simply "an abstraction" for Lenin. Concretely, it was rather "a workers' and peasants' state" and moreover "a workers' state *with a bureaucratic twist to it.*"[4] What was dangerous about the "bureaucratic twist" of the state was precisely that it engaged in practices ("a culture," Lenin said) which were inimical to full democracy and the unleashing of popular potentials for transformation toward the achievement of freedom where the state is no longer, in Marx's terms, "superimposed upon society...[but] completely subordinate to it."[5] We are confronted here with a conception of class politics as irreducible to simple sociological class location yet, at the same time, Lenin attributed the bureaucratic character of the state to the backwardness and overwhelmingly historically agrarian nature of Russian society.[6] Consequently "it will take decades to overcome the evils of bureaucracy."[7] "(In the last analysis) *struggle alone* will determine how far we shall advance..."[8]

In order to enable proletarian control over the state apparatus, two fundamental political problems needed to be solved: 1) the limitation of

---

3 In the *Critique of the Gotha Programme* (1875), Marx wrote: "Between capitalist and communist society there lies the period of the revolutionary transformation of the one into the other. Corresponding to this is also a political transition period in which the state can be nothing but the r*evolutionary dictatorship of the proletariat* [...] Since the state is merely a transitional institution of which use is made in the struggle, in the revolution, to keep down one's enemies by force, it is utter nonsense to speak of a free people's state [...] Freedom consists in converting the state from an organ superimposed upon society into one completely subordinate to it." Lenin, in his *The State and Revolution*, commented that: "socialism was termed by Marx [...] the lowest phase of communist society" and that "he consistently applies materialist dialectics, the theory of development, and regards communism as something which develops out of capitalism. Instead of scholastically invented, 'concocted' definitions and fruitless disputes over words (What is socialism? What is communism?)." (Lenin 1974: 475-476)
4 Lenin 1973a: 24. Charles Bettelheim comments that, in taking this position "Lenin thus broke openly with a problematic which was not merely that of Trotsky and Bukharin, but which had implicitly also been that the entire party, namely, the problematic which identified the Soviet state with a 'workers' state'." (Bettelheim 1976: 391)
5 See Marx 1875.
6 "In our country bureaucratic practices have [...] economic roots [within] the atomized and scattered state of the small producer with his poverty, illiteracy, lack of culture..." (Lenin 1973a: 351)
7 Lenin 1973a: 56.
8 Lenin 1973b: 52.

state bureaucratic excesses and 2) training of (non-party) workers to take over state administrative tasks. The resolution of these two problems required much closer links between the party and the masses in order for the vanguard party to ultimately rely on them. The party's reliance on the masses was made necessary by the fact that

> the dictatorship of the proletariat cannot be exercised through an organisation embracing the whole of that class because [...] the proletariat is still so divided, so degraded, so corrupted in parts (by imperialism in some countries) that an organisation taking in the whole proletariat cannot directly exercise proletarian dictatorship. It can be exercised only by a vanguard that has absorbed the revolutionary energy of that class.[9]

But "communists should control the [state]machinery they are assigned to, and not [...] that the machinery should control them."[10] Concurrently, the vanguard, in order to win "must have the sympathy of the masses"[11] and moreover it "cannot possibly exist unless we have good relations with the peasant masses."[12] Hence "what matters now is how to approach the mass, to establish contact with it and win it over, and how to get the intricate transmission system working (how to run the dictatorship of the proletariat)."[13] Indeed "we can and must find [...] methods of testing the mood of the masses and coming closer to them."[14] In order to do so successfully, the party had to acquire the support of the trade unions, the main organisations of the working masses. It was they who would help the party resolve the political problems mentioned above for they were the "'transmission belts' running from the vanguard to the mass of the advanced class and from the latter to the mass of the working people."[15]

In addition, for Lenin, "trade unions are reservoirs of the state power, a school of communism and a school of management. The specific and cardinal thing in this sphere is not administration,"[16] the bureaucratic approach of controlling the trade unions from above that Trotsky was advocating. "Trotsky's fundamental mistake is that he treats [...] *the questions* [...] *as administrative*"[17] rather than political. The role of "the Communist Party, the vanguard of the proletariat, [is to lead] the non-Party working masses educating, preparing, teaching and training the masses."[18] It does so by drawing the non-party masses

---

9 Lenin 1973a: 21.
10 Lenin 1973b: 442.
11 Ibid: 476.
12 Ibid: 489.
13 Lenin 1973a: 23.
14 Ibid: 362.
15 Ibid: 21.
16 Ibid: 98.
17 Ibid: 97.
18 Ibid: 50.

into its work: "we shall draw into Soviet work, primarily economic work, hundreds upon hundreds of non-Party people, real non-Party people from the masses, the rank and file of workers and peasants…"[19]

Lenin continued even more vehemently to warn his comrades that "if the party falls out with the trade unions the fault lies with the party and this spells certain doom for the Soviet power […] Nothing can ruin us but our own mistakes. […] There is a spirit of hostility for us among the trade union rank and file because of our own mistakes and the bureaucratic practices up on top, including myself …"[20] "The masses of organised workers are legitimately protesting and inevitably showing readiness to throw out the new officials who refuse to rectify the useless and harmful excesses of bureaucracy."[21] Should an administrative approach to the trade unions, as advocated by Trotsky and Bukharin be followed, this would threaten the dictatorship of the proletariat itself.

For Lenin, ways had to be found to enable ordinary workers to combat bureaucratic power and to defend themselves against their own state: "We now have a state under which it is the business of the massively organised proletariat to protect itself […] while we […] must use these workers' organizations to protect the workers from their state, and to get them to protect our state."[22] The point is re-iterated insistently: "the trade unions no longer have to face the class economic struggle but the non-class 'economic struggle,' which means combating bureaucratic distortions of the Soviet apparatus, safeguarding the working-people's material and spiritual interests in ways and means inaccessible to this apparatus, etc. This is a struggle they will have to face for many more years to come."[23]

But it was not just the state apparatuses that were the problem, "we must have the courage to face the bitter truth. The Party is sick. The Party is down with the fever."[24] During this period the party was becoming "overgrown" by its administrative apparatus thus undermining the power of elected officials. In his study of that period Charles Bettelheim comments that:

> The transformation of the Bolshevik Party between 1918 and 1923 […] presented a twofold aspect: on the one hand, it tended to preserve the proletarian character of party policy; on the other it tended to bestow independence upon the party's administrative apparatus and thereby increase the freedom of action of a body of officials who, in the conditions then existing, were increasingly bourgeois and petty bourgeois[25]

---

19 Ibid: 362.
20 Ibid: 58.
21 Ibid: 73.
22 Ibid: 25.
23 Ibid: 100.
24 Ibid: 50.
25 Bettelheim 1976: 309.

Lenin attempted to find a cure for the growing sickness in developing closer ties with the masses. By identifying the "honest and loyal worker [...] among the non-Party people [...] and trying them out in wider and gradually expanding fields of work, and [thus helping to] cure the evil of isolation of Communist Party cells from the masses, an evil that is in evidence in many places."[26] Moreover, in order to strengthen itself, the party should be purged "of those who have lost touch with the masses."[27] The suggestions of the non-Party masses must be sought out and taken into consideration when purging the party for "the working masses have a fine intuition, which enables them to distinguish honest and devoted communists from those who arouse the disgust of people earning their bread by the sweat of their brow."[28]

Lenin did not mince his words to his comrades when they were defending communists who upheld bureaucratic practices on the basis of their loyalty to the cause. Thus, to Bogdanov he wrote in 1921:

> We must not be afraid of the courts (our courts are proletarian) or of publicity, but must drag bureaucratic delays out into daylight for the people's judgement: only in this way shall we manage to cure this disease [...] we don't know how to conduct a public trial for rotten bureaucracy: for this all of us, and particularly the People's Commissariat for Justice, should be hung on stinking ropes. And I have not yet lost all hope that one day we shall be hung for this, and deservedly so.[29]

Finally, Lenin also turned to the masses in order to staff a specific institution whose job he hoped it would be to control the state bureaucracy more directly. This was the 'Workers' and Peasants' Inspection' (or *Rabkrin*). The "overcoming the evils of bureaucracy" required "hundreds of measures, wholesale literacy, culture and participation in the activity of the Workers' and Peasants' Inspection:"[30]

> In view of the hidebound 'departmentalism' that prevails even among the best Communists, the low standard of efficiency of the employees and the internal intrigues in the departments (worse than any Workers' and Peasants' Inspection intrigues), we cannot at the moment dispense with the Workers' and Peasants' Inspection [...] if not, it will be impossible to combat departmentalism and red tape, it will be impossible to teach non-Party workers and peasants the art of administration, which is a task that at the present time we cannot shirk either in principle or in practice.[31]

---

26 Lenin 1973a: 476.
27 Lenin 1973b: 39.
28 Ibid: 40.
29 Lenin 1977: 556.
30 Lenin 1973a: 68.
31 Lenin 1973b: 353-354.

Marcel Liebman, in his book *Leninism under Lenin*, comments that this case of the Workers' and Peasant's Inspection was "typical of the methods that were often used by the Soviet state in order to correct its own faults. When attacked by the apparently incurable disease of 'institutionitis', it tried to deal with the defects of the existing bodies by creating new ones, which did not always abolish the old bodies, but merely took their places beside them."[32]

At the end of his life then, Lenin was convinced that the only way to overcome the reactionary politics of the state bureaucracy, was a reliance of the masses of non-party workers and peasants:

> with the exception of the People's Commissariat of Foreign Affairs, our state apparatus is to a considerable extent a survival of the past and has undergone hardly any serious change [...] how did we act in the more critical moments of the Civil War? We concentrated our best Party forces in the Red Army; we mobilised the best of our workers; we looked for new forces [...] I am convinced that we must go to the same source to find the means of reorganising the Workers' and Peasants' Inspection [...] we must make the Workers' and Peasants' Inspection a really exemplary institution, an instrument to improve our state apparatus.[33]

At the same time Lenin admitted "frankly that the People's Commissariat of the Workers' and Peasants' Inspection does not at present enjoy the slightest authority"[34] and he not only planned its re-organisation but expressed the hope that the renovated Inspection will act more decisively and that "exceptional care" must be devoted to "raising it to an exceptionally high level."[35] He ended on a note exhorting his comrades to "reduce our state apparatus to the utmost degree of economy. We must banish from it all traces of extravagance, of which so much has been left over from tsarist Russia, from its bureaucratic capitalist state machine."[36]

Of course, we now know that this did not happen; Lenin's struggle was not continued, and the mass organisations gradually lost all independence from the state-party. Liebman commented in conclusion that in this manner "a regime born in a struggle for freedom and amid hopes for a libertarian society acquired, in the shape of a burdensome and authoritarian bureaucracy, what was to be one of the most lasting features of the Soviet scene."[37]

Today, these arguments of Lenin's are largely forgotten. It is assumed on 'the Left' that socialism is a goal to be attained and not a period of transition to communism during which the state power and its practices and

---

32 Liebman 1975: 323.
33 Lenin 1973b: 481, 489.
34 Ibid: 490.
35 Ibid: 495, 501.
36 Ibid: 501.
37 Ibid: 325.

subjectivities must be struggled against in order to provide the conditions for popular democracy and to give free reign to popular inventiveness. Human emancipation (freedom) cannot be achieved exclusively through the utilisation of state power, even though that power may be necessary, for it has been precisely the state that has reproduced the oppression of the majority by a minority from the moment of its rise during the Neolithic Revolution. State coercion of the bourgeoisie must therefore be complemented by the most extensive forms of popular democratic practice. Of course, the dialectic between coercion and freedom is not an easy matter to resolve politically, but addressing this dialectic is precisely what the emancipatory politics of socialism are all about. In the People's Republic of China, Mao and his allies also recognised in the mid 1960s that if a return to state capitalism was to be avoided, the state production of a bourgeois culture had to be confronted by a mass movement and mass popular democracy. This is precisely what the Cultural Revolution in that country was designed to confront.[38] In fact we should now be aware that the road followed by Lenin, to fight state bureaucracy by setting up other state institutions, cannot be successful, although this made sense within the political subjectivities of his time.

In sum, if we are interested in seriously thinking a politics of emancipation today, it is necessary for any such project to be based on independent popular movements. Having said that, the major problem of the necessary relationship between such movements and a political organisation is still the subject of historical experimentation. Past practical experiences of linking the political organisation with the masses such as the 'Mass Line' developed by Mao and the 'Return to the Source' advocated by Cabral,[39] must be analysed and subjected to critical scrutiny if we are to hold firm to the view that it is the masses who make history. In particular, this means transcending the problematic of representation that lies at the core of the party form of organisation and which is invariably statist as the party is said to 'represent' – the people, the working-class or the masses – within a state-controlled domain of politics. The problematic of representation disables the necessary constant problematising of the dialectic of movement and organisation, of theory and practice. A political subjectivity that is in essence emancipatory and dialectical is opposed to a politics of simple representation. Ultimately, as Lenin advised, this means never failing "to understand what is decisive in Marxism namely, its revolutionary dialectics."[40]

---

38 The politics of the Cultural Revolution have only recently started to be seriously studied in detail. For two extremely important books see Y. Wu (2014) and Russo (2020).
39 See *inter alia* Mao Zedong "Some Questions Concerning Methods of Leadership" (1943) and "On Coalition Government" (1945) in *Selected Works of Mao Tse-Tung Vol.3* and Cabral (1973).
40 Lenin 1973b: 476.

References

Bettelheim, Charles (1976), *Class Struggles in the USSR, First period 1917-1923*. London and New York: Monthly Review Press.

Cabral, Amilcar (1973), *Return to the Source: Selected Speeches of Amilcar Cabral*. London and New York: Monthly Review Press.

Lenin, V.I. (1973a), *Collected Works Vol. 32*. Moscow: Progress Publishers.

Lenin, V.I. (1973b), *Collected Works Vol. 33*. Moscow: Progress Publishers.

Lenin, V.I. (1974), *Collected Works Vol. 25*. Moscow: Progress Publishers.

Lenin, V.I. (1977), *Collected Works Vol. 36*. Moscow: Progress Publishers.

Liebman, Marcel (1975), *Leninism under Lenin*. London: Merlin Press.

Mao, Zedong (1967), *Selected Works of Mao Tse-Tung Vol.3*. Oxford: Pergamon Press.

Marx, Karl (1875), "Critique of the Gotha Programme," *Marxist Internet Archive*. Accessed on 28.11.2020, at https://www.marxists.org/archive/marx/works/1875/gotha/.

Russo, Alessandro (2020), *Cultural Revolution and Revolutionary Culture*. Durham: Duke University Press.

Wu, Yiching (2014), *The Cultural Revolution at the Margins*. Cambridge: Harvard University Press.

20. Lenin: A Man of Action and a Defender of the Integrity of Revolutionary Thought

Molaodi Wa Sekake

> *The dearest possession of any person is life. It is given only once, and it must be lived so as to feel no torturing regrets for wasted years, never know the burning shame of a mean and petty past; so live that, dying you had a right to say: all my life, all my strength was given to the finest cause in all the world – the fight for the Liberation of Humankind.*
> Nikolai Ostrovsky

If Lenin never had an opportunity to say, "All my life, all my strength was given to the finest cause in all the world – the fight for the Liberation of Humankind," as expressed by his fellow countryman Nikolai Ostrovsky, to commemorate him in this manner is unequivocally to state that on his behalf. Lenin used the pen to live beyond it; he died to outlive himself through his deeds and ideas. And since we can say, "Lenin is dead, long live Lenin," we cannot summarise his life, just as we cannot summon all his work in one essay – unless the immediate enterprise is to banish him from public imagination to the delight of liberal and conservative forces.

Yet that must never stymie our efforts to honour him – now and forever. We can only honour a man of Lenin's stature by locating him in history; that is, by looking at how history shaped him and how he shaped it in return. To do so is to look at moments of progress and regress; of mishaps and happiness. To go about such a task requires our blatant refusal to bury or imprison the contours of history into hagiographies. We should, therefore, visit Lenin's grave to work with him and against him (when the need arises). Like many other Left-scholars from Europe, Lenin's intellectual labours were not adequate to grasp the *ontological* question that affects racialised persons beyond Marxist political economy categories. This owes largely to the context of their political work rather than prejudice: they did not, and cannot, experience what it means to *exist* as a racialised being beyond recognising that there are colonies and colonised people.

As a result, many Left-scholars have come to treat race and racism (including sexuality) as epiphenomena, not *constitutive aspects* of colonial oppression. This is a blatant refusal to understand the 'complex' of colonialism. Out of this, we have come to live with scholars who – wittingly or unwittingly – passionately sanitise the wars of conquest and dispossession that took place in some parts of Europe, in Africa and in the Americas. No wonder we have thinkers and activists in some parts of Europe who are left-wing racists. To them it is class or nothing; anything else is a disturbance of the 'class struggle.' As such, while we go to the grave to work with Lenin on the importance of proletarian internationalism, we also need to grapple with the *philosophical* and *ontological* presuppositions that undergird European modernity. These are presuppositions that are still deeply embedded in modern philosophical and political thought.

The prevalence of racism, and particularly anti-Black racism, all over the world reflects an ugly reality that we can only overcome if we go to the root cause. A revolutionary theory must serve people, not the other way around. Orthodox Marxists, for instance, often want people to serve theory. But a revolutionary philosophy or theory should not be like a big container that we enter to receive ready-made facts about our lives; it should rather reflect our realities, experiences and aspirations. We need not shy away from these – and many other such matters – in the name of 'working class unity.' The unity of the working class must be based on authentic relations in which everyone's humanity is recognised.

Lenin Resurrected to be Killed Again

There is a paradox, created by people who believe themselves to be 'revolutionaries,' and particularly by the political elite of national liberation movements in Africa. This is the paradox of resurrecting Lenin, only to kill him again. The question, then, would be: Why not leave him where he is, in his grave, if to resurrect him is also to kill him? Perhaps, in the field of linguistics, this cannot make sense: it passes as tautology; but in the field of political power relations it serves a particular purpose. A renowned South African Black Conscious art critic, Athi Joja Mongelezi, in one of the South African national newspapers, wrote, specifically in reference to Steve Biko,[1] that he "is brought to the table of power not only to silence him, but also ultimately to discombobulate the restless masses."[2]

We can, as well, point out many occasions where Lenin has been conveniently resurrected to pacify, not agitate, the so-called 'masses.' On many of these occasions, Lenin is passionately resurrected to live against himself; to argue against himself; to speak against all that he lived for. In that way, therefore, Lenin is cowed to the cultural sensibilities and power relations that he lived all his life fighting against.

We, from South Africa, can attest to this unfortunate reality. The wrecking crew[3] that is either unwilling or unable to transform radically the social and economic order for the benefit of the poor and workers, expediently and voraciously scavenge quotes from Lenin's works. This is in pursuit

---

1 Steve Biko was a leader of the Black Consciousness movement and an ardent proponent of Black Consciousness Philosophy. He co-organized the Black People's Convention of 1972, and published *I Write What I Like* in 1978. Biko viewed white racism as the main problem facing Black people and advocated Black unity to challenge it. He was brutally killed by the Apartheid regime in 1977. In his own words: "It is better to die for an idea that will live than to live for an idea that will die," and "the most potent weapon in the hands of the oppressor is the mind of the oppressed."
2 See Mongalezi 2014.
3 See Holt 2009.

of the fig leaf of legitimacy, not for anything radical or transformative. Out of this, Lenin's works become merely promiscuous texts at the disposal of a decadent political elite, on neocolonial and neoliberal steroids. Just one example, in 2008 the then Minister of Public Enterprise, Barbara Hogan, at the National Council of the Young Communist League of South Africa, told us that she had read Lenin and Marx, yet her ministry zealously carried out neoliberal programmes that had been made official state policies in 2006.

The fact of the matter is that this type of scavenging should not be the case in a country like South Africa; a country that is in dire need of the systemic and structural transformation of unjust power relations to cater for the landless and propertyless working class, who largely consist of Black people. It should not, indeed, be the case in a country where the debt-to-GDP ratio is so unsustainably high and grows day by day; where wealth is still concentrated in a few hands, mainly in those of white males; where youth unemployment is a ticking time tomb.

On the contrary, in this era of rampant financialization of the economy, we should turn to Lenin to understand the dynamics and contradictions of finance capital, and its impact on countries and people; to analyse the changes in the global economic landscape that occurred in the 70s and 80s and the workings of neoliberal finance capital that underlie them. Lenin's *Imperialism, The Highest Stage of Capitalism,* for instance, can provide us with an understanding of crucial aspects, such as the role of Credit Ratings Agencies (CRAs) in today's global capitalist economy. The economic growth prospects of many countries are based on the amount of investment they can attract. To avoid the asymmetry of information between investors and countries, CRAs have come to play a key role in determining where investments can be made for profit. As a result of their power to make assessments and allocate credit scores to countries and corporations, CRAs are central to the well-being, or lack thereof, of many countries. In fact, they have become the 'economic hit men' of the era of neoliberal finance capital. This system has plunged many countries into debt, leading to a situation in which they have no choice but to fall into the arms of multilateral institutions such as the IMF and the World Bank. One of the tragic implications of this reality is that countries lose their sovereign power over policymaking. When that happens, democracy becomes a mockery, human sensibilities for justice and compassion are cold-bloodedly molested and human rights are unashamedly sacrificed on the altar of profit.

Instead of turning Lenin into a Trojan horse (to bluff the working class) to implement neoliberal economic and social policies, national liberation movements in Africa, such as the African National Congress (ANC) in South Africa and the Mozambique Liberation Front (FRELIMO), could refer to his works to transform radically their societies for the benefit of the poor and workers. It can neither be understandable nor justifiable to refuse to deepen the struggle against imperialism, as Lenin would have required of every oppressed and exploited territory and people. This is particularly so for a continent such as ours with a rich history of anti-colonial politics, which is still subjected to a massive capitalist imperialist rip-off. The implications of Structural Adjustment Programs (SAPs) and the ongoing pillage of Africa are in need of nothing short of a revolution in thought and action to bring radical change to this unfortunate but by no means inevitable situation.

In Africa, as in other continents where wars of liberation were relentlessly waged, the state assumed an important role in the development, or lack thereof, of a country. As such, Lenin's *State and Revolution* could have provided, and could still provide, vital insights into the nature of the state to bring about much-desired changes for the benefit of the people and workers. In South Africa, where a national liberation movement, the ANC, has been the governing party for more than twenty years (since our transition from Apartheid to democracy), there was a particular conception of the transformation of society that was centred on the state, and built on the notion of the National Democratic Revolution. Worked out in the struggle days, the belief, simply put, was that revolutionary forces would take over the state, radically transform it and then use it to also transform society, deepen, advance and defend the democratic gains.

This belief was consistent with what Marx and Engels explicitly expressed in the *Communist Manifesto*, and reiterated by Lenin in his *State and Revolution*: "One thing especially was proved by the Commune, viz., that 'the working class cannot simply lay hold of the ready-made state machinery and wield it for its own purposes.'"[4] Yet what has come of such a belief, in Africa in general and South Africa in particular, is nothing short of betrayal. The transition from Apartheid to democracy, or what the South African Communist Party (SACP) referred to as a 'democratic breakthrough', has not brought about any meaningful change in the lives of poor people and workers. In fact, a 1994 programme called the *Reconstruction and Development Programme* (RDP) was ruthlessly abandoned in favour of the neoliberal *Growth, Employment and Redistribution* (GEAR) strategy in 1996.

Since then, the state has been sheepishly beholden to neoliberal forces. GEAR was the complete opposite of RDP. By way of example, the latter advocated for increased expenditure on social and economic services to deal with poverty, unemployment and inequalities; the former, by contrast, eschewed such social value, focusing instead on inflation targeting and economic growth. GEAR was therefore a typical neoliberal programme that pushed for less state involvement in the economy, labour market liberalisation, market-centred approaches to development, trade liberalisation, etc.

In this, there was, and there is still, a belief that the economy would grow and 'trickle down' to the benefit of everyone, including the poor and workers. Instead, the economy grew (between 1996 and the early 2000s) and still grows, to the benefit of the rich few at the expense of the bulk of

---
4 Lenin 1974a: 419.

the working-class population, hence the tragic reality of 'jobless growth.' As such, the state was never going to be used to tamper with property relations and usher in radical change for the benefit of the working class. It was clear, therefore, that the 'national productive forces' (land, banks, mines, water resources, forests, etc.) would not be placed under the command of the people but would remain in the hands of the few.

To this day, we live with the fact that wealth is still concentrated in the hands of a small number of (mainly white) people. Consequently, there was no way that colonial and capitalist state-formation dynamics could have been overcome without radical or counter-hegemonic imaginations, and Lenin's *State and Revolution* could have offered just that. Instead, the political elite chose, and still chooses, to turn his works into souvenirs they only reminisce about when they talk about their former life in exile; in Moscow, Tanzania, Algeria, etc. The elite has thus come to bask in the glory of decadence at the expense of thoroughgoing transformation.

Lenin and the Integrity of Revolutionary Thought: Lessons

Capitalism in the form of neoliberalism cultivated, in the words of Fredric Jameson, the "cultural logic of late capitalism." How, then, did the Left forces, locally and globally, understand the changes in the cultural or intellectual sphere that were to justify the economic logic of neoliberal finance capital in the 21st century?

As the Soviet Union founded by Lenin and the Berlin Wall that divided East and West Germany were crumbling, there was a talk in town. It was a talk of 'post'-everything: post-history, post-politics, post-structure, post-state, post-truth, post-class, etc. In 1992, the American scholar Francis Fukuyama wrote *The End of History and the Last Man*. In the main, Fukuyama's argument was that with the collapse of the Soviet Union, signalling the end of the 'cold war,' there was no possible way of life (economically and otherwise) other than that of the United States of America. The result of these cultural and intellectual shifts, which were reflective of the changes in economic relations, was that long-held conceptual models and intellectual paradigms, such as Marxism and Psychoanalysis, came under intense scrutiny. Faced with this rewriting of history, it is not difficult to imagine some pertinent questions that could have been posed by Left-thinkers and activists:

- How are we going to talk about Lenin's State and the Revolution if we live in a 'post-state' order, or even about the revolution, when 'history' has ended (since the revolution, as Marx had once observed, is the locomotive of history)?
- What of historical materialism, when history has ended and nothing can be materially 'pinnable', 'mappable' or 'understandable', since reality is said to be that which is evanescent?

In general terms, we can say a lot of things about that period and its impact, intellectually and otherwise. Concretely, one of the important things we can point out here is that the 'cultural logic of late capitalism' neutralised many Left-thinkers and organisations. Yes, many of them gave up the revolutionary combat gear and joined the merry-go-round of intellectual trends, in which the rule of the ephemeral reigned supreme; just as national liberation movements in Africa were kissing goodbye to the notion of imperialism in their political documents and vocabulary in the 1990s. The academy and political movements, alike, were cowed into submission. If that were not the case, the task of constructing a socialist world would not have been tampered with.

As a result of this, won-over souls, in the academy for instance, underwent a mandatory baptism of questionable epistemic paradigms. The primary mission was to turn the academy into a cathedral of conformity, albeit couched in pseudo-revolutionary speak. Art, architecture and philosophy departments, for instance, began to smell the 'postmodernist fragrance' of thinking (a continuity of the bourgeoisie mode of thinking) as opposed to the 'odour of materialism' (which would have somewhat meant a challenge to the prevailing cultural and epistemic paradigms). Out of this, a materialist critique of capitalism vanished into thin air, except in the margins by daring scholars and activists such as Samir Amin and Thandika Mkandawire. In short, neoliberalism and its cultural logic were running amok. The implications of this reality forced some scholars to decry:

> I think that we scholars and publishers have allowed the moneychangers to enter the temple. We need to restrict their activities, because we cannot kick them out the way Jesus did. Of course, many universities are, in significant part, financial holding operations. Don't be shocked. So are many of our churches.[5]

Yet it was not the first time a certain idea swept people's minds in that way – either to win them over completely or to push them against the wall and, as a result, compel them to develop weird theoretical paradigms. The dynamics of the evolution of the natural and mathematical sciences, for instance, can testify to this. In fact, such realities are regular occurrences in history.

Indeed, only those with the requisite political and philosophical stamina and a single-minded sense of purpose can survive such moments – and Lenin exemplified both. Those who were swept aside or won over by the intellectual trends of the 'cultural logic of late capitalism' could have taken a leaf out of Lenin's works. In his times, that which was theoretically 'fashionable' was

---

5 Waters 2004: 5.

always subjected to intense critique. It was put through the tempest of hard-hitting yet honest and frank discussions and polemical engagements. Lenin's *Materialism and Empirio-Criticism* in 1909 and his *"Left-Wing" Communism: An Infantile Disorder* in 1920 testify to this fact. Without such processes of (self-)critique, one is likely to mistake ripples of pond water for the volcanic waves of the ocean. This is what Left-thinkers, particularly those who believed in dialectical and historical materialism, should have realised or known when it came to the 'cultural logic of late capitalism.'

Therefore we can say, without any doubt, that without Lenin's clarity of thought, single-minded sense of purpose, sensitivity to the task at hand and capacity to lead an organisation, one of the greatest events of the 20th century, the Russian October Socialist Revolution, could not have taken place. His theoretical interventions in fierce debates that were bound to shift the revolution towards a particular direction were no mere spluttering of inchoate phrases or words to hoodwink both suspecting and unsuspecting minds; rather, they were coherent critiques that informed a clear programme of action. Arguably, there is no single text by Lenin that did not seek to respond to the question at hand – from his 1899 essay *The Development of Capitalism in Russia* to his 1917 book *The State and Revolution*.

Lenin's Sense of Location

The Development of Capitalism in Russia was one of Lenin's first published texts. It was a thought from below: a concrete analysis of Russia's social and economic development. Lenin's recognition of the primary responsibility to understand the conditions of his country became the basis of his conception of the international struggle. The local informed the international. But in this too, the unique dynamics of the international were given adequate attention. There was, therefore, no 'parochial' approach to the 'international' struggle. This defined his political philosophy. In fact, the text can be said to have countered a pre-emptive war against critical thought and praxis in Russia.

According to the logic of Western European philosophical paradigms at the time, the 'universal' should always take place at the expense of the 'particular,' in order to constitute true imagination. The refusal to fall prey to such a trap says a great deal about Lenin's philosophical sensibilities in conducting revolutionary political work. Many of his comrades, on the other hand, were swept into a sea of idealism in the early 1900s, as evident in *Empiriomonism: Essays in Philosophy* by Alexander Bogdanov, inspired by the 'solipsism' of Mach and Avenarius. They were, therefore, extraordinarily desensitised to the concrete conditions of the Russian peasants and workers. In *Materialism and Empirio-Criticism*, Lenin sought to deal with such tendencies; for him, those were Russian variants of idealism that sourced their inspiration from Western European arch-idealists such as Immanuel Kant, George Berkeley, etc.

If Lenin and like-minded comrades had lowered their philosophical guard or resigned themselves to 'analytical inertia' or 'philosophical agnosticism,' the Russian Revolution could not have taken place. This is because the infatuations of the idealist faction of the Party would have made them overlook (the) concrete realities and, therefore, the necessary revolutionary tasks at hand. Lenin, however, paid adequate attention to the specific, concrete conditions that had to inform a revolutionary programme of action. This is what continents and countries still reeling from the impacts of slavery and colonialism should take into consideration if they are to transform themselves. In Africa, for instance, the persistent failure to understand the concrete realities and implications of 'enclave economies' has greatly stymied efforts at radically transforming the continent's economic and social landscape. If a self-sufficient Africa has to be created, the economic logic of the enclave must be taken into consideration and transcended. The Malawian scholar Professor Guy Mhone, for instance, laid a solid foundation for this to happen, through his insightful work on African political economy.

Lenin and the Colonial Question

In the 1920 preface to *Imperialism*, Lenin writes:

> Capitalism has grown into a world system of colonial oppression and of the financial strangulation of the overwhelming majority of the population of the world by a handful of 'advanced' countries. And this 'booty' is shared between two or three powerful world plunderers armed to the teeth (America, Great Britain, Japan), who are drawing the entire world into their war over the division of their booty.[6]

From this arose a radical conception of imperialism: "Imperialism was therefore not to be explained as merely a change in the foreign policies of the governments of the 'advanced' countries, but as a change in the nature of the capitalist relations of production."[7] The understanding was: because capitalism exploits the masses of the people in the colonies, and turns them into the proletariat, they must be organised. It was for this reason, in the main, that the Communist International in 1920 resolved that the communist parties of colonially occupied territories should work with progressive national liberation movements to weaken capitalist imperialist forces.

Lenin was well aware that it was important to understand the workings of the capitalist system, through communist formations in every country,

---
6 Lenin 1974b: 191.
7 Lorimer in Lenin 1999: 10.

at its imperialist phase. In fact, it was understood that this was vital for the principled unity of the oppressed nations and its people, to constitute far-reaching counter-hegemonic politics in pursuit of freedom. Only a leader with foresight, a practical ideologue, could have realised that colonies were important in the 'economic value chain' because they made resources available for the imperialist countries that had taken advantage of them. Lenin understood that by organising and working for the unity of the occupied territories and their nationally oppressed people, the imperialist efforts of capitalist countries would be thwarted, thereby presenting the possibility of an alternative socialist world order. It is in this context that Lenin approached the national and colonial questions.

Perhaps, in an environment in which people continue to suffer from the implications of colonialism and from the constant onslaught on their lives of capitalist imperialism – especially in Africa, Asia, Latin America and the Caribbean – it is time for the working class to organise and take up things for itself. The working classes of different countries have been let down, and continue to be let down, by governments that have sold their souls to the highest bidder. The working class must realise that beyond itself, its organisation, its unity and its capacity, it can never go anywhere; it will remain in chains with its fate determined by its exploiters. There are, however, political traditions at our disposal to carry out our mission. We must use texts such as *Imperialism, the Highest Stage of Capitalism*, and many others, to paddle ourselves out of the morass of unequal and violent settler-colonial, racist, patriarchal and capitalist imperialism. In fact, such texts can be used to break wide open the fissures of history to unleash possibilities of a free, just and equal society. The facade of the bourgeoisie liberal rights framework must be smashed. The parapet that kept, and still keeps, under wraps the deadly assumptions and stereotypes of the racist, patriarchal, homophobic, capitalist, colonial, imperialist order must be torn apart.

We have seen that Lenin's theoretical works were always directly linked to the revolutionary tasks at hand; yet we must understand his political works as part of many other counter-hegemonic traditions, such as revolutionary nationalism that anchored anticolonial struggles, from which we can and must draw inspiration. We should understand the volcanic calls of such traditions for the working class to assume the responsibility of liberating itself. We must take them as calls to a blatant refusal to be sacrificed ruthlessly on the altar of the insatiable greed of the capitalist imperialist behemoth.

Resisting any temptation to take pride in borrowed intellectual and philosophical robes, we must use Lenin's works to counter the pre-emptive war against critical thought and praxis. We must understand them as saying to us: If the murmurings of the oppressed turn into a cry for justice and equality, we must amplify them and take them to their logical end; and if they rattle the cultural and intellectual edifices of the capitalist order that has always imprisoned them, we must never stand in their way. The revolution is the cleansing of the spells cast on us by a world that has never loved us; it is to be born anew. We must not fear it. The battle cry should be amplified and taken to every cranny and nook of the world.

We must understand Lenin, through his works, as saying to us: If the 'gutter' speaks, and utters a vocabulary of lifelong refusal, of lifelong banishment from the realm of proper human life, and of tears turned into reservoirs of defiance and doggedness, let the gutter find expression. We must understand him as saying to us: Turn 'colonial plantations' and 'ghettos' into citadels of revolutionary reason and praxis to bring an end to the logics of exploitation, oppression, and dehumanisation embodied and constantly reproduced by the prevailing political economy of capitalist imperialism.

Only the working-class movement, with a single-minded sense of revolutionary purpose, can push against the stubborn frontiers of settler-colonial and capitalist imperialist power relations and imaginations. Only through the unity of the working class can a new human being, no longer made in the image of a greedy and sadistic 'master' class, come about. This is what Lenin relentlessly sought to achieve throughout his life. On the eve of so-called World War I, he constantly warned socialist formations in different countries that the working class stood to lose because those were imperialist wars. Unfortunately, the socialist bloc in Germany voted for the German state to fund the war and those in France sided with their national governments against the Russian Tsar. This, tragically, caused serious divisions and fragmentations in the international socialist camp.

In other words, Lenin understood that internationalism was not a matter of convenience; it was rather determined by the very conditions of capitalism. He realised that capitalism had assumed an international character – it had "created a world market, a world division of labour and a working class." If we are to truly roll back the frontiers of capitalist imperialist relations in this era and in the future, the disunity of the working class has to be avoided. In the context of capitalist imperialism, proletarian internationalism is the way to go until we attain a truly just and equal society.

In conclusion, we can no longer refuse to "honour the scrolls written in ash of charred bodies"[8] nor to surrender ourselves to the gifts bequeathed to us by revolutionaries who are physically no more, such as Lenin. These bequests say to us: No matter what it takes, we should always be on the side of the political, social, cultural and economic underdogs. Based on this, and amid the constant and systematic assault of capitalism on peoples' lives and the natural environment, perhaps we will finally come to the realisation that where Lenin's (s)word does not reach, capitalist imperialist violence shall not vanish. Lenin, in any event, could neither have suffered from the "torturing regrets for wasted years" nor could he have "known the burning

---

8 Matela 2020.

shame of a mean and petty past;" because he gave his life "to the finest cause in all the world – the fight for the Liberation of humankind." Lenin is dead, long live Lenin!

References
Frank, Thomas (2008), *The Wrecking Crew: How Conservatives Rule*. New York: Henry Holt and Company.
Jameson, Fredric (1989), *Postmodernism, or, the Cultural Logic of Late Capitalism*. Durham: Duke University Press.
Lenin, V.I. (1974a), *Collected Works Vol. 22*. Moscow: Progress Publishers.
Lenin, V.I. (1974b), *Collected Works Vol. 25*. Moscow: Progress Publishers.
Lenin, V.I. (1999), *Imperialism – The Highest Stage of Capitalism*. Sydney: Resistance Books.
Matela, Kahahliso (2020), "A Series of Letters to Poets," *An Irrational Diary*. Accessed on 29.06.2020, at http://anirrationaldiary.blogspot.com/2020/03/a-series-of-letters-to-poets_35.html?m=1.
Mongelezi, Athi Joja (2014), "The quiet violence of Steve Biko," *SowetanLive*. Accessed on 29.06.2020 at https://www.sowetanlive.co.za/sundayworld/lifestyle/talk/2014-09-15-the-quiet-violence-of-steve-biko/.
Sewell, Rob (2019), "Lenin and Internationalism," *In Defence of Marxism*. Accessed on 29.06.2020, at https://www.marxist.com/lenin-and-internationalism.htm.
Waters, Lindsay (2004), *Enemies of Promise: Publishing, Perishing and the Eclipse of Scholarship*. Chicago: Prickly Paradigm Press.

21. Electric Communism:
The Continued Importance of Energy to Revolution[1]

Matthew T. Huber

> *Communism is Soviet power plus the electrification of the whole country.*[2]

One of the many unfortunate aspects of the postmodern turn in the 1980s is a specific critique of modernity only in terms of cultural discourse: 'metanarratives,' ideologies of progress, and scientific rationalism.[3] As critics like Jameson and Harvey[4] point out, postmodernism emerged as a peculiar kind of 'cultural logic' largely divorced from the material foundations of social life. Another reading is that once the material foundations of industrial modernity were locked into place – at least in the advanced capitalist world where 'postmodern' theories were particularly popular – people forgot, or perhaps never *experienced*, the massive, often violent transformations wrought by 19th century industrialisation. Vladimir Ilyich Ulyanov, on the other hand, lived in a time and place where these transformations were impossible to ignore. This is why, in the famous quote above, he lays out the centrality of electricity to the communist project – a project in which Soviet power aims to "make the masses electricity-conscious."[5] While this statement likely appears technologically determinist in the wake of postmodern arguments on the fluid and contingent nature of history, Lenin's goal was simply to put into practice Marxist ideas that were largely uncontroversial at the time.

Energy, History and the Realm of Freedom

At the core of the industrial transformations so important to Marx's and Lenin's thinking is the centrality of energy. This can be catalogued in three critical domains. First, the shift from a reliance on human and animal muscle power for mechanical energy or simply 'work' – including material production and physical transport – to automatic machinery powered by fossil fuel. Of course, it was Karl Marx himself[6] who understood the significance of this shift, in his writing on the role of machinery in capital's exploitation of human (muscular) labour power.

Second, the shift from a reliance on land for all kinds of energy (most notably forests) to the decidedly non-land-intensive reserves of subterra-

---
1 I would like to thank Hjalmar Jorge Joffre-Eichhorn for his extensive feedback and helpful suggestions on previous drafts. All mistakes are my own.
2 Lenin 1974: 516.
3 See Lyotard 1984.
4 See Jameson 1991 and Harvey 1989.
5 Ibid: 517.
6 See Marx 1990.

nean fossil fuel for *heat* energy. This is not merely a question of how to warm our homes and other domestic spaces: it is about heat energy to fuel all manner of industrial processes from glass to beer making. It would take several planets' worth of forests to provide the heat energy required by the urban built environment we know today – the 'concrete jungle' of steel skyscrapers and asphalt roads. Our decidedly urban world is built through the combustion of oil, coal and natural gas.

Third, the shift from an organic to an industrial agricultural system is one in which fossil fuel-based 'inputs' take the place of what human labour and natural systems did before. It is not just tractors that replace the animal toil of ploughing, but also the chemical pesticides and fertilizers that replace the labour-intensive work of weeding, manure spreading, and other traditional activities. In the U.S., the story is dramatic: in 1790, 90% of the population worked on farms; in 1910, it was down to 35%; today it is less than 1.5%.[7] The export of industrial agriculture around the world after World War II ushered in a long period of "global depeasantisation."[8] Or as Aaron Benanav puts it, "The major global job destroyer in the 20th century was not 'silicon capitalism' but nitrogen capitalism."[9]

In fact, Bob Johnson argues that subterranean fossil fuel represents "the material substrata of our lives," what he calls "modernity's basement."[10] Problematically, however, capitalist commodity relations ensure that this material substrata is invisible: "We industrial peoples have preferred to keep our energy dependencies out of sight."[11] The result is a 'culture' increasingly unaware of the extent to which our entire systems of production and reproduction rely on industrial systems powered by fossil fuels; or in 21st century Lenin-speak, many of us are energy-unconscious.

At the core of all of these systems is electricity. While the first era of fossil fuel powered industrialisation was focused on steam and coal,[12] what some call the "second industrial revolution"[13] was based on the electrification of industrial production – most notably in the Fordist 'assembly line' powered by small efficient electric motors – and the shift to oil and internal combustion engines in the realm of transport.

The transformations brought about by electricity were impossible to ignore: not just electric lighting, but radio transmission, refrigeration, and water pumps for irrigation, among many inventions. Significantly, Lenin's life basically tracked exactly this massive expansion of electricity and its ever-growing importance as a core part of the productive forces of modern industrial capitalism.

---

7 Olmstead and Rhode 2014: 168.
8 See Araghi 1995.
9 Benanav 2019: 119.
10 Johnson 2014: xviii.
11 Ibid: xxix.
12 See Malm 2016.
13 Beaudreau 1999: 90.

These productive forces are therefore at the centre of a historical materialist understanding of the transition to socialism or communism, and hence, in Lenin's time it was an uncontroversial principle of classical Marxist theory that capitalism would play a world-historic role in developing the forces of production in such a way as to make *freedom* possible. Engels perhaps explains this most clearly:

> [I]t is precisely this industrial revolution which has raised the productive power of human labour to such a high level that – for the first time in the history of humanity – the possibility exists…to produce not only enough for the plentiful consumption of all members of society and for an abundant reserve fund, but also to leave each individual sufficient leisure so that what is really worth preserving in historically inherited culture – science, art, human relations is not only preserved, but converted from a monopoly of the ruling class into the common property of the whole of society…[14]

Likewise, Marx[15] referred to the development of these productive forces as creating the "material conditions of production which alone can form the real basis of a higher form of society, a society in which the full and free development of every individual forms the ruling principle."

The logic is straightforward: without industrial technology and automation made possible by machines and electric power, society would require a return to *muscular* or manual labour as the basis of material production. In Marx's view,[16] the "realm of necessity" would crowd out any possibility for a "realm of freedom," because most labour would be needed in agricultural and other manual production just to produce the bare minimum of subsistence.

Machine production and automation would therefore form the material basis for a communist vision of freedom based on *free time* – what Marx described as "disposable time"[17] to develop one's own human and creative capacities. Trying to apply Marx's thinking to the concrete situation of post-1917 Russia, it is no surprise that Lenin saw electricity as absolutely central to the revolutionary project of creating a communist society. Accordingly, the question was how to make this vision a reality in what was an essentially agrarian country.

---

14 See Engels 1872.
15 Marx 1990: 739.
16 Marx 1981: 959.
17 Marx 1973: 708.

Primitive Accumulation and Socialised Production: Electrifying the Revolution

Capitalism is a historically novel mode of production for one major ecological reason: it tears the bulk of the population away from the land and forces them to survive by means of money and commodity relations. Marx described this violent and bloody process as "primitive accumulation" and argued it was a necessary precondition of capitalist social relations. Yet, just as Marx saw capital's development of the productive forces as creating the material conditions for communism, he also saw "primitive accumulation" as necessary to destroy the somewhat scattered and small-scale peasant forms of production that dominated before the rise of capitalism:

> The small-holding peasants form an enormous mass whose members live in similar conditions but without entering into manifold relations with each other. Their mode of production isolates them from one another instead of bringing them into mutual intercourse.[18,19]

Primitive accumulation destroys this scattered and private form of production and at the same time *socialises* it by creating more expansive divisions of labour and harnessing the social power of scientific knowledge directly into large-scale industrial production. For Marx and Engels, only this *socialised* form of production could form the basis for what Engels described above as a production system capable of abolishing poverty and thereby deliver mass freedom. The problem with capitalism, of course, is that it socialises production but maintains private forms of appropriation. Malm brilliantly shows how the early era of coal-fired steam power – a *social* product of engineering knowledge if there ever was one – was conducive to *private* capital accumulation based on the exploitation of a surplus of workers in urban industrial districts.[20] Whereas waterpower tethered capital to the countryside – and forced them to share a hydrological commons – coal and steam allowed private capital to locate in urban areas "where labour is easily procured."[21] In other words, fossil capital is a type of socialised production for privatised appropriation *par excellence*.

Returning to Russia post-1917, the problem the Bolsheviks and Lenin faced was that Russia remained an overwhelmingly rural society when

---

18 Marx 1963: 123-124.
19 There is increasing evidence that Marx discovered the largely *communal* nature of Russian peasant production late in his life (Anderson 2010). As Marot recently described, "The mir, or peasant repartitional commune, managed the political and economic affairs of the peasantry in the villages in much of Russia, and had done so for centuries. Its officers, drawn from older, more experienced peasants, were elected in peasant assemblies, where decisions required unanimity in a great majority of cases. In their own sphere, the peasants obviously had hegemony." (Marot 2019) Although Marx became more optimistic that such cooperative forms of peasant production could inspire a communist mode of production, he did not advocate a return to rural peasant life as such.
20 See Malm 2016.
21 Malm 2016: 121.

the revolution took place. This is the reason why revolutionary economist Yevgeni Preobrazhensky, in the context of the New Economic Policy begun by Lenin after the destruction of the Civil War, advocated for a new type of "socialist primitive accumulation":

> Primitive socialist accumulation [...] means accumulation in the hands of the state of material resources mainly or partly from sources lying outside the complex of state economy. This accumulation must play an extremely important part in a backward peasant country, hastening to a very great extent the arrival of the moment when the technical and scientific reconstruction of the state economy begins and when this economy at last achieves purely economic superiority over capitalism.[22]

As opposed to capitalist primitive accumulation, however, Preobrazhensky sought the least violent way to accomplish what any Marxist should understand as necessary, "repudiat[ing] on principle all the forcible methods of capital in this sphere,"[23] while not ignoring that

> ...the idea that socialist economy can develop on its own, without touching the resources of petty-bourgeois (including peasant) economy is undoubtedly a reactionary petty-bourgeois utopia. The task of the socialist state consists here not in taking from the petty-bourgeois producers less than capitalism took, but in taking more from the still larger incomes which will be secured to the petty producer by the rationalisation of the whole economy, including petty production, on the basis of industrialising the country and intensifying agriculture.[24]

Preobrazhensky's position was highly contested, however. More tactical political thinkers were concerned that any type of economic policy that could be perceived as exploitative of the peasantry threatened the mass coalition between workers and peasants upon which the revolution apparently relied. Isaac Deutscher recounts, "Bukharin attacked the whole of Preobrazhensky's conception as 'monstrous,'"[25] and even Trotsky – who was seen as allied with Preobrazhensky – "jumped to his feet to deny"[26] the highly abstract conception of "exploiting" the peasantry. Nevertheless, despite these tactical political concerns, Deutscher points out that those too preoccupied with accommodating the demands of the peasantry were at odds with *basic* Marxist ideas: "As peasant property was in the Marxist

---

22 Preobrazhensky 1967: 84.
23 Ibid: 88.
24 Ibid: 89.
25 Deutscher 1959: 201.
26 Ibid: 200.

view incompatible with fully fledged socialism, Bukharin in fact placed a question mark over Marxist socialism at large."[27]

Millar, on the other hand, suggests that Preobrazhensky was "a careful Marxist theoretician"[28] simply trying to apply the insight of primitive accumulation as a necessary precondition of communism. He points out that Preobrazhensky's theory was explicitly presented as an abstract one that doesn't take into account the concrete conditions of Russian peasant life. Moreover, Preobrazhensky argued that the workers' state should aim "to implement primitive socialist accumulation through tax, price and financial policies"[29] in contrast to the capitalist use of violence written "in letters of blood and fire."[30] Lenin clearly respected Preobrazhensky's theoretical acumen but had characteristically acerbic views on his ability to navigate the political and strategic terrain: "All Comrade Preobrazhensky's theses are ultra- and super-academic; they smack of the intelligentsia, the study circle and the littérateur, and not of practical state and economic activity."[31]

Ultimately fatal differences of approach notwithstanding, the communist leadership, Lenin and Preobrazhensky included, clearly agreed that the countryside must be transformed to make communism possible, if needed by "melting church bells for copper and placing a light bulb in every village."[32] Therefore, the 1921-GOELRO plan, the worker state's first attempt at large-scale planning (including electrification) in the wake of the civil war and the resultant massive fuel shortages[33] set out to do precisely this. Lenin argued:

> Anyone who has carefully observed life in the countryside, as compared with life in the cities, knows that we have not torn up the roots of capitalism and have not undermined the foundation, the basis, of the internal enemy. The latter depends on small-scale production, and there is only one way of undermining it, namely, to place the economy of the country, including agriculture, on a new technical basis, that of modern large-scale production. Only electricity provides that basis.[34]

In the same speech, Lenin then transitioned into a discussion of the role of electricity in peasant life that many today would likely find vulgarly modernist and patronising. He cites a peasant using light as a metaphor: "We peasants

---

27 Ibid: 201.
28 Millar 1978: 393.
29 Ibid: 390.
30 Marx 1990: 875.
31 Lenin 1973: 238.
32 Coopersmith 2016: 155.
33 Ibid: 130ff.
34 Lenin 1974: 516.

were unenlightened...and now light has appeared among us, an 'unnatural light, which will light up our peasant darkness.'"[35] Lenin goes on to insist:

> What we must now try is to convert every electric power station we build into a stronghold of enlightenment to be used to make the masses electricity-conscious, so to speak....Besides literacy, we need cultured, enlightened and educated working people; the majority of the peasants must be made fully aware of the tasks awaiting us.[36]

Does this kind of ideology imply a modernist – and somewhat imperial – outlook towards traditional peasant modes of subsistence and culture? Yes. But, in 1920 and after, there was no doubt that Marxism was a thoroughly modernist project that sought to build socialism on the 'basis' of industrial capitalism. As a result, the Soviet leadership with Lenin at the helm needed to believe in and make sure that the peasant masses would welcome the 'enlightenment' of electrified modernity, including in the form of large-scaled educational and literacy campaigns. In any event, a few years after Lenin's death in 1924, the electrification of the country was eventually carried out at full steam, and with considerable success: "In 1920 there were ten district power stations in the country with a total power production of 253,000 kilowatts. In 1935, there were already ninety-five of these stations with a total power of 4,345,000 kilowatts."[37] In fact, despite his strong critique of Stalinism, an increasingly beleaguered Trotsky could still celebrate what revolutionary socialism had achieved: "Socialism has demonstrated its right to victory, not on the pages of *Das Kapital*, but in an industrial arena comprising a sixth part of the earth's surface – not in the language of dialectics, but in the language of steel, cement and electricity."[38]

Then again, Stalin's 1930s version of "socialist primitive accumulation," an expression that he refused to use himself, was far more violent than the one defended by Preobrazhensky – forced collectivisation and the liquidation of the kulaks as a class included. Ironically, Preobrazhensky himself ended up liquidated in 1937. Like capitalist primitive accumulation, Stalin's modernisation of the country was achieved "dripping from head to toe, from every pore, with blood and dirt."[39] Even worse, by the 1950s, many rural areas of the Soviet Union were still without access to electricity.[40]

Whether sparkling success or bloody failure, the Soviet electrification campaign was forever associated with Lenin's bold vision of electricity for all, perhaps most powerfully symbolised by the so-called 'Ilyich lamps,'

---

35 Ibid: 517.
36 Ibid.
37 Trotsky 1972: 7.
38 Ibid: 8.
39 Marx 1990: 926.
40 See Pushkova n.d.

the incandescent light bulbs that were first delivered to rural villages, some of which continue to brighten people's lives to this day.[41]

Electric Communism in the 21st Century

In a world where many of us are 'unconsciously' surrounded by electric devices, steel and automated machinery, it is easy to denounce Lenin's thinking as 'problematic.' This is especially true today when we can lay blame on the entire modernist project for the fossil fuel-fired planetary crisis of climate change. To be sure, the challenge of climate change means we must rethink Marx's and Lenin's understanding of automated industrial machinery as the basis for the 'realm of freedom.' While many seem to think that this implies a rejection of the modernist aspects of socialism in total, the challenge remains the same as it was in Lenin's time; namely, to *develop the productive force*s, but this time towards a green or zero-carbon electricity system that can power the automated machinery that makes freedom possible.

As Lenin envisaged, most contemporary engineers and energy experts agree that the answer to massive decarbonisation is not less, but substantially *more electricity*. The dictum among these experts is that we must first decarbonise electricity and then "electrify everything" that currently doesn't rely on electricity, such as transportation, and certain forms of industrial production.[42]

In the U.S., Left and socialist organisers have coalesced around a program for this type of electrifying transformation: the Green New Deal.[43] This programme proposes a massive public works project – its radical variants take the entire energy system under public ownership – to transform the electricity, transport and industrial system in accordance with the ten-year timeline set out by the Intergovernmental Panel on Climate Change. If this sounds fanciful, consider that the original 1930s New Deal aimed at and actually accomplished its own massive electrification project, increasing from 10% of rural households in 1933 to 97% by 1960.[44] In other words, it appears that Franklin D. Roosevelt clearly agreed with Lenin's advice on the importance of electricity to rural life.

In contrast to the communist electrification project, the Green New Deal is not exactly based on 'free time' for the proletariat. Rather it proposes putting the masses to work through a federal jobs guarantee that would employ a sizeable segment of the surplus populations created by global neoliberal capitalism.[45] Yet, as Daniel Aldana Cohen argues, these jobs could potentially be marshalled to revive visions of "public luxury" to

---

41 Ibid.
42 See Roberts 2017.
43 See Aronoff et al. 2019.
44 See Fleming and Lillehei 2020.
45 Although, until the recent pandemic, official unemployment had remained low, the proportion of the population in the labour force has dropped steadily over the last two decades from 67.3% in early 2000 to 62.7% today (Bureau of Labor Statistics 2020).

combat the neoliberal privatism so entrenched in our contemporary culture and politics.[46] Naomi Klein suggests that the Green New Deal could lead to shorter work-weeks so the masses can enjoy "publicly funded art and urban recreation or access to nature through new protections for wilderness."[47]

In general terms, given that a decarbonised electricity system is an obvious material condition for any semblance of a sustainable, let alone communist, society, the Green New Deal could pave the way for electrified zero-carbon automated abundance. It is after all a social democratic program. Others, however, see electricity as central to a different mode of production entirely. Bastani, for example, argues that solar power technology could provide the basis for a "fully automated luxury communism."[48] Although his proposal of asteroid mining might be a little over the top, he forcefully argues for exactly the same vision Marx, Engels, and Lenin shared of communism as a "post-scarcity" society in which poverty is abolished and leisure is available to all. He also underscores that the Left must recover a vision of socialist progress that builds on – not against – the industrial material conditions that confront the world today. More than twenty years before Bastani, during the peak of neoliberalism, David Schwartzman similarly argued that solar power represented the inexhaustible and abundant resource necessary to form the material conditions for what he called "solar communism."[49] Alternatively, there are those who think that the intermittent nature of renewable power must be combined with nuclear or other non-fossil forms of energy.[50] In short, there is no lack of innovative 'communist' ideas about how to keep our lives electrified; regardless of the *source of energy*, all of these perspectives retain Lenin's view of a future society as premised on *energy abundance*.[51]

Conclusion

Marxism and the communist project have always been about two critical issues: the material conditions of labour – how much labour is required to reproduce the material basis of society as a whole – and human emancipation. It is fanciful to think that the latter can be achieved without any of the labour-saving machinery that defined the era of industrial capitalism; and today, as in Lenin's time, that machinery is electric.

One of the greatest indictments of capitalism is that, as a system, it is so ill-equipped to deliver to the masses the material basics of existence: in 2020, a century after Lenin's call for electrification, a staggering 13% of the world population, or nearly one billion people, lack access to electric-

---

46 See Cohen 2019.
47 Klein 2019: 264.
48 See Bastani 2019.
49 See Schwartzmann 1996.
50 See Phillips 2015.
51 This view is of course at odds with much of the eco-left today, which argues for austerity and limits. For example, see Vettese 2018.

ity.[52] Of course, if Lenin had had his way "the electrification of the whole country" would have set the stage for the electrification of the whole *planet*. There can be no doubt, therefore, that Lenin would be despondent to see the planet today:burning from climate change and teeming with masses denied the enlightenment and freedom electricity can provide.

With a resurgence of political movements grounded in the Marxist (and Leninist) conception of politics, we may yet have time to make this vision of global electric communism a reality in the 21st century. Unlike the Soviet project of violent primitive accumulation, however, communists today must honour Lenin's original views on the "self-determination" of all peoples,[53] especially those in rural areas. Rural communities themselves must participate in these electrification projects. There will also need to be a broader ideological project – a new *enlightenment* project – to convince the masses in the cities and countryside that only *socialised* production systems, in contrast to small-scale local production, can create the conditions for true freedom based on time for human development. This is in fact what *humanity* as a whole so desperately needs: the species-wide democratic and social control of our productive metabolism with nature. Only such 'conscious' ecological planning based on an internationalist solidarity of the global working class and its peasant allies can rescue our planet from the ravages of global capital.

References

Anderson, Kevin B. (2010), *Marx at the Margins: On Nationalism, Ethnicity, and Non-Western Societies*. Chicago: University of Chicago Press.

Araghi, Farshad A. (1995), "Global Depeasantisation, 1945-1990," *The Sociological Quarterly*, 36(2): 337-368.

Aronoff, Kate, Battistoni, Alyssa, Cohen, Daniel Aldana and Thea Riofrancos (2019), *A Planet to Win: Why we need a Green New Deal*. London: Verso.

Bastani, Aaron (2019), *Fully Automated Luxury Communism*. London: Verso.

Beaudreau, Bernard C. (1999), *Energy and the Rise and Fall of Political Economy*. Westport: Greenwood Press.

Benanav, Aaron (2019), "Automation and the future of work 2," *New Left Review*, 120, 117-146.

Bureau of Labor Statistics (2020), "Civilian labor force participation rate." Accessed on 29.06.2020, at https://www.bls.gov/charts/employment-situation/civilian-labor-force-participation-rate.htm.

Cohen, Daniel Aldana (2019), "A Green New Deal for Housing," *Jacobin*. Accessed on 29.06.2020, at https://www.jacobinmag.com/2019/02/green-new-deal housing-ocasio-cortez-climate.

Coopersmith, Jonathan (2016), *The Electrification of Russia 1880-1926*.

---

52 See Ritchie and Roser 2019.
53 See Lenin 1977: 393-454.

Ithaca: Cornell University Press.
Deutscher, Isaac (1959), *The Prophet Unarmed: Trotsky: 1921-1929*. Oxford: Oxford University Press.
Engels, Friedrich (1872), "Part One: How Proudhon Solves the Housing Question," *Marxist Internet Archive*. Accessed on 29.06.2020, at https://www.marxists.org/archive/marx/works/1872/housing-question/ch01.htm.
Fleming, Billy, and Alexandra Lillehei (2020), "To rebuild our towns and cities, we need to design a Green Stimulus," *Jacobin*. Accessed on 29.06.2020, at https://www.jacobinmag.com/2020/04/green-stimulus-new-deal-infrastructure-buildout-coronavirus.
Harvey, David (1989), *The Condition of Postmodernity: An Enquiry into the Origins of Cultural Change*. Oxford: Blackwell.
Jameson, Fredric (1991), *Postmodernism, or, the Cultural Logic of Late Capitalism*. Durham: Duke University Press.
Johnson, Bob (2014), *Carbon Nation: Fossil Fuels and the Making of American Culture*. Lawrence: Kansas University Press.
Klein, Naomi (2019), *On Fire: The Burning Case for a Green New Deal*. New York: Simon and Schuster.
Lenin, V.I. (1977), *Collected Works Vol. 20*. Moscow: Progress Publishers.
Lenin, V.I. (1973), *Collected Works Vol. 33*. Moscow: Progress Publishers.
Lenin, V.I. (1974), *Collected Works Vol. 31*. Moscow: Progress Publishers.
Lyotard, Jean-Francois (1984), *The Postmodern Condition: A Report on Knowledge*. Minneapolis: University of Minnesota Press.
Malm, Andreas (2016), *Fossil Capital: The Rise of Steam Power and the Roots of Global Warming*. London: Verso.
Marot, John (2019), "The New Economic Policy Was the Alternative to Stalinism," *Jacobin*. Accessed on 29.06.2020, at https://www.jacobinmag.com/2019/12/new-economic-policy-stalinism-nep-bolsheviks-october-revolution.
Marx, Karl (1963), *The Eighteenth Brumaire of Louis Bonaparte*. New York: International Publishers.
Marx, Karl (1973), *Grundrisse*. London: Penguin Books.
Marx, Karl (1981), *Capital Vol. 3*. London: Penguin Books.
Marx, Karl (1990), *Capital Vol. 1*. London: Penguin Books.
Millar, James R. (1978), "A Note on primitive accumulation in Marx and Preobrazhensky," *Soviet Studies*, 30(3), 384-393.
Olmstead, Alan L., and Paul W. Rhode (2014), "Agricultural Mechanisation," in Neal K. Van Alfen (ed.), *Encyclopedia of Agriculture and Food Systems*. Amsterdam: Elseveir, 168-178.
Phillips, Leigh (2015), *Austerity Ecology and the Collapse-Porn Addicts*. London: Zero Books.
Preobrazehnsky, Evgeny (1967), *The New Economics*. Oxford: Oxford University Press.

Pushkova, Darya (n.d.), "Of Russian origin: The Ilyich Lamp," *Russiapedia*. Accessed on 29.06.2020, at https://russiapedia.rt.com/of-russian-origin/the-ilyich-lamp/.

Ritchie, Hannah, and Max Roser (2019), "Access to energy," *Our World in Data*. Accessed on 29.06.2020, at https://ourworldindata.org/energy-access.

Roberts, David (2017), "The key to tackling climate change: electrify everything," *Vox*. Accessed on 29.06.2020, at https://www.vox.com/2016/9/19/12938086/electrify-everything.

Schwartzman, David (1996), "Solar communism," *Science & Society*, 60(3), 307-331.

Trotsky, Leon (1972), *The Revolution Betrayed: What Is the Soviet Union and Where Is It Going?* New York: Pathfinder Press.

Vettese, Troy (2018), "To freeze the Thames," *New Left Review*, 111, 63–86.

22. City of Lenin and the Social(ist) Life of a River: Gendered Enviro-Technical History of Leninabad/Khujand and the Syrdarya

Mohira Suyarkulova

This essay starts with an image. It is most probably a staged photograph by a TASS[1] photographer, Simchenko, made in 1975 depicting "holiday-makers on the beach of the Tajik Sea" (*Tadzhikskoe more*). In the foreground of the picture sits a young woman wearing a one-piece swimming suit, her long hair falling down her back and head covered with a shiny gold-embroidered *duppi* (skull-hat), which indicates her Tajikness and perhaps the status of a young bride. She is seated on a brightly coloured, richly ornamented carpet – another deliberate visual cue pointing us to the 'oriental' location

---
1 *Telegrafnoe Agentsvo Sovetskogo Soyuza* (Telegraph Agency of the Soviet Union, today: *Informatsionnoye agentstvo Rossii TASS*) is a major new agency, founded in Russia in 1904.

of the shot. In the background, three other young women are seen playing in the water, wearing even more daring swimsuits.

This image represents at least four promises of communism in Soviet Central Asia rooted in the Soviet modernising project in the region. The first is the promise of transformation of the region's nature through large-scale water infrastructure projects, which the Tajik Sea itself represents. The second promise is connected to the first and refers to economic development through electrification and industrialisation; the water dams and hydropower stations built on them had the dual purpose of agricultural irrigation and electricity production that would power the new industries. The carpet the young Tajik woman is sitting on was produced at the factory recently built near the new artificial water reservoir, which would mostly employ local women. Third, and again connected to the previous two, was the promise of gender emancipation and new ideals of bodily autonomy best illustrated by the liberated women of the Soviet 'orient'[2] enjoying themselves on the beach. Finally, the dam that created the artificial sea for hydropower production and irrigational use was named 'Friendship of the Peoples' (*Druzhba narodov*) to signify yet another promise of the Soviet project – to overcome ethnic divides through the processes of rapprochement (*sblizheniie*) and merger (*sliianiie*) into a transnational community of Soviet, and ultimately all working people of the world.

In this essay I will reflect on these promises of communism in the city of Khujand in the north of Tajikistan, which between the years 1936 and 1991 was known as Leninabad – the City of Lenin. I do so through an examination of the social(ist) life of the Syrdarya river and the ways in which human-river interactions are shaped by the grand narratives of Soviet and post-Soviet politics in gendered ways. From the early Leninist vision of "all power to the Soviets plus electrification of the whole country," to the post-Soviet realities of neoliberal globalisation, de-industrialisation and labour migration, this paper uses the socio-enviro-technical and affective history of the river as a vehicle for narrative.

I myself was born in Soviet Tajikistan's capital, Dushanbe, at the beginning of the last decade of the Soviet Union. My childhood until the collapse of the USSR and the start of the Tajik civil war very much resembled the idealised image of the successes of the Soviet development project. My maternal grandparents were both medical doctors and both of my parents had higher education. Women in my family were capable and successful and my mother and aunts brought up children on their own thanks to the support system of kindergartens and after-school programmes. My brother and I would spend the school holidays in the pioneer camps in the mountains,

---

2 Although part of the European tradition of studying, imagining and depicting the "Orient," Soviet Orientalism fused this undertaking with a Marxist view of the world and the universalising modernisation project. This knowledge was somewhat paradoxically used in service of nation-building projects in Soviet Central Asia. For more, see: Schimmelpenninck van der Oye 2014, Battis 2015, Bustanov 2017.

where everyone would learn how to swim in a swimming pool filled with icy water from the glaciers that also feed the rivers in the valleys. Nonetheless, as a child I never travelled to the north of the republic, where the city of Leninabad (now Khujand) is located. Hence, I was only introduced to the Syrdarya later in my life.

In fact, because my family had to flee Tajikistan during the Civil War in early 1993, I only returned to the country to do fieldwork for my PhD in the 2000s and later in the 2010s for a postdoc project. That is why the research for this essay, like for all of my other academic work, is not purely conducted out of academic curiosity, but has deep personal and political significance, helping me to make sense of the world around me – past and present.

"Taming the Rivers" and Reclaiming the Hungry Steppe: the Grand Transformation of Nature and the Socialist Development Project

Tajikistan's history of electrification dates back to the 1920s, when the newly established Tajik ASSR (at that point still a part of the Uzbek SSR) was established within the revolutionary Soviet state. Vladimir Lenin believed in the essential role of electrification for successful communist development. The Central Soviet administration created the State Commission for Electrification of Russia (GOELRO) and a plan for the implementation of electrification called the "Russian SFSR Electrification Plan." This was "mankind's *first* integral state plan of economic development on the basis of electrification."[3]

Electrification plans for Central Asia were drafted with the direct involvement of Lenin, and the Central Asian Water Administration based in Tashkent, Uzbekistan, was created to supervise the projects in the region, which was directly governed by the Central Asian Bureau of the Russian Communist Party Central Committee This plan foresaw the exploitation of water resources for hydropower production and the establishment of a single power grid for the whole region. One of the principles of the plan most relevant to Central Asia was the intention to build "electric power stations on the outskirts of the country, in the former backward non-Russian areas, and the establishment of new seats of industry."[4]

As a result, Central Asia, along with other Soviet regions, became a "laboratory of socialist development," whereby large-scale hydropower projects were designed and implemented as part of an ambitious "hydraulic mission" called upon to "light the way to progress and civilisation."[5] Tajikistan is a predominantly agricultural mountainous country with glacier-fed rivers and little fertile land, without significant oil or gas reserves. Therefore, when the first dams were being constructed these were intended

---

3 Steklov 1965: 11 in Sakal 2016.
4 Sakal 2016: 9.
5 See Kalinovsky 2018.

primarily for irrigation and land reclamation, to support the Soviet Union in achieving cotton independence from the hostile capitalist world. However, the Second World War, which led to the evacuation of factories and plants from European parts of the USSR to Central Asia (mostly to Soviet Uzbekistan), shifted the focus of the dam-construction projects from irrigation for cotton fields to industrialisation and electricity production. This is how the Kairakkum hydropower project, which created the 'Tajik Sea' near Leninabad, came into being.

Flora Roberts describes the controversy between the Tajik and Uzbek SSRs that accompanied the process of the planning of the dam on the Syrdarya river near the administrative border of the two republics during the 1940s. Although the dam and the resulting water reservoir (which would inundate about a quarter of all fertile land the republic held) along with the hydropower plant (HHP) were to be located entirely in Tajik territory, the chief beneficiary of the Tajik Sea would be Soviet Uzbekistan.[6] For the Tajik leadership at the time, the focus remained on agriculture and production of cotton rather than with the industrial development prioritised by Uzbekistan. By way of compensation, the Uzbek SSR 'gifted' its Tajik neighbour a piece of land in the Hungry Steppe for the lost lands in the Kairakkum.

The new dam bearing the name of 'Friendship of the Peoples,' and the 'Tajik Sea' created by the dam, were finally inaugurated with much pomp and celebration in April 1956.[7] This marked a new era of post-Stalinist development in Tajikistan, which Artemy Kalinovsky defines as the period when the "decolonisation" of Soviet Central Asia was completed.[8] During the Cold War, Central Asia became prominent in global politics as a showcase for the success of the socialist path of development for former colonies that were gaining independence in the post-war period. This empowered the new leaders of the region's republics to negotiate new terms of development (away from agriculture/cotton production and towards industrialisation) through appeals to Leninist principles of nationality policies and use of anti-colonial rhetoric. Kalinovsky argues that, "While Central Asian party leaders almost certainly did not think of their republics as 'colonies' of Moscow or dream about political independence, they did feel material and cultural inequality not only relative to Moscow but to each other. In a sense, the wave of decolonisation occurring beyond the USSR's borders provided the impetus to complete the 'decolonisation' of the Central Asian republics within a Soviet framework."[9]

Thus, we can see that rivers and their multiple uses (for agriculture, for electricity production, for fishing and recreation) were at the heart of Soviet

---

6 See Roberts 2018.
7 Ibid.
8 See Kalinovsky 2018.
9 Kalinovsky 2013: 192.

Along the new course. Lithograph by V. Pilpeniuk. From Ogni Nureka [Lights of Nurek], *ed. V.I. Dashkevich. Dushanbe: Irfon, 1974.*

modernisation projects in the Tajik SSR. This was part of the heroic narrative of the "great transformation of nature" – harnessing elementary forces in service of humanity and the building of a communist future.[10] In his analysis of the Soviet environmental utopias, Mikhail Myl'nikov identifies three distinct periods of Soviet environmental ideologies and policies: early Soviet conservationist ethics (1917-1930s) gave way to the 1948 Stalinist plan for the "transformation of nature," which initiated the "great construction projects of communism," whereby nature was viewed as a hostile agent that needed to be tamed/conquered for the needs of the country's economy, accompanied by the cult of the almighty Soviet worker.[11]

This vision included the mission to 'tame' rivers in the service of socialist development – building a system of canals, dams and hydropower stations, and regulating their flow for industrial and agricultural use. Stalinist "gigantomania" was replaced, in turn, by a new paradigm of harmonious coexistence between humans and nature.[12] At this point – in the late 1950s to early 1960s – Vladimir Ilyich Lenin unexpectedly became the central figure of Soviet environmentalist propaganda and a large number of articles, brochures and books were published in which Lenin was valorised as a great example of the love for nature and its rational use.[13] In 1960, an open letter signed by academicians V.N. Sukachev and A.L. Yanshin in *"Vokrug sveta"* [Around the World] magazine announced the creation of a new youth movement "For a Leninist approach to nature" (*Za leninskoe otnoshenie k prirode*). Subsequently, *"Yunyi Naturalist"* [Young Naturalist]

---

10 Myl'nikov 2017: 466.
11 Ibid: 470-471.
12 Ibid: 478.
13 Ibid.

magazine began publishing a regular column under the same title.[14] It was during this period that leading Soviet academics expressed their opposition to the projects of diverting the flow of the Siberian rivers to reclaim the lands in the steppes of Middle Asia and Kazakhstan for agriculture.

While Soviet scholars and political commentators during the Cold War framed environmental issues as a class-based problem in a capitalist world, the Soviet Union had a host of its own environmental disasters, many of which resulted from extremely ambitious projects (mostly originating during the Stalinist period) bordering on science fiction.[15] During the 1980s, as the new policies of perestroika and glasnost were introduced under Mikhail Gorbachev's leadership, new public discussion of the ecological disasters that resulted from the "great transformation of nature" projects, the arms race, and rapid industrial development finally began taking place.[16] This resulted in multiple protests against dams and electrification projects in some socialist states and Soviet republics. In Tajikistan, the local intelligentsia expressed opposition to the plans for the construction of the Roghun HPP, resulting in changes to the plans for the height of the dam.[17] Interestingly, until the very last years of the Soviet Union's existence, appeals were still being made for a return to the Leninist principles in environmental management. Thus, for instance, B. Ioganzen and E.V. Logachev wrote in 1990 in their book *V.I. Lenin i sovremennyie ekologicheskiie problemy* [V.I. Lenin and Contemporary Ecological Problems]:

> Nature acts according to its own objective laws, and humans must learn these, in order to act in unison with nature, to avoid doing irreparable damage. If the lessons from Friedrich Engels and Vladimir Ilyich Lenin were implemented, there wouldn't be the tragedy of Chernobyl, nor desiccation of the Aral Sea, the products of agriculture would not be poisoned by pesticides and other chemicals.

In short, the rivers of Tajikistan, as in the rest of Central Asia, had important work to fulfil in the great project of constructing an 'actually existing socialism' and in the process had to undergo certain transformations while themselves transforming people's lives. As Flora Roberts aptly noted: "Perhaps there is not much that the people of Khujand [Leninabad] experienced in the course of the Soviet years that did not also, for a time at least, leave its mark on the river that runs through the city, a (mostly) silent witness to its joys, upheavals and tribulations."[18] Yet while the river was changed as part of the modernist developmental projects of the 20th century, this process was not gender-neutral and thus affected local men and women differently.

---

14 Ibid: 479.
15 Ibid: 482.
16 Ibid: 487.
17 Suyarkulova 2014.
18 See Roberts 2016.

Towards the Emancipation of the Women of the Soviet 'Orient': The Working Mother Contract

Monument to Lenin on the right bank of Syrdarya in Leninabad. From Soviet Tajikistan: Photo Album. *Dushanbe: Irfon, 1984.*

In the Soviet periphery, which included the new Tajik Republic (promoted to the level of full Soviet Socialist Republic in 1929), the electrification effort, along with policies of sedentarisation, collectivisation, indigenisation (*korenizatsiia*) and the assault on oppressive traditions, like polygyny, child marriages, women's seclusion and veiling (*hujum*), formed part of other policies called upon to develop the 'backward' regions of the former Tsarist empire, to "raise the level of culture in the countryside and to overcome, even in the most remote corners of the land, backwardness, ignorance, poverty, disease and barbarism."[19] While the "backwardness" of the region was seen mainly in its Islamic heritage, essentially feudal relations of production and colonial oppression under tsarist Russia, women were perceived by the Bolsheviks as an especially oppressed group within these societies. Consequently, a series of compensatory policies were designed in order to rectify past wrongs and to emancipate local women, many of whom joined the women's movement despite the great cost and personal risk associated with such activism. As a result, in the first decades of Soviet rule in the region countless women activists were brutally murdered.[20] Thus, Lenin's commitment to electrification in Central Asia, as elsewhere in the Soviet Union, was also embedded in the gender-based emancipatory project of the liberation of women. Women were mobilised to become new Soviet citizens. They were to be relieved from the hardship of household toil by new technologies and socialised childcare, and thus able to engage fully in the economic, political, social and cultural life of the society.[21]

Negar Behzadi and Lucia Direnberger point out the complex, contradictory and hybrid nature of the Soviet ideology and policy of the liberation-through-work project with regard to Tajik women during the post-war period up to

....
19 Lenin 1920: 335.
20 See Kamp 2011.
21 See Shchurko 2016.

perestroika.²² They argue that Tajik women were largely excluded from certain types of work (which required higher qualifications, relocation to the cities and/or involved interactions with unrelated males) and were predominantly employed in agriculture – a 'third' or 'in-between space' located "between the domestic and the public, the Tajik and the Soviet, and the traditional and the modern."²³ Kolkhoz work was considered a type of non-work, was gendered and ethnicised through the association of Tajik women with the home and the rural, and became the dominant mode of productive employment for local women due to the necessity to 'protect' them from a sexualised/Russified urban outside space, thereby reinforcing the very same traditional notions of shame and honour that the Soviet liberation of women was meant to overcome. Within this framework, Tajik femininity was defined in opposition to Russian femininity, the latter being identified as urban, professional and licentious.²⁴ While men could be employed in professions requiring technical knowledge like driving a tractor in the kolkhoz, women were the primary manual workforce, picking cotton, tilling the soil in their kitchen gardens, looking after animals, and so on – i.e. they were doing jobs that were not mechanised.

Women picking pomegranates. From Soviet Tajikistan: Photo Album, *1984.*

---

22 See Behzadi and Direnberger 2020.
23 Ibid: 3.
24 Ibid: 12.

There were, of course, some 'progressive' (*peshqadam*) women who successfully challenged social expectations and control thanks to the Soviet valorisation of education and work outside of the home "with in some instances a sense of accomplishment as well as pride and pleasure regarding their ability to move, both socially and spatially."[25] At the same time, motherhood remained a socialist duty for women upon which career advancement and access to opportunities was often conditional.[26] Indeed, motherhood was glorified in Soviet society and mothers of many children were valorised as 'heroines.' Only later, during the perestroika years, the double burden that all Soviet women experienced began to be discussed openly, as well as the difficult labour conditions, poverty, lack of education and poor health of Tajik women. A 1988 article in *Kommunist Tajikistana* exposed the high rates of anaemia among Tajik women due to frequent births, poor nutrition and exposure to defoliants and pesticides in the cotton fields.[27] Their multiple hardships notwithstanding, Tajik women continued to labour away until the USSR, and with it the project of women's emancipation, suddenly collapsed in 1991, ushering in a series of fundamental transformations for both Tajik women as well as the rivers of the soon-to-be independent Republic of Tajikistan.

Tajikistan in the Age of Neoliberal Capitalism: A New Gender Contract

When Tajikistan suddenly and reluctantly became an independent state in 1991, the country underwent dramatic transformations, including a vicious civil war (1992-1997), in which the number of estimated casualties varies between 50,000 and 500,000, and with up to 20% of the population becoming internally displaced persons and refugees. The war also impacted heavily on the lives of Tajik women and continues to have a lasting gendered effect.[28] Unsurprisingly, the processes of establishing order after the conflict, the nation-building and 'transition' to market capitalism were not gender-neutral either. In fact, gender largely served as an organising principle in post-Soviet Tajik society. Poverty, brought about by dispossession during the transition years and the rolling back of the welfare state, resulted in the rise of early marriages, the seclusion of women, and the loss of prestige of education.[29] Furthermore, the image of the 'proper' Tajik woman (as well as the 'proper' Tajik man), her role in the reproduction of the nation and culture, was of great importance for the new nationalist project,[30] led by president Emomali Rahmon(ov). Over the years, Tajikistan has become an autocratic kleptocracy, where the elites advance a narrative of the Tajiks as the true Aryans with a

---

25 Ibid: 8.
26 Ibid: 12.
27 Ibid: 8.
28 See Roche 2017.
29 Bozrikova 2002: 57.
30 See Temkina 2008 and Suyarkulova 2016.

civilising mission in the region, while close to a million Tajiks (mostly men) work as migrants in Russia to sustain their families at home. In these conditions, possible life scenarios for Tajik women have become rather limited.

Kristen Ghodsee, a historian of socialist countries, in her book *Why Women Have Better Sex under Socialism* writes that the "collapse of state socialism in 1989 created a perfect laboratory to investigate the effects of capitalism on women's lives."[31] In the case of the former Soviet republics of Central Asia, a number of common neoliberal policies aimed at "refamilisation" have driven women back into domesticity, away from the public sphere and productive work.[32] This was usually framed as a return to the "authentic" pre-Soviet way of life and the honourable traditional values of the nation.

The gender contract of late socialism was described by Anna Temkina as that of a "working mother."[33] She defines a gender contract as a "dominant prescriptive model which differentiates activities based on gender/sex and age, defining one's status, rights, duties and responsibilities in the sphere of production and reproduction."[34] In contrast to Soviet times, today's new gender contract for women is primarily of a sexual and reproductive nature. In post-Soviet Tajikistan, the patriarchal order is reproduced both publicly and privately through a key cultural code, which sets the configuration of the gender/age hierarchy and everyday gendered practices – a marriage arranged by parents.[35] Gendered expectations of propriety are enforced by the family through control of the "correct" gender display of its women: their dress, appearance, adherence to norms of proper conduct.[36] Men's "honour" is performed through control over women of the family.[37] In this changed context, Tajik women find themselves mobilised as a different type of political subject – no longer as subjects of liberation but rather as the beneficiaries of interventions by international development projects, funded by foreign governments, charitable foundations, or financial institutions like the World Bank and the International Monetary Fund.

With regards to energy production, independent Tajikistan has gone through similar fundamental changes. In the age of neoliberal development, access to clean and affordable energy has been reframed as one of the Sustainable Development Goals. It is theorised within this framework that having access to energy empowers communities, especially women within those communities, and contributes to poverty reduction, health and wellbeing, climate action, and gender equality.[38] In Central Asian states most of the communities, even the most remote mountainous ones, had benefited

---

31 Ghodsee 2018: 11.
32 Ibid: 68.
33 Temkina 2008: 34.
34 Temkina and Rotkirch in Temkina 2008: 26.
35 Ibid: 37.
36 Ibid: 83.
37 Harris 2004: 73-80.
38 See Kim and Standal 2019.

from state-supplied electricity from at least the 1970s, but affordability, reliability and access to energy supply suffered greatly during the transition years.[39] A similar development has occurred throughout the region. For example, Kim and Standal in their study of the political economy of energy and gender in rural Naryn, Kyrgyzstan, found that the new discourse of "energy security and economic growth through export of energy" deprioritised "people's access and need for electricity" thus resulting in "a profound neglect of gender concerns in contemporary Kyrgyz energy politics."[40]

This finding is echoed in the work in Tajikistan of Diana Ibañez-Tirado, whose ethnographic study revealed how contemporary large hydropower projects by the Tajik government, and the resulting forced taxation of the population to complete the construction of the Roghun HPP,[41] are experienced as "everyday disasters" by common people:

> The ongoing effects of such disastrous events overlapped with pre-existing constant electric blackouts and shortages of water that meant that many women and children had to fetch water from far from home, or procure wood to cook on fires in outdoor kitchens. Constant debt and chronic illnesses, combined with a lack of sustainable sources of income and affordable medical care, were also cited by my informants as disasters that were not eventful but rather constant aspects of people's daily lives.[42]

Moreover, people across the country were forced to buy Roghun shares under the threat of losing their job if state employed, having their business closed down, or as students not being allowed to sit their exams or enrol the following year. As a result, "many workers (*korgar*) acquired bank loans (*qarz*) and requested urgent remittances from their relatives working in Russia to help pay for the stock."[43]

While the government declared the completion of the high dam for a huge hydropower station a national idea and a sacred mission of each Tajik citizen,[44] the promised gains of the project are not likely to trickle down

---

39 See Gullette and Feaux de la Croix 2014.
40 Kim and Standal 2019: 5.
41 Roghun dam and HPP is a Soviet era project to be constructed on the Vakhsh river in Tajikistan. First proposed in 1959 and designed in 1965, the dam was envisioned as the highest dam in the world at 335 meters. Construction began in 1976, was opposed by local intelligentsia during the perestroika years, and was eventually frozen after the collapse of the USSR. In 1994, Russia agreed to complete the project, but failed to fulfil its promise, resulting in the abrogation of the agreement. Another unsuccessful deal with a Russian aluminium company was signed in 2004. Neighbouring Uzbekistan also opposed the construction of the dam, fearing that use of water upstream for electricity generation would compromise its cotton fields yields. Following a World Bank assessment, a deal was made with an Italian company to finally complete the project. In October 2016 Emomali Rahmon officially launched the construction of the dam. Far from being only an infrastructure project, the Roghun dam and HPP have become the national idea of the new Tajik state (Suyarkulova 2014).
42 Ibañez-Tirado 2015: 550-551.
43 Ibid: 555.
44 See Suyarkulova 2014.

to them, because the main benefits from the increased energy production would accrue to the Tajik Aluminium Company (TALCO) – Tajikistan's main consumer of electricity. Although TALCO is formally a state-owned company, it pays no taxes to the state budget and through a complex tolling system and corrupt offshore money laundering schemes siphons off untold amounts of national wealth, benefiting a small group of ruling elites.[45] In summary, the dam, which was opposed in late Soviet times on environmental grounds and because it would result in a loss of cultural heritage sites, is now celebrated as the ultimate promise for the development of modern Tajikistan, while the Leninist principles of environmentalism and socialist development ideals are left far behind. Meanwhile, it is often the women of Tajikistan who have to bear the human costs of these elites' ambitions.

After Lenin: Social Life and Death on the Syrdarya River in Khujand

When I arrived in Khujand in the summer of 2017, I had a hard time finding an apartment to rent as a single woman travelling alone. The real estate agent I approached tried calling different landlords and kept repeating that I was a 'decent' (*poryadochnaya*) woman. At first, I was confused and did not understand why he kept referring to me like that; later, a Khujandi friend explained that the 'season' at the Tajik Sea had started and that prostitutes from all over the country were flocking to the city to make money. After hours of waiting and phone calls in the stuffy office, the agency managed to find me an apartment in one of the residential *mikrorayons* on the right bank of the Syrdarya. As I conducted my research on river-human interactions in the former city of Lenin, it became increasingly obvious to me that these interactions continue to have a gendered nature and create distinct moral geographies of the city and its surroundings.

In stark opposition to the Soviet image with which I began this essay and my own childhood memories, I observed that the river banks within the city as well as the shoreline of the Tajik Sea were nowadays marked as almost exclusively male spaces. The city beach, the teahouses and speakeasies hidden under the bridge were all sites of homosocial conviviality and recreation. When I travelled to a picnic area by the Tajik Sea with a group of young men, I realised that all the women on the beach were fully clothed in the traditional Tajik dresses and *izors* (long undergarments covering the legs). While the men looked rather comfortable stripped to their underwear when they swam and sunbathed, the women were covered up and apparently did not know how to swim. As I continued my observations and had conversations with regulars of the city beach, it became clear that the water's edge is seen as a place where the rules of sexuality and gender are at risk and therefore need to be enforced. The spaces of interaction between

---

45 See Heathershaw 2011.

the river and humans are viewed as spaces for the pleasure of boys and men, while modesty codes for women mean that their presence in these spaces is always fraught.

In morbid irony, the only point of interaction between the river and the women of Khujand are the cases of death by drowning through suicide in the river. Sughd province has the highest suicide rate in Tajikistan. Indeed, the suicide rate, especially among female youth, was so alarming that local authorities commissioned a study in collaboration with a team of scholars from Columbia University and UNICEF in 2013. According to this study, "girls and young women in Sughd region are subject to a disproportionately high risk of suicide. In contrast to the ratio of suicides committed by men to those of women in the developed Western countries, which is 4:1, as well as the average ratio for Central Asian region at 3:1,[46] the ratio of men who committed suicide to that of women in Sughd region was 1:1.2."[47] In addition, the researchers identified gendered violence against women and girls as the primary cause of suicides in the province:

> This data shows that the level of education of girls, who attempted or committed suicide, was lower than that of the girls from the control group. The data also demonstrates that forced marriages often take place in the Sughd region. Moreover, a significant share of the participants of this study considered this practice an important factor in the rise of suicide rates, especially among girls. This data also allowed to reveal other specific risk factors among women. For instance, women from families, where it is considered necessary to beat up a woman if she talked to a man, who was not her relative, are twice as likely to engage in suicidal behaviour than women from other families.[48]

The authors of the report conclude that "gender issues [...] are of strategic importance for the protection of the vulnerable groups of the population of the Sughd region, especially girls. It is possible that suicide is viewed as a viable alternative to what girls perceive as a life in the conditions of cruel treatment, when the human freedom to take important, life-defining decisions, such as choosing a spouse, education and friends, is limited."[49]

Moreover, Tajik women's behaviour, mobility and appearance are not only subject to control by their relatives, but also regulated by government intervention. In 2016, a decree prohibiting "Islamic" or "foreign" dress was adopted and actively enforced in the country.[50] And in 2018, the Ministry of Culture of Tajikistan published a colourfully illustrated "Book of Recommendations"

---

46 WHO 2011b.
47 UNICEF 2013: xii.
48 Ibid: xiii.
49 Ibid: xiv.
50 See Ibañez-Tirado 2016.

for Tajik women on acceptable dress, prohibiting long black Arab-style Islamic gowns and head-coverings, while also advising against overly revealing "European" fashions. The book consists of eleven sections, suggesting outfits for civil servants, every-day and weekend ensembles, as well as getups for festive occasions, yet failing to suggest clothing for sport or swimming.

In her analysis of why the patriarchal order remains functional in Tajikistan, Anna Temkina argues that it guarantees Tajik women security and safety in times of uncertainty: "A woman in Tajikistan found herself in a system of physical and economic security/safety within the kinship and community network, [where she] was largely protected from state interference into the private sphere of family and from the unpredictability of family life and lives of her children."[51] Yet despite repeated patriarchal claims to protect 'their women,' we can see that both in public and private spheres, women's bodies are claimed as the bearers of 'honour' of the family and the nation, and that the waters of the Syrdarya give the final embrace to countless women who were never allowed to frolic freely with their sisters on the shore of the Tajik Sea. Meanwhile, the monument to the leader of the revolution who promised liberation to Tajik women, which once stood on the right bank of the Syrdarya river in the former city of Lenin, has been replaced with the statue of Ismail Somoni, the new father of the nation.

Following the fall of the Soviet Union, gendered narratives and norms became a way to order society in Tajikistan, frequently robbing women of the possibility to be educated, to choose their own path in life, and often of life itself. Yet contrary to the patriarchal fantasies of past, present and future, everywhere in Tajikistan I met strong, independent, hard-working women, who work the fields, defend human rights, run businesses, teach at schools, staff most hospitals, serve in public office and work abroad to provide for their families. In a way, these women run the country. I long for the day when it is them, and not the men who currently dictate the length of their skirts, who decide their own destinies and those of their country.

References

Battis, Matthias (2015), "Soviet Orientalism and Nationalism in Central Asia: Aleksandr Semenov's Vision of Tajik National Identity," *Iranian Studies*, 48(5), 729-745.

Behzadi, Negar Elodie, and Lucia Direnberger (2020), "Gender and ethnicity in the Soviet Muslim peripheries: a feminist postcolonial geography of women's work in the Tajik SSR (1950-1991)," *Central Asian Survey*, 39(2), 202-219.

Bustanov, Alfrid K. (2017), *Soviet Orientalism and the Creation of Central Asian Nations*. New York: Routledge.

Ghodsee, Kristen R. (2018), *Why Women Have Better Sex Under Socialism:*

---

51 Temkina 2008: 106.

And Other Arguments for Economic Independence. New York: Nation Books.

Gullette, David, and Jeanne Féaux de la Croix (2014), "Mr Light and people's everyday energy struggles in Central Asia and the Caucasus: an introduction," *Central Asian Survey*, 33(4), 435-448.

Harris, Collette (2004), *Control and Subversion: Gender Relations in Tajikistan.* London: Pluto Press.

Heathershaw, John (2011), "Tajikistan amidst globalisation: state failure or state transformation?, *Central Asian Survey*," 30(1), 147-168.

Ibañez-Tirado, Diana (2016), "Gold teeth, Indian dresses, Chinese lycra and 'Russian' hair: embodied diplomacy and the assemblages of dress in Tajikistan," *Cambridge Journal of Anthropology*, 34 (2), 23-41.

Ibañez-Tirado, Diana (2015), "Everyday disasters, stagnation and the normalcy of non-development: Roghun Dam, a flood, and campaigns of forced taxation in southern Tajikistan," *Central Asian Survey*, 34(4), 549-563.

Kalinovsky, Artemy M. (2018), *Laboratory of Socialist Development: Cold War Politics and Decolonisation in Soviet Tajikistan.* Ithaca: Cornell University Press.

Kalinovsky, Artemy M. (2013), "Not some British colony in Africa: politics of decolonisation and modernisation in Soviet Central Asia, 1955-1964," *Ab Imperio*, 2/2013, 191-222.

Kamp, Marianne (2011), "Femicide as Terrorism: The case of Uzbekistan's unveiling murders," *in* Elizabeth D. Heineman (ed.), *Sexual Violence in Conflict Zones: From the Ancient World to the Era of Human Rights.* Philadelphia: University of Pennsylvania Press, 56-72.

Kim, Elena, and Karina Standal (2019), "Empowered by electricity? The political economy of gender and energy in rural Naryn," *Gender, Technology and Development*, 23(1), 1-18.

Lenin, V. I. (1974), *Collected Works Vol. 30.* Moscow: Progress Publishers.

Myl'nikov, Mikhail (2016), "Utopiia sovetskogo ekologicheskogo proekta i 'zelenyi' kommunizm" [The utopia of Soviet ecological project and 'green' communism], *in* Georgy Mamedov and Oksana Shatalova (eds.), *Poniatiia o sovetskom v Tsentral'noi Azii [Concepts of the Soviet in Central Asia]*, STAB Almanac. Bishkek: STAB-Press.

Roberts, Flora (2016), "Towards an environmental history of Soviet Leninobod." Paper presented at international symposium "The Social History and Anthropogenic Landscape of the Syr Darya River Basin: Exploring an Environmental Archive," Tashkent, Uzbekistan, April 18-19, 2016.

Roberts, Flora (2018), "A controversial dam in Stalinist Central Asia": Rivalry and 'Fraternal Cooperation' on the Syr Darya," *Ab Imperio*, 2/2018: 1-25.

Roche, Sophie (2017), "Tajik women during the civil war: the breast of the shahid mother had milk," *Central Asia Analytics Network.* Accessed on 29.06.2020, at https://caa-network.org/archives/9168.

Sakal, Halil Burak (2016), "'Socialist rivers' and the environmental history of Central Asia in the Cold War." Paper presented at international symposium "The Social History and Anthropogenic Landscape of the Syr Darya River Basin: Exploring an Environmental Archive," Tashkent, Uzbekistan, April 18-19, 2016.

Schimmelpenninck van der Oye, David (2014), "The Curious Fate of Edward Said in Russia," *Études de lettres,* 2-3, 81-94.

Shchurko, Tatsiana (2016), "'Zhenshchina Vostoka': Sovetskii gendernyi poriadok v Tsentral'noi Azii mezhdu kolonizatsiei i emancipatsiei" ['Woman of the Orient': Soviet gender order in Central Asia between colonisation and emancipation], *in* Georgy Mamedov and Oksana Shatalova (eds.), *Poniatiia o sovetskom v Tsentral'noi Azii [Concepts of the Soviet in Central Asia],* STAB Almanac. Bishkek: STAB-Press.

Suyarkulova, Mohira (2014), "Between national idea and international conflict: the Roghun HPP as an anti-colonial endeavour, body of the nation and national wealth," *Water History,* 6, 367-383.

Suyarkulova, Mohira (2016), "Fashioning the nation: gender and politics of dress in contemporary Kyrgyzstan," *Nationalities Papers,* 44(2), 247-265.

Temkina, Anna (2008), *Seksual'naia zhizn' zhenshchiny: mezhdu podchineniiem i svobodoi.* [Sexual Life of Woman: Between Submission and Freedom]. Saint Petersburg: European University in St. Petersburg.

UNICEF (2013), *Issledovaniie rasprostranennosti i dinamiki samoubistv sredi detei i molodykh liudei (v vozraste ot 12 do 24 let) v Sogdiiskoi oblasti Tadzhikistana* [A study of the scope and the dynamics of suicide among children and young people (ages 12 to 24) in Sughd region of Tajikistan]. Dushanbe: Tajikistan.

23. A Whole River of Blood: Lenin and Stalin

Ronald Grigor Suny

Both Lenin and Stalin were sincere revolutionaries. They were both committed to fundamental political and social transformations of the imperial society in which they lived. The shared vision that emerged from their understanding of Marxism and the dynamics of capitalist development in the Russian Empire led them to believe that a liberal democratic revolution was possible in Russia despite the weakness of the bourgeoisie, the overwhelming demographic dominance of the peasantry, and the small number of true proletarians. Confidence and courage, patience and determination characterised them both. They were undeterred by the evidence that peasant common sense was hostile to socialism and indifferent to democracy, for the revolution would be made in cities by factory workers and aided ultimately by allies from outside the country. But fundamental to how Russia would progress to socialism was the question of how the eighty percent of the population that lived in the villages would adjust to the socialists in the Kremlin. As Marxists they understood that the present order could not be transformed without violence, including the deployment of terror against those who resist, and they were prepared to use the weapons of war in what they conceived as a struggle for emancipation.

Revolutions, like wars and other moments of crisis, upset and reset the prevailing common sense, but in the case of 1917-1921 the old order was destroyed, momentarily replaced by chaos and destruction, until a new order, after the cataclysms of World War, revolution, and civil war, could be built. After revolution, however, came a kind of restoration. The peasants of Russia took control of the vast spaces of the countryside, re-established their communal organisation of life and property, now free of landlords and Stolypin freeholders. Those peasants who had taken advantage of Prime Minister Stolypin's reforms, and left the peasant commune to create their own farmsteads in the years before the World War, soon found that the newly emancipated peasantry would not tolerate the breakup of the commune. The old order before Stolypin was basically restored. At no time in the five centuries past had the peasants been so firmly in charge of the major resource of Russian life, the outputs of agriculture, as they were in the 1920s. The Bolsheviks sat atop a sea of villagers, and Lenin understood that if Communists did not prove to be competent managers they could be swept aside by a massive jacquerie. To maintain their precarious hold on power the Communists made major concessions: to the peasantry, the New Economic Policy (NEP) that granted them dominion over their produce after paying a tax in kind; and to the non-Russian peoples, the policy of *korenizatsiia*, the promotion of national cultures and national cadres. Violence subsided; the police withdrew; and a public sphere of limited liberties was permitted. Instead of socialism a modified state capitalism was established that aided the rebuilding of the decimated economy and brought a degree of acquiescence in the rule of the Soviets. No international socialist revolution came to the aid of the Soviet Union; instead the USSR existed as a pariah state in a hostile capitalist and colonial world system.

Social and economic concessions ran parallel to political tightening of the party over fundamental decision-making. With the exception of the Communist Party, all political parties – including socialist parties – were effectively outlawed. In the same month, March 1921, that the party adopted NEP, the Red Army crushed the rebellion of the Kronstadt sailors, and Lenin guided the Tenth Party Congress to issue the ban on factions within the party. Fearful of dissenting Communists and no longer trusting the urban workers, party leaders hobbled intraparty discussion and democracy.

Pragmatic to the point of seizing whatever opportunity was at hand, Stalin deftly usurped Leninism soon after his mentor's death with his speeches that became *Foundations of Leninism*. At first the enthusiastic defender of NEP, the close ally of pro-peasant Nikolai Bukharin and gradualism, he later became a radical opponent of the state capitalist path and the fiercest foe of concessions to either peasants or non-Russian peoples. His pell-mell war on the peasants in the campaigns of collectivisation of agriculture and dekulakisation, and his insistence on the highest rates of industrial production no matter what the cost to labourers or materials, abandoned the cautious and more accommodating approach of Lenin's last years and resurrected the more reckless policies of the Civil War. Stalin resorted to the wide deployment of violence, substituting instruments of coercion for persuasion and concessions. While dressing in the garb of Lenin and justifying his revisions of Bolshevism in the language of the founders, Stalin revised, suppressed, and even reversed much of the legacy of Lenin. Internationalism turned into nationalism; the promotion of non-Russians was steadily replaced by overlays of Russification; the *smychka* [alliance] between the workers and the peasants was buried in the ferocity of collectivisation; radical transformation of the family and the liberation of women ended with reassertion of the most conservative 'family values.' And one by one, almost all of Lenin's closest associates fell victim to the self-proclaimed keeper of the Leninist flame.

Trotsky's famous phrase that "a whole river of blood" separates Bolshevism from Stalinism also separates much of the Left historiography of the USSR from most liberal and conservative writers. Those who emphasise the continuity between Leninism and Stalinism indict the revolution and the democratic and socialist aspirations of 1917 with the horrific consequences of Stalin's "revolution from above" and the massive use of state terror in a time of peace. They tend to see violence as embedded in the regime from beginning to end without distinguishing one period from another. Conservative authors like Martin Malia and Richard Pipes, or the contributors to the infamous *Black Book of Communism,* fail to consider that revolutionary terror deployed during civil war, as difficult as it is to reconcile with the ambition to create a democratic and socialist society, is justified by more pragmatic political arguments than is the exercise of massive, arbitrary killing in the 1930s, the aim of which appears to be the creation of an autocratic regime and a sense of security required by elite paranoia. Civil War violence subsided during NEP until it was revived by men and women in black leather coats in the brutal collectivisation campaigns in the early 1930s. Once Stalin consolidated his hold over the party, arbitrary arrests, fabricated conspiracies, and show trials metastasised into mass killing, death by famine, and the effective elimination of almost all of Lenin's closest comrades.

Emphasising the differences between Lenin and Stalin, the Left, nevertheless, has often been reluctant to recognise the continuities and connections between Leninism and Stalinism. Both were revolutionising processes, unwilling to accept backward Russia as it was (here they differ from many traditionally authoritarian dictatorships). But both were as well conservative, restorative efforts – in Lenin's case to restore a war-torn, devastated country, stabilise a fragile modernising regime floating on a sea of potentially hostile peasants, and create political legitimacy based on more than victorious revolution. In Stalin's case, the party-state was anxious to re-establish hierarchies, affirm certain traditional values like patriotism, patriarchy, more traditional gender roles, and family values, while destroying the independent power of peasants and workers in its headlong campaign to rapidly industrialise the country. The revolution and the restoration were both evident in the 1930s, with the revolution powerfully present in the First Five-Year Plan period, and the restoration dominating in the mid-1930s. The contradictions between those aspects of Stalinism that extended the revolutionary, egalitarian and participatory impulses of 1917 and those that resurrected stratification and authoritarianism remained in irresolvable tension with one another until the demise of the USSR.

Both continuities and ruptures coexist in the history of Bolshevism, from its inception in 1903 through its seventy-year dominion in Russia. Having studied for decades the pre-revolutionary career of Stalin, I have been struck by how the language and political culture of Bolshevism was shaped by the personality and polemical style of its first leader, Vladimir Lenin. Here is a passage from my forthcoming book, *Stalin: Passage to Revolution,* that illustrates the potency of language in shaping the history of the party, and eventually the Soviet state:

[After the defeat of the Revolution of 1905], Bolshevism continued to attract the most radicalised young intellectuals and embittered workers as it had in the revolutionary years 1905–1907 and would again when the labour movement revived in 1912. Leninists were generally perceived to be the more militant and aggressive of the two Social Democratic factions.

There was a romantic, even millenarian impulse that propelled many into the perilous pursuit of revolutionary change, and when in the years after 1907 Lenin edged pragmatically toward combining underground revolutionary activity with exploitation of the new legal institutions, the 'left' Bolsheviks resisted what looked like accommodation with the existing order. This pattern would repeat itself in the future – in 1918 in the crisis over Russia's surrender to imperial Germany at Brest-Litovsk, and again in 1921 in the transition from the radical program of 'War Communism' to the moderation of the New Economic Policy. On several occasions Lenin would tear into what he called "left-wing infantilism," even as he zealously fought against those on his right, like the Menshevik "liquidators," whom he feared were abandoning the revolutionary struggle altogether. But in his "war on two fronts" Lenin was particularly strident and uncompromising in his reflexive readiness to use the most offensive language to caricature his opponents. This was a trait that his disciple Koba [Stalin] shared. Because of Lenin's great stature among his comrades, he encouraged a rhetoric and culture within the faction of bitter, exaggerated accusation and condemnation that in post-revolutionary years would have fatal effects on those who had employed it so loosely in less consequential circumstances.[1]

Consider Stalin's own language in letters to Molotov half a decade before he launched the great purges of 1936-1938: "The behaviour of Sergo (and Iakovlev) in the story of the 'completeness of production' is impossible to call anything else but anti-party, because it has as its objective goal the defense of reactionary elements of the party *against* the CC VKP(b)."[2] Or: "It is absolutely essential to shoot Kondrat'ev, Groman and a pair of other bastards (*merzavtsy*)...It is absolutely essential to shoot the group of wreckers in meat production and to publish this information in the press."[3] In May of the most sanguinary year, 1937, Stalin wrote to his chief executioner, Ezhov: "One might think that prison for Beloborodov is a podium for reading speeches, statements which refer to the activities of all sorts of people but not to himself. Isn't it time to squeeze this gentleman and make him tell about his dirty deeds? Where is he, in prison or in a hotel?"[4]

For Lenin, dictatorship and terror were necessary but undesirable means to a desired end; for Stalin they became both means and the end. Lenin's various regimes were adjustments to harsh realities; Stalin's autocracy was declared by him to be socialism. Stalinism was both an outgrowth of aspects of Lenin's Bolshevism and a malignant perversion of the original aspirations of the founders and the revolutionary masses who came out onto the streets in 1917. There was no inevitability in the degeneration of the revolution. Ultimately, those who rose in the party made choices that

---

1 Suny 2020: 413.
2 Lih, Naumov and Khlevniuk 1995: 234.
3 Ibid: 200.
4 Starkov 1993: 29.

proved fatal to both democracy and socialism, the two goals of revolution that must progress together.

References

Lih, Lars T., Naumov, Oleg V., and Oleg V. Khlevniuk (1995) (eds.), *Stalin's Letters to Molotov*. New Haven: Yale University Press.

Starkov, Boris A. (1993), "Narkom Ezhov," *in* J. Arch Getty and Roberta Thompson Manning (eds.), *Stalinist Terror: New Perspectives*. Cambridge: Cambridge University Press, 21-39.

Suny, Ronald Grigor (2020), *Stalin. Passage to Revolution*. Princeton: Princeton University Press.

24. The Revolutionary Personality and the Philosophy of Victory – Commemorating the 150th Anniversary of Lenin's Birth

Wang Hui

The "Modern Prince" and the Revolutionary Personality

Following the collapse of the Soviet Union and the socialist states of Eastern Europe, various social movements have emerged throughout the world. The 21st-century socialism of Latin America, for example, along with peasant armed struggles in South and East Asia,[1] have sought to sustain the revolutionary heritage of the 20th century. Yet under new conditions, the prospects for such movements remain unclear. In the advanced capitalist societies and the so-called transitional countries, none of the large-scale social protest movements such as Occupy, or the numerous labour movements, has been able to alter in any fundamental way the state of 'depoliticisation' that has arisen since the end of the Cold War. Social inequality, financial crises, the spread of epidemics, ecological destruction, and political crises caused by the advance of globalisation have arisen time and again, yet such premonitions of disaster – in which the "weakest links" of global capitalism are plainly visible – have so far failed to galvanise any overt political force that might be able to shatter these links. The political landscape of the contemporary world, it appears, has not yet escaped the shadow of the defeat of the socialist experiments of the 20th century. As Alain Badiou states, "The second [communist] sequence is over, and it is pointless to try to restore it."[2]

Simultaneously, the tide of neoliberalism has given rise to nationalist and populist trends. Most shocking is that, amidst these trends, many labourers who have lost their jobs and social protections have become adherents of right-wing politics. At precisely the moment that liberals decry the rise of populism, why is it that left-wing politics has lost the support of workers in the 'rust belts' and fallen into a state of complete impotence? Why is it that innumerable resistance movements lack any clear political capacity or direction, succumbing instead to the pitfalls of racism, xenophobia and identity politics? In addition to the departure of the vanguard party and larger-scale class movements, the most easily identifiable reasons include a weakness of leadership, an absence of tactical and strategic discussion of left-wing theory, and a decline in debate about concrete paths for social transformation. It is to these three interwoven elements – which, indeed, constitute the core political legacy of the 20th century – that we will turn our attention in this essay.

---
1 Including those in Nepal and India.
2 Badiou 2008: 29-46. According to Badiou, the period from the October Revolution of 1917 until the end of the Great Proletarian Cultural Revolution in 1976 constitutes the "second sequence," following the Paris Commune, in which the communist hypothesis was put into practice. Badiou argues that the primary content of this sequence (Marxism, the workers movements, mass democracy, Leninism, the vanguard party, and the socialist state apparatus) has ceased to be applicable.

Let us begin, then, with the issue of leadership. How are we to understand the power of leadership in revolutionary and reformist movements? Gramsci, in his *Prison Notebooks*, argues that Machiavelli's *The Prince* should be understood as "an historical exemplification of [...] a political ideology expressed neither in the form of a cold utopia nor as learned theorising, but rather by a creation of concrete fantasy which acts on a dispersed and shattered people to arouse and organise its collective will." Gramsci believed that "the modern prince, the myth-prince, cannot be a real person, a 'concrete individual' but is rather 'the political party' – the first cell in which there come together germs of a collective will tending to become universal and total. In the modern world, only those historico-political actions which are immediate and imminent, characterised by the necessity for lightning speed, can be incarnated mythically by a concrete individual."[3] Following this logic, the political party is the soul of modern politics. Yet it is also true that, because of the necessary relationship between the political party and state power, the entire history of the political party has been accompanied by "statification,"[4] bureaucratisation and depoliticisation. While the organisational framework of the political party and its position within the state system are today as stable as ever, the political party in the true sense of the word has thus already come to a premature end.

At the same time, as scholars of the Russian and Chinese revolutions will know, at critical historical moments in the circuitous path of these revolutions, the leaders who employed now legendary methods to accomplish their aims cannot be equated merely with the political party as such. On the contrary, at many historical junctures, Lenin, Mao and other revolutionary leaders found themselves in a state of *opposition to* their own party and at odds with its political direction. These revolutionaries were able to gain positions of leadership in the party only through protracted and, at times, bitter political and theoretical struggle. Indeed, in the case of Lenin, this almost perpetual struggle was a hallmark of his leadership, evinced for example in his insistence on maintaining internal party democracy even under the most dangerous and difficult conditions. This insistence was informed by Lenin's theoretical-practical conviction that to abolish open and frank intra-party debate, criticism, and self-criticism, would have extinguished the party's life force by abandoning the principle of democratic centralism – as he clearly articulated in the preface to *What Is To Be Done?*, citing Ferdinand Lassalle's letter to Marx of 24 June 1852: "[P]arty struggles lend a party strength and vitality; the greatest proof of a party's weakness is its diffuseness; and the blurring of clear demarcations; a party becomes stronger by purging itself [...]"[5] The long list of

---

3 Gramsci 1992: 129.
4 It is in this sense that I advanced the thesis of the "premature end of the political party" – that in a period where class and class politics persist and have expanded, the political party has come to a premature end as a result of statification. (See Wang Hui 2006: 687)
5 Lenin 1977a: 346.

Lenin's internal party antagonists is testament to this theoretical and political struggle: Bernstein, Plekhanov, Potresov, Maslov, Zinoviev, Kautsky, Luxemburg, Trotsky, Bukharin, Stalin... In a similar vein, Mao Zedong even dared, towards the end of his life, to oppose the entire system of the party, proclaiming that he stood together with the People. This unequivocal commitment to the active promotion of self-renewal within the political party and the ongoing reconstruction of relations between the party and the People was made possible by the exceptional political force exhibited by both of these leaders, by what we may call their *revolutionary personality*. In practice, the three actors – party, People and revolutionary leader – existed in a relationship of tension with one another: what delineates the revolutionary personality is a relentless dedication, through political struggle, to sustain and enhance the key interlinkages within this complex relationship.

It is undoubtedly true that the revolutionary personality as it was embodied by Lenin would have a profound influence on the long history of the Chinese Revolution. The Marxist theorist Li Dazhao, one of the founders of the Chinese Communist Party, viewed Lenin and Sun Yat-sen as the two revolutionary leaders of the Chinese Revolution, ascribing to both men the characteristics of the revolutionary personality:

> Because Mr. Lenin himself thought about Mr. Sun Yat-sen, we can view them in comparative terms. Mr. Sun Yat-sen was a man possessed of tremendous personality. Whether friend, follower, or enemy, all acknowledge his greatness. Lenin's personality was likewise tremendous. Whether friend, follower, or enemy, all acknowledge his greatness; in Russia there are those who are opposed to the Communists and who oppose Communism, yet they hold Lenin as an individual in great esteem. With respect to their revolutionary spirit, these two men likewise have much in common: when Lenin encountered setbacks, he did not lose hope or sink into despair. So too with Sun Yat-sen, he personally said that, after the second revolution failed and he had to flee to Tokyo, all those beneath him were falling into despair, and yet he himself insisted that the revolution had not failed, and so they should not fall into despair, but, rather, try again, and do better! Thus, the spirit of Lenin is the spirit of Sun Yat-sen, which is the spirit of the revolutionary! So too must we bear this spirit in mind!"[6]

Li Dazhao believed that the primary commonality between Lenin and Sun Yat-sen was their revolutionary personality, a force that transcended

---

6 Li 1999: 641.

the category of class interests, so that not only did they gain the recognition of their friends and followers, but so too did they force their enemies to acknowledge their strength. A further point of commonality between the two: they were eternal revolutionaries who showed no fear of failure. This observation is in accordance with the perspective of Lu Xun. On 12 March 1926, Lu Xun released his essay 'On the First Anniversary of Mr. Sun Yat-sen's Death' in Citizen News, in which he wrote:

> I recall that not long after Sun Yat-sen's death last year, there were some muckrakers who voiced some sneering remarks about Sun Yat-sen...yet regardless of such sneers, Sun Yat-sen's life, from beginning to end, was a life of revolution, even in the face of failure, it was still revolution; after the formation of the Chinese Republic, he was dissatisfied, and did not rest on his laurels, but rather continued to work for the completion of the revolution. Even on the eve of his death, he said: the revolution has not yet succeeded, all our comrades must strive on! [...] He was an eternal, total revolutionary. Whatever he did, it was all for revolution. However much men hereafter might disparage or snub him, everything he did, to the end, was for the revolution.[7]

In short, the revolutionary is a "totality." No matter what they do, "everything is for the revolution." This is synonymous with Trotsky's views on revolutionary art and literature put forward in *Literature and Revolution*, which Lu Xun summarised as follows: "even if revolution is not the subject matter, you must nonetheless take the consciousness embedded within the new things created by the revolution as the point of departure; otherwise, even if revolution is the subject matter, there can be no revolutionary art and literature." Thus, in order to create revolutionary art and literature, it is first necessary to become a revolutionary person; to conduct a revolution, it is first necessary to become a revolutionary person. Sun Yat-sen, and thereby Lenin, was precisely this kind of revolutionary person: "to the end, he constantly led new revolutionaries forward, and collectively strove for the completion of revolutionary work."[8]

Identifying the "Weakest Link":
The "Second Nature" of the Revolutionary Personality

In Lenin's epoch, in addition to expressing personal commitment and individual self-cultivation, the revolutionary personality also embodied a capacity to grasp the primary contradiction and throw oneself into action,

---

7 Lu Xun 2005: 306.
8 Ibid.

which we may term a "second nature." This requires that, at the same time as the revolutionary engages in actual movements, they must also enter into intense theoretical work, in order to be able to distinguish the moment for action amidst a complex and shifting reality, convince and even attack mistaken positions within the same camp, and conceive of revolutionary strategy and tactics. Trotsky observed that "in the *Iskra*, I believe, Lenin for the first time expressed the thought, that in the complicated chain of political action one must always seek out the central link for the moment in question in order to seize it and give direction to the whole chain. Later, too, Lenin returned to this thought quite often, even to the same picture of the chain and the ring. This method passed from the sphere of the conscious, as it were, into his unconsciousness and finally became second nature."[9] Lenin's totalising analysis of the situation and concrete grasp of the facts was, in the final analysis, subordinate to what he took to be the determining "link" of the given moment, to such an extent that, in concrete action, he often placed to one side any matters that directly or indirectly conflicted with the central task. "This 'defect' was only the reverse side of his faculty of the greatest inward mobilisation of all his forces, and exactly this faculty made him the greatest revolutionary of history."[10]

That which Trotsky termed seeking out the central link for the moment in question in the complicated chain of political action, in order to give direction to the whole chain, demarcates a certain capacity to assess the entire epoch. In his January 1915 article 'Under a False Flag,' Lenin advanced a methodology for distinguishing the specific features of an epoch:

> We are undoubtedly living at the juncture of two epochs, and the historic events that are unfolding before our eyes can be understood only if we analyse, in the first place, the objective conditions of the transition from one epoch to the other. Here we have important historical epochs; in each of them there are and will always be individual and partial movements, now forward now backward; there are and will always be various deviations from the average type and mean tempo of the movement. We cannot know how rapidly and how successfully the various historical movements in a given epoch will develop, but we can and do know which class stands at the hub of one epoch or another, determining its main content, the main direction of its development, the main characteristics of the historical situation in that epoch, etc. Only on that basis, i.e., by taking into account, in the first place, the fundamental distinctive features of the various 'epochs' (and not single episodes in the history of

---

9 See Trotsky 1925.
10 Ibid.

individual countries), can we correctly evolve our tactics; only a knowledge of the basic features of a given epoch can serve as the foundation for an understanding of the specific features of one country or another.[11]

Of course, this understanding of the epoch requires a precise reading of the national situation. In this sense, the "second nature" of the revolutionary personality is not an abstract internationalism or a pure ideal but is rather an internationalism with deep roots in national life. On 23 April 1923, Trotsky released an article in *Pravda* to commemorate the fiftieth anniversary of Lenin's birth. What is significant about this rather short article, entitled 'Nationalism in Lenin,' is that its core content is not internationalism but rather Lenin's "high degree" of "national" character": "He is deeply rooted in the new Russian history, makes it his own, gives it its most pregnant expression, and thereby reaches the height of international action and international influence." Trotsky argues that, in addition to an attunement to materialism, revolutionary leaders require "that mysterious creative power that we call intuition: the ability to grasp appearances correctly at once, to distinguish the essential and important from the unessential and insignificant, to imagine the missing parts of a picture, to weigh well the thoughts of others and above all of the enemy, to put all this into a united whole and the moment the "formula" for it comes to his mind, to deal the blow. This is intuition to action. On the one side it corresponds with what we call penetration." Trotsky understood that emphasising these "nationalist" specificities of Lenin was liable to shock certain people, and so he further explained: "[T]o be able to direct such a revolution, without precedent in the history of peoples, as is now taking place in Russia, it is most evidently necessary to have an indissoluble organic connection with the main strength of popular life, a connection which springs from the deepest roots. [...] Just because the social revolution, that has long had its international theoretical expression, found for the first time in Lenin its national embodiment, he became, in the true sense of the word, the revolutionary leader of the proletariat of the world."[12]

Lenin's theory of imperialism was precisely such a living development of his methodology of recognising the epoch. His great work – *Imperialism, the Highest Stage of Capitalism* – does not deal with China to any significant extent, but its theoretical analysis provided the precondition for the renewal of the Chinese Revolution. If it might be said that the unevenness of the imperialist world system gave rise to a series of "weakest links" within that system, then so too did the internal fractures created by a situation of competition among great powers create a series of "weakest links" within China itself, thereby creating the conditions for national revolution: "the

---

11 Lenin 1974: 135-157.
12 See Trotsky 1925.

great speculative coup of international capitalism, not fully ripened for international co-operation, [is] still hampered by the necessity under which the groups of capitalists lie, of using national feelings and policies to push their special interests."[13] As such, at the same time as they launched "the joint attack of Western Powers in China," their practice of using proxy wars to engage in mutual struggles and competition within China also created civil wars and fragmentation. The process by which France, Russia, Germany, Britain, Japan, the United States and other great powers struggled for international supremacy proceeded in tandem with their dividing-up of China. These two historical processes had as their common aim the acquisition of monopoly control over investment and excavation in different areas through the use of political and military occupation, in order that these imperialist powers might accrue superprofits. Thus, there exist in the imperialist epoch two kinds of "weakest link." One is that which Lenin described in these terms: "uneven economic and political development is an absolute law of capitalism. Hence, the victory of socialism is possible first in several or even in one capitalist country alone."[14] The other consists of the cracks and fissures created by the situation of uneven economic and political development within a country, as well as the contradictions between the agents of imperialism amongst the oppressed people. This latter kind of "weakest link" provided the conditions for the survival and development of the forces of the Chinese Revolution in the vast expanse of the countryside as well as in the border regions between provinces and in peripheral regions.

The "weakest link" not only marks the weak points in the ruling order, but also indicates the possibility of rupturing that system. Thus, the "weakest link" cannot exist of its own accord but relies on the formation of a revolutionary force. The revolutionary forces of the twentieth century did not exist in isolation within a single state or territory, but were national, class, strata and territorial movements which possessed deep international linkages with one another. In other words, without revolutionary forces and a revolutionary theory committed to rupturing with the ruling order, the "weakest links" would simply not exist; without being able to conceptualise the "weakest links" of the capitalist world-system and the "weakest links" of national state power together, it is difficult to form revolutionary strategy and tactics. With respect to the revolutionary situation, if imperialism is understood solely as an economic phenomenon rather than as rooted in the situation of political and military competition that emerges from economic demands, and if one fails to grasp that, between the old colonial policy and the new imperialism there exists no sharply-defined boundary, then, as a result, it is impossible to form a concrete strategy and tactics for resisting imperialism. In this sense, without revolutionary strategy and tactics, the weakest link cannot become the "weakest link" in the full sense of the word.

---

13 Hobson 2016: 309.
14 Lenin 1974: 339-43.

Thus, being able to truly discern who comprises the revolutionary forces, or locating the point of departure for developing revolutionary forces, creates the premise for being able to discern the "weakest link."

Today, we are closely familiar with Lenin's analysis of the Eastern Question and the Chinese Revolution during the period from around the 1905 Russian Revolution until the 1911 Xinhai Revolution. Through his theory of imperialism and advocacy of national self-determination in the period before and after the outbreak of the First World War, as well as his assessment of "advanced Asia, backward Europe," Lenin integrated the Eastern Question – from the Balkan Crisis to the Chinese Revolution – into his analysis of the newest stage of international capitalism. In his famous work *The Right of Nations to Self-Determination*, Lenin wrote: "In Eastern Europe and Asia the period of bourgeois-democratic revolutions did not begin until 1905. The revolutions in Russia, Persia, Turkey and China, the Balkan wars – such is the chain of world events of *our* period in our 'Orient.'"[15]

In actual fact, the position of the Russian Revolution on the national question was closely linked to the process of the "Awakening of Asia." Nevertheless, before the Northern Expedition,[16] with the exception of a small minority (for example, the representative of the Comintern and founder of both the Chinese Communist Party and the Communist Party of Indonesia, Dutchman Hans Sneevliet) there were very few in the various levels of leadership who sought to link the Chinese and Russian revolutions in a more concrete fashion. They might well have agreed with Lenin's view on unevenness and the weakest link in the imperialist epoch, but they had not yet integrated this theory into the search for a revolutionary force in China. The Comintern revolutionary M.N. Roy opposed Lenin's strategy of the united front, arguing that Sun Yat-sen was a schemer and reactionary.[17] Then, at the Congress of the Toilers of the Far East (held in Moscow in January 1922), Zinoviev voiced his dissatisfaction with Sun Yat-sen seeking support from the United States, and sharply criticised the bourgeois orientation of the Chinese Nationalist Party. Even Trotsky only began to take an interest in the Chinese Revolution in the 1920s, especially following the outbreak of the Shanghai workers' uprisings.

Lenin's assessment was radically different, however. In 1925, Karl Radek, who later became President of Moscow Sun Yat-Sen University, published an article in *Pravda* commemorating the death of Sun Yat-sen, in which he paid special attention to the following: "One day in 1916, at the time when the First World War was at its height, some Bolsheviks gath-

---

15 Lenin 1977b: 106.
16 The Northern Expedition was launched by the National Revolutionary Army in 1926 to combat the Northern Warlord Government, based on an alliance between the communists and the Kuomintang (KMT), with Soviet support. It led to the establishment of a KMT government in China in 1928, following the expulsion of the communists by the KMT in 1927.
17 Bergere 1998.

ered together at Berne to discuss problems of self-determination of nations. Lenin, who was at the conference, suddenly made a proposal that the Bolsheviks unite with the Chinese Revolution in the future. His proposal at the time seemed to be an idiot's impossible dream! Just imagine, the Russian proletariat will join with millions of Chinese to fight! Among those five or six Bolsheviks present at the meeting, who among them imagined that if they had lived long enough, they would see this dream materialise."[18] At Lenin's direction, from November 1922 to February 1923, the Fourth Congress of the Comintern passed the 'Theses on the Eastern Question,' and, after analysing the natural errors of the Chinese Communist Party, advocated cooperation between the Communists and the Nationalists and the formation of a united front.[19] In January 1923, representative of the Soviet government Adolph Joffe had discussions with Sun Yat-sen in Shanghai, resulting in the Sun-Joffe Joint Declaration. Under the premise of acknowledging Sun Yat-sen's view that communism and the Soviet governmental system were not applicable to China at that time, the Declaration formally began the first period of cooperation between the Communists and the Nationalists, and the Nationalist policy of alliance with Soviet Russia, cooperation with the Communists, and support of the workers and peasants. On the basis of his understanding of the totality and specificity of the imperialist epoch, and his concrete grasp of different social conditions, Lenin overcame the clear divergences between the ideology of Sun Yat-sen and the Chinese Revolution on the one hand, and the Communist movement on the other, and discovered the potential of the Chinese Revolution and its consistency with the Russian Revolution.

This point deeply influenced Li Dazhao and the first generation of Chinese Communists, whose conception of the world and of internationalism was also deeply rooted in national life. In his aforementioned talk at a meeting commemorating the second anniversary of Lenin's death, Li Dazhao offered a perspective that would appear inconceivable to a 'pure' Marxist or Communist:

> Leninism is the theory and strategy for the proletarian revolution in the imperialist epoch. The ideology of Sun Yat-sen is the theory and strategy of the revolution of oppressed peoples in the imperialist epoch. In theoretical terms, the ideology of Sun Yat-sen and Leninism can be linked and combined with one another, and so too in strategic terms are they consistent with one another. Therefore, it can be said that Leninists are precisely followers of the ideology of Sun Yat-sen; and followers of the ideology of Sun Yat-sen are, in turn, Leninists! Their ideologies are both revolutionary

---

18 Sheng 1971: 15.
19 Ibid: 10.

ideologies...their ideas and tremendous personalities are without differences.[20]

As a committed communist who, at that moment in Chinese history, was also the most theoretically advanced in Marxism, Li Dazhao asserted that "had Sun Yat-sen been born in Russia, he would absolutely have been a Lenin; had Lenin been born in China, he would absolutely have been a Sun Yat-sen! Their ideologies may appear different from each other on the surface, but in actual fact it is just a matter of their environments being different. Sun Yat-sen and Lenin share the same goal. But alas, Sun Yat-sen's environment did not allow him to achieve success in the same way as Lenin!"[21] Li Dazhao did not seek to eliminate or blur the differences between the revolutions led by Lenin and Sun Yat-sen, but rather located points of intersection and commonalities amidst a structure of difference and even opposition. He did so within a political logic constituted by the interactive relationships between the global situation and conditions within each country. As a result, through a process of acknowledging a common enemy, he was able to expand the category of friends and enemies, and so constitute a broad front.

Mao and Lenin, or People's War and the Coronavirus

On 28 April 1927, two weeks after Chiang Kai-Shek launched his 12 April coup in Shanghai, Li Dazhao was murdered in Beijing by the Fengtian clique warlord Zhang Zuolin. Five months later, the Autumn Harvest uprising led by Mao Zedong was also defeated, prompting a retreat into the Jinggangshan mountains in Jiangxi, and the creation of the first revolutionary base area and China's soviet government. Under the guidance of Lenin's theory of the "weakest link," this began a new stage in the Chinese Revolution. As distinct from Lenin's primary focus on theorising the unevenness between states within the imperialist world-system, Mao Zedong's focus was on the modes of expression of this uneven system within a single state. His analysis began from the unique character of China: "The long-term survival inside a country of one or more small areas under Red political power completely encircled by a White regime is a phenomenon that has never occurred anywhere else in the world. There are special reasons for this unusual phenomenon. It can exist and develop only under certain conditions."[22]

This uniqueness was explored through a systematic analysis: first, of the indirect, or non-direct, character of imperialist rule in China, from which arose the constant wars and divisions between the varied White governments.[23] It was in this respect that China uniquely differed both from

---
20 Li 1999: 641.
21 Li 1999: 641.
22 Mao 1965: 64.
23 Ibid.

the internal state structure of imperialist countries, as well as from the situation in those colonies directly ruled by imperialism, therefore being a state of combined and uneven development. Second, the conditions for the existence of Red political power did not simply consist in the fact of there being a vast, impoverished peasantry (one of the forms of a stage of combined development of capitalist and non-capitalist modes of production). More important still was that in some locations there existed revolutionary experience and mobilisation.[24] Third, the long-term survival of these small Red areas was determined by whether there existed the development of a nationwide revolutionary situation.[25] Fourth, if there existed no "regular Red Army of adequate strength," and only local Red Guards, then it would not have been possible to produce a situation in which one might set up an independent political regime, especially over the long term.[26] Finally, if there existed no powerful revolutionary organisation, or if, in spite of the existence of such an organisation, its policy was completely wrong, then Red political power could not exist.[27] In actual fact, whilst Mao Zedong's analysis was not understood by the highest leaders of the Chinese Communist Party at that time, his writing nonetheless provided strategy and tactics for an actual struggle, and so too did he use the form of theoretical analysis to conduct struggle and debate with other positions within the party.

Mao's strategy and tactics drew directly from Lenin's theoretical analysis of the imperialist epoch. The title 'A Single Spark Can Start A Prairie Fire' recalls the title of Lenin's newspaper, *Iskra*. In the vast expanse of the Chinese countryside, People's War consisted precisely in the forging of an unprecedented revolutionary force based on the peasantry, through practices of armed struggle, land reform, and the amalgamation of armed struggle, social reform, the united front, and the building of the party and of political authority. People's War does not designate a purely military concept but rather a political category. Under the unique conditions of twentieth-century China, People's War emerged as the process for the production of a new kind of political subject, as well as the process for the production of political structures and forms of self-expression adequate to that political subject. In the course of People's War, the representative relationships of the modern political party were fundamentally transformed. The birth of a political subject based on the peasants as its primary component, and with the worker-peasant alliance as its external political form, compelled the formation or transformation of all political forms, including the border region government, the political party, the peasant association, trade union and so on. The general principles of People's War include: first, that only through relying on and mobilising the masses is it possible to conduct war;

---

24 Ibid: 65.
25 Ibid: 66.
26 Ibid.
27 Ibid: 66-7.

second, that not only is it necessary to have a great conventional army, but so too must there be local armed detachments and militias; third, that the category of the militia designates a political process that is centred on land reform and the construction of political power, which has close links with the military struggle.

In the process of fighting against the new Coronavirus, the Chinese Communist Party has made a series of eye-catching appeals to this tradition, by conceiving of the struggle against the virus as "a People's War, a Total War, a Preventative War." Preventative War refers to the aim of the struggle, whereas People's War and Total War point to the character of the struggle. This People's War is embodied in mass-based forms of control and prevention that link the community, family, work unit and individuals to different levels of government in a vertical fashion. The Total War expresses that this struggle is a total mobilisation of the state system and state capacities. The People's War of the twentieth century, on the other hand, was a fundamental method of overcoming the total wars of the imperialist states, and so People's War and Total War are, in fact, mutually opposed categories. In the 21st century, however, when an epidemic compels total state mobilisation, the party has made multiple appeals to the model of People's War in order to constitute a new model of vertical as well as horizontal social mobilisation.[28] Many commentators in the West have ascribed China's process of fighting the epidemic to "authoritarianism" and yet have been unable to identify the capacities of "People's War" within the framework of national mobilisation, and have also failed to disentangle the complex relationship between People's War and Total War. Under conditions of emergency, might these re-emergent capacities of People's War be able to become more than mere methods of state mobilisation, re-igniting the agency and active role of the People, and once again compelling unity between the People and the "Modern Prince"? Under contemporary conditions (economic, technological, media communication) might these capacities be able to resolve the rupture of old political and social forms, and provide a motivating force for new ones? At a moment when the media and intellectual elites are hurriedly discussing how the coronavirus will transform the world order, it is necessary to re-state the following historical experience: without a new politics a new order cannot emerge. Thus, the question remains: What is to be done?

---

28 In the first stage of fighting the epidemic, provinces from all over China sent more than 40,000 medical personnel to Wuhan, thirteen cities in Jiangsu province each sent a medical team to the city of Xiaogan in Hubei province, and streets, residential compounds, villages, schools, factories and diverse commercial organisations were organised into basic units to fight the epidemic. Moreover, in rural areas, the fundamental force of existing structures of social organisation, combined with the power of the state administration via the sending of cadres to villages and townships in recent years, has allowed for a series of preventive measures that managed to contain the spread of the virus. In any case, in the absence of a vaccine against the Coronavirus, the problems of mobilisation and organisation are key to understanding how China was able to gain victory in the early stages of the anti-epidemic struggle.

The Eternal Revolutionary and the "Philosophy of Victory"

Reiterating what was stated at the beginning of the text, the contemporary world, it appears, has not yet escaped the shadow of the defeat of the socialist experiments of the 20th century. In general terms, every setback and every loss of hope is accompanied by dismay and melancholy. When historians, philosophers and other observers use defeat as their point of departure to look back on the twentieth century, should we not also seek to reflect on those new understandings of defeat and victory that emerged, developed and transformed in tandem with the consciousness of that century? Lenin himself had his fair share of bitter failure and defeat both before and after the 1917 revolution – it was precisely these experiences that shaped him as a revolutionary activist, and out of which his tactical versatility would emerge: "If from Lenin's numerous strategic lessons we wish to remember something with especial clearness, let it be what he calls the policy of the great changes: Today on the barricades and tomorrow in the seat in the Third Duma, today a summons to world revolution, to the international October revolution, and tomorrow negotiations with Kiihlmann and Czernin to sign the disgraceful peace of Brest-Litovsk. [...] And when the sound of the storm reaches here from the west, and it will resound, then whatever burdens us, bookkeeping, calculation, and NEP, we will answer without hesitation and without delay: We are revolutionaries from head to foot, we were so, we remain so, we shall remain so to the end."[29]

Similarly, the Chinese Revolution also resulted in a rich set of reflections on the question of defeat and victory. These reflections emerged from the internal course of the revolution to redefine the contents of the revolution itself. Lu Xun's "literature of resisting hopeless" and Mao Zedong's formulations of "from victory to victory" and the "philosophy of victory" comprise two examples of literary and philosophical articulations concerning hope and hopelessness, defeat and victory, and so too do they mark the personality types of two revolutionaries and their respective "political philosophies." In my view, the "philosophy of victory" is a series of historical reflections born from totally immersing oneself in collective struggle. It is, therefore, the strategic reflection of a revolutionary subject, in which sacrifice and tragedy are dealt with under the aegis of a program of action oriented towards victory. It entirely rejects those elements of isolation, meaninglessness, and feelings of insurmountable exhaustion that belonged to the intellectual and literary spheres during and after the May Fourth movement.[30] The "philosophy of victory" is rooted in the cruel and

---

29 See Trotsky 1925.
30 An anti-imperial and cultural movement led by intellectuals and students, named after the mass demonstration in Beijing on May 4, 1919 protesting the decision of the Versailles Peace Conference, which transferred former German concessions in the Shandong province to Japan. The May Fourth Movement was composed of two movements: a new cultural movement marked by the publication of *Youth Magazine* (later renamed *New Youth*) in 1915, which promoted cultural enlightenment, new literature and the vernacular movement; and the student movement of May 4th 1919, which marked the beginning of a new

tragic history of collective struggles, but it is also embodied in the strategic consideration of seeking victory in a context of defeat. Failure is not only the mother of success, but also the logical point of departure for the "philosophy of victory." To begin from defeat means seeking to discern once again the "weakest link" in a situation of difficulty, and developing a strategy and tactics through which one can defeat the enemy and gain victory, and in so doing, reconstruct the relation between oneself and the enemy as part of the process of creating a new conjuncture of forces. This process is, in actual fact, one of reconstructing the self, or the subject.

Mao Zedong's "Why Is It That Red Political Power Can Exist in China?" (5 October 1928), "The Struggle in the Chingkang Mountains" (25 November 1928), "A Single Spark Can Start a Prairie Fire" (5 January 1930) and other texts, signify precisely this emergence of the "philosophy of victory." For subsequent literary authors who described the twists and difficulties of the revolutionary process, this philosophy provided a lifeline of optimism expressed by the formulations "from victory to victory" as well as "the future is bright, the road is tortuous." In August 1949, on the eve of the founding of the People's Republic, Mao looked back on Chinese history since the 1840s and declared, in a manner that brooked no disagreement: "how different is the logic of the imperialists from that of the people! Make trouble, fail, make trouble again, fail again [⋯] till their doom; that is the logic of the imperialists and all reactionaries the world over in dealing with the people's cause [⋯] Fight, fail, fight again, fail again, fight again [⋯] till their victory; that is the logic of the people, and they too will never go against this logic."[31] This process of struggle, defeat and eventual victory is not only the logic of the people, however, it is also the process for creating the people as a revolutionary subject. By way of example, the resistance struggles following the Opium War could not be completed by a single group of people, as between successive subjects of resistance there exist important differences. Yet the logic of struggle-defeat-struggle constitutes these different sectors into a "People" that grows in strength and maturity on a daily basis, and which strides from struggle and defeat towards victory. Thus, the "philosophy of victory" has, as its guiding orientation, the implementation of the people and their will.

In other words, the true standard for the assessment of defeat is not defeat in and of itself, but rather whether the logic of struggle is able to persist and endure. Lu Xun defined Sun Yat-sen as an "eternal revolutionary" – a revolutionary defined through constant defeat, whereby "victory" does not designate a final conclusion but rather emerges through a process of being defeated and broken and yet still continuing to fight.[32] The reason that the "philosophy of victory" is optimistic is that such a philosophy is,

---

democratic revolution in China, and prompted the establishment of the Chinese Communist Party (CCP).
31 Mao 1961: 428.
32 Lu Xun 2005: 306.

from beginning to end, linked with an understanding of the dialectics of predicament, and with a strategic practice that is itself rooted in this understanding. Victory is not an abstract future, does not reside in an abstract utopia, but rather lies precisely in concrete practice and in the dialectical analysis of the balance of forces between ourselves and the enemy. Consequently, while the "philosophy of victory" is a philosophy of action, it does not entail the supremacy of the will. Quite the opposite, it situates the will for victory and an analysis of the situation in the antagonism and transformation of contradictions, thereby actively intervening in these very same processes.

Lu Xun's "literature of resisting hopelessness" rejects the worldview of optimism, but it does not oppose collective struggle; it does not locate hope in any subjective category but seeks to explore a path to the future amidst the wide expanse of the world. The "literature of resisting hopelessness" clearly differs from any "literature of optimism," but it has certain points of commonality with the "philosophy of victory." The "philosophy of victory" in the Chinese Revolution was at first born amid pools of blood and bitterness, through an analysis of a situation of defeat that was highly disadvantageous for the revolutionary forces. The countryside (not the cities) and the border regions (not the centre) became the location for the development of revolutionary strategy, but the demarcation of this new space arose precisely from a situation of defeat and the wide disparity between "our" forces and those of the enemy. The logic of victory lies in continued action, exploration and struggle, and is therefore radically different from a blind optimism or a metaphysical hope. The degeneration of the "philosophy of victory," that is, the transformation of the "philosophy of victory" into different forms of the "literature of optimism," arises precisely from abandoning the analysis of a highly disadvantageous situation of defeat, and the consequent rejection of truly strategic and concrete tactical reflections. As soon as this process of reflection is discarded, action will in all likelihood lose its direction, and hope will come to be invested in the inevitability of victory or an abstract future.

In conclusion, the revolutionary personality represents the personification of "resisting hopelessness" and "towards victory." In this respect, these revolutionary personalities approximate "mythic characters" (and for this reason they have repeatedly been thrust into the "secular world" by being stigmatised). Yet, if you will permit me to borrow Gramsci's language once more, the fullest mode of expression of "myth" is not that of a political party that organises the collective will, or the leader of such a party, but is rather the promoter of the real forms of action of an organised force that show that the collective will is already working effectively. This kind of personality, which can only emerge through action, is capable of inspiring people to excavate the future under their own feet unyieldingly and uncompromisingly, even in a situation without hope, and so promote the political maturity of the movement. Lenin's *What Is To Be Done?* is precisely such a paradigm of the "philosophy of victory": under disadvantageous conditions, we must closely analyse the specificities of the epoch, the relationship between immediate tasks and our fundamental objectives, and, through both theoretical research and tactical struggles, further the mutual amalgamation of political and practico-economic dimensions of the entire struggle, in order that we might unite dialectically the tasks of the period and the final objective within a concrete framework encompassing theory, strategy and action.

In an era that is post-revolution and post-political party, the aim of re-posing the question of the revolutionary personality as one of the political legacies of the twentieth century is not to advocate the worship or function of an individual, but to provide inspiration and encouragement for political renewal. In an epoch where the political system based on the political party has fallen into a universal crisis at both the international and national level, surely the revelation that this great legacy has to offer us is how we might – based on already existing elements and in the face of new conditions – constantly re-pose the question of "what is to be done," and in so doing compel ourselves to uncover possibilities for radically new political, economic and social organisation.

Translated from the original Mandarin Chinese by Ben Kindler

References

Badiou, Alain (2008), "The Communist Hypothesis," *New Left Review*, 49, 29–46.

Bergere, Marie-Claire (1998), *Sun Yat-sen*. Stanford: Stanford University Press.

Gramsci, Antonio (1992), *Selections from The Prison Notebooks of Antonio Gramsci*. New York: International Publishers.

Hobson, John Atkinson (2016), *Imperialism: A Study*. New York: Routledge.

Lenin, V.I. (1977a), *Collected Works Vol. 5*. Moscow: Progress Publishers.

Lenin, V.I. (1977b), *Collected Works Vol. 20*. Moscow: Progress Publishers.

Lenin, V.I. (1974), *Collected Works Vol. 21*. Moscow: Progress Publishers.

Li Dazhao 李大钊 1999 [1926], "Zai liening shishi er zhounian jinian dahui shang de yanshuo" 在列宁逝世二周年纪念大会上的演说 [Talk at a meeting commemorating the second anniversary of Lenin's death]. In *Li Dazhao quanji di si juan* 李大钊全集第四卷 (Collected works of Li Dazhao volume four), 640-42. Shijiazhuang: Hebei jiaoyu chubanshe.

Lu Xun 鲁迅 2005 [1926], "Zhongshan xiansheng shishi hou yi zhounian" 中山先生逝世后一周年 [On the first anniversary of Mr. Sun Zhongshan's death]. *In Lu Xun quanji di qi juan* 鲁迅全集第七卷 (Collected works of Lu Xun volume seven), 305-307. Beijing: Renmin wenxue chubanshe.

Mao, Zedong (1965), *Selected Works of Mao Zedong, Vol. 1*. Peking: Foreign Languages Press.

Mao, Zedong (1961), *Selected Works of Mao Zedong, Vol. 4*. Peking: Foreign Languages Press.

Sheng, Yueh (1971), *Sun Yat-sen University in Moscow and the Chinese Revolution: A Personal Account*. Kansas: University of Kansas Center for East Asian Studies.

Trotsky, Leon (1925), "Lenin," *Marxist Internet Archive*. Accessed on 01.07.2020, at https://www.marxists.org/archive/trotsky/1925/lenin/index.htm.

Wang Hui (2006), "Depoliticized Politics, Multiple Components of Hegemony, and the Eclipse of the Sixties," *Inter-Asia Cultural Studies*, 7.4.

25. In the Shadows of Never-Ending Warfare:
On the Use-Value of Lenin Today[1]

Darko Suvin

> *People for the most part (99 per cent of the bourgeoisie, 98 per cent of the liquidators, about 60–70 per cent of the Bolsheviks) don't know how to <u>think</u>, they only <u>learn words by heart</u>. They've learnt the word "underground." Firmly. They can repeat it. They know it by heart. But <u>how</u> to change <u>its forms</u> in a new situation, how to learn and think <u>anew</u> for this purpose, this we do not understand.*
> V.I. Lenin: "Letter to Inessa Armand"[2]

1. Why Lenin?

There is a wonderful apocryphal anecdote, which I often quote in these horrific years of devolving imperialist slaughters. It is an imaginary dialogue between Shklovsky[3] and Trotsky, for all their blind spots still the most intelligent Formalist and the most intelligent Leninist of that spacetime:

> Shklovsky said to Trotsky, "I'm not interested in what flag flies on the fortress. I write about perception and literature and don't care about war."
>
> Trotsky replied, "But war cares about you."

Why write today about Vladimir Ilyich Lenin? This should be obvious but isn't. It is not so much because of a (very necessary) piety towards him, as towards all our Great Left Ancestors, from Lucretius and Mo Zi through the pivots of Spinoza, Hegel and Marx, up to – and I mention only those nearest and most sympathetic to me – Brecht, Benjamin, Gramsci, Mao, Castro, Ho, Tito, and Kidrič?[4] It is <u>because of us</u>: for Lenin's major international achievement was contracting out of the huge and quite symptomatic carnage of the first capitalist and imperialist World War, a harbinger of all the subsequent mass killings, where genocide returned from the colonies to the continent of metropolitan imperialism as a sign that any real liberalism was over at home too. Not so coincidentally, this was meant to militarise the disciplining of working classes:

---

1 Versions of this text have appeared in *Communism, Poetry: Communicating Vessels* (2020) and *Coiled Verbal Spring: Devices of Lenin's Language* (2018).
2 Lenin 1973: 131 (translation: A. Rothstein).
3 Viktor B. Shklovsky (1893-1964), the most daring and seminal Russian Formalist of the years 1915-28, also a Renaissance-type genius who wrote fiction and scenarios for movies. He invented the concept of *ostranenie*, refunctioned by Brecht as *Verfremdung* (I discuss this in "Parables and Uses of a Stumbling Stone"). There are oodles of writings on him and Formalism online, see to begin with the fundamental Erlich.
4 See more on the last two in my *Splendour, Misery, and Possibilities: An X-ray of Socialist Yugoslavia* (2016).

> Anyone can understand that war and conquest without and the encroachment of despotism within mutually support each other; that money and people are habitually taken at will from a people of slaves to bring others beneath the same yoke; and that conversely war furnishes a pretext for exactions of money and [...] for keeping large armies constantly afoot [...] In a word, anyone can see that aggressive rulers wage war at least as much on their subjects as on their enemies, and that the conquering nation is left no better off than the conquered.[5]

Turning masses of plebeians into cannon and bomb fodder, "[w]ar was the true government of Europe [and the world – note DS] from 1914 onwards."[6] Destruction of people, commodities, and nature needed for quicker circulation of capital would henceforth be on a permanent mass basis: World War II 1936-45, III during the Cold War after 1945, and IV from Libya and Iraq on in this glad new century.

Emphatically, we cannot afford to disregard THE major historical anti-war gesture in modern history, one that earned Lenin the sympathies of millions in the whole world regardless of all else. To this we must add the defeat of fascist global domination in World War II, for it pivoted on the role of the USSR which, for all its horrible counter-revolutionary carnages, retained enough inbuilt elements of the original plebeian Leninism to make that war a supreme example of a just one: still carnage but obviating centuries of ruling fascism. And today, with exponentially more destructive technology threatening all vertebrate life on Earth, humanity is in a zero-sum conflict with perpetual warfare American-style (also British, French, and, as of Yugoslavia and Afghanistan, German and pan-European-style): either we'll get rid of it, or it will get rid of us.

Of course, we need other teachers too, supplementing and where need be modifying him, but the Lenin experience remains central. With him we must begin in the wake of Marx: all else follows. We need communism for many reasons,[7] but the most pressing one is to stop warfare and other sources of mass killings (for example in the present use of the "corona" disease by all our rulers for surveillance) as well as eco-destruction. Our dire need is for "survival studies" or salvational politics. An indispensable foundation stone for it is enlightening ourselves and others. The manifold popular icons of "Lenin's little light bulb" in the years of Soviet Russia's electrification[8] are therefore an allegory for our time.

---

5 Rousseau 1991: 90-91.
6 Russo 2016: 163.
7 What people mean by communism is here crucial, surely not the entirely "statalised" travesty of Stalin's type nor PR China today. I use it in the sense of Marx – see my essay "15 Theses" in *Splendour*.
8 See Suvin 2017b.

Photos: The Light Bulb Of Ilyich (Lampochka Ilicha)

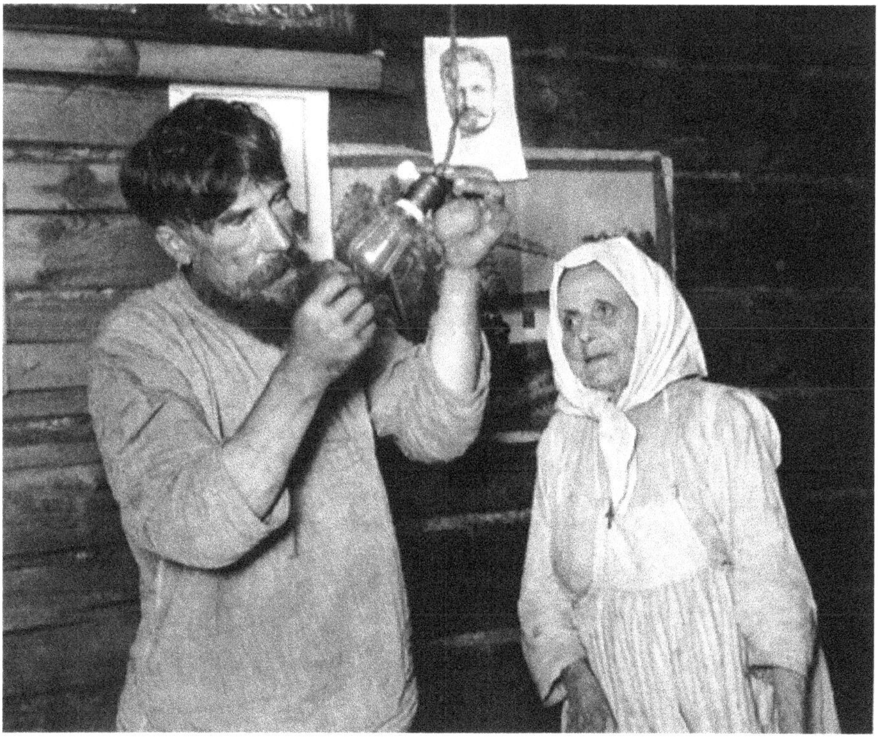

2. The Context of Lenin: An Age of Never-Ending Imperialist Warfare

The texts Mayakovsky commissioned for the special issue of the LEF (*Left Front of the Arts*) periodical in 1924 and recently translated into English – I think for the first time in almost a century – in the welcome book *Coiled Verbal Spring: Devices of Lenin's Language*[9] are, understandably for a beginning, focused on Lenin's briefer signed articles. They do not deal with possibly his most important signed work, *The State and Revolution*, except for a reference to why it wasn't finished, nor do they mention the unsigned but clearly his "Decree on Peace" (depersonalised to function as a government declaration). This Decree will bear repetition and meditation today when we would sorely need it again, with updates on covert economic and informational warfare. It had eleven meaty – and for that conjuncture quite precise and exhaustive – paragraphs, but I present here only extracts from five:

Decree on Peace

> The workers' and peasants' government, created by the Revolution of October 24-25 and basing itself on the Soviet of Workers', Soldiers' and Peasants' Deputies, calls upon all the belligerent peoples and their government to start immediate negotiations for a just, democratic peace.
>
> By ... such a peace the [workers' and peasants'] government means an immediate peace without annexations (i.e., without the seizure of foreign lands, without the forcible incorporation of foreign nations) and without indemnities.
>
> The [workers' and peasants'] government considers it the greatest of crimes against humanity to continue this war over the issue of how to divide among the strong and rich nations the weak nationalities they have conquered, and solemnly announces its determination immediately to sign terms of peace to stop this war on the terms indicated...
>
> The government proposes an immediate armistice to the governments and people of all the belligerent countries, and, for its part, considers it desirable that this armistice should be concluded for a period of not less than three months...

---

[9] A rather different variant of this essay was written as the Afterword to the book *Coiled Verbal Spring* sparked, edited, and introduced by Sezgin Boynik; it was much helped by our protracted discussions. I approach Lenin also in my essay "What and How" from Communism, Poetry, where this article was first published, and glance at him in a number of other places in that book; in particular, another very important use of Lenin, his doctrine of the mediating and guiding party, to my mind by no means a dead issue, is discussed in my essay there "What Is."

> While addressing this proposal for peace to the governments and peoples of all the belligerent countries, the Provisional Workers' and Peasants' Government of Russia appeals in particular also to the class-conscious workers of the three most advanced nations of mankind and the largest states participating in the present way, namely, Great Britain, France, and Germany. ... [We trust] that the workers of the countries mentioned will understand the duty that now faces them of saving mankind from the horrors of war and its consequences, that these workers, by comprehensive, determined, and most vigorous action, will help us to conclude peace successfully, and at the same time emancipate the labouring and exploited masses of our population from all forms of slavery and all forms of exploitation.

Notice that, in this – in all senses – diplomatic document, the usual rhetorical expedients or devices analysed by the Formalists have been maximally dampened down. Since you do not vituperate people with whom you want – at least ostensibly – to conclude an accord, there is no mention of capitalism or imperialism, none of economics. His March 1917 *Letters from Afar* sentence cited in the Boynik ed. book by Tynyanov, "Russian capital is merely a branch of the worldwide 'firm' which manipulates hundreds of billions of rubles and is called 'England and France'," is for the purpose at hand left unmentioned. But knowing full well that the accord would be against the interest of the governments and ruling classes bent on conquest, so that you must have a Plan B, you do not pull your punches either. In the final paragraph, there is a change of language from a diplomatic governmental declaration dealing in nations and borders to a kind of – yet unborn – Third International exhortation: it invokes the tradition of workers' struggles in France, the UK, and Germany to make it clear on whom the real hope for peace depends – and who will be separately approached to realise it.

This shows very clearly what most of the translated exegeses also stress: in Lenin there is no disjunction between language and liberatory action. His permanent underlying motto was What Is To Be Done (by persuading people and listening to the people): even in public governmental documents where he had to contend with the rulers' bureaucratic tradition of employing language to hide, twist, and obfuscate matters. To this should be added his recurring terms of middle-range <u>situation</u>, fusing spacetime and orientation, and tactical <u>task</u>, which is precisely That Which Is To Be Done primarily and immediately, now and without a doubt. It echoes immemorial activist wisdom, say by Dōgen, 13th C founder of Sōtō Zen: "The statement 'When time comes' means 'The time is already now, and there is no room for doubting it.'"

Alas, the optimistic trust in "Western" working classes proved to be mainly mistaken, though these were strong enough to prevent direct intervention against the Soviets by the "Western" armies in the ensuing Civil War (except for relatively minor actions against Arkhangelsk and Vladivostok).

Thus, the context for Lenin is his winning the peace with the Central Powers and then the Civil War against the "Western" allies: it is the existence of a potentially communist USSR. But the absence in the final paragraph of the USA – an important, and eventually decisive, belligerent nation since April 1917 – indicates a limit to the Decree and (I'm afraid) to Lenin's experiential horizon. Not only: it was a limit of the whole European socialist and then communist tradition, perhaps visible in the fact that its major ecumenical literary critic, Georg Lukács, never wrote anything of note about American literature and culture.

3. Two Limits of Lenin

I'm not drawing up here an encompassing balance sheet for Lenin's writing and actions, which would have been largely positive. But I find two significant places where I politically disagree with his argumentation, though they can still be used as awful warning.

The first one seems philosophical, it concerns his book *Materialism and Empirio-criticism* of 1909, where the worthy goal of preventing demoralisation after the 1905 defeat led to a simplified collapsing of positions in modern physics (e.g. of Mach) to their supposed political effect of relativist demobilisation. Lenin at that point knew little and probably cared less about physics; with his usual – but here oversimplified – vigour he was guarding the "scientificity" of Marx and Engels as a backbone of confidence into a possible revolution. This opened the door to a quite untenable theory of arts and sciences subjectively "mirroring" an objective reality – that is, to a mechanical materialism later warmly espoused by harmful Stalinist inquisitors into sciences and arts. It amounted to a ban on radical innovation within Marxism and communism quite uncharacteristic of Lenin's own major achievements. He would correct his philosophical bearings after an intense bout of reading Hegel, at the dark time of the inglorious fall of the social-democracy into supporting the world war – see the most revealing notes in his *Philosophical Notebooks* (wrongly so titled by editors under Stalin, it should have really been *Notebooks on Hegel*).

Even more harmful was Lenin's insistence at the 1921 Party congress on a ban on currents or "factions" within the communist party, reversing the whole tradition of vigorous interior debates in the first two Internationals. True, he thought this was a temporary measure for one year only in view of introducing NEP as a major "retreat;" but the remedy turned out to be worse than the disease and provided the major plank for Stalinist orthodoxy after 1928. In its consequences it was a truly epochal miscalculation.

4. Lenin's Importance for Us

What about the Lenin possibly alive today? I shall use here the second major clarification of Lenin at the time of the LEF issue, Lukács' 1924 booklet *Lenin – A Study of the Unity of His Thought*. I shall take from Lukács's partly dated work a main theme sparked by it, though going beyond it: capitalist degeneration.

His central thesis seems to be that Lenin "saw the problems of [his] age as a whole: the onset of the last phase of capitalism ... [and t]he actuality of the revolution [as human salvation.]"[10] For him, as for Marx, "the concrete analysis of the concrete situation is [...] the culmination of all genuine theory, its consummation, the point where it therefore breaks into practice."[11]

But what did Lenin see his age as? Lukács mentions an intriguing and for us most apposite debate on the Left in Russia after the failed 1905 revolution: should that period be seen as after the revolution's defeat (that is, we are in 1849) or before the decisive revolution (we are in 1847 and all is still open), as Lenin obviously believed and worked to accomplish. Today we could pose this as: are we in 1915 or even in 1939 – a nadir of horror yet on the eve of a political salvation – or are we in 1991 – the unstoppable downward slide of humanity's anti-utopian perdition, of a piece with the Nazi decade (though hypocritically disguised) only with no efficient alternative?

My favourite definitional slogan of Lenin's is: "Socialism is Soviet power plus electrification of the whole country" (remember "Ilyich's little light bulbs"?) Were we to generalise the sturdy and vivid examples from his writing, they would amount to full democracy from below (accompanied by suitable political institutions) and full use of ecologically safe science and technology available to all. On the most difficult road toward this – think of all the bankers, generals, and the millions of their mercenaries in media etc. who murder to prevent it – we need two, three, many Lenins: no doubt, updated for a post-cybernetic etc. age, taking into account the different technologies of ruling hardwares and softwares, but with the same unswerving dedication as and some approximation to the genius of Vladimir Ilyich's.

However, there is a most important difference from the age of Lenin in today's epoch (humankind's position) under the far-off stars, nanophysical AI armies, and capitalist banks – so that he remains a necessary but, alas, no longer sufficient guide. How can we begin sketching in the basis for a present-day guide?

It would be easy to compile here a representative list of the rising bourgeoisie's huge and permanently needful humanising achievements – pivoting on the French, American, and Industrial revolutions, best praised in *The Communist Manifesto* – and what happened to them in history. It may be enough to suggest the concepts and practices of Enlightenment, citizenship, republicanism, global interchanges, hygiene and antisepsis, longer life-span for a majority, universal elementary schooling and easy access to middle and higher schooling, urbanisation, easier transport and communication, and so

---

10 Lukács 1970: 10-11 (translation: Nicholas Jacobs).
11 Ibid: 42-43.

on and on – in sum, the twin peaks of easier living, made possible by industrial productivity, and happiness ("a new idea in Europe," said Saint-Just). Why do I call them "permanently needful?" Because – although they were first memorably formulated and fitfully tried in and around the three bourgeois revolutions I mentioned (and in a number of precursors) – they in fact foundered under a capitalist rule indelibly marked by plundering dispossession, colonialist violence, and metropolitan exceptionalism that then necessarily went in each country hand in hand with internal racism and exploitation. The possible universally valid achievements of the bourgeoisie were left to be picked up by socialists and communists – as is implied in the whole Lenin event. To be sure, I do not wish to claim exclusive vanguard status for North Atlantic revolutions here as they sedimented into the infamous "modernisation theory:" the West as against the Rest[12] is not the universal norm in relation to which all vectors toward easier living and happiness from other political spacetimes – say tribal society, or Asia, or the Haiti of Toussaint l'Ouverture, or the Yugoslavia of Tito, or the Cuba of Castro – would be particular and peripheral. If one believes, as Lenin did when he could afford it, in plebeian democracy from below (the Soviets, or ruling through councils of working people) then all anti-capitalist vectors towards this have the same dignity wherever and whenever they might happen; and Europe, including Russia, just happened to industrialise and form a conscious proletariat first, so as to reach some formulations which remain indispensable.

Thus, if the bourgeois wave's humanly useful peak was 1848 for Western Europe and 1865 for the USA – later in most other places – then the reflux or devolution of capitalism after that in all matters of disalienation is glaring. True, there was a subsidiary but very important upward blip of antifascism and the Welfare State ca. 1933-73, which put paid to the crassest threat of fascism and demonstrated that a reasonably sane and good life was now technically possible for all; I was raised and formed by it and do not at all wish to minimise the achievements of both the Leninist thrust and the Keynesian response (half mirror image, half co-optation to prevent worse for the co-opters). But on the whole, both in the ongoing world wars and in the triumph of financial turbocapitalism from the 1970s on, all the positive achievements of the bourgeoisie and capitalism are one by one being taken back, as if to console us for its forthcoming passing.

As different from Lenin, our problem is that we can't be sure whether the coming new epoch of relations in and around human production – what Yeats memorably called the new beast slouching toward Bethlehem – will be less or more monstrous: will it be communist enlightenment and poetic justice[13] or fascist savagery fusing slavery, serfdom, and exploitation with the highest technology? One could today make a very long negative list on the model of the following one a generation ago: it is not by chance that major

---

12 Cf. Sakai 1997 & 2005.
13 That I argue for in *Communism, Poetry*.

technological progress "[has led] to disastrous outcomes: pesticides increase pests; hospitals are foci of infection; antibiotics give rise to new pathogens; flood control increases flood damage; and economic development increases poverty."[14] To crown all, in lieu of democracy and the citoyen, after 2008 capitalism's legitimate son of fascism is returning, and some approximation of its yearning for total control from the rulers downward is present in how all States cope with the COVID pandemic. The bourgeois dispensation turns out to be a recipe for the world's most successful transmutation of progress into regress or happiness into misery, and capitalist profitable productivity a recipe for mega-titanic destruction!

This is what we absolutely must start from: the taking back of the reasons for the Communist Manifesto's glorification of the bourgeoisie. Following Lenin's style of writing and working, our negation of the systematic negativity grasping at us ought to be phrased as: If we don't do such-and-such in proper pragmatic ways to re-establish revolutionary horizons, we are lost. Humanity is lost. No halfway measures will help it, only a consistent Leninianism 2.0: for the alternative is, in Jack London's felicitous image, generations of an "iron heel" of mass killings and ecocide.

References

Boynik, Sezgin (ed.) (2018), *Coiled Verbal Spring: Devices of Lenin's Language* [with texts by Mayakovsky, Shklovsky, Eikhenbaum, Yakubinsky, Tynyanov, Tomashevsky, Kazansky, Kruchenykh]. Helsinki: Rab-Rab Press.

Erlich, Victor (1981), *Russian Formalism.* New Haven: Yale University Press.

Lenin, V. I. (1917), "Decree on Peace," *Marxist Internet Archive.* Accessed on 26.11.2020, at www.marxists.org/archive/lenin/works/1917/oct/25-26/26b.htm.

Lenin, V.I. (1973), *Collected Works Vol. 35.* Moscow: Progress Publishers.

Levins, Richard (1996), "Ten Propositions on Science and Antiscience," *in* Andrew Ross (ed.), *Science Wars.* Durham: Duke University Press, 180-91.

Lukács, Georg (1970), *Lenin: A Study of the Unity of his Thought.* London: New Left Books.

Rousseau, Jean-Jacques (1991), "Abstract and Judgement of Saint-Pierre's Project for Perpetual Peace," *in* Stanley Hoffmann and David P. Fidler (eds.), *Rousseau on International Relations.* Oxford: Clarendon Press, 53-100.

Russiapedia, "Of Russian Origin: The Ilyich Lamp." Accessed on 26.11.2020, at https://russiapedia.rt.com/of-russian-origin/the-ilyich-lamp/.

Russo, Alessandro (2016), "The Sixties and Us," *in* Alex Taek-Gwang Lee

---

14 Levins 1996: 180-181.

and Slavoj Žižek (eds.), *The Idea of Communism 3*. London: Verso, 137-78.

Sakai, Naoki (1997), *Translation and Subjectivity*. Minneapolis: University of Minnesota Press.

Sakai, Naoki (2005), "Civilizational Difference and Criticism: On the Complicity of Globalization and Cultural Nationalism," *Modern Chinese Literature and Culture*, 17.1, 188-205.

Suvin, Darko (2016), *Splendour, Misery, and Possibilities: An X-ray of Socialist Yugoslavia*. Leiden: Brill.

Suvin, Darko (2017a), "Parables and Uses of a Stumbling Stone," *Arcadia*, 5.2, 271-300.

Suvin, Darko (2017b), *Lessons from the Russian Revolution and Its Fallout*. Belgrade: Rosa Luxemburg Foundation Southeast Europe.

Suvin, Darko (2020), *Communism, Poetry: Communicating Vessels*. Toronto: Political Animal.

26. Lenin – Which Lenin?

Slavoj Žižek

The majority of radical Leftist thought in recent decades has been caught in the trap of oppositionalism: it adopts as self-evident the claim that true politics is only possible at a distance from the state and its apparatuses: the moment an agent immerses itself fully into state apparatuses and procedures (like parliamentary party politics), the authentic political dimension is lost. (From this standpoint, even the Bolshevik triumph – taking power in Russia in October 1917 – appears a self-betrayal.) But is there in such a stance not an indelible aspect of avoiding responsibility? Withdrawal into non-participation in power is also a deliberate act since one is aware that somebody else will have to do it, and the dirtiest thing is to leave to another the dirty job and then, after the job is done, accuse this other of unprincipled opportunism. (Among others, Eamon de Valera did this when he let Michael Collins conduct the 'dirty' negotiations with the British which led to the Free Irish State, and then, after profiting himself from it, accusing him of treason.) An authentic political agent is never afraid to take power and assume responsibility for what is going on, without resorting to excuses ("unfortunate circumstances," "enemy plots," or whatsoever). Therein resides Lenin's greatness: after taking power, he knew the Bolsheviks found themselves in an impossible situation (with no conditions for an actual "construction of Socialism"), but he persisted, trying to make the best out of total deadlock.

The true dimension of a revolution is not to be sought in the ecstatic moments at its climax (one million people chanting in the main square…); one should rather focus on how the change is felt in everyday life when things return to normal. This is why Trotsky lost against Stalin: after Lenin's death, the population of the Soviet Union was slowly emerging from ten years of hell (World War I, civil war) with untold suffering, and people longed for a return to some kind of normalcy – this is what Stalin offered them, while Trotsky, with his permanent revolution, promised them just more social upheaval and suffering.

In a vague but pertinent homology, we can say that the construction of the enemy in an antagonistic relation plays the role of Kant's schematism: it allows us to translate theoretical insight (awareness of abstract social contradictions) into practico-political engagement. This is how we should read Badiou's statement that "one cannot fight capitalism": one should "schematise" the fight into activity against concrete actors who work like the exposed agents of capitalism. However, the basic wager of Marxism is precisely that such a personalisation into an actual enemy is wrong – if it is necessary, it is a kind of necessary structural illusion. So does this mean that Marxist politics should permanently manipulate its followers (and itself), acting in a way it knows is misleading? Marxist engagement is condemned to this immanent tension, which cannot be resolved by claiming that now we fight the enemy and later we will move to the more fundamental overhaul of the system itself. Left populism stumbles upon the limit of fighting the enemy the moment it takes power.

In a situation like today's, Left populism's fatal flaw is clearly visible: its weakness is precisely what appears to its partisans as its strength, namely the construction of the figure of enemy and the focus on the struggle against it. What is needed today are above all positive visions of how to confront our problems: the threat of ecological catastrophes, the destabilising implications of global capitalism, the traps of the digitalisation of our minds... In other words, what is needed is not just to fight big financial institutions but to envisage new modes of financial politics, to provide feasible answers to the question: OK, so how would you organise finances if you gain power? It's not just to fight against walls and for open borders but to envisage new social and economic models that would no longer generate refugees. Today, more than ever, our system is approaching such a deep crisis that we can no longer just bombard it with our demands, expecting that it will somehow manage to meet them while continuing to function smoothly.

Instead of just focusing on antagonism, it is therefore crucial for a Leftist government today to define a role for the private sector, to offer the private sector precise conditions under which it can operate. As long as (at least a large part of) the private sector is needed for the smooth functioning of our societies, one should not just antagonise it but also propose a positive vision of its role.

Perhaps, then, instead of the increasingly boring variations on the topic of "distance from the state," what we need today is a return to Lenin – but which Lenin? Here is how, two years before his death, when it became clear that there would be no pan-European revolution, and that the idea of building socialism in one country was nonsense, Lenin viewed the situation:

> What if the complete hopelessness of the situation, by stimulating the efforts of the workers and peasants tenfold, offered us the opportunity to create the fundamental requisites of civilisation in a different way from that of the West European countries?[1]

One should take note of how Lenin used here a class-neutral term "to create the fundamental requisites of civilisation," and how, precisely when he accentuates the distance from West European countries, he clearly refers to them as the model. Communism is a European event, if there ever was one. When Marxists celebrate the power of capitalism to disintegrate old communal ties, when they detect in this disintegration the opening of the

---
1 Lenin 1973: 478.

space of radical emancipation, they speak on behalf of the emancipatory European legacy. Walter Mignolo and other post-colonial anti-Eurocentrists (quite correctly) dismiss the idea of Communism as European and, instead of Communism, propose that the resistance to global capitalism resort to ancient Asian, Latino American, or African traditions. There is a crucial choice to be made here: do we resist global capitalism on behalf of the local traditions it undermines, or do we endorse this power of disintegration and oppose global capitalism on behalf of a universal emancipatory project? The reason anti-Eurocentrism is so popular today is precisely because global capitalism functions much better when its excesses are regulated by some ancient tradition, when global capitalism and local traditions are no longer opposites but are on the same side.

To put it in Deleuzian terms, Lenin's moment is the "dark precursor," the vanishing mediator, the displaced object never at its own place, between the two series, the initial "orthodox" Marx's series of revolution in the most developed countries, and the new "orthodox" series of the Stalinist "socialism in one country," and then of the Maoist identification of the Third World nations with the new world proletariat. Here, the shift from Lenin to Stalinism is clear and easy to determine: Lenin perceived the situation as desperate, unexpected, but as such one that had to be creatively exploited for new political choices; with the notion of "Socialism in one country," Stalin re-normalised the situation into a new narrative of linear development in "stages." That is to say, while Lenin was fully aware that an "anomaly" had happened (revolution in a country which has no presuppositions for developing a socialist society), he rejected the vulgar evolutionist conclusion that revolution took place "too early," so that one can only take a step back to developing modern democratic capitalist society, which will then slowly create conditions for socialist revolution, claiming that – to refer back to the crucial passage quoted above – this very "complete hopelessness of the situation" offers "the opportunity to create the fundamental requisites of civilisation in a different way from that of the West European countries."[2] What Lenin is proposing here is effectively an implicit theory of "alternate history": under the "premature" domination of the force of the future, the same "necessary" historical process (of modern civilisation) can be (re)run in a different way.

And is such an approach not needed today more than ever? All the threats that haunt us, from environmental disasters to viral epidemics, from digital control to chaotic migrations, indicate the urgency to "create the fundamental requisites of civilisation in a different way," through a new internationalism that will open up the path to radical change.

References
Lenin, V.I. (1973), *Collected Works Vol. 33*. Moscow: Progress Publishers.

---

2 Ibid.

27. For Comrade Lenin on his 150th Birth Anniversary[1]

Vijay Prashad

Vladimir Ilyich Ulyanov (1870-1924) was known by his pseudonym – Lenin. He was, like his siblings, a revolutionary, which in the context of Tsarist Russia meant that he spent long years in prison and in exile. Lenin helped build the Russian Social Democratic Labour Party both by his intellectual and his organisational work. Lenin's writings are not only his own words, but the summation of the activity and thoughts of the thousands of militants whose paths crossed his own. It was Lenin's remarkable ability to develop the experiences of the militants into the theoretical realm. It is no wonder that the Hungarian Marxist György Lukács called Lenin "the only theoretician equal to Marx yet produced by the struggle for the liberation of the proletariat."[2]

Building a Revolution

In 1896, when spontaneous strikes broke out in the St. Petersburg factories, the Socialist Revolutionaries (SR) were caught unawares. They did not know what to do. They were disoriented. Five years later, V. I. Lenin wrote that the "revolutionaries *lagged behind* this upsurge, both in their 'theories' and in their activity; they failed to establish a constant and continuous organisation capable of *leading* the whole movement."[3] Lenin felt that this lag had to be rectified.

Most of Lenin's major writings followed this insight. He worked out the contradictions of capitalism in Russia (*The Development of Capitalism in Russia*, 1896), which allowed him to understand how the peasantry in the sprawling Tsarist Empire had a proletarian character. It was based on this that Lenin argued for the worker-peasant alliance against Tsarism and the capitalists. When the Russian Revolution of 1905 collapsed, Lenin took to *Novaya Zhizn* (12 November 1905) to argue that the "survivals of serfdom" formed a "cruel burden on the whole mass of the peasantry;" the "proletarians under their red banner," he wrote, "have declared war on this burden." It was not enough, Lenin argued, for the workers to fight for the peasants' demands, and it was not enough for the independent demands of the peasantry – for land – to be met; what was necessary was to deepen the unity between the workers and the peasants in the fight "against the rule of capital" and for socialism. There was no sense in being naïve about the fact that there were class relations within the "peasantry," and that the small farmers had their own vested class interests in their small private holdings. Lenin's study emphasised the differentiation of the peasantry, in order to understand that the small farmers had a closer class allegiance to the landlords in terms of the defence of private

---

1 Editor's note: This text was simultaneously published in Prashad 2020.
2 Lukács 2009: 13.
3 Lenin 1977a: 397.

property and in terms of the right to exploit landless agricultural workers. Lenin saw with steely-eyed clarity that the development of worker-peasant unity had to fully grasp the complexities of the countryside, otherwise the movement for socialism would be derailed in a petty bourgeois direction.

Opponents of Tsarism other than the Bolsheviks (such as the Social Democrats, the agrarian radicals, the SR, and the Mensheviks) stopped far short of the socialist project. Lenin understood from his engagement with mass struggle and with his theoretical reading that the social democrats – as the most liberal section of the bourgeoisie and the aristocrats – were not capable of driving a bourgeois revolution let alone the movement that would lead to the emancipation of the peasantry and the workers. His theoretical assessment was elaborated in *Two Tactics of Social Democracy in the Democratic Revolution* (1905). *Two Tactics* is perhaps the first major Marxist treatise that demonstrates the necessity for a socialist revolution, even in a "backward" country, where the workers and the peasants would need to ally to break the institutions of bondage and advance society into socialism.

These two texts from 1896 and 1905 show Lenin avoiding the view that the Russian Revolution could leapfrog capitalist development (as the populists – *narodniki* – suggested) or that it had to go through capitalism (as the liberal democrats – the Kadets, for example – argued). Neither path was possible or necessary. Capitalism had already entered Russia, a fact that the populists did not acknowledge; and it could be overcome by a worker and peasant revolution, a fact that the liberal democrats disputed. The 1917 Revolution and the Soviet experiment proved Lenin's point.

Having established that the liberal elites would not be able to lead a worker and peasant revolution, or even a bourgeois revolution, Lenin turned his attention to the international situation. Sitting in exile in Switzerland, Lenin watched as the Social-Democrats capitulated to the warmongering in 1914 and delivered the working-class to the world war. Rosa Luxemburg, equally dismayed, wrote, "The global historical appeal of the Communist Manifesto undergoes a fundamental revision and, as amended by Kautsky, now reads: proletarians of all countries, unite in peace-time and cut each other's throats in war!"[4] Frustrated by the betrayal of the social democrats, Lenin wrote an important text – *Imperialism, the Highest Stage of Capitalism* – which developed a clear-headed understanding of the growth of finance capital and monopoly firms as well as inter-capitalist and inter-imperialist conflict. It was in this text that Lenin explored the limitations of the socialist movements in the West, with the labour aristocracy providing a barrier to socialist militancy; and the potential for revolution in the East, where the "weakest link" in the imperialist chain might be found. Lenin's notebooks show that he read 140 books and 213 articles in English, French, German and Russian to clarify his thinking on contemporary imperialism.

---

4 Luxemburg 1915.

Clear-headed assessment of imperialism of this type ensured that Lenin developed a strong position on the rights of nations to self-determination, whether these nations were within the Tsarist Empire or indeed any other European empire. The kernel of the anti-colonialism of the USSR – developed in the Communist International (Comintern) – is found here.[5]

The term 'imperialism,' so central to Lenin's expansion of the Marxist tradition, refers to the uneven development of capitalism on a global scale and the use of force to maintain that unevenness. Certain parts of the planet – mostly those that had a previous history of colonisation – remain in a position of subordination, with their ability to craft an independent national development agenda constrained by the tentacles of foreign political, economic, social and cultural power. In our time, new theories have emerged that suggest that the new conditions no longer can be sustained by the Leninist theory of imperialism. Antonio Negri and Michael Hardt, for instance, argue that there is no geopolitical rivalry left, that there is only the extension of the sovereignty of the constitution of the United States on a world-scale. This is what they call Empire. What the people – the "multitude" – must do, they suggest, is to contest the terms of this constitution but not the fact of its global aspiration. Others argue that the world has flattened, so that there is no longer a Global North that oppresses a Global South, that the elites of both regions are part of a global capitalist order. This is the kind of theory that Karl Kautsky advanced in the name of 'ultra-imperialism.' Lenin responded sharply to Kautsky and this theory of 'ultra-imperialism,' saying that Kautsky noted that "the rule of finance capital lessens the unevenness and contradictions inherent in the world economy, whereas in reality it increases them."[6] Elements of Lenin's text are, of course, dated – it was written a hundred years ago – and would require careful reworking. But the essence of the theory is valid: the insistence on the tendency of capitalist firms to become monopolies, the ruthlessness with which finance capital drains the wealth of the Global South and the use of force to contain the ambitions of countries of the South to chart their own development agenda.

Finally, Lenin spent the period from 1893 to 1917 studying carefully the limitations of the party of the old type – the social democratic party. If you spend any time in Lenin's *Collected Works* during the decades before the 1917 Russian Revolution, you will find thousands of articles and reports on how to strengthen mass work and party building. In Lenin's 1899 text – *Our Programme* – he makes the point that the party must be involved in continuous activity and not rely upon spontaneous or initial (*stikhiinyi*) outbreaks. This continuous activity would bring the party into intimate and organic touch with the working-class and the peasantry as well as help to germinate the protests that then might take on a mass character. It was this

---

5 See Riddell, Prashad and Mollah 2019.
6 Lenin 1974: 272. See also Kautsky 1970.

consideration that led Lenin to work out his understanding of the revolutionary party in *What is To Be Done?* (1902). Lenin developed bold ideas for the construction of a worker-peasant party, including the role of the class-conscious workers as the vanguard of the party and the importance of political agitation amongst workers to develop a genuinely powerful political consciousness against *all* tyranny and *all* oppression. The workers need to *feel* the intensity of the brutality of the system and the importance of solidarity.

These texts – from 1896 to 1916 – prepared the terrain for the Bolsheviks and Lenin to understand how to operate during the struggles in 1917. It is a measure of Lenin's confidence in the masses, and his theory, that Lenin wrote his audacious pamphlet *Can the Bolsheviks Retain State Power?* This was written a few weeks before the seizure of power. As events unfolded in 1917, Lenin constantly tried to theorise the dynamic of change. The revolution of February 1917 had overthrown the Tsar; it had brought to power the liberals. Lenin tracked two developments of equal importance: first, that the liberals – under Kerensky – were preparing to betray the revolutionary aims and return Russia to the war, and therefore to retain the entire Tsarist system; second, that the revolutionary proletariat – and its main parties – remained alert and active, and had strengthened their political form through the Soviets. The worker-peasant controlled Soviets became a centre of 'dual power' against the liberal-dominated Duma (Parliament). What this meant to Lenin, as he wrote in several of his essays in this period, was that the Soviets had to defend the revolutionary aims and to take power. In September 1917, Lenin wrote that for a Marxist, "insurrection is an art;" Lenin and the Bolsheviks marshalled their forces, and in October 1917 they struck, and *completed* the Russian Revolution of 1917.

Building a State

No revolution is 'completed' just by seizing power. There was much work to be done in the immediate period after Lenin and his comrades took control of the collapsed Tsarist state. A close reading of Lenin's *State and Revolution* (1918) anticipates the problems faced by the Soviets in their new task – they could not only inherit the state structure, but had to "smash the state," build a new set of institutions and a new institutional culture, create a new attitude by the cadre towards the state and society.

The most important text here is *The Immediate Tasks of the Soviet Government* (April 1918), which lays out the agenda for the USSR in its first few years. The other texts show Lenin's general attitude towards state construction and to the challenges faced by the USSR – surrounded by hostile powers – in this period. Lenin's *Better Fewer, But Better* (1923), written towards the end of his life, is one of the most honest and reasonable texts on the problems faced by the new government and society.

In his last public appearance – at the Moscow Soviet on November 20, 1922 – one can see Lenin's personality in full display. There is Lenin's confidence and his humanness. There is Lenin's honesty and his ambition:

> We still have the old machinery, and our task now is to remould it along new lines. We cannot do so at once, but we must see to it that the Communists we have are properly placed. What we need is that they, the Communists, should control the machinery they are assigned to, and not, as so often happens with us, that the machinery should control them. We should make no secret of it and speak of it frankly. Such are the tasks and the difficulties that confront us – and that at a moment when we have set out on our practical path, when we must not approach socialism as if it were an icon painted in festive colours. We need to take the right direction, we need to see that everything is checked, that the masses, the entire population, check the path we follow and say, 'Yes, this is better than the old system.' That is the task we have set ourselves. Our Party, a little group of people in comparison with the country's total population, has tackled this job. This tiny nucleus has set itself the task of remaking everything, and it will do so. We have proved that this is no utopia but a cause which people live by. We have all seen this. This has already been done. We must remake things in such a way that the great majority of the masses, the peasants and workers, will say, 'It is not you who praise yourselves, but we. We say that you have achieved splendid results, after which no intelligent person will ever dream of returning to the old.' We have not reached that point yet… Socialism is no longer a matter of the distant future, or an abstract picture, or an icon. Our opinion of icons is the same – a very bad one. We have brought socialism into everyday life and must here see how matters stand. That is the task of our day, the task of our epoch.[7]

By 1921, Lenin's health had deteriorated dramatically. In May 1922, he suffered his first stroke. He died on 21 January 1924 at the age of 53. Over a million people came to pay homage to Lenin over three cold days in January before he was interned in a mausoleum in Red Square, where his body remains.

---
7 Lenin 1973: 443.

Everything that Lenin wrote a hundred years ago is not to be taken as gospel. It is a guide. Circumstances change, developments must be studied carefully. It was Lenin who taught us that "the very gist, the living soul of Marxism [is] a concrete analysis of a concrete situation."[8] What we learn from Lenin is his method and his discipline, his sharp awareness of class in terms of his understanding of politics and policy. Revolutions do not repeat themselves in all their particulars, nor do revolutionary processes. Different historical conjunctures, the concrete situations, require different historical revolutionary dynamics. We have Lenin over our shoulders; he is our inspiration and model.

References
Kautsky, Karl (1970), "Ultra-Imperialism," *New Left Review*, 59, 41-46.
Lenin, V.I. (1973), *Collected Works Vol. 33*. Moscow: Progress Publishers.
Lenin, V.I. (1974), *Collected Works Vol. 22*. Moscow: Progress Publishers.
Lenin, V.I. (1977a), *Collected Works Vol. 5*. Moscow: Progress Publishers.
Lenin, V.I. (1977b), *Collected Works Vol. 31*. Moscow: Progress Publishers.
Lukács, Georg (2009), *Lenin: A Study on the Unity of His Thought*. London: Verso.
Luxemburg, Rosa (1915), "Rebuilding the International," *Marxist Internet Archive*. Accessed on 29.06.2020, at https://www.marxists.org/archive/luxemburg/1915/xx/rebuild-int.htm.
Prashad, Vijay (2020), *Lenin 150*. New Delhi: LeftWord.
Riddell, John, Prashad, Vijay and Nazeef Mollah (eds.) (2019), *Liberate the Colonies. Communism and Colonial Freedom, 1917-1924*. New Delhi: LeftWord Books.

---

8 Lenin 1977b: 166.

I Believe in Yesterday:
A Photographer's Note on Remembering an Alternative Future

Johann Salazar

"Socialism for the rich and capitalism for the poor" declared a post that popped up on my computer screen and it seemed somehow appropriate as I sat down to write this note on our project to photograph the statues of Lenin in Kyrgyzstan. The quote was invoked, this time, in criticism of the proposed bailout scheme to infuse funds into the US economy to mitigate the effects of the current Coronavirus pandemic, which has brought most of the world to a standstill and threatens to cripple economies. The pandemic has brought into focus the need for support systems that ensure healthcare, food, and shelter for all, in the process adding a new layer of relevance to our project that intended to mark the 150th birth anniversary of Lenin, the founding father of the Soviet Union – a place where there was a serious attempt at, and arguably some success in, providing for the basic needs of everyone.

Unfortunately, the pandemic also prevented our much-anticipated return to Kyrgyzstan in early 2020 and so I must introduce the caveat that I make the following comments and observations based on what was initially intended to be purely a scoping visit of approximately 10 days that took place in the autumn of 2019. In fact, it was my first time in Kyrgyzstan and my first visit to any place that was formerly part of the Soviet Union. Given the brevity of our stay, we spent most of our time looking for 'Lenins' in the capital city Bishkek with a few excursions to nearby towns, in a car borrowed from our friends Dastan and Darika, flanked by the beautiful snow-capped Ala-Too mountains, listening to Belle and Sebastian,

> ...Ooh! Get me away from here I'm dying
> Play me a song to set me free
> Nobody writes them like they used to
> So it may as well be me...

I was born in Bombay, India, only a few years before the end of the Soviet Union and as such have no living memory of it. Although I do remember there being some mention of it in school, unsurprisingly considering that India and the USSR were close allies,[1] most of what I heard came from US-American TV, films, and video games, and in many of these the USSR and more specifically the KGB were often the "bad guys." And so, when Hjalmar invited me to collaborate on this project, I was immediately excited and also a bit nervous given that I am far from an expert on Lenin or

---
1 For an overview of India-USSR relations, see Mastny 2010 and Duncan 1989.

Leninism and knew close to nothing about Kyrgyzstan. I therefore thought it best to approach the project through the one thing that I was most familiar with about the Soviet Union: cameras and lenses. The first camera I ever bought myself was a used Japanese Pentax Spotmatic which came fitted with a Soviet made Helios 44m-4 lens. I loved that lens and continued to use it long after I retired the camera. It was important to me because it allowed me access to photography at a time when it would otherwise have been impossible on my shoestring budget. Thus, in my mind, the USSR, from an early age, has been associated with cameras that are affordable and good.

So when I was thinking about how I would like to shoot our project in Kyrgyzstan, I knew that I had to use old Soviet made cameras for at least some of it. I also hoped it would allow me to connect with the project on a personal level, both emotionally and materially. The only Soviet camera I owned at the time was my futuristic looking Zorki[2] 10, a model that was awarded the gold medal at the 1965 Leipzig World Fair.[3] Its Roman script, 'made in USSR' markings, and film speed indicators in DIN numbers instead of the Soviet standard GOST numbers, all reveal that it was produced for export – a sign that despite the 'iron curtain' the West did engage with the Soviet Union. Later I acquired an FED[4] 5 – a series that was the Soviet answer to the Leica – from old stock that shipped from Poland and then, upon arrival in Kyrgyzstan, I bought a simple and sturdy Zenit M3 SLR camera at a flea market in Bishkek. Generally, the Zenit SLRs are very popular as "these Russian cameras have introduced thousands of newcomers to SLR photography [...] [B]ecause you have to do everything manually yourself before taking a picture, the camera offers a lesson in using aperture, shutter speed and such like."[5] In keeping with the conditions of simplicity and affordability, I loaded them with consumer-grade Fujifilm C200 film and a few trial rolls of Svema color 135, rumoured to be repackaged Soviet era film. These criteria were important to me because they represent a democratising of photography that predates the age of the camera phone. The affordability of these cameras, even in their own time, allowed more people the opportunity to pursue photography not only in the USSR but also in the West, for example in Britain where in 1980 it was found that "in a very high proportion (92 per cent) of cases, a Zenith was the first SLR camera to be owned by its purchasers."[6] This was no accident; on the contrary, photography was seen as an important part of the Soviet project of emancipation. For Anatoly Lunacharsky, the Commissar of Enlightenment of the recently formed USSR, photographic literacy was

---

2 Meaning sharp-sighted in Russian.
3 http://www.sovietcams.com/index.php?734747805.
4 The FED cameras take their name from "Iron" Felix Edmundovich Dzerzhinsky and were built in a factory that was formerly a children's commune. Although joining the Bolsheviks belatedly, Dzerzhinsky became one of Lenin's right-hand men, and as such headed the Soviet secret police tasked with the ruthless repression of political enemies.
5 Wilmott cited in Hill and McKay 1988: 120.
6 Hill and McKay 1988: 119.

essential to realising the vision of the new nation. He is believed to have said, in 1926, "Just as every forward-looking comrade must have a watch, so must he be able to handle a camera. This will surely happen with time. Just as the USSR achieved universal literacy in general, so too will it have photographic literacy in particular."[7]

Curiously, the experimental energy that animated the early Soviet photographers[8] was recently rediscovered when a group of Viennese students stumbled across a Soviet LOMO LC-A, sparking off a movement of spontaneous and unrestrained photography that has come to be known as Lomography. The LOMO brand that gives the camera its name is derived from the Leningrad Optical Mechanical Association (Ленинградское Оптико-Механическое Объединение) that was awarded the prestigious Order of Lenin on numerous occasions. The newly founded Lomographic Society International made subtle nods to the Soviet project with the publication of the "revolutionary 'Lomography Manifesto'"[9] that encouraged photography that was "quick, direct, and shameless."[10] Although LOMO clearly flirts with capitalism – it is, after all, in the business of producing and selling camera equipment and photographic film – it is also the reason why there exists today an enormous number of self-styled 'revolutionary photographers' whose craft and tools could be said to surreptitiously carry forward the name of Lenin.

In Kyrgyzstan, on the other hand, Lenin is not hidden. In fact, he still stands tall in places of prominence across the landscape, which is, of course, what brought us to the country to begin with. When Hjalmar first told me that Kyrgyzstan had dozens of Lenin statues left I, ever the sceptic, immediately did a quick search online to establish if this was in fact true. To my surprise I found a Wikipedia page that listed all the Lenin statues around the world, organised by country and the respective cities that hosted them. Except for Kyrgyzstan. Instead of a list there was just one line: "Nearly every city and village in the country has a Lenin statue, usually located in the central square."[11]

Given the apparent ubiquity of Lenin in Kyrgyzstan, it did not take us long to find the very first statue of him, towering three storeys above us, and indeed located in the vicinity of Bishkek's central square. In the days that followed we found an additional ten statues of varying sizes, a large mosaic, and many other monuments, streets, and countless pieces of paraphernalia that carried Lenin's likeness or name. Walking the streets of Bishkek in search of Lenin it was another Lennon, however, whose words were echoing in my head. In one of his last interviews, John Lennon, whose work I am far more familiar with than that of Vladimir Lenin, said, "As

---

7 See Reischl 2018.
8 See Lodder 2014.
9 https://www.lomography.com/about/history.
10 See Lomographic Society 1992.
11 https://en.wikipedia.org/wiki/List_of_statues_of_Vladimir_Lenin.

far as overthrowing something in the name of Marxism or Christianity, I want to know what you're going to do *after* you've knocked it all down. I mean, can't we use *some* of it? What's the point of bombing Wall Street? If you want to change the system, change the system. It's no good shooting people."[12] The reason these words came to mind is because what is striking about Bishkek is that many of the old Soviet-era buildings remain standing, some still performing the role originally assigned to them, and unlike in other former Soviet republics that underwent systematic decommunisation, still bearing their Soviet symbology. There were sickles and hammers aplenty though they now stood under a Kyrgyz flag. Exactly why this decommunisation did not take place, I was unable to find out. Perhaps, the Kyrgyz are not satisfied simply with iconoclasm for its own sake. Perhaps they had more immediate concerns to worry about. Or perhaps they even appreciated them.

In any case, the Kyrgyz landscape in and around Bishkek is sprinkled with reminders of Soviet triumphs in science, sports, industry and infrastructure: from stylishly designed bus-stops dotting deserted highways, to monuments to success in the space race. Among the ones that left a strong impression on me were the memorials to those who lost their lives in the Second World War, which in the post-Soviet space is referred to as the Great Patriotic War, a reminder of the enormous price paid by the USSR, which incurred 95 per cent of the military casualties among the Allied powers, and also of the tremendous contribution of the Red Army, which inflicted on the Nazis three-quarters of their wartime losses.[13] The fact that many of these monuments included statues of people with Asian features was something that caught my attention, especially since I am aware of the erasure of the contribution of people of colour to the war effort, for instance, the contribution of Indian soldiers who fought under the British flag in both WWI and WWII.[14]

This brings me to the issue of race. Among the buildings that continue to serve their old purpose are the housing complexes, the typical Soviet Khrushchvovky, many of which sport a work of art of some kind. On the side of one such building was a mural of three children walking hand in hand, each of a different ethnicity – One Asian, One Russian and One Black. It was this "internationalist" mural that came to mind a few months later when I was listening to a segment of a podcast titled 'Black in the USSR'[15] in which Yelena Khanga discusses her experience of growing up as a black woman in the Soviet Union. What was interesting was the care she took to emphasise that, although she did have some difficult encounters due to the colour of her skin, these were the result of ignorance and not racism. To hear

---

12 Cited in Sheff 2000.
13 See Tharoor 2016.
14 For a brief overview, see Tharoor 2016 and Gupta 2017 for WWI and WWII respectively.
15 See Berry 2020.

her speak made me, also a person of colour, feel like there was something drastically different about her experience that possibly traced its heritage to the Soviet commitment to anti-colonialism and universal emancipation.

Perhaps it is experiences like these that explain the existence of a certain nostalgia for the USSR in post-Soviet Kyrgyzstan. As a matter of fact, a survey conducted in 2013 showed that 61% of those interviewed believed that the breakup of the Soviet Union did harm to their country. Despite official decommunisation, this appears to be the case in many of the former Soviet republics. Significantly, this opinion seems to be more widespread among the older population – those who have a lived experience of the USSR.[16] This partially explains the presence of flea markets and antiques shops with Soviet memorabilia aplenty that, in a place infrequently visited by outsiders, can rely only on the domestic market for their wares; the other, unfortunate, side of this being that many people in Kyrgyzstan today are forced by poverty to sell whatever little they have, a lot of which happens to be old Soviet stuff. By way of example, Valentina and Alexander, an ethnic Russian couple and the owners of one of the antiques shops that we visited, concluded after a long discussion that things were better now, although this was clearly a conclusion that Alexander, a passionate collector of coins of different countries and eras, had difficulty committing to. He stood pensive and quiet in his shop filled with souvenirs from their Soviet past until his wife woke him out of his reverie, gently reminding him to "smile Alexander." On the other hand, a local taxi driver, Nurkan, who helped us locate another Lenin statue in Bishkek, said that for him "Lenin is like God." It is this diversity of opinion within Kyrgyzstan about the USSR that, for me, makes the question of the Kyrgyz' relationship with their Lenin monuments a particularly interesting one. What is the use of a monument that evidently was the product of a personality cult designed to propagate and sustain the Soviet project, now that the Soviet Union has ended? What dreams do these statues keep alive? What lessons do they teach? We hope to explore some of these questions when we return to Kyrgyzstan in the near future, but for now they remain unanswered.

Speaking of Soviet nostalgia, during our time there I also took several photos of Hjalmar alongside Lenin because I was intrigued by his fascination with Lenin and the USSR, a fascination that was and continues to be shared by many people outside the post-Soviet space. For instance, I know that Jawaharlal Nehru, the first Prime Minister of India, was very impressed by the early successes of the USSR. Consequently, much of India's own technological progress and the country's '5-year plans' were inspired by Soviet Union policies. Even B.R. Ambedkar, the chief architect of India's constitution, did not deny the achievements of the USSR despite being critical of the means used to achieve them. In an essay comparing (the) Buddha

---

16 See Mastracci 2017.

and Marx, he wrote, "It has been claimed that the Communist Dictatorship in Russia has wonderful achievements to its credit. There can be no denial of it. That is why I say that a Russian Dictatorship would be good for all backward countries. But this is no argument for permanent Dictatorship." Ambedkar also argued that the goals of communism were similar to those of Buddhism, but where Lenin sought to achieve them by force Buddha sought to do so "by persuasion, by moral teaching, by love."[17] He believed that Buddha had established a type of communism in the Buddhist Sangha. Similar claims have of course been made of the early Christian communities. For me, this congruence is important for two reasons: first, because it highlights the relevance of the shared goal of ending human suffering that detractors of Communism discard along with it; and second, because it informs my understanding of how this better world can be achieved without violence.

Today, we see traces of two very different visions of a 'better world' competing for space in Bishkek. This is evident in the different styles of architecture, ways of dressing, and even in the graffiti, some of it in English, including one that read 'West is the best' (although what 'west' its authors were talking about specifically is unclear). Or perhaps this is precisely why photography is such an appropriate medium for this project, because even though it makes a claim to the truth, what it actually offers is merely a shard of truth shrouded in perspective. During my time in Kyrgyzstan, it soon became clear to me that I was not photographing a person but rather the likeness of a person on which many ideas were and continue to be projected, both from within the (former) Soviet Union and also from without. Therefore, to further highlight the many distortions of the man and the tenuousness of our knowledge of the past, we also ventured to intentionally distort some of the images of Lenin in the Kyrgyz public space, some of which we have included in this book.

This still leaves us with the question of how we must remember Lenin on the 150th anniversary of his birth. One possible response occurred to me as a result of a visit to a town called Kant, where we were led to a Lenin statue that was locked inside the compound of a factory by two young women named Nika and Yulia, both of whom were palpably excited to meet and talk with two strange-looking foreigners strolling around in their hometown. Walking there, we asked them what they knew about Lenin and without skipping a beat, Nika, the more talkative of the two, said, "Well, I know he is a human being."[18] So, there we are. After all this time and all the effort put in by friends and foes alike to make him either superhuman or supervillain, it's about time we finally treat Lenin simply as a man. If we

---

17 Speech delivered at the closing session of the Fourth Conference of the World Fellowship of Buddhists in the State Gallery Hall in Kathmandu (Nepal), on 20th November 1956.
18 Hjalmar points out that the word she used, "tshelavek," means both human being and man in the general, patriarchal sense of the word. It does not literally refer to a biological man, which is "mushchina."

can do that, we can both admit his flaws and, at the same time, give credence to the value of the better world he envisioned.

A vision, in fact, that is starting to appear, at least to some people across the globe, more attractive than the world we are living in today. The goal of ending human misery, regardless of whether we choose to arrive at it through Buddhism or Christianity or Communism, is one that is eclipsed by the profit motive in our present capitalist system. Here I return to the words of Ambedkar who as a member and leader of the Dalit community, regarded as untouchables in India, spent a lifetime fighting for their equality: "Society has been aiming to lay a new foundation [that] was summarised by the French Revolution in three words, Fraternity, Liberty and Equality. The French Revolution was welcomed because of this slogan. It failed to produce equality. We welcome the Russian Revolution because it aims to produce equality. But it cannot be too much emphasised that in producing equality society cannot afford to sacrifice fraternity or liberty. Equality will be of no value without fraternity or liberty." In short, we cannot ignore the atrocities that were committed in the USSR, but in the same breath we cannot use them to undermine its successes. For me, it is enough to blame the former on its leaders and credit the latter to its people. It is what I imagine Lenin would have wanted.

References

Ambedkar, B. R. (2014), *Dr. Babasaheb Ambedkar Writings and Speeches Vol. 3*. New Delhi: Dr. Ambedkar Foundation.

Berry, Emanuele (2020), "Black in the USSR," *This American Life*, 694. Accessed on 29.06.2020, at https://www.thisamericanlife.org/694/get-back-to-where-you-once-belonged/act-one-13.

Duncan, Peter J.S. (1989), *The Soviet Union and India*. London: Royal Institute of International Affairs.

Fricke, Oscar (1979), "The Dzerzhinsky Commune: Birth of the Soviet 35mm Camera Industry," *History of Photography*, 3(2), 135-155.

Gupta, Diya (2017), "Why remembrance of Indian soldiers who fought for the British in World War II is so political," *The Conversation*. Accessed on 29.06.2020, at https://theconversation.com/why-remembrance-of-indian-soldiers-who-fought-for-the-british-in-world-war-ii-is-so-political-86885.

Hill, Malcolm R., and Richard McKay (1988), *Soviet Product Quality*. London: Palgrave Macmillan.

Lodder, Christina (2014), "Revolutionary Photography," *Museum of Modern Art Internet Publication*. Accessed on 29.06.2020, at https://www.moma.org/interactives/objectphoto/assets/essays/Lodder.pdf.

Lomographic Society (1992), Lomography [The Lomography Manifesto]," *Wiener Zeitung*. Accessed on 29.06.2020, at http://www.fotomanifeste.de/manifeste/1992-lomographischegesellschaft-thelomographymanifesto.

Mastny, Vojtech (2010), "The Soviet Union's Partnership with India," *Journal of Cold War Studies,* 12, 50-90.

Mastracci, Davide (2017), "Former Soviet Citizens Support the USSR," *Medium.com.* Accessed on 29.06.2020, at https://medium.com/@DavideMastracci/former-soviet-citizens-support-the-ussr-afdcb10c2225.

Reischl, Katherine M. H. (2018), "In the Soviet School of Photography: Lessons in Photographic Literacy," *Modernism/modernity.* Accessed on 29.06.2020, at https://modernismmodernity.org/articles/soviet-school-photography.

Sheff, David (2000), *All We Are Saying: The Last Major Interview with John Lennon and Yoko Ono.* New York: St. Martin's Griffin.

Tharoor, Ishaan (2016), "How the Soviet Union helped save the world from Hitler during World War II," *Independent.* Accessed on 29.06.2020, at https://www.independent.co.uk/news/world/the-soviet-union-helped-save-the-world-from-hitler-a7020926.html.

Tharoor, Shashi (2015), "Why the Indian soldiers of WW1 were forgotten," *BBC Magazine.* Accessed on 29.06.2020, at https://www.bbc.com/news/magazine-33317368.

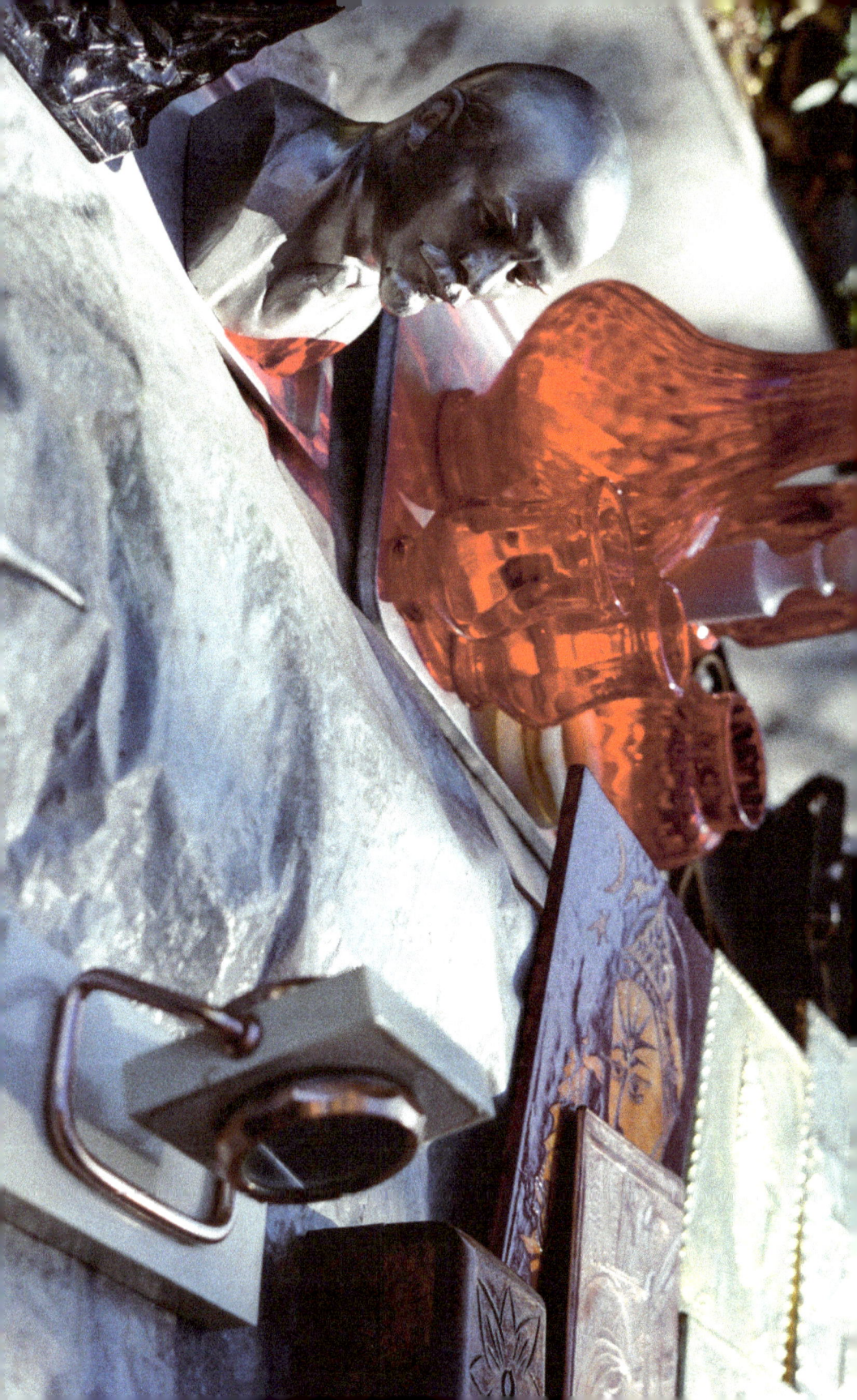

To Those Born After

Bertolt Brecht

I.

Truly, I live in dark times!

The innocent word is foolish. A brow unfurrowed
Bespeaks indifference. S/he who laughs
Has not yet heard
The terrible news.

What times are these, when
A talk about trees is almost a crime
As it silently shrouds so many evils!
S/he who walks calmly across the road
Can surely no longer be reached by friends
Who are in need?

True: I still earn my keep.
But believe me, this is pure chance. Nothing
I do gives me the right to a full belly.
Fortune has spared me. (When my luck runs out
I will be lost.)

They tell me: eat and drink! Be happy for what you have!
But how can I eat and drink, when
I wrest what I eat from the hungry and
Owe my glass of water to one who thirsts?
And still I eat and I drink.

Would that I were wise.
The old books tell us that to be wise is to
Forgo the struggles of the world and
Live out this brief time without fear
To get by without violence
To repay evil with good.
The wise do not satisfy their desires but forget them.
All of this I cannot do:
Truly, I live in dark times!

II.

Into the cities I came in the time of chaos
As hunger reigned.
Among the people I came in the time of uprising
And I rose with them in outrage.
So passed the time
Given to me on earth.

Eating my meals between battles
I slept among murderers
Loved indifferently
And had no care for nature.
So passed the time
Given to me on earth.

The streets in my time led to the swamp
A spoken word might betray me to the slaughterers
I was capable of little. But the rulers
Would feel safer without me, that much I hoped.
So passed the time
Given to me on earth.

My strength waned. Our destination
Far off in the distance
Was clearly visible, yet for me
Could hardly be reached.
So passed the time
Given to me on earth.

III.

You, who will rise from the flood
In which we have foundered
Do not forget
When you speak of our weaknesses
The dark time
You have been spared.
Did we not endure, changing country more often than our shoes
The wars of the classes, despairing
That there was only injustice and no outrage?

Yet we know:
Even the hatred of baseness
Distorts the features.
Even anger at injustice
Hoarsens the voice. Oh we,
Who wished to lay the ground for kindness
Could not ourselves be kind.

But you, when the time comes at last
That wo/man is helper to wo/man
Think of us
With forbearance.

Translated from the original German by Patrick Anderson

During the first months of his regeneration, he used to spend almost all his time reading; but this lasted only a little more than six months. When he saw that he had acquired a systematic style of thought in the spirit whose principles he found to be correct, he said to himself:
'Reading is now a secondary matter:
from this time forth I am ready for life.'

What is to be done? – Nikolai Chernyshevsky

The Central Committee

Kevin B. Anderson is a Professor of Sociology at University of California, Santa Barbara. He is the author of *Lenin, Hegel, and Western Marxism: A Critical Study* (University of Illinois Press, 1995), *Foucault and the Iranian Revolution: Gender and the Seductions of Islamism* (with Janet Afary, University of Chicago Press, 2005), and *Marx at the Margins: On Nationalism, Ethnicity and Non-Western Societies* (University of Chicago Press, 2010/2016), and is the co-editor of the *Rosa Luxemburg Reader* (with Peter Hudis, 2004), *Karl Marx* (with Bertell Ollman, 2012), and the *Dunayevskaya-Marcuse-Fromm Correspondence* (2012, with Russell Rockwell). Currently, he is working on a study of Marx's late writings on non-Western and precapitalist societies and gender. He teaches graduate seminars in classical social theory, contemporary social theory, and Marx and Marxism.

Alain Badiou was born in 1937 in Rabat, Morrocco. He studied at the Ecole Normale Supérieure (ENS), graduating with a Masters in Philosophy. He was Professor of Philosophy at the University of Paris VIII and then at ENS (Ulm). He is the author of three novels and eight plays, as well as a large number of political, aesthetic (including *Five Lessons on Wagner*) and philosophical works. In all, he has published over one hundred titles, many of which have been translated into a variety of other languages. Three of his books have enjoyed considerable success: *Ethics* (1993), *In Praise of Love* (2003), and *The Meaning of Sarkozy* (2007). Three works constitute, in his own eyes, his major philosophical contribution: *Being and Event* (1988), *Logics of Worlds* (2006), and *The Immanence of Truths* (2018).

Roland Boer is the first foreign national to be appointed to an ongoing position in a School of Marxism Studies in China. He now works at the School of Marxism Studies at Dalian University of Technology, in China's Northeast. In the past, his publications have focused on developments in European and Russian Marxism. At present, he is engaged in Chinese-language research on Socialism with Chinese Characteristics and the project of the Reform and Opening-Up.

Atilio Alberto Boron, born in 1943 in Buenos Aires, is an Argentine political scientist and sociologist. He holds a PhD in Political Science from Harvard University and is currently the director of the Centro de Complementación Curricular in the Faculty of Humanities and Arts at the National University of Avellaneda, Argentina. He is Doctor Honoris Causa of several universities in Argentina and Venezuela. In 2004 and 2009, he was awarded the Casa de las Américas Ensayo Ezequiel Martínez Estrada Prize and the International José Martí Prize, respectively. In the English language, some of his publications include *Empire and Imperialism: A Critical Reading of Michael Hardt and Antonio Negri* (2005) and *Twenty-First-Century Socialism: Is There Life After Neo-Liberalism?* (2014).

In Spanish, he recently published *América Latina en la geopolítica del imperialismo (2012)* and *El hechicero de la tribu. Mario Vargas Llosa y el liberalismo en América Latina* (2019).

Michael Brie, born in 1954 in Schwerin, Germany, is a philosopher and political scientist. He is senior fellow at the Institute for Critical Social Analysis of the Rosa Luxemburg Foundation in Berlin and president of the foundation's Scientific Advisory board. His areas of research interest include the history and theory of socialism and state socialism, the problems associated with the socio-ecological transformation of modern societies in the age of the organic crisis of financial-market capitalism, and the perspectives of a solidarity society. In 2019 he published *Rediscovering Lenin. Dialectics of Revolution and Metaphysics of Domination* (Palgrave Macmillan).

Charles Buxton has been living in Bishkek since 2002, and until 2018 was regional representative of INTRAC (International NGO Training & Research Centre) working with civil society across the five ex-soviet countries of Central Asia. Earlier, he worked for VSO (Voluntary Service Overseas) in a similar position covering East Europe and the former Soviet Union. Prior to that, he was active for 20 years in community development in East London. With a degree in Russian, Charlie has published three books aimed at bringing together practical lessons from international development and a Left view of the Soviet experience: *The Struggle for Civil Society in Central Asia: Crisis and Transformation* (Kumarian, 2011); *Russia and Development: Capitalism, Civil Society and the State* (Zed, 2014); and *Ragged Trousered NGOs: development work under neoliberalism* (Routledge, 2019). He is now the director of a public foundation, Books for Development, set up in 2019 in Bishkek.

Elvira Concheiro Bórquez holds a PhD in Sociology. Since 1977 she has been affiliated with the National Autonomous University of Mexico, where she is a professor in the Faculty of Political and Social Sciences and the postgraduate program of Latin American Studies, and lead researcher at the Centre for Interdisciplinary Research of Science and Humanities. On two occasions, she was invited to be associate researcher at universities in France (Paris X-Nanterre and Paris I-Sorbonne). Her most recent publications include *Reencuentro con Marx; El comunismo: otras miradas desde América Latina y Congresos Comunistas. México 1919-1981; Antología del Pensamiento Crítico Mexicano Contemporáneo (2014)*, and the edited volume *Marx revisitado: posiciones encontradas*. In addition, she has published dozens of book chapters, articles and essays on a variety of issues concerning political sociology as well as Marxist and Left critical theory.

Jodi Dean teaches political theory in Upstate New York, USA. Her most recent books are *The Communist Horizon, Crowds and Party*, and *Comrade: An Essay On Political Belonging*, all published by Verso.

The Central Committee

Owen Hatherley was born in 1981 in Southampton, England. He writes regularly on architecture, culture and politics for *Architectural Review, Dezeen,* the *Guardian,* and the *London Review of Books.* He is the author of ten books: *Militant Modernism* (Zero, 2009), *A Guide to the New Ruins of Great Britain* (Verso, 2010), *Uncommon – An Essay on Pulp* (Zero, 2011), *Across the Plaza* (Strelka, 2012), *A New Kind of Bleak* (Verso 2012), *Landscapes of Communism* (Penguin 2015), *The Ministry of Nostalgia* (Verso, 2016), *The Chaplin Machine* (Pluto Press, 2016), *Trans-Europe Express* (Penguin, 2018) and *The Adventures of Owen Hatherley in the Post-Soviet Space* (Repeater, 2018). He received a PhD from Birkbeck College in 2011 for a thesis on *The Political Aesthetics of Americanism.* He has also edited and introduced an updated edition of Ian Nairn's *Nairn's Towns* (Notting Hill Editions, 2013), written texts for the exhibition *Brutalust: Celebrating Post-War Southampton,* at the K6 Gallery, and contributed a long essay and picture research to Christopher Herwig's *Soviet Metro Stations* (Fuel, 2019). Between 2006 and 2010 he wrote the blog 'Sit Down Man, You're a Bloody Tragedy.' He is the culture editor of *Tribune.*

Matthew T. Huber is Associate Professor of Geography at Syracuse University. His work focuses on the relationships between energy, capitalism, and the politics of climate change. His first book *Lifeblood: Oil, Freedom and the Forces of Capital* (University of Minnesota Press, 2013) examined oil's role in powering a specific form of suburban privatism and neoliberal populism in the United States. He is currently working on a book for Verso on the intersection of class and climate politics. He is a regular contributor to *Jacobin Magazine* and has written for other popular outlets such as *The Trouble, The American Prospect,* and *Toxic News.*

Wang Hui is Director of the Tsinghua Institute for Advanced Study in Humanities and Social Sciences. He teaches at Tsinghua University, Beijing as Distinguished Professor of Literature and History, has published extensively on Chinese intellectual history and literature, and is actively engaged in debates on Chinese historical and contemporary issues. His books have been translated into various languages; in English his works include *China's Twentieth Century* (2015), *China From Empire to Nation-State* (2014), *The Politics of Imagining Asia* (2010), *The End of Revolution* (2009) and *China's New Order* (2003). His four-volume work *The Rise of Modern Chinese Thought* (2004, in Chinese) is regarded as one of the most important contributions to modern Chinese scholarship over the past two decades. Wang Hui is the recipient of numerous awards such as the 2013 Luca Pacioli Prize, which he shared with Jürgen Habermas, and the 2018 Anneliese Maier Research Award.

Vashna Jagarnath has a PhD in History. She is a former Deputy Dean at Rhodes University and currently works in the office of the General Secretary of the National Union of Metal Workers of South Africa (NUMSA).

She is also the Deputy General Secretary of the Socialist Revolutionary Workers Party. In a private capacity, Vashna is the director of Pan Africa Today and Friends of the Workers as well as Senior Research Associate at the Centre for Social Change. She publishes regularly in the South African public sphere.

Benjamin Kindler is a PhD candidate in modern Chinese literature at Columbia University, and is currently completing a dissertation under the title "Writing to the Rhythm of Labour: The Politics of Cultural Labour in Revolutionary China, 1942-1976." His academic work is concerned with the problem of how to envisage a new cultural subject and a new practice of writing in the course of the Chinese Revolution, especially in the context of struggles surrounding the contents of communist labour and the task of overcoming the division between mental and manual labour. He otherwise enjoys translation and is deeply committed to bringing contemporary intellectual discussions in mainland China to an international audience.

Aisuluu Kokoyeva is a journalist. She graduated from the Faculty of Journalism at the Kyrgyz State National University in Bishkek and has worked for various state and non-government newspapers and websites. A member of the Union of Writers and Central Asia PEN-club, she writes poems and prose, and translates from Russian into Kyrgyz. In 2014, Aisuluu published the book "A woman's diary," and in 2016, a semi-fictional, semi-documentary book about a village teacher in the Toktogul (mountain) region of Kyrgyzstan. Her literary works and articles have been featured in the media and read aloud on radio. In 2016 she was awarded 2nd place in a Radio Azattyk/Liberty Blog competition celebrating 25 years of Kyrgyzstan's independence.

Tora Lane holds a PhD in Russian Literature, is associate professor in comparative literature and head of research at CBEES, Södertörn University. She specialises in Russian modernism, and Soviet and post-Soviet literature. She has published several articles on the poetry of Tsvetaeva, the prose of Andrei Platonov, and on aesthetic issues related to Soviet literature. Her publications include *Rendering the Sublime: A Reading of the Fairy Tale Poem "The Swain" by Marina Cvetaeva* (2009, dissertation), *Disorientations: Philosophy, Literature, and the Lost Grounds of Modernity* (ed. with Marcia Sá Cavalcante Schuback) and *Andrei Platonov. The Forgotten Dream of the Revolution* (2018).

Ursina Lardi, born in 1970 in Samedan, Switzerland, is a theatre, film and television actress. She studied acting at the "Ernst Busch" theatre school in Berlin. She has worked in Germany's leading theatres, including the Schauspiel Frankfurt, the Deutsches Schauspielhaus Hamburg, the Berliner Ensemble and the Staatstheater Stuttgart. Since 2012 Lardi has been a regular ensemble member at the Schaubühne Berlin. She has played the principal role in various Schaubühne productions, such as *Compassion: The History of the Machine Gun* by Milo Rau, a performance about the limits of our compassion and European humanism; *Lenin*, also by Milo Rau; *Oedipus the Tyrant* by Romeo Castellucci; and *The Marriage of Maria Braun* by Thomas Ostermeier. In 2017, she received the Hans Reinhart Ring, the highest award in Swiss theatre. For her role in *Traumland*, Lardi was voted Best Actress at the Swiss Film Awards in 2014. She also performed in Michael Haneke's *The White Ribbon*, which received both a Golden Globe and a Golden Palm. In the 2020-2021 season, Milo Rau and Ursina Lardi join forces again for *Everywoman*, in which Lardi plays a woman who is confronted with her own mortality and realises that she has to change her life.

Georgy Mamedov, born in 1984, is a communist and LGBT activist, curator and educator based in Bishkek, Kyrgyzstan. He teaches history and theory of modern and contemporary art at the American University of Central Asia in Bishkek and chairs the board of the leading Central Asian LGBT organisation "Labrys Kyrgyzstan." His most recent artistic projects include collaboration with the Dutch Werker Collective on the project "A Gestural History of the Young Worker" for the Fifth Industrial Biennial of Contemporary Art in Yekaterinburg, Russia (2019) and the lecture-performance "Delirious Blues: A Philosophy Letter from the Low Life" presented at the Parliament of Bodies edition at the Bergen Assembly in 2019. Georgy has co-authored and co-edited a number of publications including a pioneer Russian-language collection of feminist and queer sci-fi "Utterly Other" (Bishkek 2018), the book *Queer Communism is Ethics* (Moscow 2016), and the almanac *Concepts of the Soviet in Central Asia* (Bishkek 2016). In 2015, Mamedov was awarded the French Order of Arts and Letters.

Michael Neocosmos is Emeritus Professor in Humanities at Rhodes University in South Africa and Distinguished Visiting Scholar at the University of Connecticut Humanities Institute in the United States. He is the author of many articles and several books including *From Foreign Natives to Native Foreigners: Explaining Xenophobia in South Africa* (Dakar: Codesria, 2010) and *Thinking Freedom in Africa: Toward a Theory of Emancipatory Politics* (Wits University Press, December 2016). This last book was awarded the Frantz Fanon Prize for outstanding work by the Caribbean Philosophical Association in 2017. He is currently working on a book provisionally titled *The Dialectics of Emancipation in Africa* to be published by Daraja Press as well as on *An Anthology of African Political Thought from Ancient Egypt to the Present* to be published by Codesria.

Vijay Prashad is the Director of Tricontinental: Institute for Social Research, and Chief Editor, LeftWord Books (Delhi). He is the editor of *Lenin: Selected Writings*, New Delhi: LeftWord Books, 2018.

Matthieu Renault is an Associate Professor in philosophy at the University Paris 8 Vincennes-Saint-Denis, and a member of the Laboratory of Studies and Research on Contemporary Logics of Philosophy (LLCP). His research focuses on the relations between philosophy and non-European societies, the (post)imperial history of knowledge formations and their re-appropriation from minority standpoints. He authored: *Frantz Fanon. De l'anticolonialisme à la critique postcoloniale* (Éditions Amsterdam, 2011), *L'Amérique de John Locke. L'expansion coloniale de la philosophie européenne* (Éditions Amsterdam, 2014), *C.L.R. James. La vie révolutionnaire d'un "Platon noir"* (La Découverte, 2016), and *L'empire de la révolution. Lénine et les musulmans de Russie* (Syllepse, 2017).

Marcos Del Roio, PhD in Political Science at FFLCH-USP, is Professor of Political Science at the Faculty of Philosophy and Sciences at UNESP (campus of Marília), where he focuses primarily on the areas of Political Theory of Socialism and Worker Policy. He is the editor of the journal *Novos Rumos*, and director of the Astrojildo Pereira Institute. He has published books, book chapters, and articles in Brazil and abroad. In 2015, he published *The Prisms of Gramsci: The Political Formula of the United Front* (Brill).

Thomas Rudhof-Seibert, an activist since the early 1970s, is a philosopher and author. He is a human rights advisor and South Asia Coordinator for the Frankfurt-based political relief organisation *medico international*, a board speaker of the *Institut Solidarische Moderne* (ISM), a member of the scientific board of the Rosa Luxemburg Foundation, and a militant of the *Interventionistische Linke* (IL). In his writings, Seibert configures a political philosophy of the May 68-revolution based on non-dogmatic Marxism, existentialism and post-structuralism, thereby contributing to an 'ecology of existence'. Recent book publications: *Zur Ökologie der Existenz* (Hamburg 2017), *Kritik und Aktualität der Revolution* (Vienna/Berlin 2017, with Martin Birkner). His work is accessible in German at: www.thomas-seibert.de.

Maurico Sandoval Cordero, born in San José, Costa Rica, loves cinema and is a leftist militant. He works as a researcher and teacher at the Facultad Latinoamericana de Ciencias Sociales, Sede Académica Costa Rica (FLACSO Costa Rica). He is dedicated to sociopolitical analysis, specifically to issues related with violence and political organisation in Latin America. He is a specialist in areas such as political theory, epistemology and the structuring and history of knowledge in Latin America, and is part of the Working Group "Herencias y perspectivas del marxismo" of the *Consejo Latinoamericano de Ciencias Sociales* (CLACSO).

Molaodi Wa Sekake is a social activist. He holds a diploma in political and social development (Workers College, Durban), a Bachelor of Social Science in Sociology and Industrial Studies, and a Postgraduate degree from the University of KwaZulu-Natal. He is currently pursuing a Master's degree in Development Studies at the University of the Witwatersrand. His areas of study include political economy, labour relations and urban development. Wa Sekake has a keen interest in various art forms including music, literature, fine art and poetry. He is intrigued by artistic activism, where art is used as a tool to effect change. He has authored a number of essays in magazines. His two-volume work, *Socialism NoMuntu Omusha – Taking the Oath of Revolutions* is soon to be published.

Ronald Grigor Suny is William H. Sewell, Jr. Distinguished University Professor of History at the University of Michigan and Emeritus Professor of Political Science and History at the University of Chicago. He was the first holder of the Alex Manoogian Chair in Modern Armenian History at the University of Michigan, where he founded and directed the Armenian Studies Program. He is author of *The Baku Commune: Class and Nationality in the Russian Revolution*; *The Making of the Georgian Nation*; *Looking Toward Ararat: Armenia in Modern History*; *The Revenge of the Past: Nationalism, Revolution, and the Collapse of the Soviet Union*; *The Soviet Experiment*; *"They Can Live in the Desert But Nowhere Else": A History of the Armenian Genocide*; *Red Flag Unfurled: History, Historians, and the Russian Revolution*; and co-author with Valerie Kivelson of *Russia's Empires*. He has finished a biography of the young Stalin – *Stalin: Passage to Revolution* – for Princeton University Press and a series of historiographical essays on Stalinism and Soviet history – *Red Flag Wounded: Stalinism and the Soviet Experiment* – for Verso Books. He is currently working on a book on the recent upsurge of exclusivist nationalisms and authoritarian populisms: *Forging the Nation: The Making and Faking of Nationalisms.*

Darko Suvin is Professor Emeritus at McGill University in Montreal, Canada. He is best known for several works of criticism and literary history devoted to science fiction and Brecht, as well as his work in the field of post-Yugoslav studies. He is also a published poet, in multiple languages, and a Fellow of the Royal Society of Canada (Academy of Humanities and Social Sciences).

Mohira Suyarkulova is a queer communist and feminist activist scholar living and working in Bishkek, Kyrgyzstan. She holds a PhD in International Relations from St Andrews University. Mohira is an "undisciplined scholar," who has been hosted by departments of political science, social anthropology, sociology and, now, psychology. Her research interests lie in the intersection of politics, arts and activism. Most recently she led a participatory action study of the sexual lives of LGBTQ people in Bishkek with the aim of creating a queer sex education curriculum. Currently she is working on a Leftist manual on happiness alongside her colleagues and comrades Nina Bagdasarova and Georgy Mamedov.

Oxana Timofeeva is professor at the "Stasis" Center for Philosophy at the European University at St. Petersburg, leading researcher at Tyumen State University, member of the artistic collective "Chto Delat?" ("What is to be done?"), deputy editor of the journal "Stasis," and the author of the books *History of Animals* (London: Bloomsbury Academic, 2018; Maastricht: Jan van Eyck, 2012; trans. into Russian, Turkish, and Slovenian), *Introduction to the Erotic Philosophy of Georges Bataille* (Moscow: New Literary Observer, 2009), *How to Love a Homeland* (Cairo: Kayfa ta, 2020; trans. into Arabic), and other writings.

Slavoj Žižek, born in 1949 in Ljubljana, Slovenia. Bachelor of Arts (philosophy and sociology, 1971), Master of Arts (philosophy, 1975), and Doctor of Arts (philosophy, 1981) at the Department of Philosophy, Faculty of Arts, University of Ljubljana. Doctor of Arts (psychoanalysis, 1985) at the Université Paris-VIII. Doctor Causa Honoris at the University of Cordoba, Argentina (2005).

The Politburo

Hjalmar Jorge Joffre-Eichhorn is a German-Bolivian theatre maker, compulsive reader – printed books only – and reluctant writer. Since 2010, he has been feeling at ease in the post-Soviet space, particularly in Kyrgyzstan and Ukraine. After much ideological soul-searching, he now considers himself a decolonial communist. Hjalmar is still hopeful of one day being able to read Lenin in the original Русский язык. If and when he succeeds, he shall treat everyone around him to a shot of vodka or cognac. Or two. In the meantime, la lucha continúa.

Patrick Anderson loves words – their sound, look, meaning, origins – and has been a student of language throughout his life. He is unsurprisingly an aficionado of cryptic crosswords, and spends far too much time perusing etymological databases. Patrick has lived, worked and studied in five continents, and devotes most of his professional life to supporting people and communities to navigate the world with courage, dignity and passion.

Johann Salazar is an independent researcher and photographer with a background in Sociology and Anthropology. His current interests include visual storytelling, science communication, and issues of identity and belonging.

The Politburo thanks Lars Holthusen, Bolek, Marjan Jukic, Deepana and Sophia Anderson, Roderick Anderson, Rita Pais, Petra Eichhorn-Peters, Nico Peters, Jana Düring, Sonne Ince, Isabela Lemos, Christina Schütze, Tracy L. Hunter, Agnieszka Cwielag, Sabrina Keller, Patricia de Menezes Cardoso, Emiliana Marques, Daria Davitti (Rest in Power, Ugo!), Marco Túlio Andrade, Maria Mercone, Rubxn Solís, the Afghanistan Human Rights and Democracy Organization (AHRDO), Tiago Castela, Phil Butland, Firoze Manji, Kate McDonnell, Dianne Kirby, Marc Weinblatt, Claudia and Bodo Fischer, Kai Rüter, Jörn Rohde, Jorge Joffre-Arteaga, Ursula Zienow, Nancy Joffre, Reinaldo Imaña, Rufina Condori and Alcira Arteaga vd. de Joffre (Rest In Power) for the various forms of patient, essential support they extended during the composition of this book.

Lenin150 (Samizdat)

Index

1956 CPSU Congress 113
26th of July Movement 69
Abahlali baseMjondolo 54-55
Abstract Revolutionism 62
Adamczak, Bini 7, 42
Affirmative Action 92
African National Congress 215
Agriculture 106, 226, 229-230, 241, 243, 245, 255-256
Agribusiness 186
Algebra 66
Alienation 6, 84, 126-127, 131, 164, 286
Alliances 61, 63, 68-69
All-Russia Newspaper 128, 131
Althusser, Luis 114-115
Anarchism 80, 172-173, 179, 183-184
Antagonism 15, 35, 103, 105-107, 178, 275, 292
Anti-Japanese War 107
Antiphysis 184, 186-187
Apartheid 54-55, 216
Appassionata xix
Arendt, Hannah 167
Allende, Salvador 67, 73
Ambedkar, B.R. 307-309
Amin, Samir 218
Argentina 40, 67, 73, 89, 91, 319
Aristotle 192-195
Armand, Inessa 5, 279
Asthmatic Solidarity xiii
Austerity 171, 233
Autonomism 44
Axelrod, Pavel 69
Backwardness 72-73, 88-89, 106, 195, 197, 204, 229,
                                        240, 244, 257, 265, 268, 296, 308
Badiou, Alain 155, 176, 261, 291
Baku Congress 100
Balabanoff, Angelica 4
Ban on Factions 284
Barwicka-Tylek, Iwona 193
Bastani, Aaron 233
Bataille, George 159
Batista, Fulgencio 69
Batken 3
Battle of Ideas, The 76
Bay of Pigs Invasion 69
Beatles, The 192, 199
Bebel, August 92

Benjamin, Walter 4, 279
Bensaïd, Daniel .... xvii, 4, 41
Berardi, Bifo .... xii-xiii, 4
Bergson, Henri 192
Berkeley, George 219
Bernstein, Eduard 153, 263
Bettelheim, Charles 204, 206
Biko, Steve 214
Bishkek .... xix, 3, 140, 303-308, 320, 322-323, 325
Black Consciousness 214
Bloch, Ernst 33, 192
Bogdanov, Alexander 153, 193, 207, 219
Boggs, Grace Lee 98
Bokonbaev, Joomart .... xi, xvii, 140-141
Bolshaia Sovietskaia Entsiklopedia 107
Bolshevik (party) 16, 23, 26, 36, 52, 62, 69-70, 89, 105, 114-115, 157, 165,
                              178, 206, 228, 244, 255, 258, 269, 279, 296, 298, 304
Bolshevisation 61
Bolshevism 32, 69, 128, 138, 181-182, 184-185, 193, 256-258
Bolsonaro, Jair 31
Brecht, Bertolt 1, 6, 159, 279, 325
Breton, André 180
Brie, Michael 114, 117
British Gay Left Collective 119
Brodsky, Iosef 167
Buddhism 308-309
Bukharin, Nikolai 23-24, 64, 99, 105, 203-204, 206, 229-230, 256, 263
Bureaucracy 18, 52, 204, 206-208
Cabral, Amilcar 209
Capitalism .... xviii, 2, 4, 12, 18, 24, 31, 33-35, 55, 57, 63, 66-68, 71, 73-75,
    81, 84, 88-89, 91-93, 99-100, 104, 106, 119, 149-152, 182, 204, 209, 215,
    217-222, 226-233, 246-247, 256, 261, 266-268, 283, 285-287, 291-293,
    295-297, 303, 305
Capitalist Degeneration 285
Castration 126
Castro, Fidel 43, 67, 69, 76, 279, 286
Caucasus 31, 115, 198
CCCP 1
Central Asia .... xi, 140, 198, 239-244, 247, 250, 320-324
Centralisation .... xviii, 88, 100-101, 174, 179, 262
Central Única dos Trabalhadores (CUT) 90
Césaire, Aimé xiii
Chauvinism 17, 115, 117, 119, 197-198
Chávez, Hugo 73-74
Chavismo 76
Che Guevara 43, 66, 75
Chernobyl 243
Chernov, Viktor 70, 153

Index

Chernyshevksy, Nikolai 130, 316
Chevengur 163-168
Chiang Kai-Shek 270
Chile 39, 45-46, 67, 81, 89, 91
China 15, 31, 44, 63, 80, 98, 103, 107, 209, 266-272, 280, 319, 321-322
Chinese Nationalist Party 268
Christianity 85, 149, 306, 309
Chto Delat 159
Churchill, Winston 73
Civil War 5, 16, 32, 35-36, 61, 106, 111, 114, 195, 198, 203-204,
        208, 229-230, 239-240, 246, 255-257, 267, 284, 291
Class Consciousness 16, 35, 51, 67, 69, 73, 97-98, 111, 130, 168,
        174-180, 264, 273, 298
Class Struggle 24, 39, 54-57, 69, 71-74, 83, 89-93, 118-121, 125, 128-131, 138,
        164, 172-184, 205-206, 213, 216-217, 221, 283, 295-296
Claudín, Fernando... 62
Climate Change 39, 186, 232, 234, 247, 321
Cold War 2, 31, 217, 241, 243, 261, 280
Collectivisation 106, 132, 231, 256-257
(Anti-)Colonialism 4, 17, 43, 45, 55-56, 76, 87, 90, 93, 111, 171, 173,
        196-198, 213, 216-217, 220-222, 241, 244, 256, 267, 286, 297, 307, 327
Commodified Romance 125
Communist Attractor 6-7
Communist Desire 7, 125-128, 130-132
Communist Horizon .... xvii, 7, 39, 43, 120, 287
Communist League 183, 215
Communist Necessity 7
Compromises 63-64, 68-70, 72-73, 198
Comrade(-ship) .... xi, xii, xiii, xviii, xix, xx, 4-5, 7, 45-47, 62, 83, 97, 107, 115,
        119, 125-133, 139, 149, 156-159, 166, 196-197, 206-208, 219-220, 257-258,
        264, 298, 305
Conditions of Admission to the Communist International 61
Congress of the Toilers of the Far East.. 268
Contradictions (antagonistic, non-antagonistic) 17, 25, 32-36, 57, 66, 97,
        100-101, 103, 105-107, 111, 114-118, 122, 183-184, 204, 215, 257, 264, 267,
        275, 291, 295, 297
Coronavirus (COVID-19) .... xviii, 39, 51, 54-55, 118, 171, 179-180,
        185-187, 270, 272, 280, 287, 303
Correa, Rafael 73
Costa Rica 39
Cotton (Monoculture of).. 198, 241, 245-246, 248
Cohen, Daniel Aldana... 232
Collins, Michael.. 291
Colombia 55, 91
Communist Party of Great Britain... 81
Corbyn, Jeremy 83
Courtois, Stéphane 193
Credit Rating Agencies... 215

Crisis of Marxism 40
Critical Solidarity .... xviii, 6, 111
Cuba 41, 44-47, 62-63, 69, 75-76, 89, 286
Cultural Revolution... 140, 209
Danton, Georges 12
Decommunisation 306-307
Decree on Peace 282, 283
Defeat 3-4, 39-41, 46, 62-63, 89-90, 129, 191, 257, 261,
270, 273-275, 280, 284-285
De-Imperialisation 197
Dekulakisation 256
Deng Xiaoping 103
Departmentalism 207
Depeasantisation 226
Derrida, Jacques 177, 199
De-Stalinisation 115
Deutscher, Isaac 79, 229
Developmentalist State 90
Dialectics 3, 5, 13, 25-26, 32, 36, 40, 62, 74, 89, 97-101, 103-105,
107, 111, 116-118, 126, 128, 156, 165-166, 182-185, 193-194, 199, 204, 209,
219, 231, 275-276, 320, 323
Dictatorship of the Proletariat 24, 106, 174, 177, 203-206
Doctrinairism 74-75
Dōgen 283
Dogma 25, 44, 47, 61, 65, 67-68, 74-75, 90, 116-117, 158, 164-165, 171, 324
Dual Power 44, 46, 298
DuBois, W.E.B. xi
Duma 26, 51, 70, 273, 298
Dunayevskaya, Raya 98-99
Dushanbe 111, 239
Dzerzhinsky, Felix 115, 304
Eastern Europe 39, 44, 91, 166, 261, 268-269
Easter Uprising 99
Echeverría, Bolívar 40
Economic Struggle 174-178, 206
Economism 120-121, 172-173, 175-176, 179-181, 187
Ecosocialism 33, 35, 233, 320
Egypt 15, 323
Einstein, Albert 192
Ejército Zapatista de Liberación Nacional (EZLN) 39, 91
Electrification 225, 230-234, 239-240, 243-244, 280, 285
Engels, Friedrich .... xiii, xviii, 25, 67, 87-90, 92-93, 97-98, 103,
107, 130, 173, 184, 216, 227-228, 233, 243, 284
Epistemology 26, 92, 105, 114, 324
Epoch .... xii, 18, 25, 34, 36, 179, 186, 264-269, 271, 276, 284, 286, 299
European Left 31-36, 62-63, 218-219, 284, 292-293
Exile 5, 33, 46, 51, 53, 82, 125-126, 132, 217, 295-296
Existentialism 181, 183, 324

Index

Fabergé Easter Egg 53
Failure .... xxiii, 7, 19, 31, 62, 66, 93, 165, 169, 178-179, 231, 264, 273-274
February Revolution 15-17, 34, 53, 69, 129, 298
FED 5 (camera) 304
Federici, Silvia 149-154
Fernández, Alberto 40, 74
Fink, Bruce 126
Finland Station 53
First International 13
First Wave Governments in Latin America 40-41, 44
Fisher, Mark 4, 6
Five-Year Plan .... xi, 16, 257
Floyd, George .... xi, xii
Folk Politics 44
Forbearance 1, 6, 315
Formalism 279, 283
Fossil Capital 228
Fourth International 81
France 16, 62-63, 81, 191, 204, 222, 267, 283, 320
FRELIMO (Mozambique Liberation Front) 215
French Revolution 15, 309
Fridays for Future 31
Fukuyama, Francis 6, 217
Fully Automated Luxury Communism 233
Gandhi, Mahatma 192, 199
Garner, Eric .... xi, xii
Gender .... xviii, 101, 114, 118, 120, 150, 154, 157, 159, 181,
238-239, 244-251, 257, 319
George, Lloyd 73
Georgia 114-115, 197-199, 325
Georgian Affair 114
Germany 12, 32, 34, 52-53, 63-64, 72, 130, 149, 174, 217,
222, 258, 267, 273, 280, 283
Ghodsee, Kristen 92, 247
Global Governance 185
Global North 297
Global South 47, 100, 297
GOELRO 230, 240
Goethe, Johann Wolfgang von 159
Gorbachev, Mikhail 243
Gorky, Maxim 106
Gorz, André 181
Gramsci, Antonio 43, 62, 68-69, 159, 262, 275, 279, 324
Grant, Ted 79
Great Proletarian Cultural Revolution 261
Green New Deal 232-233
Guatemala 39
Guiadó, Juan 74

Hall, Stuart 4
Hardt, Michael 181, 297, 319
Hartmann, Heidi 120-121
Harvey, David 225
Hauntology 6
Hegel, Georg Wilhelm Friedrich 32, 89, 97-101, 103-107, 159, 184,
186, 194, 279, 284, 319
Hegel Notebooks 97-100, 284
Historical Materialism 40, 74, 194, 217-219
Hogan, Barbara 215
Hölderlin, Friedrich 5
Honduras 39
Hook, Sidney 99
Hughes, Langston xi
Human Rights 6, 215, 251, 324
Hungary 63, 79
Hybrid Wars (Fifth-Generation Warfare) 62, 75
Hydropower 239-241, 248
Icon(isation) 5-6, 145, 280, 299
Identity Politics 111, 114, 117-121, 261
Imperialism xii, 13, 15-17, 32-33, 35, 40, 43, 56, 62, 64, 74-76, 88-89, 97, 99-101,
104, 114, 116, 120-121, 196-198, 205, 215-216, 218, 220-222, 255, 258,
266-274, 279, 282-283, 296-297
India 55, 81, 98, 192, 198, 261, 303, 306-309
Indigenisation (Korenizatsiia) 244
Indonesia 81, 268
Industrialisation 106, 225-226, 239, 241
Inequality of the Oppressor Nation 116-121
Inquisition 149, 154
International Monetary Fund 247
Internationalism 11, 111-112, 116-118, 214, 222, 256, 266
Ireland 74, 99-100
Iskra 69, 265, 271
Italy 63, 81
James C.R.L. 98-99, 195
Jameson, Fredric 217, 225
Japan 62, 98, 107, 220, 267, 273
Jim, Irvin 57
Jobless Growth 217
Johnson-Forest Tendency 98-99
Jonsson, Stefan 167
Julius Caesar 2
Kadets 193, 296
Kamenev, Lev 23
Kairos 197
Kalinovský, Artemy 240-241
Kant, Immanuel 97, 185, 219, 291, 308
Katusky, Karl 33, 70, 72, 89, 97, 101, 153, 263, 296-297

Karensky, Alexander	298
Khanga, Yelena	306
Kidrič, Boris	279
Kruschev, Nikita	113
Kierkegaard, Søren	183
Kingdom of Ends	185
Kirchner, Cristina Fernández de	40, 73
Kirghiz SSR	xvii, 1, 141
Klein, Naomi	233
Kolkhoz	245
Kollontai, Alexandra	4
Konspiratsiia	157, 195
Kremlin	255
Kronstadt	80, 256
Krupskaya, Nadezhda	xix, 4, 125-126, 128-129, 131-132, 139, 145
Kulak	231, 256
Kun, Béla	63
Kurechin, Sergey	112-113
Kyrgyzstan	xvii-xix, 1, 3, 6, 140-141, 248, 303-308, 322-323, 325
Labour Party	18, 80-85, 295
Lacan, Jacques	xvii, 126
Lafargue, Paul	151
Lassalle, Ferdinand	262
Leading Class	68
LEF (Left Front of the Arts)	282, 285
Leftism	61-63, 65, 70, 76
Left-Wing Melancholia	2, 40
Legal Forms of Struggle	68
Leninabad (Khujand)	238-241, 243-244
Lenin Cult	1, 24, 163, 242, 307
Leninist Killjoy	3
Leninitis	2
Lenin Lamp	231, 281
Lenin Moment	171-172, 178-179, 182, 293
Lenin Monuments	xvii, xix, 1, 3, 6, 24, 111, 121, 163, 244, 251, 305-307
Leninist Approach to Nature	242
Lennon, John	305
Li Dazhao	263, 269-270,
Liebknecht, Karl	32, 63, 191
Liebman, Marcel	208
Lih, Lars T.	157, 195
Locomotive (of History, of the Revolution)	5, 156
LOMO (Ленинградское Оптико-Механическое Объединение)	305
Lomographic Society International	305
Long March, The	107
Lorde, Audre	xi
Lucretius	279
Lukács, György	98-99, 200, 295

Lunacharsky, Anatoly 143, 145, 304
Luther, Martin 12
Luxemburg, Rosa 32, 63, 72, 101, 165, 263, 296, 319, 320, 324
Lu Xun 264, 273-275
Machiavelli, Niccolò 197, 262
Macri, Mauricio 73-74
Maduro, Nicolás 73-74
Magic 120, 149-160
Malm, Andreas 228
Mao Zedong 17, 103, 107, 209, 262-63, 270-274, 279, 293
Marcuse, Herbert 99
Mariátegui, José Carlos 46, 47
Marikana Massacre 55
Martí, José 76
Martov, Julius 69, 70, 132, 153
Marx, Karl .... xvii, 3, 7, 11-13, 18, 23-26, 32, 39-41, 47, 66, 67, 88-92, 97-101,
    103-107, 114, 117, 119-122, 130, 138, 150, 156, 163-165, 173, 182-184,
    193-195, 203-204, 209, 213-217, 225-234, 239, 255, 261-263, 269-270,
    279-280, 284-285, 291-293, 295-299, 306, 308
Marxism-Leninism 25, 40, 195
Maslov, Petr 263
Mass Line 209
Mass Strike 51-52, 81-82, 89, 157, 191, 295
Materialism 97-99, 129, 194, 218, 266, 284
Mausoleum 146, 299
Mayakovsky, Vladimir 2, 4, 282
May Fourth Movement 273
Means of Production .... xiii, 18-19
Mensheviks 35, 70, 104, 114, 193, 203, 258, 296
Mental Health 5, 118
Merleau-Ponty, Maurice 181-183
Metaphysics (Aristotle) 194
Mexico 39, 46, 83, 89, 91, 185
Mhone, Guy 220
Militant, The (organisation) 82-83
Militant, The (publication) 79
Mir (peasant commune) 228, 255
Miracle 140-160
Mkandawire, Thandika 218
Modernisation .... xi, 231, 239, 242, 286
Mongelezi, Athi Joja 214
Monopoly Capitalism 100, 267, 296
Morales, Evo 7, 73, 91
Moscow 5, 24, 51, 61, 81, 115, 136, 140, 143, 217, 241, 268, 299
Motley Formations 46
Movimento dos Trabalhadores Sem Terra (MST) 90
Mo Zi 279
Multitude 181

Index

Mushroom Hoax 112-113, 121
Müller, Heiner 146
Münzer, Thomas 12
Myl'nikov, Mikhail 242-243
Narodnaya Volya 52, 130
Narodniki 193, 296
Natanson, Mark 70
National Question 23, 34, 100, 106, 114-119, 197-198
Negri, Antonio 181, 297
Nehru, Jawaharlal 307
Neoliberalism .... xix, 6, 31, 35, 39, 56, 67-68, 90-92, 117-121, 145,
 171, 215-218, 232-233, 239, 246-247, 261
Neolithic Revolution 18, 209
New Deal 232-233
New Economic Policy (NEP) 5, 106, 203, 255-257, 273, 284
Newspeak 167
NGO-isation 56
NKVD 80
Ni una Menos 91
Nicaragua 63
Nicholas II 51-53
Non-Party Workers 207-208
Novaya Zhizn 295
Nucleus of Political Desire called Lenin 41-47
NUMSA 55, 57
Objective Conditions 104, 265
October Revolution .... xvii, 19, 36, 61, 67, 69-70, 79, 89, 92, 105-106,
 114, 129, 143, 179, 219, 261, 273, 282, 291, 298
O'Farrell, John 80
Opportunism 64-76, 172, 187, 291
Ordzhonikidze, Sergo 115
Organisation 16, 19, 31, 39-49, 52, 56-57, 63-74, 114, 125-133, 156,
 171-188, 195, 208-209, 255, 270-276, 295
Osh 3, 140
Osmonov, Alykul 141
Ostrovsky, Nikolai 213
Other, The 126-132
Oxygenic Communism .... xi-xiii
Paris Commune 44, 101, 130, 261
Parti Communiste Français 181
Partido dos Trabalhadores (PT) 90
Party-Movement 44
Patriarchy 4, 54, 114, 119-121, 246-251, 257, 308
Peace, Land, Bread 51-57
Peasantry 13, 69-70, 106, 141, 195-197, 228-290, 255, 271, 295-297
People's Republic of China 31, 44, 63, 209, 261-277, 280
People's War 270-272
Pepetela 4

Perestroika 243-248
Peru 39
Petrograd 16, 19, 35, 53
Petty Bourgeoisie 56, 63, 70, 120, 197, 206, 229, 296
Philistine 153, 156
Philosophy of Victory 273-276
Physis 184-187
Photographic Literacy 304-305
Phronesis 193-200
Plato 192-194, 199
Platonov, Andrei 4, 163-169
Plekhanov, Georgy 69, 89, 97-98, 104, 153, 193, 263
Plutarch 2
Poland 63, 304
Political Contingency 42, 46
Political Therapy 5, 152
Politics of Truth 176
Poll Tax 80-83
Popular Front 67
Populism 261, 292
Porcaro, Mimmo 171-172
Portugal 81, 87
Positive Hallucinations 5
Postmodernism 91-92, 218, 225
Potresov, Alexander 59, 263
Pravda 266, 268
Preobrazhensky, Evgeny 229-231
Primitive Accumulation 87, 149, 228-231, 234
Professional Revolutionaries .... xi, 157, 165, 176-179
Proletariat .... xvii, 11-13, 17, 24, 43, 51-52, 57, 61-64, 67, 70-72, 75, 88-89, 106, 111, 128-132, 140, 168, 174-183, 187, 195, 197-198, 203-206, 220, 232, 266, 269, 293, 295, 298
Propaganda 68, 72, 82, 165, 242
Propaganda of the Deed 184
Provisional Government 17, 35
Psychoanalysis 127-131, 217
Publicity 175-177, 184, 207
Pushkin, Alexander 1, 141
Putin, Vladimir 100, 113
Pyatakov, Georgy 23
Pyatoe Koleso 112
Queer Communism 119-121
Rabocheye Dyelo 173
Race 98, 114, 181, 213, 306
Racism 54, 119, 213-214, 221, 261, 286, 306
Radek, Karl 64, 268
Rahmon, Emomali 246, 248
Ramaphosa, Cyril 54

Ramones, The 149
Rasputin 52
Rau, Milo 143-145
Reagan, Ronald 6
Realm/Kingdom of Freedom 3, 225-227, 232
Realm of Necessity 227
Rearguard 6
Red Army 61-63, 114, 140, 208, 256, 271, 306
Red Terror 113, 255-257, 304
Reed, John 23
Reid, Jimmy 84
Repression 34, 52, 55
Return to the Source 209
Revolutionary Personality 6, 261-276
Revolutionary Socialist League 81
Right to Disillusionment 4-5
Right-Wing Nationalism 40, 121, 261
Rishikesh Ashram 192
Roberts, Flora 241, 243
Roosevelt, Franklin D. 232
Roy, M.N. 268
Russia .... xi, 2, 11-13, 15-19, 23, 26, 34-36, 51-53, 57, 61-62, 70, 89, 104-105,
    125, 130-131, 143, 149, 157, 165, 169, 173, 195-198, 203, 208, 219, 227-228,
    238, 244, 247-248, 257-258, 263, 266-270, 283, 285-286, 291, 295-297, 308
Russian Empire 43, 114-115, 197, 255
Russian Social Democratic Labour Party 70, 295
Russification 116, 256
Salmond, Alex 84
Santos, Boaventura de Sousa 6
Sartre, Jean-Paul 181-187
Sayle, Alexei 80
Sblizheniie 239
Schwartzman, David 233
Scientificity 284
Scioli, Daniel 73-74
Scotland 81, 83-84
Second Coming 163, 168
Second International 33, 97, 99, 104
Secret Speech 80
Sectarianism 44, 67
Self-Determination 91, 114, 119, 197, 234, 268-269, 297
Self-Optimisation 5
Separation 126-127, 130-131
Sereni, Emilio 26
Serge, Victor 4, 79
Sheridan, Tommy 83
Shivji, Issa 56
Shklovsky, Viktor B. 279

Show Trials .... xi, 81, 257
Siberia .... xi, 125, 132, 243
Sieger-Gen 3
Simbirsk 2
Sliianiie 239
Smychka 203, 256
Social Democracy 34-35, 173, 179, 183-184, 195, 296
Socialism or Barbarism 2.0 7
Socialist Primitive Accumulation 229-231
Socialist Realism 141
Socialist Revolutionaries 295
Socialist Revolutionary Workers Party 55
Solar Communism 233
Solidarność 79
Solidarity .... xviii, xix, 3, 6, 56-57, 82, 111, 115, 121, 156-159, 171,
 185-186, 198, 234, 298
Solzhenitsyn, Aleksander 79
Sophia 192-195, 200
South Africa 53-57, 214-216
South African Communist Party 216
Soviet Nostalgia 307
Soviets 16-19, 26, 35, 52, 69, 92, 101, 131, 256, 286, 298
Spectre of Communism .... xix, 2, 7, 41
Spinoza, Baruch 150, 279
Spontaneity 99, 156, 165, 173-180
Stalin, Joseph 16, 23-25, 67, 80-81, 90, 98, 113, 115, 117, 143,
 196-198, 200, 231, 255-259, 263, 280, 284, 291, 293
Stalinism 25, 181, 231, 241, 242-243, 255-259, 284, 293
State, The 15-19, 24-25, 32, 34, 40, 42, 44, 46, 52-56, 74, 87, 89-92, 98-101,
 106, 115-116, 131, 150-151, 163-165, 172, 175, 184-185, 193, 196-197,
 199, 203-210, 216-217, 229-230, 240, 243, 246-249, 256-257, 261-262, 267,
 270-272, 286, 291-293, 298-299
Steel, Mark 80
Stiob 112
Stolypin, Pyotr 255
Structural Adjustment Programs 216
Struve, Peter 69, 153
Sukhanov, Nikolai 35, 153
Sun Yat-sen 263-264, 268-270, 274
Switzerland 32-33, 53, 104, 129, 149, 296
Syr Darya 238-251
Taaffe, Peter 79
Tajik Civil War 111, 239
Tajikistan 111, 238 251
Tajik Sea 238-241, 249-251
TALCO 249
Tanzania 217
TASS 113, 238

Technic 151-152, 156
Temkina, Anna 246-247, 251
Tenth Party Congress 256, 284
Testament 5, 24, 115, 196
Thatcher, Margaret 6, 82-83
Third International (Comintern) 45, 61, 172, 268-289, 297
Thunberg, Greta 32
Tito, Josip Broz 159, 279, 286
Tokombaev, Aaly 141
Tomsky, Mikhail 198
Totalitarianism 167-169
Trade Union 15, 51, 55, 57, 72, 91, 106, 205-206, 271
Traverso, Enzo 2, 40
Treaty of Brest-Litovsk 64, 258, 273
Trotskyism 73-74, 79-81, 98-99
Trotsky, Leon 11-13, 23, 34, 63, 67, 70, 74, 79-81, 83, 97, 101, 114, 143,
        153, 203-206, 229, 231, 256, 263-266, 268, 273, 279, 291
Trump, Donald 31, 74, 76
Turkestan 198
Turusbekov, Zhusup 141
Tynyanov, Yuri 283
Tynystanov, Kasym 141
United Kingdom 31, 62, 283
Ukraine 31, 100, 197
Ulyanov, Aleksander 52
Ulyanova, Maria xi
Ultrabolshevism 181-185
Ultra-Imperialism 33
UNICEF Study Tajikistan 250
United Front 57, 268-271
USA 62, 118, 217, 276, 268, 284, 286, 297
Use-Value 4, 7, 279
USSR .... xi, xii, 1, 6, 44, 79, 80, 84, 100, 112-113, 149, 167, 197, 239,
        241, 246, 248, 256-257, 280, 284, 297-298, 303-309
Utopia 2, 4, 33, 34, 68, 157, 159, 169, 192, 229, 242, 262, 275, 299
Utopian Spark 166-167, 169
Uzbekistan .... xi, 240-241, 248
Valera, Eamon de 291
Vanguard 6, 51, 61, 71-72, 90, 98, 100, 165, 174, 178-179,
        195, 205, 261, 286, 298
Venezuela 40, 62, 74-76, 91
Vertov, Dziga 140
Vietnam 44, 63
Voluntarism 62, 172
Wales 81
Wallerstein, Immanuel 40, 66
Washington Consensus 90
Weakest Link 43, 105, 261, 264-270, 274, 296

Weber, Max 65
Wisdom of Lenin 191-201
Witch (-hunt, -craft) 149-160
Woods, Alan 79
Workers' and Peasants' Inspection (Rabkrin) 207-208
Workers' State 91, 204, 230
Working Class 12, 52, 55-57, 69, 72, 81, 90, 92, 100, 115, 121, 125, 128-131, 178, 181, 214-217, 221-222, 234, 279, 283
World Bank 54, 247-248
World War I 32, 36, 52, 99, 222, 268, 291
World War II (Great Patriotic War) 98, 140, 181, 226, 241, 280, 306
Wright, Erik Olin 33
Zavaleta Mercado, René 45-47
Zenit M3 SLR (camera) 304
Zetkin, Clara 63, 153
Zinoviev, Grigory 23-24, 263, 268
Žižek, Slavoj .... xx, 5, 39, 166, 171, 186
Zola, Emile 173
Zorki 10 (camera) 304

www.ingramcontent.com/pod-product-compliance
Lightning Source LLC
Chambersburg PA
CBHW042118300426
44117CB00021B/2981